HEALTH CARE OPERATIONS MANAGEMENT

A Systems Perspective

James R. Langabeer II, MBA, PhD

Professor, Health Informatics, Management,
and Emergency Medicine
The University of Texas Health Science Center
Houston, TX

Jeffrey Helton, PhD, CMA, CFE, FHFMA

Assistant Professor, Health Care Management
College of Professional Studies
Metropolitan State University of Denver
Denver, CO

JONES & BARTLETT
LEARNING

World Headquarters
Jones & Bartlett Learning
5 Wall Street
Burlington, MA 01803
978-443-5000
info@jblearning.com
www.jblearning.com

Production Credits
VP, Executive Publisher: David Cella
Publisher: Michael Brown
Associate Editor: Lindsey Mawhiney
Editorial Assistant: Nicholas Alakel
Production Manager: Tracey McCrea
Senior Marketing Manager: Sophie Fleck Teague
Art Development Editor: Joanna Lundeen
Art Development Assistant: Shannon Sheehan

Manufacturing and Inventory Control Supervisor: Amy Bacus
Composition: Cenveo Publisher Services
Cover Design: Kristin E. Parker
Manager of Photo Research, Rights & Permissions: Lauren Miller
Cover Image: © Steve Design/ShutterStock, Inc.
Printing and Binding: Edwards Brothers Malloy
Cover Printing: Edwards Brothers Malloy

Library of Congress Cataloging-in-Publication Data
Langabeer, James R., 1969- , author.
  Health care operations management : a systems perspective / James R. Langabeer, Jeffrey Helton.—Second edition.
    p. ; cm.
  Includes bibliographical references and index.
  ISBN 978-1-284-05006-6
  I. Helton, Jeffrey, 1961-, author. II. Title.
  [DNLM: 1. Hospital Administration—methods. 2. Efficiency, Organizational. WX 157.1]
  RA971.3
  362.11068—dc23

  2014033878

6048
Printed in the United States of America
19 18 17 16 15   10 9 8 7 6 5 4 3 2

About the Authors

James R. Langabeer II, PhD, MBA

Dr. James Langabeer is a professor of informatics, health care management, and emergency medicine at the University of Texas Health Science Center at Houston. He has spent most of his career focused on quality improvement and information technology in hospitals and health care. His career has involved hospital executive administration, information technology startups, management consulting, and health

care research and teaching. Dr. Langabeer was the founding chief executive officer of Greater Houston Healthconnect (the regional health information network serving Southeast Texas) and helped move the organization from concept to reality. He was the executive vice president of a technology and consulting firm based in Boston that was widely touted as "best of class" in thought leadership on predictive modeling and business intelligence. He has lived and/or worked extensively in Boston, London, Paris, Rotterdam, and Tel Aviv, as well as Houston. He has served on the faculties of the University of Texas, Boston University, and Baylor College of Medicine.

Dr. Langabeer has served as principal investigator on many national research projects. He has been funded by the American Heart Association, the U.S. Centers for Disease Control, Health and Human Services, and many other agencies and foundations. He has more than 85 publications that can be found in some of the highest-rated management and clinical journals such as the *Journal of Emergency Medicine, American Heart Journal, Pediatrics, Health Care Management Review, Quality Management in Health Care,* and *Health Care Management Science.*

Dr. Langabeer earned his PhD from the University of Lancaster in England in management science, an EdD in leadership from the

University of Houston, and an MBA from Baylor University. He is also an Emergency Medical Technician with Advanced Cardiac Life Support certifications, a Certified Management Accountant, and a Fellow in the Healthcare Information and Management Systems Society.

Jeffrey Helton, PhD, CMA, CFE, FHFMA

Dr. Jeffrey Helton is an assistant professor of health care management at Metropolitan State University of Denver. He also holds an adjunct faculty appointment in health care management at The George Washington University and in health informatics at the University of Denver and health informatics at the University of Texas School of Biomedical Informatics. The majority of his career has been spent as

Courtesy of Jeffrey Helton

chief financial officer for several health care systems across the United States, where he led several turnarounds of organizations previously in bankruptcy or receivership. During his career as a financial executive, he identified several operational challenges in hospitals and health plans that required development of staffing standards, labor management processes, and internal financial controls to restore financial stability to organizations. He has since supported other health care organization turnarounds as a consultant, assisting in the analysis of labor costs and development of labor control programs.

As a part of his consulting work, Dr. Helton has also served as chief financial officer of the Disaster Housing Assistance Program on behalf of families displaced from their homes as a result of Hurricanes Katrina and Ike. As custodian for more than a quarter billion dollars in federal funds, he became a Certified Fraud Examiner and provided fraud prevention assistance to the agencies assisting victims of these natural disasters. He has also used his background in fraud detection to assist several health care organizations in developing fraud prevention and detection programs and has provided material support to many health care fraud prosecutions, resulting in multiple millions of dollars in recovered fraud losses.

Dr. Helton is a Fellow of the Healthcare Financial Management Association, where he serves on its board of examiners. He also volunteers his financial management expertise to the Association of University Programs in Health Administration, where he serves on its finance committee and as treasurer of the Health Care Management Division of the Academy of Management and a member of the finance committee of the Colorado Association of USA Track and Field. He is a Certified Fraud Examiner and a member of the board of advisors for the Association of Certified Fraud Examiners. Dr. Helton is also a Certified Management Accountant.

Dr. Helton earned his PhD in public health management from the University of Texas School of Public Health, an MS in hospital and health administration from the University of Alabama at Birmingham, and a BS in business administration from Eastern Kentucky University. He is a journal article reviewer for *Healthcare Financial Management, Journal of Healthcare Management, Social Science and Medicine,* and *Journal of Public Health Management and Practice.*

Table of Contents

List of Figures and Tables

Figures

Tables

New to the Second Edition

In recent years, there has been a heightened awareness of the effect that efficient and successful management of the health care organization can provide. New federal policies and new payer reimbursement models are just two examples of how the industry is changing. The discipline of health care operations management is key to the success of these changes and to organizations in general. Operations management focuses on improving clinical and administrative processes, streamlining costs, and ensuring high-quality outcomes while optimizing available resources—all of these are critical to organizations that are struggling to compete and survive in an era of constrained reimbursements. The first edition of this book was widely adopted by universities throughout the world, and due to demand and our desire to make operations management current and relevant, it seemed an appropriate time to introduce the second edition. This revision of the book offers an expanded coverage of quality, financial, and systems management.

We would like to thank Jones & Bartlett Learning for their leadership in publishing this second edition. We would also like to thank the thousands of readers and dozens of professors who read the first edition and offered their opinions and insights for revisions. We truly appreciate your help with and continued support of this second edition.

The encouragement of friends and family helped us complete this book, which was quite an undertaking! We would also like to acknowledge the wonderful editorial assistance from Elizabeth Vogler, MA from the University of Texas School of Biomedical Informatics. She was tremendously helpful in organizing chapters and giving all of the material a final read.

Many changes, improvements, and additions were made in response to valuable comments by readers and users. First, there were several errors in the text and these have all been fixed. Dr. Jeffrey Helton, a significant researcher in health care finance and operations management, was added as a coauthor to the text to provide greater coverage on certain topics. All chapters were made current in terms of statistics and updated references and were edited for the purpose of clarifying some material, correcting a few minor errors, improving language and syntax, and generally updating material. Some chapters were merged and combined, and a few new chapters were created. In all, the second edition contains 17 chapters, which will allow the academic reader to complete one chapter per week during the semester. The more significant changes are encapsulated as follows:

- Chapter 1, "Health Care Operations and Systems Management," was augmented greatly by the addition of sections on management decision making. Because the ultimate purpose of operations management tools and methods is to improve decision outcomes, we felt it was appropriate to expand the discussion of decision making.
- Chapter 2, "Health Care Marketplace," provides greater detail on current health policies and their effect on the health care environment. There is a discussion of the Affordable Care Act and other relevant federal policies.
- Chapter 3, "Health Care Finance for the Operations Manager," was expanded and reworked to include new reimbursement models, information on how payers reimburse provider organizations, and an examination of how an organization is paid can effect operations management.
- Chapter 4, "Quality Management," provides significantly more detail on Six Sigma and Lean methods, which have been continuously increasing in adoption in recent years.
- Chapters 5 and 6 were updated and augmented with additional theory around operations research and practical examples.
- Chapter 7, "Operational Metrics in Health Care Organizations," is a new chapter that details the key metrics in operations management. These metrics include discussion of full-time equivalent, adjusted patient days, and other productivity metrics. Additional details on sources of labor data to enhance the accuracy of calculating labor management metrics are also included.

- Chapters 8 through 10 were updated and information was consolidated.
- Chapters 11 through 15 represent the supply chain management areas. These chapters were consolidated where needed and also revised and improved. They include greater coverage of forecasting and supply chain management systems.
- Chapter 16 blends a new component focused around operational analysis and benchmarking and provides integrative examples for operations management. Because analysis and comparison of units to others has become so widespread, we felt it important to add sections on how to make proper comparisons.

Preface

Although less than 5% of the American population currently works in a health care system, the overwhelming majority of adults have been a patient or a guest at a hospital, clinic, or physician's office. Of those, while most remember the quality and care given by nurses and physicians, many have left the facility with an overwhelming feeling of disdain for the inefficient and time-consuming business processes. Excessive wait times, lack of coordination among different departments, duplicate entry of personal information in multiple manual forms, unfriendly facilities, and general lack of customer service are typical attributes assigned to health care organizations. Although outcome data suggest that the quality of medical care is improving for most types of illness, the attention to detail in day-to-day operational management has not kept pace.

In a time when hospitals' financial situations are increasingly being called into question, hospitals are now starting to get serious about creating operational efficiencies to become more competitive and financially viable. Do hospitals and clinics exist to make profits? Some do; however, most do not. Either way, if hospitals are to survive dismally poor health care economics, escalating costs, and increasing competitive pressures, they must apply sound business management. This will ensure that hospitals earn the reasonable return on investment necessary to continue to invest in and upgrade buildings, programs, and employees.

A very active debate continues at the national level, primarily focused on health policy research. New programs and policies centered around the concepts of "pay for performance," quality and accreditation, flawed government funding mechanisms, federal and state regulations, publication and sharing of outcome data with the public, and other aspects of the U.S. health care system continue to address structural issues that affect the quality and costs of care in general. In addition, behavioral research into physician judgment and mechanisms to encourage elimination of unnecessary tests and treatments will likely change medical education in the future. All of these can help improve the industry's economics and market structure. But, for now, hospitals and systems must continue to look internally at their own operations and management to adapt and thrive in current conditions. Hospitals cannot wait for policy to address the structural issues driving health care costs—they must apply inspired management to improve organizational performance today.

Principles of operations management, whether they focus on productivity or supply chain management, are common in other industries but have yet to really catch on in health care. There has been a reluctance to admit the applicability of business optimization techniques to the health care industry in general. This, coupled with the lack of sophistication and management education on the part of health care managers, limits the ability to fully understand and utilize the concepts, methods, and techniques offered.

Up until about two decades ago, business managers in health care were considered low-level "paper pushers." Senior administrators at most hospitals tended to be clinically trained and did not see as much value in managing business issues as medical ones. Of course, at that time most hospitals were reimbursed fully for all operational costs and capital costs, plus a small margin. With guaranteed profits, there was not a big drive for efficiency and productivity management. Times have changed.

However, most books on health care business management still focus primarily on issues of either governance or finance—both of which are important topics but alone are not comprehensive. Coverage of revenue cycle issues such as reimbursement, patient billing, coding, and collections are well addressed, as are basic accounting and financial reporting topics. Similarly, governance issues such as improving physician relations are well documented. Yet, as important as these topics are, it leaves most of business operations fairly uncovered.

This text focuses on the practical application of operations management techniques in health care organizations, including hospitals, clinics, multiple-hospital systems, and other facilities in an integrated delivery network. For clarity purposes, however, the term *hospital* is widely used in this book, and it refers broadly to any large organizational entity—*hospital* is simply easier to use as the unit of measure than *integrated delivery network, health care system, clinic,* or the like. Hospitals remain the predominant hub of the health care system, and they employ the majority of workers and resources, so they make more lucid examples for most concepts illustrated here. The tools and techniques used in this text, however, are just as relevant to other health care facilities.

This book concerns itself primarily with the topics that have not been extensively treated in health care texts, which are the operational components of health care. These include all areas that help hospitals improve productivity, reduce cycle times, measure performance, analyze activities, compare organizations to others, improve cost management, and generally create business value by converting resources into services. Hospital operations management concerns itself with a few key themes, all of which will be covered in this text: productivity analysis, supply chain management, business process and service design, quality management, inventory management, technology and systems, operational planning and scheduling, and performance improvement. All of these are traditional operations research topics that, when applied to hospitals and health care organizations, cover the majority of resource consumption.

This book was written to help practicing executives and administrators, as well as students in undergraduate and graduate health care administration programs, understand the importance of sound operational management by using business strategy and logistics to create a competitive advantage for their organization. It presupposes that there will be a growing need for improved cost efficiencies and economics in the coming years, and this mindset is required if hospitals are to survive competitive pressures. The significance and role of business professionals in health care will continue to evolve and improve over time, and therefore it is mandatory that the skills and expertise of hospital business officers continue to improve.

The framework for this book uses a practical perspective of operations management and attempts to set a path for hospitals to pursue a strategy of operational excellence. Therefore, the problems this book addresses are those that are integrated around operations and logistics management, as displayed in **Figure P1-1**.

This book will help hospital and health care administrators to address important operational and day-to-day issues in this rapidly evolving industry. This book should be used as a reference guide for those working in hospital administration, clinic management, performance improvement, and all other areas of management and it serves three purposes:

1. Present concepts and techniques about improving daily operations capabilities and capacity in health care.
2. Educate students and administrators on the value of clinic and business operations, with a strong focus on analytical models for decision making.
3. Help health care organizations improve their performance and outcomes.

It is our hope that this book will stimulate significantly more research and publication on mastering operations research in health care and using advanced techniques to drive improved competitiveness into health care.

PART I

Operations, Systems, and Financial Management

Part I of this text provides the reader with a foundation of operations management and explains its role in improving health care's financial and business condition. Health care activities and processes are complex. To perform optimally, they must be managed as a system. Operations and systems management requires knowledge of process improvement, quality, finance, and many other business practices. As a service industry, financial outcomes are driven primarily by labor and supply costs, so an understanding of the income statement and the use of key ratios to manage these areas is provided. Understanding the concepts of operations management, and its relationship to financial margins, is also explored.

Chapter 1 offers an overview of the discipline of operations and systems management and that of management in general. Goals of operations management, from cost reduction to network optimization, are described, as well as the key functions and roles performed by operations managers. This chapter sets the stage for the rest of the text.

Chapter 2 provides an introduction to the health care marketplace. Because health care organizations are businesses, they must generate revenues and sustain themselves financially, as organizations do in other industries. This chapter defines the hospital and health care organization and discusses the nature of its goods and services. This chapter provides an overview of some of the significant health policies that affect patient operations, including the Affordable Care Act. The concept of health care production, distinct from operations, is also explored.

Chapter 3 provides a structured introduction to health care finance for the operations manager. An understanding of the drivers of improved financial performance is essential to effective operations management. This chapter addresses how hospitals earn revenue, and it defines the basic terms used in health care finance. Of great importance, it explains the key external financial statements that represent the financial condition of the organization, which are used as data sources for a variety of operational analyses in this text.

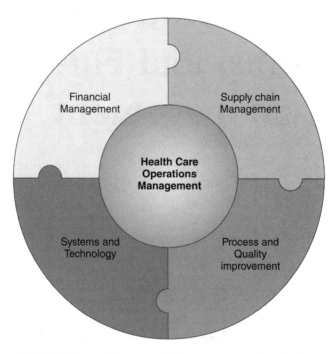

FIGURE P1–1 Operations Management in Health Care

Health Care Operations and Systems Management

GOALS OF THIS CHAPTER

1. Describe the need for improved decisions and management systems.
2. Define health care operations management.
3. Describe the roles and responsibilities of health care operations managers.
4. Examine the management decision-making process.
5. Understand the goals of operations management.
6. Describe the management discipline and where operations management fits.

Health care operations management is a discipline that integrates scientific principles of management to determine the most efficient and optimal methods to support patient care delivery. Today, most hospital positions are roles that involve the coordination and execution of operations. This chapter provides the rationale for operations management and describes its evolving role in helping hospitals become more competitive.

THE ROLE OF HEALTH CARE OPERATIONS MANAGEMENT

Health care operations is about management of interconnected processes, or systems. A **system** is a set of connected parts that fit together to achieve a purpose.

Health care operations and systems management is the set of diverse and inter-related activities that allow for diagnosis, treatment, payment, and administrative management in health care facilities.

Most hospitals are nonprofit in nature. Nearly 80% of hospitals are considered nonprofit and exist solely to serve the community in which they operate, down from 85% a few years ago. As nonprofits, these organizations are exempt from most federal and state taxation and are not expected to show continuous positive growth rates or large profit margins, as most publicly traded firms do. However, if a hospital or health care organization cannot show some return on the capital or dollars invested, there will be negative consequences. For example, failure to show reasonable margins will likely cause the public bond market (which finances most health care growth today) to assign subpar credit ratings; therefore, the bonds themselves will have poor yields, making hospitals less than stellar investments for bondholders.

Most important, the term *limited profit margins* implies that there will be fewer dollars to invest back into the business to ensure that buildings are updated, equipment is replaced and technology is modern, and clinical programs will continue to expand and be enhanced. Without these investments, hospitals will likely be unable to attract the most qualified physicians and administrators, which will continue the downward spiral. While some hospitals and health care systems wait for changes in the public health policy to save them, the more competitive and successful hospitals are acting now to protect their margins.

In this era of continual pricing pressures affecting the top line of the income statement, and with a large majority of all hospitals reporting negative profit margins, it is essential that hospitals begin to look toward more sophisticated business strategies to succeed. Differentiated marketing programs and strategies, broader use of advertising, and more careful and precise long-term planning about service lines are all strategies that must be utilized (Rovin, 2001).

Equally as important, there must be a broader adoption of operations management techniques into hospital business affairs. Monitoring and maximizing labor productivity for all medical support and allied health professionals is critical to maintaining salary expenses. Incorporating queuing theory and scheduling optimization methods helps drive waste and cycle time out of hospitals. Incorporating logistical and supply chain management techniques helps reduce operational expenses, eliminate excess safety stocks, and generally improve working capital management. Most important, using technology to further automate and streamline all processes in hospital operations can help reduce costs and maximize efficiencies.

Hospitals and other health care organizations cannot rely on extrinsic factors (such as health policy, federal payer regulation changes, or shifts in managed care market structures) to change their margin potential. Although these are important issues, they are covered in other texts and will evolve regardless of the managerial behavior that hospitals employ. However, equally significant to these macro-level issues are the micro-economic and organization factors that can be affected by operations and logistics management. Operations management can help organizations today.

Think of health care profit margins as a balloon, where a variety of extrinsic, or external, factors cause deflationary pressure from the outside. On the inside is the set of decisions and management systems put in place to combat these pressures and essentially inflate the balloon, or expand the margin. In effect, operations management is the set of intrinsic, or internal, processes and decisions that help address costs, process, technology, and productivity. Strategic management, although equally important, is not a focus of this text. **Figure 1–1** shows conceptually the margin-expansion role that operations management plays.

Health care is primarily a service sector, in that the industry provides intangible or nonphysical "goods," as opposed to physical objects that can be seen or touched. Hospital services primarily deliver care through providers to patients and therefore lack a manufacturing or assembling process. These services are unique and somewhat differentiated from other hospitals, knowledge based, and have high levels of customer interaction. Of course, there is a physical good that

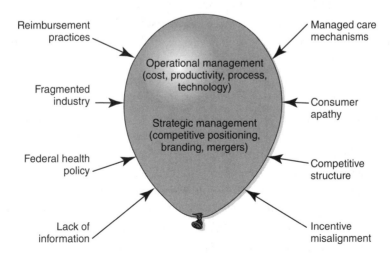

FIGURE 1–1 Operations Management Counters the Extrinsic Pressures Deflating Health Care Margins

accompanies the service, which is the focus of supply chain management in hospitals that procures, replenishes, and stores medical supplies and pharmaceuticals as well. In this regard, hospitals have a mix of both tangible and intangible characteristics. All of these attributes make health care operations management somewhat different from industries that strictly produce and market physical goods or widgets.

Health care operations management can therefore be defined as the quantitative management of the supporting business systems and processes that transform resources (inputs) into health care services (outputs). Inputs are defined as resources and assets such as labor and capital, including cash, technology, personnel, space, equipment, and information. Outputs include the actual production and delivery of health care services. Quantitative management implies a heavy use of analytical and optimization tools, as well as extensive use of process and quality improvement techniques to drive improved results.

Health care operations management is a discipline of management that integrates scientific or quantitative principles to determine the most efficient and optimal methods to support patient care delivery. This field is relatively new to health care, but it has existed in other industries for nearly 100 years.

KEY FUNCTIONS OF HEALTH CARE OPERATIONS MANAGEMENT

The scope of health care operations management includes all functions related to the management systems and business processes underlying clinical care. This includes extensive focus on the following: workflow, physical layout, capacity design, physical network optimization, staffing levels, productivity management, supply chain and logistics management, quality management, and process engineering. **Table 1–1** summarizes these key functions and illustrates some of the critical issues and questions that must be addressed for the health care enterprise.

Health care operations management includes all of these business functions and provides job opportunities for those with titles such as administrator, scheduling manager, operations supervisor, vice president of support services, quality manager, operations analyst, director of patient transportation, procurement manager, management engineer, inventory analyst, facilities manager, supply chain consultant, and so on. Nurses, technicians, and other health providers also play a key role in managing service operations. Operational management positions in hospitals will continue to grow as the need for increased cost efficiency and accountability rises.

Table 1–1   Key Functions and Issues in Health Care Operations Management

Operations Management Function	Objective or Issue to Consider
Workflow process	• Are there too many departments or people performing the same task? • Do we have an end-to-end map of our major business processes? • How many manual processes exist? • Are there ways to reduce cycle time, steps, and choke points for key processes? • Can we improve speed and patient satisfaction?
Physical layout	• Are our facilities designed with the consideration of speed, capacity, traffic flow, and operational efficiency? • Are unit or floor layouts designed to eliminate redundancy (e.g., safety stock on all resources)?
Capacity design and planning	• How can we reduce bottlenecks to improve patient throughput for each area? • In which cases should we increase the use of technology to improve labor productivity?
Physical network optimizations	• Where should we position appropriate par locations, pharmacy satellites, warehouses, and supplies to minimize resources and costs? • Do we strategically utilize vendors and their facilities? • How can we design and position optimal locations for clinics or resources to ensure lowest total costs?
Staffing levels and productivity management	• How much output can we expect from our staff? • Have we maximized the use of automation and electronic commerce to increase productivity? • Have we implemented sophisticated analytical models to optimize labor and resource scheduling?
Supply chain and management	• Have we built collaborative planning and forecasting logistics processes to standardize items and reduce total costs? • Should we operate *just in time*? • Do we use automated, optimized replenishment of medical–surgical supplies to increase turns and asset utilization? • How much inventory of each item do we need? • Do we use perpetual inventory systems to ensure stringent internal controls and accurate financial reports?
Quality, planning, and process improvement	• Do we use advanced tools for tracking projects? • Are we measuring the right performance indicators to bring visibility to trends and exceptions? • Do we know how we compare to our key competitors? • Have we identified the quality issues that affect our customer satisfaction and efficacy goals, in addition to efficiency, costs, and speed?

THE NEED FOR OPERATIONS MANAGEMENT

The *Future of Emergency Care* report series produced by the Institute of Medicine of the National Academies describes the problems facing health care today, especially the emergency care arena. The report outlines several recommendations for solving the current crisis, and one key recommendation notes, "Hospitals should reduce crowding by improving hospital efficiency and patient flow, and using operational management methods and information technologies" (Institute of Medicine, 2006, p. 2).

Others outside of the health care industry have also identified weaknesses in how health care managers administer the processes and systems. IBM has recognized that the service sector must focus more on applying management science to improve processes and outcomes and is collaborating with universities to implement what it calls *services science*. Irving Wladawsky-Berger, IBM's Vice President for Technical Strategy and Innovation, was quoted in *The New York Times* as saying,

> All those processes [in a hospital] get done in a relatively ad hoc way. If we want to apply information technology and engineering discipline to improve the quality of the service to reduce errors and to improve productivity, you need people who know how to design a hospital system. (Holstein, 2006, p. 10)

Clearly, even those on the periphery of the health care system understand the complexity and the lack of sophistication that currently exist in the industry.

Many other researchers and associations have called for operations management to help drive improvements and efficiencies in the health care system (Herzlingertt, 1999). The purpose of this text is to help students and practitioners do just that.

GOALS OF THE OPERATIONS MANAGER

The operations manager may hold any number of the job titles discussed earlier, but generically the term *operations manager* will be used to describe all such positions in this text. A clinic manager who ensures that processes are in place so that patients efficiently move from registration to treatment rooms to payment is an operations manager. An administrative director who oversees financial operations is an operations manager. An operations manager is any individual who directs and transforms processes to improve the delivery of patient care. What else do operations managers do? They have a variety of broad goals and functions in the hospital, including all of the following: reduce costs, reduce variability and improve logistics flow, improve productivity, improve quality of customer service, and continuously improve business processes. These are outlined in more detail in the following sections.

Reduce Costs

The primary role of operations managers is to take costs out of the health care system. Finding waste, improving utilization, and generally stabilizing and reducing the overall cost of delivering services are essential functions. A hospital with appropriate tracking and management systems—that can isolate all personnel, material, and other resources utilized for delivery of care—will be much more likely to reduce costs because it understands the underlying cost structure. Identifying costs and eliminating unnecessary waste and effort is at the forefront of an operations manager's priority list.

Reduce Variability and Improve Logistics Flow

Operations managers continuously look for the most efficient and optimal paths for movement of resources, whether those resources are physical or information flows. Similarly, there is a continuous focus on reducing variability. **Variability** is the inconsistency or dispersion of inputs and outputs. Variability threatens processes because it results in uncertainty, too many or too few resources, and generally inconsistent results. If there are 10 patients typically seeking care in a specific clinic within a certain time period, and then 20 appear the following period, it will be difficult to staff, control waiting times, and manage patient flows.

Improving flow means seeking higher throughput or yields for the same level of resource input. **Throughput** is the rate or velocity at which services are performed or goods are delivered. If a hospital typically sees four patients an hour and can increase throughput to six per hour, this is a 50% improvement in logistical flow and throughput. Similarly, if patient volumes double but a hospital maintains the same historical inventory levels of pharmaceutical supplies, this represents significant improvement in material flow, because assets have higher utilization and turns.

Staffing and resource consumption should be tied directly to patient volumes and workload: If patient volumes increase, so too should resources. Unfortunately, many health care facilities do not understand patient volumes and the variability that exists from hour to hour and day to day. Managing this variability allows an adjustment to staffing mix and scheduling to accommodate the changes, without staffing at the peaks (which causes excessive costs), staffing for the valleys or low points (which will cause long lines periodically due to limited resources and therefore service quality issues), or staffing for the average (which is the most common suboptimal approach). **Figure 1–2** shows how variability changes over time, which necessitates both capacity and demand analyses.

Logistics is defined as the efficient coordination and control of the flow of all operations, including patients, personnel, and other resources. The role of operations managers is to facilitate improved logistics and throughput by using streamlined process and facility designs to increase capacity, workflow, and throughput.

Improve Productivity

Hospitals have a tendency to hire additional staff faster than in other industries. This is partly driven by the highly structured organizations that are common in health care and partly because of the historical lack of focus on costs. In years past, hospitals were reimbursed by the government and other payers on a "cost-plus" basis—meaning that whatever the cost to deliver, hospitals would be fully reimbursed along with a small profit margin.

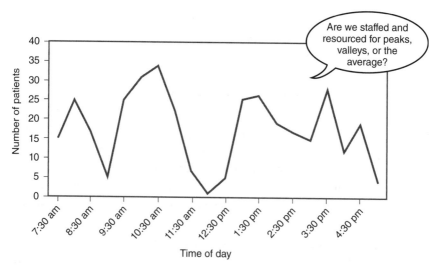

FIGURE 1–2 Variability Creates Chaos and Inefficiency

When pricing is guaranteed to cover costs, there is not a tendency to be overly cost conscious. Even though the industry continues to move toward a prospective payment system and managed care, the mentality and behavior of many hospitals have been slow to adapt. **Productivity** is defined as the ratio of outputs to inputs. Improving productivity implies a search for higher levels of output from all employees and other assets. This is one of the most vital roles of an operations manager.

Improve Quality of Customer Service

Health care cannot become so focused on cost and efficiency that quality starts to diminish. Improved quality implies reduced medical errors and improved patient safety, in addition to higher levels of patient satisfaction. Maintenance and improvement of high quality and service levels, both from patient care and other business services (such as the cafeteria or admissions), are expected from an operations manager. Across all industries, higher-quality services lead to the ability to secure higher prices, which drives increased market shares and operating margins (Buzzell & Gale, 1987).

Ensuring that services continue to improve patient satisfaction levels while simultaneously reducing response and waiting times are key deliverables to providing higher-quality services. The **cost–quality continuum** refers to a theoretical trade-off in which a focus on one side of the equation leads to diminishing returns on the other. A focus on costs may lead a hospital to reduce services provided, which may affect overall quality. Operations professionals must balance both and help to make optimal decisions on many fronts.

Continuously Improve Business Processes

In highly structured organizations, business processes tend to be unique to each department and are not highly cross functional or integrated. The operating room in one hospital may handle procurement of goods one way, while the same hospital's gynecology department handles it another. There is typically no sharing of best practices internally, standardization of processes that can lead to improved learning and economies of scale, and very little multidepartment workflow automation. Each department in large hospitals today operates as an independent business, which creates multiple efficiency problems. The role of operations management is to find ways to carry out business processes while improving process efficiency and effectiveness. **Figure 1–3** shows the operations management process of converting inputs into outputs.

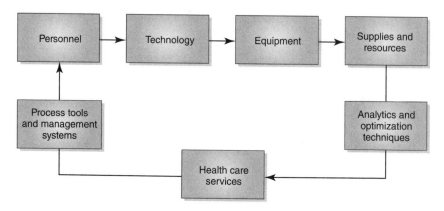

FIGURE 1-3 The Operations Management Process

COMPETITIVE ADVANTAGE OF OPERATIONS

Overall, if a hospital is successful at delivering on each of these goals throughout the facility, it will deliver improved operational effectiveness. **Operations effectiveness** is a measure of how well the organization is run. It considers both the efficiency of resource inputs and usage and the effectiveness of overall management in achieving desired goals and outcomes (Kilmann & Kilmann, 1991). **Operational excellence** is a term often used to describe a business strategy that focuses exclusively on maximizing operational effectiveness.

A hospital that is operationally effective is heading toward increased competitiveness. **Competitiveness** is management's ability to respond to environmental changes (such as changes in reimbursement practices) as well as competitors' actions (such as adding new facilities or expanding existing service lines). If a hospital can achieve a competitive edge or advantage over other hospitals—and sustain this position—it will have higher operating margins and be able to continue improving, expanding, and surviving. Operations management is critical to this outcome.

Competitiveness is often driven by innovation. **Innovation** is the continuous search for a way to do new things or to do current things better. Organizations innovate by using new technologies or finding ways to change the playing field so that processes that once were considered essential are no longer necessary. The electronics industry is an example in which firms continuously innovate. A firm that was competitive based on analog technology had its perspective of the world shaken up considerably when digital technology was created, and the products that the firm once made became completely irrelevant. In addition, continuous innovation often results in hypercompetition, which ultimately is characterized by economics wherein both prices and costs decline (D'Aveni, 1994). For example, when digital video disc players were first introduced, prices were nearly $1,000. Today, they can be purchased for as little as $30 in discount stores. The prices of smartphones, tablets, televisions, laptops, and many other electronics all follow the same pattern. In health care, innovation also helps to improve competitiveness.

FACTORS DRIVING INCREASED HEALTH CARE COSTS

Imagine that rather than a health care organization's annual budget increasing between 5% and 15% (the range of industry average annual changes), expenses could be maintained and even show signs of deflation, or negative price/cost growth. This would be very beneficial to a hospital's financial condition if it could reduce costs and maintain similar pricing levels.

The historical argument justifying continuously growing health care inflation rates typically focuses on five points:

1. Consumers are aging and living longer and are increasingly utilizing a greater number of services than in prior years.
2. The costs of medical technology and equipment continue to rise, and this represents a growing percentage of capital budgets for most organizations.
3. The labor costs of key resources (such as physicians and nurses) are governed by market shortages for these positions, which have increased steadily in the past few decades.
4. Prices of pharmaceuticals, which represent a sizable portion of medical treatment plans, continue to escalate to cover high costs of research and development, long U.S. Food and Drug Administration approval cycles, and generally high industry margins for pharmaceuticals.
5. Emphasis on strict managed care, which appeared to be the predominant model a decade ago, is slowly shifting and diminishing in practice.

The result has been a steadily increasing cost of care. For example, the Bureau of Labor Statistics tracks inflation growth through its consumer price index, a mathematical calculation of the average pricing changes over time, using a market basket approach. The general consumer price index for all items in years 1999 through 2005 showed an increase of less than 14% over 7 years, or around

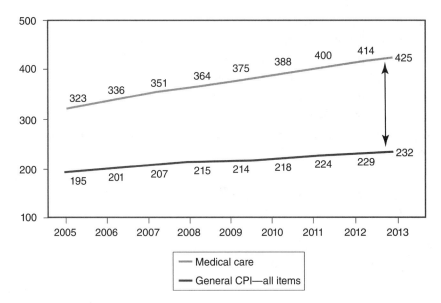

FIGURE 1–4 Controlling Exponential Price Increases in Health Care
Data from U.S. Department of Labor, Bureau of Labor Statistics, 2014.

2% per year (Bureau of Labor Statistics, 2014). Compare that with the cost of medical care, which rose nearly 30% in that same time period—almost double that of all the other goods tracked. **Figure 1–4** shows this growth over time.

Overall spending for health care in the United States has risen steadily. In 1993, health care costs represented 13% of the national gross domestic product; in 2006, this number increased to more than 16.5%; and today it is nearly 18–19% of the gross domestic product. Economists project that this will double again in the next decade (Heffler et al., 2005). While some hospitals wait for the national debate to continue, it is important to first look at the intrinsic factors in the organization that are driving excessive costs: redundancy, inefficiency, bureaucracy, waste, paper, limited productivity, lack of performance monitoring, poor deployment of information technology, and generally unsophisticated levels of management.

LEARNING FROM OTHER INDUSTRIES

Although health care is unique and has its own set of challenges, hospitals can learn a great deal from other industries that have evolved faster due to technology or process innovation, industry economics, more aggressive competition, reduced barriers to entry and exit, or just better trained business managers. For example, if managers looked at a hospital as being similar to the retail industry, they could better understand how to lay out floors, design configurations to achieve more efficient movement and handling, and use analytical forecasts to drive all aspects of the business. There is a lot to learn from the more operationally effective industries. The tools and techniques that are most similar should be borrowed and applied to health care where appropriate.

For example, in the airline industry, thousands of planes move through the sky fairly seamlessly. Planes land every few seconds at major airports throughout the world, and yet there are very few accidents (as a percentage of total flights), very high levels of on-time rates (given numerous factors such as weather and security), and very little lost baggage. Nearly 650 million passengers boarded planes in 2013 in the United States alone (Bureau of Transportation Statistics, 2014). Airlines have learned to operate using speed and volume as an advantage. When an airplane lands, there is very little time before it must be turned around and readied to take off to another destination. This changeover process allows less than 30 minutes, on average, to completely refuel, check maintenance and mechanical conditions, validate aviation systems, restock food and supplies, change over personnel, and unload and reload hundreds of passengers. Think of this changeover as it relates to the process a hospital goes through when changing out beds after a patient is discharged (i.e., admitting and bed management process). A lot can be learned from how another industry approaches a somewhat similar problem. **Table 1–2** summarizes what operations managers in health care can learn from other industries.

Table 1–2   Teaching from Other Industries

Retail	Building layout and configuration, customer flows, use of forecasts and planning, electronic commerce
Airlines	Scheduling, logistics, strategic pricing (yield management)
Chemicals	Efficiencies, economies of scale, extensive use of linear programming and quantitative modeling
Electronics	Technology innovation, product life-cycle management, pricing strategy
Telecommunications	Command and control center

PRINCIPLES OF MANAGEMENT

Operations management is one discipline in the broader field of management. According to most theorists, management concerns itself with four key functions: planning, organizing, leading, and controlling. **Planning** involves the establishment of goals and a strategy to achieve them. In health care, planning can be strategic (such as deciding which geographic region to invest in a new facility), or it can be operational (such as how many employees to have on staff for each shift). **Organizing** includes making decisions about which tasks will be done, where, when, and by whom. Organizing uses a variety of tools, such as an organizational chart to manage people's roles and reporting relationships, process flowcharts for improving activities, and Gantt charts for managing projects. **Leading** includes motivating employees, building support for ideas, and generally getting things done through people. Providing direction and clarification of expectations, as well as the role of change management, or preparing the organization for changes to come, are instrumental in providing leadership in hospital operations management. **Controlling** includes all tasks to monitor and track progress toward goals, ensure performance improvement, and make corrective changes in strategy where necessary. The use of status reports, budgets, procedures, and a multitude of other tracking tools is useful in helping enhance management control.

Managers wear many hats and play many roles. They may serve as a figurehead, make decisions, reward employees, and handle conflicts and solve problems. Managers help plan tasks, organize and direct them, and continually adjust and control. Henry Mintzberg (1973), one of the earliest researchers on management processes, described the nature of a manager's work as grouped around three key themes: informational, decisional, and interpersonal. Informational refers to collecting, monitoring, and disseminating information from the external and internal environments to work teams. Decisional refers to making key decisions for the organization, such as allocation of scarce resources, rewards and penalties for employees, and negotiations with employees and others. Interpersonal includes training and motivating employees, serving as a spokesperson, facilitating communication exchanges among various groups, and serving as a liaison.

The study of management continues to evolve. It has moved through a variety of schools of thought: from scientific management to process focused to human behavior to decision or management sciences theory to social and open systems (Certo & Certo, 2005). These schools of thought represent different contexts or perspectives on which a manager's role and tasks should be based. For example, the systems theory schools emphasize that a manager views the organization as a living organism, which is changing and adapting and that operates by an integrated network of open processes. Behavioral schools tend to view management from a psychological aspect, highlighting the importance of understanding what motivates employees and how human and cognitive factors influence work environments.

For purposes of operations management and looking for ways to improve operational effectiveness, the school of thought that is most relevant is that of scientific management.

THE SCIENTIFIC AND MATHEMATICAL SCHOOLS OF MANAGEMENT

Operations management seeks to apply quantitative and analytical techniques to achieve the goals of reduced costs, higher quality, higher productivity, improved processes, and improved logistical flows. The role of mathematics started to drive concepts of industrial efficiency in what is now known as the scientific management era, which began prior to the turn of the 20th century.

Scientific schools of thought historically focused on use of concepts such as time and motion studies, which measured how long business processes took, seeking ways to reduce the variability of the results and continuously shrinking the times and associated costs. Early work by Frank and Lillian Gilbreth helped drive a focus on continual improvements—finding ways to do things faster and with fewer resources. In fact, the Gilbreths' research has had a profound effect on health care as well (Gilbreth & Carey, 1966). In the early 1900s, they were credited as observing the productivity of surgeons and found that the introduction of changes in both staffing and workflow could significantly alter physician productivity. The introduction of a surgical nurse—to help provide surgical instruments and supplies when needed in order to free up the surgeon, thereby improving overall productivity—was one of the key recommendations made. In addition, the Gilbreths recommended other hospital improvements, such as a tray to hold common surgical instruments. These are just two of the contributions made by scientific management to health care.

Frederick Taylor, one of the original management researchers and the "father of scientific management," was often quoted as saying that scientific management is a great "mental revolution" (Matteson & Ivancevich, 1996). By this, he meant that a scientific approach encourages a different perspective or outlook that can change management behaviors and results. This revolution led to some key concepts, such as specialization, division of labor, and mass production. The concept of **specialization** suggests that if people repeatedly perform just one task, they will be able to perform that task faster and with higher quality than others, because they have repeated exposure to the process and have learned from their experiences. Specialization, in many regards, is what leads hospitals to structure their organization around units such as nursing or materials management. Continued specialization helps to produce well-defined roles and tasks, concentrated work efforts, and higher efficiencies. This is also known as **division of labor**. **Mass production** is the creation of rapid production processes through the use of assembly-line techniques. Mass production has been embraced by most other industries, but, in many respects, it is not relevant in health care.

The scientific era has been shown to have several failings and issues, which led to other schools of thought. The lack of focus on human behavior, alignment of employee rewards with those of the organization, and understanding the need for job rotations and expansion all are major issues that well-rounded managers must consider. Thus, many of the analytical concepts of scientific management remain vital to health care operations management. First, scientific management suggests the need for a strong understanding of processes, their costs and resource utilizations, constraints, and cycle times. Second, scientific management encourages an initial focus on understanding expected outcomes and subsequently designing management systems and business processes around this operational strategy. Third, the variability of processes has to be smoothed out and consistently managed. Finally, scientific management shows that in many cases quantitative approaches can help create mathematically optimal results for common management decisions and problems. These four fundamental concepts are the foundation of the operations management discipline.

MANAGEMENT DECISION MAKING

Management decision making is a process in an organization in which decisions are made (Yates, 2003) and reflects the major processes involved in managing the work of organizations (Szilagyi & Wallace, 1990). Decisions are the output of the process and are typically described as a choice between two or more alternatives (Rowe, Boulgarides, & McGrath, 1984). Decisions can also be described as an "action" taken as a result of a process. As Hoch and Kunreuther (2001) stated, "The strength or weakness of managerial decisions is the linchpin of the business enterprise" (p. 9).

Herbert Simon (1960), one of the first researchers on decision making in organizations, described the decision-making process as having three steps:

1. Finding occasions to make a decision.
2. Finding possible courses of action.
3. Choosing among many options.

Browne (1993) described it similarly as that "which occurs at the highest level of an organization" (p. 2). Schwenk (1988) described management or strategic decisions as ill structured, nonroutine, important to the organization, involving large resource commitments, and generally very complex. A traditional management decision process, adapted from Browne, is shown in **Figure 1–5**.

Decision-making theory has been defined by many perspectives: sociology, psychology, economics, engineering, and business. Because management decisions are made within organizations, organizational theorists early on shaped the field by suggesting a rational approach where decision makers make decisions in the best interests of the organization and emphasize "information processing." More recently, there has been a strong emphasis on decision making as a behavioral process, as decisions are made by individuals, where personality and judgment represent both a source of bias and influence on decision processes.

Harrison (1987) described decisions as either "routine and programmable" or "complex and unique." If decisions are routine, then they are procedural and can use computation and rational models for decision support. This area is well suited for operations research methods. The latter is more unstructured and relies more on judgment and general problem-solving approaches. This method has typically been considered to emphasize behavioral processes over quantitative ones, because they involve ambiguity, conflict, negotiations, and bias created by the interaction of individuals and personalities.

Similarly, Allison (1971) outlined three perspectives on strategic decision making: rational, organizational, and political.

1. *Rational.* Barnes (1984) was one of the earlier researchers in this area, which defines decisions as the product of a "conscious choice." The rational, conscious choice emphasizes a "search and selection" process that has limited alternatives, maximizes decision outcomes, and adjusts for risks. Other researchers have outlined structured methods for organizational decision makers to follow to reach optimal or maximizing outcomes (see Christensen, Andrews, Bower, Hammermesh, & Porter, 1982).

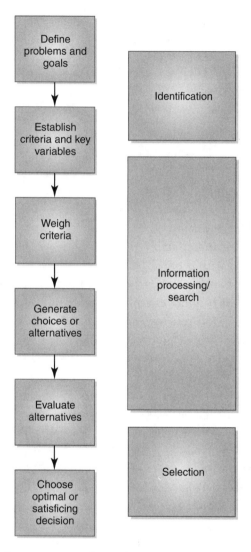

FIGURE 1–5 Traditional Decision-Making Process

2. *Organizational.* Henry Mintzberg (1978) is generally recognized as one of the leading researchers on decision making from an organizational theory perspective. This views decisions as the outputs of organizational processes, not individual ones, and includes adapting astrategy to the environment. The organizational approach emphasizes *satisficing*. **Satisficing** is a process of making a less than optimal decision, but one that can be supported and is acceptable because it meets the minimal criteria (e.g., the decision is reached quickly, is adequate, and/or is the result of

consensus between parties). Satisficing terminates the search for alternative processes early. Ambiguity plays a critical part, as does the concept of randomness, which leads to models of decision making that are less than rational and that can be described as "organized anarchies" or "garbage can" models (March & Olsen, 1979).

3. *Political.* From this perspective, decisions are the result of bargaining among individuals attempting to achieve their own personal goals (Abell, 1975). This includes social, nonprofit, educational, and other organizations. Political models tend to redefine the decision processes, structures, and goals on a continual basis, making evaluation difficult. Behavioral concepts, such as the roles of judgment, biases, emotions, and heuristics, are often a component of this perspective. Bazerman (2005) is one of the prominent researchers on individuals and behavior in decision-making processes.

From both the organizational and political perspectives, the concept of bounded rationality has emerged. Bounded rationality suggests that humans or individuals have only a limited, finite capacity to understand all of the options available to them and process them in an evaluation mode (Simon, 1979). Bounded rationality can also be described as limits on a human's ability to process and interpret large volumes of data (Bazerman, 2005). Theory suggests that while rational models think all alternatives are known, they usually are not and there is no known probability or consequences of the actions. In addition, goals are changing and the process is not always as sequential as it would appear. The complexity of decision processes is also often used to describe why rational models are not appropriate.

There are two components of bounded rationality: search and satisficing (Simon, 1979). Search refers to how extensively a decision maker searches for information to guide decision making (Tiwana, Wang, Keil, & Ahluwalia, 2007). Simon envisioned an "aspiration point" where managers determine what is "good enough." This process of terminating the search process without incorporating more extensive information is called *satisficing*, as discussed earlier. This can create biases and risks for managers.

The concept of trade-offs is related to satisficing (Simon, 1965). Trade-offs represent a cognitive process of balancing the pros and cons of attributes or decision criteria in an effort to accept less of something to get more of something else (Luce, Payne, & Bettman, 2001).

Browne (1993) described four models or perspectives in decision theory: normative, descriptive, analytical, and behavioral. Normative models, or prescriptive models, describe what managers should be doing to produce optimal outcomes.

Browne suggested that normative models are the contributions of scientific management. Simon (1965) argued that rational models of management science are valuable contributions toward normative decision-making theory. Descriptive models describe what actually occurs in organizations, not what should occur. Analytical models, which are the contribution of management science, involve risk and uncertainty in quantification and in the role of modeling decisions and predicting outcomes. Finally, behavioral models examine the roles of bias and cognition in humans, as well as how information is processed and used.

As theory has established, decision making is not necessarily a rational search and evaluation process, where alternatives are clearly defined, evaluated, and then the best alternative is selected. Brunsson (1985) argued that decision making is less about finding the right choice and more about giving an impression of rationality in organizational processes. He also described other more common irrational processes used by managers. In decision sciences, decisions are sometimes categorized into one of two types: routine or complex. Routine decisions have been described as "programmable" and are sometimes associated with selection and evaluation methods that can be mechanized or automated (Harrison, 1987). These routine decisions are often supported by methods such as operations research. The more complex the decisions are, the greater the use of intuition or judgment in the process, and presumably the less likely that methods such as operations research will be used. Discussion in strategic management literature about the role of intuition versus analytics touches on this subject but does not comprehensively address the role of quantitative methods using the routine-complex dimension (Miller & Ireland, 2005).

In summary, organizational decision-making processes are complex and appear to be variable in nature. In addition, the complexity of the decision and the cognitive capacity of the decision makers both influence the form of decision processes. As a result, some health care organizations may find a quantitative component of operations management decision making more useful or relevant, while others may value it to a lesser extent.

POWER AND DECISION MAKING IN HEALTH CARE

Decisions in health care do not follow the traditional, logical processes used in industrial organizations. In other industries, where profit maximization and shareholder wealth are the primary motives, decisions are usually driven by goal alignment for both managers (those who run the business) and owners (shareholders who invest in equity or debt and have a claim on the profits and assets). Decision making tends to follow cost-benefit models and focus on risk minimization, cash flows, and return on investment. Although disputes and conflicts may arise because of incomplete or imperfect information (as described in the agency theory of economics), these disputes can typically be minimized by changing incentives, behaviors, and structural mechanisms.

In health care, however, there is incomplete alignment of goals between different agents, or managers, in the organization because of three issues:

1. *Goals are unclear.* There are clinical goals, financial goals, educational or academic goals, societal goals, community goals, and so on. The ambiguity that exists in terms of priorities and focus makes goals much less acute than in other industries.

2. *Organizations are complex.* In industrial organizations, the organization is clearly focused on the key aspects of buying, making, selling, and moving products to the marketplace. In health care, reporting relationships often involve complex matrices and dual-reporting structures. This is not the "command and control" structure, focused on speed and efficiency of decision making, that might work in other places.

3. *Relationships are ambiguous.* Many business units in health care are interconnected, but they often behave as if they were not. Independent departments and providers help create an environment that is less team focused than in other industries, making relationships important for purposes of mutual support as allies. There are also continuous power struggles in the health care arena between different factions of employees. This creates ambiguity in decision making.

Physicians are typically the most dominant players, given their clinical expertise and control over the "production" of health care services, and they have a very substantial role in most major organizational decisions (Young & Saltman, 1985). Power conflicts with nurses and other providers are frequent and have developed (for structural reasons) in the struggle for control over patients, their care, and overall patient management processes (Coombs, 2004). As such, several formal power bases have emerged: business managers, who increasingly are becoming more professional and sophisticated; physician leadership, which historically dominates the power pendulum; and nursing leadership, which may have the most intimate knowledge of patients and their needs.

Those who control the "production" process in most industries tend to have the most influence and can control decision making for many things. In the production of health care (i.e., delivery of treatments and provision of care) physicians are by far the dominant players, yet their role in most operational management processes in most hospitals is waning as professional business managers evolve.

Decision making in teaching hospitals and academic medical centers is even more complicated due to the introduction of another dominant party: academic faculty and researchers (Choi, Allison, & Munson, 1986). In the largest hospitals, this complexity in decision making is complicated by large business infrastructures, which may employ hundreds or thousands of individuals in all types of support functions from admissions to patient finance to facilities.

Three characteristics define this complexity of decision processes: problematic preferences, unclear technology, and fluid participation (Cohen, March, & Olsen, 1972). These characteristics, together with "streams" of both problems and choices, can be combined in unclear decision processes in a "garbage can," where they can often address the wrong problems at the wrong time. This garbage can tends to allow issues and solutions to resurface in strange ways, which often results in a lack of clarity and focus.

With all of these dominant players and complexities, many hospitals have become large bureaucracies. These bureaucracies make it difficult to make important decisions, address financial and business issues, change behaviors and business processes, and implement new technology.

Sophistication in operations and logistics management requires not only understanding concepts and their application to health care, but also understanding the persuasive and leadership characteristics necessary to navigate the bureaucracy, influence dominant power groups, engage support for ideas, and ultimately gain approval for and acceptance of changes. These changes will come only if business executives achieve more dominant power positions, which can evolve only as operations and logistics executives are recognized for their contributions, specialized education, professional expertise, and leadership skills. Collaboration within these multidisciplinary organizations is just one way to retain more control in the decision-making process.

THE ROLE OF TECHNOLOGY

With its focus on improvements, operations management rests highly on the use of technology and automation. Many new technologies—including mobile devices, handhelds, scanning capabilities, asset tracking, database management, health information exchanges, and electronic health records—help managers improve their capture of data and transform it into improved decisions. Decisions about capital investment in new information and management systems are always at the forefront of the modern operations manager's mind. Technology should be considered whenever quality and efficiency is low. Processes that are repetitive in nature and that can be replaced by less expensive automation are also suitable for a technology investment. Technology often serves one of three roles:

1. Automate manual processes.
2. Improve transaction processing capabilities.
3. Improve the quality of analysis, reports, and decisions.

Technology has the ability to substantially alter the economics of a process. Processes that can be mechanized allow for faster production or delivery, with less resource usage—two keys to improving operational effectiveness. The decision to substitute capital, or technology, for labor—especially in areas of business support services—is the only way to reduce processing and transactional costs over the long run.

TRENDS IN OPERATIONS MANAGEMENT

There are several trends that are being widely considered and adopted in hospitals. These are depicted in **Table 1–3**, and the trends correspond to the role or function of operations management most closely related to it.

Table 1–3   Roles and Trends in Health Care Operations Management

Primary Role of Operations Managers	Evolving Trends
1. Reduce costs	Standardization Optimization Resource tracking systems
2. Reduce variability and improve logistical flow	Integrated service delivery Analytics Supply chain management
3. Improve productivity	Information technology; mobile devices; asset and patient tracking systems Return on investment
4. Provide higher-quality services	Evidence-based health care Six Sigma
5. Improve business processes	Outsourcing Globalization

Outsourcing is the contracting of an outside firm to perform services that were once handled internally. Outsourcing is common in many industries, and in health care it has been used successfully for cafeteria operations, bookstore management, investments, and even nursing and other clinical care areas. Outsourcing is not a new concept, but it has a slow adoption rate in health care, where decisions such as these are often difficult to make, especially when they result in the dismissal of employees from hospital payrolls. However, outsourcing, when used selectively to target the right areas, can be beneficial from a cost perspective.

Outsourcing relies on the notion that a hospital should focus on its core competencies—delivering clinical care—and not on some of the less mission-centric functions, such as housekeeping, materials management, finance, and information technology. When analyzing pre- and postperformance improvement, the evaluation of internally performed or selective outsourcing costs must be undertaken to ensure that all options are explored and the most operationally effective process remains.

Integrated service delivery is another trend that has developed over the past few years. Many researchers have pointed to the excessive cost of care as being driven by the medical community's continued desire for specialization and concentration on discrete diseases and treatments, rather than integrative, comprehensive care (Porter & Teisberg, 2006). In response to this, hospitals are looking for ways to push care toward more integrative medicine, including higher sharing of information, resources, and collaboration. The effect on operations management will include redesign of business processes and changes in the number and frequency of logistics networks.

Supply chain management is the integrated management of all products, information, and financial flows in a network designed to pull products from manufacturers to consumers. In health care, there has been widespread adoption of improved sourcing and inventory techniques, designed to lower overall supply expense ratios (which typically account for 25% to 50% of all hospital costs). Significantly more detail about the use of supply chain and logistics management will be covered elsewhere in the text.

Another trend in health care operations management is globalization. The world is becoming smaller, and vendors from all around the globe are competing for business in retail and other industries. Health care has only recently felt the effects, but this trend will continue. When firms look for outsourcing opportunities (e.g., in information technology), they are now able to turn to vendors as far away as Ireland and India to help manage their information technology operations infrastructure. Medical care that may once have required on-site specialists is now only a television away, allowing physicians to practice medicine without setting foot in the hospital. Vendors for certain medical supplies, pharmaceuticals, and equipment are emerging and starting to compete for business as potential suppliers, requiring hospital managers to understand global logistics. As more and more hospital services become automated, the location of the technology does not matter. This is the true result of globalization, and it will require adjustments by hospital management.

Investments in a hospital's information technology infrastructure are common today. Electronic medical records, computerized physician order entry, enterprise resource planning, picture archival communication systems, supply chain management, and many other systems are much more prevalent today than in years past. Investments in many lesser-known technologies for admissions, cashiering, inventory management, and even bed management are also becoming more common.

The basic premise of most technologies is that they provide some return that, when quantified, is greater than the costs associated with it. In some cases, this is simple to calculate, as when a system creates known financial value and has well-defined costs. In others, when the information technology produces vague benefits (such as extending a system's end of life or improving clinical quality), the returns are more difficult to measure and quantify and thus are more complex if creating a cost-benefit comparison. Regardless, the trend in leading hospitals is to conduct thorough return on investment analyses that clearly define the pre- and postenvironment and then make comparisons of the delivered or earned value for the project.

The growth in deployment of resource tracking systems is also interesting. Information systems and technology are being developed specific to health care to allow for tracking of patients, equipment, supplies, pharmaceuticals, bed occupancy, and much more. Microprocessor chips, bar-coding technology, global positioning systems, and radio frequency identification systems are all technologies that are being slowly adopted in larger hospitals. Many of these use existing wireless frequencies and infrastructure, so they are becoming easier to implement at lower costs. These tracking systems allow for closer monitoring of utilization patterns, location analysis, stationary or down times, and logistical flows, which thus helps better manage the number, type, and mix of resources required. Improved operational effectiveness results from improved utilization and higher asset productivities.

Another trend that is being followed closely in operations management is that of standardization. **Standardization** is the use of consistent procedures, resources, and services to achieve consistent results across multiple departments. In a system or network, standardization suggests that two hospitals could use the same basic medical supplies for multiple procedures, rather than a wide variety of them, which helps reduce inventory and purchasing costs and creates some economies of scale. Standardization also refers to the use of common standards for information systems, as well as personnel and operational processes. Standardization helps ensure alignment among departments, promote familiarization and learning curves, and reduce the number of transactions processed—all of which result in lower costs and higher productivity.

Finally, many hospitals practice what is called *evidence-based health care.* **Evidence-based medicine** applies the scientific method to medical practice and seeks to quantify the true outcomes associated with certain medical practices by applying statistical and research methods (Centre for Evidence-Based Medicine, 2014). Evidence-based health care, as it applies to logistics or operations, emphasizes that prior to decisions being made, the options are conscientiously analyzed for the effects each would have on operations. For example, if a certain piece of equipment needs to be replaced, evidence-based medicine suggests that the true costs and outcomes associated with this item be carefully analyzed over time; a replacement piece of equipment undergoes the exact same controls to guarantee and quantify the total effect of this change on the system. Evidence-based health care, in its use of quantitative methods and in seeking to comprehensively analyze operations, is completely in alignment with operations management theory. The use of quality management processes such as Six Sigma, which attempts to improve processes and outputs through continuous improvement techniques, is beginning to gain a solid foundation in the health care industry.

CHAPTER SUMMARY

Operations management is the quantitative management of the supporting business systems and processes that transform resources into health care outputs. Operations management is about coordinating diverse, complicated activities into a comprehensive system. It is focused on achieving operational effectiveness—defined as lower costs, higher productivity, and continuous process improvement. There are five key goals of the operations manager: reduce costs, reduce variability and improve logistics flows, improve productivity, improve quality of customer service, and continuously improve business processes. Operations management is a field within the discipline of management, and it evolved initially from the scientific management school of thought. The process of management decision making supports the choices for how operations management occurs. The decisions made affect the quality and efficiency of operations. With the increased emphasis on efficiency and quality in health care organizations, operations management has progressed to become more comprehensive and valuable. There are several evolving trends that are changing health care operations.

KEY TERMS

Competitiveness

Controlling

Cost–quality continuum

Decision making

Division of labor

Evidence-based medicine

Health care operations management

Innovation

Leading

Logistics

Mass production

Operational excellence

Operations effectiveness

Organizing

Outsourcing

Planning

Productivity

Satisficing

Specialization

Standardization

System

Throughput

Variability

DISCUSSION QUESTIONS

1. What is operations management in health care?
2. How is health care representative of a system?
3. What are the five key goals of operations managers?
4. Does operations management affect a hospital's competitive advantage?
5. What are three of the key trends affecting hospital operations?
6. Who is considered the "father" of scientific management?
7. How are decisions made in organizations?
8. What are the basic steps of a rational management decision-making process?
9. What are the common sources of cost increases in health care?
10. How does the medical care consumer price index relate to cost increases for other items?
11. What four things can be learned from scientific management?
12. What are the three reasons decision-making processes in health care are more ambiguous than in other organizations?
13. How does evidence-based medicine support operations management techniques?

EXERCISE PROBLEMS

1. Health care organizations routinely make complex organizational decisions. As an example, a decision to modify the physical layout or space of a department, or alter the schedules of a nursing unit, will affect patient care in many ways. Because so many stakeholders are involved, which process for making management decisions do you think will be followed? How would you use the decision-making process to make important decisions such as this in an organization?

2. Richmond Community Hospital currently receives more than 10,000 boxes of pharmaceutical supplies per month. All of these items are manually inspected and logged to ensure adequate receipt prior to payment. Eight employees manage receipts and deliveries, while four employees manually record and track them. A new software package that allows automated scanning of bar codes will replace all or some of the employees used for manual tracking, or at least allow redeployment to other areas of the hospital. What are some of the key questions that must be explored to fully understand the effects of technology and whether a capital investment should be made to substitute capital for labor?

REFERENCES

Abell, P. (Ed.). (1975). *Organizations as bargaining and influence systems.* New York, NY: Halstead Press.

Allison, G. T. (1971). *The essence of decision: Explaining the Cuban missile crisis.* Boston, MA: Little, Brown.

Barnes, J. (1984). Cognitive biases and their impact on strategic planning. *Strategic Management Journal, 5*(2), 129–137.

Bazerman, M. H. (2005). *Judgment in managerial decision making* (6th ed.). New York, NY: Wiley.

Browne, M. (1993). *Organizational decision making and information.* Norwood, NJ: Ablex.

Brunsson, N. (1985). *The irrational organization: Irrationality as a basis for organizational action and change.* New York, NY: Wiley.

Bureau of Labor Statistics. (2014). *CPI detailed report tables, January 2014.* Retrieved from http://www.bls.gov/cpi/cpid1401.pdf

Bureau of Transportation Statistics. (2014). *Airline activity: National summary (U.S. flights).* Washington, DC: U.S. Department of Transportation. Retrieved from www.transtats.bts.gov

Buzzell, R. D., & Gale, B. T. (1987). *The PIMS principles: Linking strategy to performance.* New York, NY: The Free Press.

Centre for Evidence-Based Medicine. (2014). *What we do.* Retrieved from www.cebm.net/what-we-do/

Certo, S. C., & Certo, S. T. (2005). *Modern management* (10th ed.). New York, NY: Prentice Hall.

Choi, T., Allison, R. F., & Munson, F. C. (1986). *Governing university hospitals in a changing environment.* Ann Arbor, MI: Health Administration Press.

Christensen, C. R., Andrews, K. R., Bower, J. L., Hammermesh, R. G., & Porter, M. E. (1982). *Business policy: Text and cases.* Homewood, IL: Irwin.

Cohen, M. D., March, J. G., & Olsen, J. P. (1972). A garbage can model of organizational choice. *Administrative Science Quarterly, 17*(1), 1–25.

Coombs, M. A. (2004). *Power and conflict between doctors and nurses: Breaking through the inner circle in clinical care.* New York, NY: Routledge.

D'Aveni, R. A. (1994). *Hypercompetition: Managing the dynamics of strategic maneuvering.* New York, NY: The Free Press.

Gilbreth, F. B., & Carey, E. G. (1966). *Cheaper by the dozen.* New York, NY: Cromwell.

Harrison, E. F. (1987). *The managerial decision-making process.* Boston, MA: Houghton Mifflin.

Heffler, S., Smith, S., Keehan, S., Borger, C., Clemens, M. K., & Truffer, C. (2005). Trends: U.S. health spending projections for 2004–2014. *Health Affairs, 10,* 79–93.

Herzlinger, R. (1999). *Market-driven health care: Who wins, who loses in the transformation of America's largest service industry.* New York, NY: Perseus Books.

Hoch, S. J., & Kunreuther, H. C. (Eds.). (2001). *Wharton on making decisions.* New York, NY: Wiley.

Holstein, W. J. (2006, December 3). And now a syllabus for the service economy. *The New York Times,* p. 10.

Institute of Medicine. (2006). *The future of emergency care: Key findings and recommendations.* Washington, DC: National Academy of Sciences.

Kilmann, R. H., & Kilmann, I. (1991). *Making organizations competitive: Enhancing networks and relationships across traditional boundaries.* San Francisco, CA: Jossey-Bass.

Luce, M. F., Payne, J. W., & Bettman, J. R. (2001). The emotional nature of decision trade-offs. In S. J. Hoch & H. C. Kunreuther (Eds.), *Wharton on making decisions* (pp. 17–36). New York, NY: Wiley.

March, J. G., & Olsen, J. P. (1979). *Ambiguity and choice in organizations.* Bergen, Norway: Universitests Forlaget.

Matteson, M. T., & Ivancevich, J. M. (1996). *Management and organizational behavior classics* (6th ed.). Homewood, IL: Irwin.

Miller, C. C., & Ireland, R. D. (2005). Intuition in strategic decision making: Friend or foe in the fast-paced 21st century? *Academy of Management Executive, 19*(1), 19–30.

Mintzberg, H. (1973). *The nature of managerial work.* Reading, MA: Addison-Wesley.

Mintzberg, H. (1978). Patterns in strategy formulation. *Management Science, 24*(9), 934–948.

Porter, M. E., & Teisberg, E. O. (2006). *Redefining health care: Creating value-based competition on results.* Boston, MA: Harvard Business School Press.

Rovin, S. (2001). *Medicine and business: Bridging the gap.* Gaithersburg, MD: Aspen.

Rowe, A. J., Boulgarides, J. D., & McGrath, M. R. (1984). *Managerial decision making.* Chicago, IL: Science Research Associates.

Schwenk, C. R. (1988). The cognitive processes in strategic decision making. *Journal of Management Studies, 25*(1), 41–55.

Simon, H. A. (1960). *The new science of management decision.* New York, NY: Harper & Row.

Simon, H. A. (1965). Administrative decision making. *Public Administration Review*, *25*(1), 31–37.

Simon, H. A. (1979). Rational decision making in business organizations. *American Economic Review*, *69*(4), 493–513.

Szilagyi, A. D., & Wallace, M. J. (1990). *Organizational behaviour and performance*. New York, NY: HarperCollins.

Tiwana, A., Wang, J., Keil, M., & Ahluwalia, P. (2007). The bounded rationality bias in managerial valuation of real options: Theory and evidence from IT projects. *Decision Sciences*, *38*(1), 157–181.

Yates, J. F. (2003). *Decision management*. San Francisco, CA: Jossey-Bass.

Young, D. W., & Saltman, R. B. (1985). *The hospital power equilibrium: Physician behavior and cost control*. Baltimore, MD: Johns Hopkins University Press.

Health Care Marketplace

Those who find themselves working as business professionals in a health care setting for the first time will undoubtedly be overwhelmed on the first day of employment. The first thing to notice is that there is a much greater focus on medical activities than business activities in most facilities. Another first impression is that the layout and design of workflow and facilities are often extremely inefficient, cluttered, and almost an afterthought. The information systems in all but the most advanced hospitals have not yet discovered or adopted electronic commerce, process automation, and real-time operational reporting, as expected in retail or manufacturing industries. In addition, hospitals have not yet begun to focus on key business issues as have almost all other industries over the past few decades. This is good news for those just joining the industry, because it promises significant change and opportunities for improvement.

Before operations management can help make a difference in health care—using quantitative tools and techniques to drive improvements across all areas of the business—it is important to understand the context of the modern hospital: what it is, how it started, and where it is going.

HOSPITALS ARE BIG BUSINESS

Hospitals are large and complex organizations and differ from most traditional organizations in many ways. First, hospital missions focus on the more abstract goals of improving community health or curing and eliminating disease. Other types of companies typically have a two-pronged mission of maximizing profits and satisfying stakeholders, which helps to clearly focus employees and others on efficiencies, revenues, and cost reductions.

Hospitals also offer an intangible product, unlike a widget that can be easily packaged and sold. This service, which is somewhat unique and not widely available, distinguishes the production of health care from the production of other goods.

Typically, hospitals are not profit-maximizing entities, and historically most have not been overly concerned about negative margins or breakeven income statements. Most other organizations focus solely on maximizing the wealth of the owners or shareholders and to a lesser degree on the social or public benefits that are derived from the production of their goods or services.

In addition, the primary performance outcome of a hospital is measured in terms of quality, which is abstractly determined by a wide range of mortality and morbidity indicators and not by business metrics such as economic value, return on investment, or net income. This lack of focus on the more common financial metrics separates health care from most other industries, which use indexes that daily monitor the efficient flow of information about the organization and communicate the value generated, as in a stock exchange. As a by-product, there is very little free flow of information about most health care organizations, and this lack of perfect information further distinguishes the health care industry.

Of great importance is that hospitals are governed to a large degree by professionals who lack formal training in business management, unlike other firms where those educated and professionally trained in business disciplines clearly govern all aspects of the business. This is one of the primary reasons the financial and business implications of key decisions may become secondary to the more relevant medical issues that dominate most physicians' mind-sets. The business managers who are recruited are often not trained as well in business or financial acumen as those graduates who tend to migrate toward the traditional profit industries, such as energy or banking.

Health care facilities also commonly work on a 24-hour-per-day basis, creating obvious labor and scheduling inefficiencies. Some industrial organizations do this as well, but they do so only to the extent that the decision to remain open generates positive cash flow. Decisions about hours in health care are driven largely by societal needs and expectations for round-the-clock medical service and availability of care at all times.

Finally, hospitals have community and other stakeholder interests that create goal ambiguity. In most towns, hospitals are as sacred as a church or civic building and are not admired as much for their economic engine as for their healing powers.

Nonetheless, hospitals have to manage the same set of business resources as any other type of organization, from financial resources to personnel, equipment, supplies, technology, and facilities. Hospitals employ hundreds or even thousands of people, with payrolls that can reach several hundred million dollars. They serve as a marketplace and are suppliers of valuable services to hundreds of customers daily. They are buyers, procuring a vast array of supplies, pharmaceuticals, and technology. To function efficiently, hospitals have to manage people, money, time, and business processes. They are economic engines that generate significant cash flows and provide economic value for their organization and their community. In short, hospitals are a business. Managing these business affairs, then, is a difficult challenge, and historically there has not been much focus in this area.

Nearly 5,800 hospitals operate today, employing almost 5.5 million people and managing gross revenues of more than $500 billion (American Hospital Association, 2013; Bureau of Labor Statistics, 2004). These are significant resources, requiring dedicated and trained business managers who can help ensure appropriate fiscal responsibility, maintain overall costs, improve productivity, and ensure positive operating margins.

While the size of hospitals varies—anywhere from 10 beds to more than 1,000 beds—the administrative organizations and operational managements are quite similar. Some have a large network of outpatient clinics, while others focus exclusively on inpatient surgeries and treatments. There may also be differences in funding sources, types of services offered, or mix of patients served, but the overall aim of business operational management should be similar. Finding methods and means for improving business operations should be the primary goal of business officers in hospitals.

WHAT IS A HOSPITAL?

A hospital is an organization devoted to delivering patient care, and it serves as the central hub for the entire health care industry. There is at least one hospital in nearly every city, and larger cities may have several dozen. Historically, hospitals were viewed as a "facility" placed to serve those who needed overnight stays (i.e., primarily inpatient) or surgery, or who were otherwise extremely sick. The very early definition of hospitals was as a place people went to die, but as the quality of care has improved so too have the national health outcomes, measured primarily in terms of morbidity and mortality rates. Consequently, fewer people go to hospitals to die than to get well or to prevent illness.

The basic definition of a **hospital** typically involves providing services clustered around three key terms: observation, diagnosis, and treatment (Griffin, 2006). **Observation** involves analyzing or studying patients and running tests and checks—all of which ultimately lead to a diagnosis. The **diagnosis** is the physician's or medical provider's explanation for the cause or source of the problem or symptoms. **Treatment** is the course of action that the hospital will take to make the patient better, lessen the symptoms, or otherwise care for the patient. All of the services that a hospital provides are typically organized around at least one of these areas.

The health care industry has become somewhat more integrated, or consolidated, in recent years. **Horizontal integration** refers to consolidation, mergers, acquisitions, or alliances among several competitive or cooperative hospitals. Horizontal integration has resulted in a large number of multihospital systems, defined as an organized system of hospitals that share central services, common ownership of assets, and/or centralized governance and management. **Vertical integration** refers to the acquisition or alliances of other parties involved in other phases of the health care value chain, such as payers, clinics, or physicians. Physician–hospital alliances and hospital-sponsored health maintenance organizations (HMOs) are common structures within vertically integrated systems. Whether vertically or horizontally integrated, an **integrated delivery network** refers to any combination or integration between a hospital and other providers or partners in the health care industry that works together collaboratively across a spectrum of care to provide more competitive and comprehensive services.

In economic terms, the "production" capabilities (i.e., the conversion of supplies, labor, and other resources into medical services) of health care are performed by physicians, nurses, technicians, and a host of other allied health professionals. Physicians, of course, have traditionally retained most of the power in health care because they have long played the dominant and central role. They are the most academically qualified, spend the longest time in training programs, and have the most systematic view of disease and anatomy. A physician is also called a *medical doctor* or simply a *doctor* in most places.

The new role of the hospital is evolving, as hospitals have extended their ownership and influence from a "facility" to a "system," which may include multiple buildings, offices, or practices distributed throughout a large geographic area. Hospitals now often include ambulatory or outpatient clinics, physician offices, treatment centers, and other services that are not necessarily housed in the primary hospital. Hospitals have come a long way since the construction of the first hospital, the Pennsylvania Hospital in Philadelphia, in the mid-1700s.

From a business perspective, it is important to understand the type of hospital in order to understand its mission, background, and orientation. There are several ways to classify hospitals, but the most common is by ownership type, type of service or specialty offered, and length of stay.

Most hospitals in the United States are primarily considered **community hospitals**, in that they are available for use by an entire community. Community hospitals represent the significant majority of all hospital-based care and include all nonfederal, short-term hospitals, whether they are for-profit, nonprofit, or public. When people think of the "typical" hospital, they are thinking of the community hospital. Community hospitals focus on short-term stays, usually fewer than 30 days, and **acute care**, defined as being focused on a specific episode or event requiring care. Sometimes both for-profit and nonprofit community hospitals are grouped together and called *private hospitals*, to distinguish them from public and government-owned facilities. In addition, churches control some of these private nonprofit hospitals. Well-known health care systems are controlled by the Baptist, Catholic, Protestant, and Seventh Day Adventist religions. Besides community, there are federally owned hospitals, such as the Veterans Administration, which manages a network of more than 150 hospitals and nearly 1,000 clinics and other facilities (Department of Veterans Affairs, 2006).

Hospitals listed with the American Hospital Association (2006) fall into one of four classifications:

1. General (providing a broad range of services for multiple conditions).
2. Specialty (services for a specific medical condition, such as oncology).
3. Rehabilitation (focused on restoring health).
4. Psychiatric (providing care for behavioral and mental disorders).

Historically, hospitals have been owned by either nonprofit, church, or government agencies and have been considered organizations offering public or social goods. This mix has been changing over the past three decades. In 1976, approximately 13% of community hospitals were for-profit or investor owned. In 1986, there were nearly 15%; in 2006, there were 17% investor owned; and in 2012, 19% of all hospitals were investor owned (American Hospital Association, 2013). As this mix shifts, a higher level of competitiveness and financial

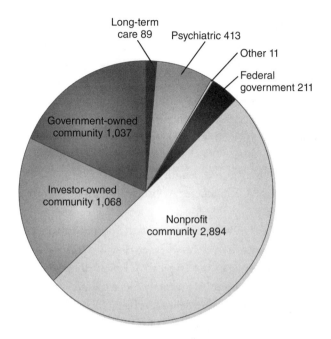

FIGURE 2-1 Hospital Breakdown by Ownership Type, 2012

Data from American Hospital Association, 2013.

focus will continue. The largest for-profit hospital systems are Hospital Corporation of America, Tenet, Health Management Associates, Triad, and Community Health. Of these, the most prominent, Hospital Corporation of America, had annual revenues exceeding $33 billion in 2012 with nearly 204,000 employees in 162 hospitals (Hospital Corporation of America, 2005). **Figure 2-1** shows the hospital breakdown by type in 2012.

TEACHING HOSPITALS

The largest major hospitals tend to fit into another classification called **teaching hospitals**, which suggests that a fairly large percentage of resources are devoted to academic and research missions, in addition to patient care.

Teaching hospitals were once thought of as the "cornerstone" of the American health care system (Iglehart, 1993). As the health care industry continues to evolve, this leadership role may be in jeopardy, as teaching facilities struggle to gain a competitive position with the other entities in the industry, including group practices, independent primary care clinics, and ambulatory surgery centers.

Teaching facilities are usually the largest, most sophisticated hospitals in the predominantly urban markets they serve (Langabeer & Napiewocki, 2000). They are almost always significantly larger than their non-teaching-hospital competitors in terms of number of employees, types of service lines offered, number of beds, number of admissions and discharges, size of financial budget, and most other measures of scale. Teaching hospitals have significantly more resources invested in facilities and technologies to provide advanced treatments for the unusually complex cases that they serve.

Teaching hospitals are committed to the principles of higher education. This means that the medical doctor–practitioners are primarily teachers and research faculty members who are affiliated with an accredited school of medicine, whose goal is to educate and formally train licensed medical doctors. Currently, there are more than 126 university medical schools accredited by the Association of American Medical Colleges in the United States and another 16 in Canada. Teaching hospitals offer medical residencies—training programs specially designed to instruct graduate medical trainees in clinical settings before they are legally licensed to practice medicine. Most major teaching hospitals have at least four residency programs. The Council of Teaching Hospitals of the Association of American Medical Colleges maintains a list of more than 400 major hospitals and many more "minor" ones (i.e., those with fewer than four residency programs). The Council of Teaching Hospitals membership requirements include a documented affiliation agreement with a medical school accredited by the Liaison Committee on Medical Education. For a complete listing of all of the major teaching hospitals, see Appendix A.

The other core component of academic medicine is a focus on applied clinical and even basic biomedical research that can help improve the ability to observe, diagnose, and treat patients in the future. Advancing knowledge for new treatments, practices, and techniques will help improve the state of practice in the future and is a critical academic concern for teaching hospitals.

Many factors distinguish a teaching hospital from other community hospitals. First, they are the largest and have the broadest scale and scope (as discussed earlier). Second, they train physicians and provide research, which are not always well reimbursed and funded. Third, they have complex organizations because they are typically partnered with medical schools and academic health centers, which have collaborative arrangements. Fourth, they have more stakeholders than most community hospitals, given the broader mission that they serve. Fifth, given their three-pronged mission (research, education, and patient care), they tend to have a more financially difficult time balancing all three needs than most single-focused community hospitals. **Figure 2–2** shows the percentage of funding that hospitals received industrywide in 2012.

What does all of this mean for hospitals? It means that hospitals have to become focused on all aspects of the profit margin. We are entering an era of competitiveness in health care, where efficiency and margins have to become primary performance indicators. Hospitals will have to continue to squeeze all possible revenue from each procedure delivered and negotiate using competitive and analytical data on costs and outcomes to maximize pricing rates in the **Charge Description Master**, which lists all prices for all services and supplies the hospital provides. On the cost side, hospitals have to reduce total cycle time and service delivery time; automate as much of the business process as possible; reduce labor costs associated with service lines that have low reimbursements; and, by using the most sophisticated budgeting and financial tools, continually drive improvements to the bottom line.

Together, reimbursement rates represent gross patient revenues for a hospital, but deductions are nearly always taken by payers for volume, exclusions, and pricing discounts to reflect the payer's contractual terms. In addition to gross patient revenues, a significant source of revenue for hospitals comes from donations and fundraising efforts, parking and cafeteria operations, gift shops, and

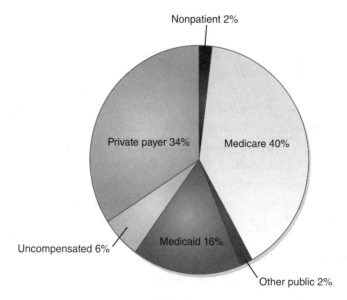

FIGURE 2–2 Funding Sources for U.S. Hospitals, 2012
Data from Centers for Medicare and Medicaid, 2005.

especially interest and investment income. According to 2005 data from the Centers for Medicare and Medicaid Services' National Health Statistics Group, 7% of all health care reimbursement was from other private sources such as these. The typical hospital has significant working capital: Large amounts of cash are constantly moving in and out of accounts. Investing these dollars wisely often means the difference between a hospital that makes money and one that does not. Without all of these sources of nonoperating revenues, most U.S. hospitals would have significantly negative overall profit margins annually.

Many thought that the advent of managed care created devastating turbulence in hospitals, but managing the hospital business will only become more difficult.

HOSPITAL BUSINESS OPERATIONS

The management of hospital business operations can be broken down into a few major roles and responsibilities, including finance and accounting, business logistics and supply chain management, physical plant or facilities, human resources, information technology, and business planning and performance improvement. There are several job opportunities in each of these areas for a typical hospital.

Finance and Accounting

Finance and accounting represents a large and growing portion of health care. Finance professionals are responsible for managing a wide variety of functions, including accounting, billing, collections, financial reporting, payroll, treasury and cash management, investment management, records management, budgeting, and accounts payable. While some of these focus on transaction processing, such as accounting, payables, and payroll, others are more focused on analysis and reporting, such as investments and budgeting. Financial analysts, accountants, and other professionals can find many challenges in this area of health care.

Logistics and Supply Chain Management

Supply chain management is one of the fastest growing sectors in health care. The search for cost savings of key resources and supplies and for better management of goods and services in the physical supply chain is responsible for creating job opportunities for analysts and professionals interested in a wide number of fields, including purchasing, receiving, inventory, transportation, distribution, logistics, and laundry and linen.

Physical Plant or Facilities

As hospitals continue to expand beyond just single, multifloor buildings, the need for additional resources and different types of facilities expertise keeps growing. Many hospitals are part of systems or networks with several facilities, each of which has a need for design, planning, construction, maintenance, housekeeping, and security operations. Roles for architects, engineers, and general business managers to help run these business support services continue to increase.

Human Resources

The average hospital employs about 1,000 people, although that number can range from 50 to more than 10,000. As large employers, there is continued need for business skills focused on providing general personnel management, as well as specialized services such as recruitment, compensation, and benefits. Organizational development and training are also common in larger hospitals.

Information Technology

Information needs require management of telecommunications, data services, information reporting, systems project management, and infrastructure support. Significant improvements in labor productivity can be gained by investing appropriately and wisely in technology to automate manual processes, as well as other technologies to improve access to information and workflow.

Business Planning and Performance Improvement

Although not typically a department in smaller hospitals, there is a much stronger focus on continuous improvement today given the financial condition and competitive environments most hospitals face. As this occurs, there has been a strong rise in demand for professionals who can help provide internal analyses and decision support in areas such as strategic planning, business process reengineering, process improvement, competitive intelligence, performance benchmarking, accreditation preparation, and quality management. This area is a small but growing opportunity for students and other professionals with keen analytical, people, and facilitation skills.

Each of these areas involves substantial levels of resources and commitment. By no means are these all of the opportunities for those interested in business careers in hospitals, but they are some of the most common.

HOSPITAL POLICIES AND REGULATIONS

Hospitals operate within strict financial, legal, and regulatory environments. The high-stakes products and services resulting from hospital operations are a matter of health and, often, of resuming a measure of quality of life. As such, hospital administrators must have a strong background in and understanding of health care policies and regulations and how they affect business operations. **Policies** provide broad guidelines that are used to create specific procedures within a system, whereas **regulations** are authorized instructions for how something should be carried out.

Contemporary policy influence can be traced back to the **Health Insurance Portability and Accountability Act (HIPAA) of 1996**. HIPAA established national standards to protect personal health information and outlined safeguards for transmitting and storing **protected health information**—defined liberally as including any information that can be used to discover the identity of an individual patient. Examples of protected health information include a patient's name, address, social security number, date of birth, insurance number, or medical record number. HIPAA changed the business processes of hospitals, doctors' offices, and health care insurance enities by affecting the way they communicate information surrounding patient care. All employees working in a health care environment must recognize HIPAA implications. Similar to a credit report, under HIPAA, patients are given explicit ownership of their information. Patients may request copies of their health records, or charts, as well as changes to amend incorrect information. In addition to providing patients with access to their medical records, HIPAA also restricts the uses for which patient information can be exchanged among providers. These restrictions allow the exchange of patient information for physicians to treat a patient, for insurance companies to pay for care, and for the administrative or operational duties of patient care. It is against most hospital policies and procedures to access or discuss patient information outside of these contexts.

Another modern **act**, or enacted health care law, that has had significant influence on health care operations is the **Health Information Technology for Economic and Clinical Health (HITECH) Act**. This act was signed in 2009 by President Barack Obama to stimulate and encourage greater efficiencies in health care for the United States. HITECH's main focus is to develop a national health information technology infrastructure. The concept of health information technology was brought to national awareness when President George W. Bush proclaimed his vision for all Americans to have a personal electronic health record by 2014. Although the United States has not met the original goal laid out by President Bush, the HITECH Act has hastened progress. A specific goal of the HITECH Act is to assist physicians and hospital systems to convert paper health records to electronic ones. To offset the cost of purchasing new technology, the act allowed a financial incentive provision for using the technology in a way that creates enhancements in the quality of efficient patient care. Depending on the population demographics served, eligible providers may receive payments up to $44,000 from Medicare and up to $65,000 from Medicaid. In order to collect these incentives, providers must use their electronic records to send prescriptions to pharmacies electronically, exchange patient information with another provider electronically, or otherwise use their electronic systems to track certain quality metrics designed to enhance patient care. In addition to financial incentives for purchasing and utilizing new technology, HITECH will enact penalties for noncompliance with electronic standards beginning in 2015. Public reimbursement programs such as Medicaid and Medicare will penalize hospitals that do not convert from paper records to electronic ones with a 1% reduction in payments in 2015 and a 3% reduction in 2017 and in all subsequent years thereafter. This will have substantial ramifications in the financial operating controls of any health care system.

CHAPTER SUMMARY

Hospitals represent society and community interests, but they are also a business. They consume significant resources and require extensive management over a wide range of functions. There is variety in patient populations, with some hospital specialization. In general, hospitals serve the following patient needs: general acute illness or trauma, specialty diseases such as cancer, rehabilitation, or psychiatry. Teaching hospitals are another class with a large percentage of resources dedicated to academic research and higher education. Managing these resources and functions requires employees new to the industry, and those currently employed, to upgrade their knowledge of finance, management, business operations management, and health care policy to help the industry continue to thrive, as well as to weather the turbulence that threatens a hospital's ability to survive. Only by using all available advanced tools, methods, and techniques will hospitals be able to use business operations management to improve their competitiveness and financial position in the health care industry.

KEY TERMS

Act	Horizontal integration
Acute care	Hospital
Charge Description Master	Integrated delivery network
Community hospitals	Observation
Diagnosis	Policies
Health Information Technology	Protected health information
for Econimic and Clinical Health	Regulations
(HITECH) Act	Teaching hospitals
Health Insurance Portability and	Treatment
Accountability Act (HIPAA) of	Vertical integration
1996	

DISCUSSION QUESTIONS

1. Is health care a "business"?
2. What are five of the key factors that distinguish a hospital from other industrial organizations?
3. Define an "average" hospital in terms of size (employees, revenue, beds).
4. Which types of hospitals exist, and whom do they serve?
5. What is the role of a teaching hospital in the health care industry?
6. What makes governance of academic hospitals more complex than that for community hospitals?
7. Which recent policies or acts have influenced health care operations management?

REFERENCES

American Hospital Association. (2006). *Guide to the health care field.* Chicago, IL: Author.

American Hospital Association. (2013). *Hospital statistics.* Chicago, IL: Author.

Bureau of Labor Statistics. (2004). *2004 career guide.* Washington, DC: U.S. Department of Labor.

Centers for Medicare and Medicaid Services. (2005). *Monthly trend report for Medicare, Medicaid, and SCHIP.* Washington, DC: U.S. Department of Health and Human Services.

Department of Veterans Affairs. (2006). *Organizational briefing book.* Washington, DC: Author.

Griffin, D. (2006). *Hospitals: What they are and how they work* (3rd ed.). Sudbury, MA: Jones and Bartlett.

Hospital Corporation of America. (2005). *2005 annual report.* Retrieved from http://media.corporate-ir.net/media_files/irol/63/63489/pdfs/05AnnualReport.pdf

Iglehart, J. K. (1993). The American health care system: Teaching hospitals. *New England Journal of Medicine, 329*(14), 1052–1056.

Langabeer, J. R., & Napiewocki, J. (2000). *Competitive business strategy for teaching hospitals.* Westport, CT: Quorum Books.

CHAPTER 3

Health Care Finance for the Operations Manager

GOALS OF THIS CHAPTER

1. Discuss the concept of a hospital as a business and the need for financial management of health care businesses.
2. Define how health care organizations are paid for services.
3. Understand the varying types of reimbursement to hospitals and the operational challenges of these payment methods.
4. Describe the three primary financial statements and what they measure.
5. Define working capital and discuss how operations management influences it.
6. Identify sources of financial data for use in operational analyses.

The health care industry today is second only to national defense in its share of the U.S. economy, totaling 17.2% of the gross domestic product as of 2012, with estimates going as high as 19.6% by 2021. The rapid growth of health care costs—for which hospitals account for 31.5%—is an area of great concern for government leaders and may become the cause of future constraints on payments to hospitals (Centers for Medicare and Medicaid Services, 2013). Considering some of the unique characteristics of the hospital organization, limits in payment growth, or even outright reductions in payments, pose a significant challenge for the operations manager in today's health care organization

HOW HOSPITALS ARE PAID

Providers of health care services (and hospitals in particular) are in many ways unique in the U.S. economy in that they routinely provide services for which they incur costs at the time of service but are not paid for those services for a period of weeks or months thereafter. Because providers pay the costs of rendering care at or before the time of service, payments to the provider are usually termed **reimbursements**. The gap in time between the provision of services and reimbursement for those services is a result of the organization of the U.S. health care system where a third-party insurer (usually called the **payer**) pays for services on behalf of the patient. Although the patient may have some nominal amount to pay for hospital services, the vast majority of payments for hospital services come from third-party payers.

Payers for hospital services are generally classified as government or nongovernment insurers. There are two major government insurers that together fund the majority of hospital services: Medicare and Medicaid. **Medicare** is the federal government health insurance plan that offers care to more than 40 million patients who are elderly, disabled, or with end-stage renal disease. Medicare has three primary components: Parts A, B, and D. Part A provides inpatient hospital coverage for participants, as well as some posthospital treatment and hospice care. Part A is paid for by a required payroll tax deduction from the entire American population. Part B is a supplemental insurance program that requires monthly premium contributions by the participant and covers physician services, emergency room services, and outpatient visits. Part D is Medicare's prescription drug benefit program, which offers discounts on outpatient drugs to lower-income seniors and disabled individuals. Of the three parts, Medicare Part A funds the largest portion of hospital reimbursements.

The federal government also funds and oversees Medicaid. **Medicaid** is designed to meet the health care needs of certain individuals with low incomes or disability who otherwise may not have the ability to pay for care. General tax revenues from both federal and state governments finance this insurance program, where the federal government funds the majority of costs (between 50% and 83%, depending on the state) and states pick up the remainder. The federal portion of the funding formula is inversely related to per capita state income, where wealthier states pay a larger proportion of Medicaid costs in those states. States are otherwise able to control their own policies, so reimbursement for services (and which services are reimbursed) varies from state to state.

Nongovernment payers are called **commercial insurers** and collectively fund between 30% and 40% of the nation's hospital services. The majority of these commercial insurance plans in the United States are made available as an employment benefit. Because commercial insurers represent the interests of many employers in the economy, they exert significant influence on the health care marketplace, aggressively negotiating discounted fees for services in exchange for patient referrals. In addition, commercial insurers have adopted policies to control the level of patient access to services and even which services are reimbursed to providers. Some such insurers are organized primarily around the management of health care access and cost and are called **managed care** organizations.

Each of these different types of payers has a certain degree of leverage based on the size of its network, the number of enrollees or members in the plan, and the number and type of patients covered. Therefore, each payer has a varying level of ability to influence and establish hospital reimbursements. The same services and supplies provided to two different patients may have the same prices billed on the hospital invoice for both patients, but the ability for a hospital to collect the total amount is entirely based on the individual payer that is reimbursing the hospital. One payer might cover 60% of all costs billed, while another might reimburse the entire amount. Negotiations, settlements, and preestablished reimbursement programs for all payers govern the extent to which costs will be reimbursed.

In general, Medicaid is considered to be the payer that reimburses the lowest for all services—in most cases not even fully reimbursing providers for the total cost to deliver care (in 2012, this approximated 85% of the costs of providing care). Other payers may reimburse at cost for specific services that may be specialized or hard to find but reimburse significantly less for services that are very competitive and general. Also, despite passage of the Patient Protection and Affordable Care Act of 2010 (PPACA), in excess of 10% of the U.S. population remains uninsured. Such individuals often pay very little, if any, of the costs of their care and receive only the minimal amount of care necessary to treat an emergency condition under federal law. To the extent that a hospital has a mission of serving the poor and uninsured, the demand for strong financial management to support operations management can determine if a hospital can stay in business.

FROM RETROSPECTIVE TO PROSPECTIVE

Since the introduction of the prospective payment system (PPS) by Medicare in 1983, there have been continued financial pressures placed on hospitals. Prior to this legislation, Medicare paid hospitals on a retrospective or cost-plus reimbursement system. In this context, **retrospective** literally means to look backward at all costs incurred. This means that regardless of the total cost to deliver services, including both operational and capital components, insurers would fully compensate actual costs, plus a component to represent a small profit margin. In an era where revenue was unconstrained, there was no need for cost efficiencies or fiscal discipline in spending or utilization patterns. **Fee-for-service (FFS)** was the original reimbursement method used by commercial insurers, where hospitals are paid directly for every service performed—essentially a "piece rate" system. Later iterations of this payment methodology called for discounts off of provider routine fees. FFS payment creates an incentive for health care providers to expand the number of services offered in order to increase collected fees. Rapid growth in payments to hospitals in the late 1960s and throughout the 1970s precipitated a call for changes away from both the retrospective and FFS methods of payment to hospitals, resulting in PPS only a few years later.

Prospective payment represents a methodology in which fee schedules are calculated based on treatment type or illness classification and are paid in advance of the treatment without regard to actual costs incurred. Since implementation of PPS, hospitals have endured a variety of reimbursement practices, all aimed at reducing costs and improving efficiency. One such practice is capitation. **Capitation** is a method of reimbursement that transfers financial risk of care to the provider and away from health plans or insurers by limiting payments to a fixed-dollar amount. Capitation reimburses the provider on a per-member per-month basis, such that a flat payment is made per capita to a defined population for a specified menu of services over a specific period of time. Although capitation is very favorable to the payer, it creates a strong incentive on the part of the provider to limit the amount of services offered to the patient.

Per diems are fixed daily payments to cover all services and procedures performed. They are essentially daily rates that limit the exposure for a payer but provide revenue caps for the hospital. They are effective in some cases, but much like FFS payment, per diems create an incentive for a hospital to treat patients longer, generating higher average lengths of stay, in order to maximize revenue.

Closely related to the per diem method is the **case rate**, which is a prospectively determined amount that is paid for all services associated with a hospital admission, regardless of the costs for that occasion of care. Case rates are often used for specific types of services, such as childbirth or organ transplants. A similar payment method—on which the original PPS was formed—is the use of diagnosis-related groups to adjust case rate payments to reflect the expected resource needs of a particular patient's condition. The **diagnosis-related group (DRG)** is a classification scheme primarily used for inpatient treatment that categorizes all patients through principal and secondary diagnosis, procedures provided, age, sex, and other factors. Although DRGs are the basis for payment under Medicare, they are also used by several commercial insurers and payers because of their comprehensive classification schema.

Under the DRG system, hospital rates are set based on the patient's illness and the length of time required to treat that illness in an inpatient setting. Many private insurers prefer fixed per diems for inpatients, where a fixed daily "allowance" is provided for all services performed and supplies consumed. Private insurers tend to use negotiating and contract management processes to establish pricing; they use contracts where negotiated discount provisions are based on market coverage, type of service, and volume of activity. In general, the use of a standard fixed rate reimbursement for each type of service performed, adjusted for case complexity, is the standard for most hospitals.

The per diem, case rate, and DRG mechanisms all relate to reimbursement for inpatient hospital services. Similar approaches apply to outpatient and ambulatory facilities where fixed, prospective amounts are paid for outpatient services such as diagnostic testing, emergency room visits, and ambulatory surgery procedures. These services are usually reimbursed on a flat per procedure rate that varies by the type of service, similar to the case rate mechanism used for inpatient care. Similar to the DRG mechanism, outpatient per procedure fees may be adjusted to reflect the relative severity or resource intensity of services using the **Ambulatory Payment Classification (APC)** system. Under prospective payment mechanisms, including per diem, case rate, DRG, per procedure, and APC mechanisms, providers have an incentive to limit the operating costs incurred to provide services.

Passage of PPACA introduced a new model of health care delivery that mixes many of the payment mechanisms mentioned here—the **Accountable Care Organization (ACO)**. An ACO is a group of various health care providers (sometimes called a *network*) who share financial responsibility for the care of a designated group of patients on behalf of an insurer. Providers may be reimbursed for services using any of the methods described here, though the payment amounts may be reduced to account for patient satisfaction or quality of care incentives built into ACO payment agreements. However, the overarching theme for reimbursement in an ACO is toward cost reduction for a population. That cost reduction focus will lead to lower direct payment rates to providers, with possible additional payments for meeting ACO incentive goals. Similarly, the ACO may be responsible for penalties if incentive goals are not met. Much like a capitation payment, the ACO arrangement in general creates an incentive to reduce the amount of care provided and maintain a fairly static level of operating costs.

The financial implications from use of prospective payment mechanisms for hospital reimbursement are enormous. The risk and pressure of holding costs below collected net revenue is being transferred from the payer to the provider. This change calls for a different type of administrator and the need for managing costs, maximizing staff productivity, and limiting unnecessary processes.

PROFIT MARGINS

Profit margins are found by subtracting expenses from revenues, and they represent the residual value to fund future operations and capital investment. Since the 1980s, the average profit margins for community hospitals have been extremely unsatisfactory. Economics suggest that with long-term industry profit margins near 0% on average, hospitals exit the market because it is unattractive to both new entrants and current organizations. Hospitals exit through bankruptcy, acquisition by a competitor, or simply dissolution. According to financial statements filed by hospitals in their annual reports to the Centers for Medicare and Medicaid Services (2014), more than one-third (34.6%) of all hospitals experienced negative profit margins during 2012.

That is exactly what continues to happen over time to U.S. hospitals. Significant consolidation of both beds and hospitals continues each year. In 1991, there were greater than 5,300 community hospitals and more than 920,000 beds. In 2001, that number had dropped to nearly 4,900 hospitals and 840,000 beds (American Hospital Association, 2006). By 2012, the decline in the number of hospitals had stabilized, with 4,999 in operation at that time, although the number of beds in operation had declined slightly to 800,566 (American Hospital Association, 2013). Meanwhile, demand continues to rise. The number of admissions rose from 31 million in 1997 across all community hospitals to nearly 35 million in 2004 and remained at that level in 2012 (American Hospital Association, 2006, 2013). The rise in outpatient volumes has grown even more quickly, to nearly 101 million visits in 2012 (Centers for Disease Control and Prevention, 2014). **Figure 3–1** shows the change in hospital demand and supply over recent years.

When supply is consolidated yet demand remains strong, pricing and margins typically rebound. That is exactly what we have seen in hospitals recently.

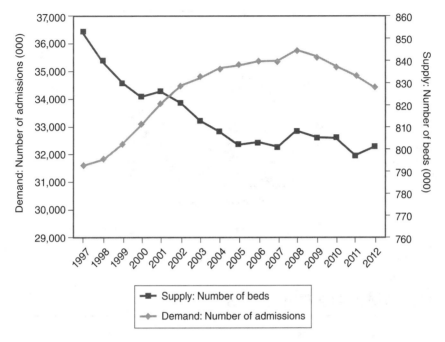

FIGURE 3−1   Hospital Industry Economics: Inpatient Supply Falling and
Demand Rising (Community Hospitals)

Data from American Hospital Association Trendwatch Chartbook, 2014.

Profit margins shrank from around 4% in 2001 to 2.7% in 2012. While supply is starting to stabilize (the number of community hospitals has remained around 4,900 for the last 8 years), the industry is seeing declines in profit margins after some increases in the prior decade (see **Figure 3−2**). It is hoped that this trend will moderate, although payment decreases mandated under PPACA will challenge the operations management field to maintain margins at current levels.

Yet this tells only half of the story. Some research suggests that nearly 50% of large hospitals have negative operating margins (Langabeer, 2006). Investment income and ancillary sources of revenue can typically contribute between 20% and 50% of total margins for an average hospital. Therefore, real operating income margins at current levels are usually between 0.5% and 1.5% across the board. With the continued rising cost of medical technologies, equipment, and other capital costs, sustaining an organization for the long term at single digit margins is nearly impossible.

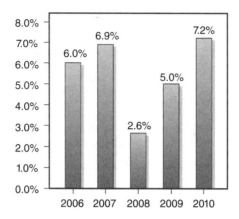

FIGURE 3–2 Average Hospital Profit Margins
Data from Modern Healthcare, 2012.

INCOME STATEMENTS

It is important to understand all of the components of a hospital's financials. This includes being able to look at all of the key statements—income statement, balance sheet, and cash flow—in order to utilize metrics and line items to fully understand a hospital's operation. The **income statement** is one of the most important, because it measures a hospital's profitability by tracking revenues, expenses, and margins. It works off of the basic accounting principle:

Revenues – Expenses = Profit margin

Beginning with the top line of the income statement, a hospital reports gross revenues. Gross revenues represent the gross or total billings to all government and private insurers for patient care activities. Gross revenue is typically reported separately for outpatient and inpatient activities. Gross revenue is the sum of all services rendered, through bills issued to payers for every DRG, current procedural terminology, and Healthcare Common Procedure Coding System code. These codes represent the hospital, professional, and technical services provided, and they are billed based on the pricing maintained in each hospital's **Charge Description Master (CDM)**. This CDM is a listing of all services and prices that the hospital delivers; it is essentially a price list, based on gross charges to be billed to payers. An assumption for private payments or for co-pays or other out-of-pocket costs is that all billings that are the patient's responsibility will be paid in full.

A hospital's gross billings, however, do not represent what will be realized, given that sizable discounts are taken based on contract negotiations (i.e., for private insurers) and for other rate caps, allowances, exclusions, or limitations. A discount or **deductions** category appears that reflects an allowance for payments that will likely not be collected. This could be because of exclusions, contractual adjustments, discounts, or other deductions for the difference between what is billed and what the insurer will pay. Deductions for many hospitals in 2012 averaged between 30% and 70%, depending on the payer mix and types of services offered. For example, if a hospital's CDM shows a price for a specific service, such as a chest x-ray for $2,500, that is the gross revenue expected and would be consolidated with all other services performed to calculate the top line on the income statement. Based on the payer mix represented in the services offered in a specific period, there would be an adjustment to discount this based on the reality of what the payer will reimburse. For instance, if the $2,500 service was reimbursed by a payer at $1,000, then $1,500 would appear in the deductions line accumulated with all other deductions, and $1,000 would be added to net patient revenue.

The difference between gross revenues and discounts and deductions is what is called *net patient revenues*. **Net patient revenues** are the actual expected revenues (gross revenues less deductions and allowances) for a hospital system and are more commonly used for hospital comparisons than gross revenues. Net patient revenue is the same as operating revenue.

Under the expense side of the income statement, hospitals typically place their highest expenses first, followed by lesser categories. For instance, if personnel expense was $17 million and supply expense was $15 million, then personnel expense would be the first expense category reported.

Depending on the level of detail that a hospital reports internally and externally, all expense categories can be hidden or aggregated to "total operating expense." Typically, the major categories that should be itemized include medical supply and drug expense, personnel or labor expense, administrative expense, general service expense, teaching expense, nursing, depreciation, and other operating expense. In other statements, the separate major divisions are detailed individually, such as intensive care unit, emergency, or obstetrics/gynecology. The two largest operating expenses in most hospitals are typically personnel and supplies. Labor expenses can account for nearly 60% of all costs, while supply and pharmaceutical expenses typically average around 20% to 30%.

The difference between net patient revenue and total operating expense is operating income or operating margin. Operating margin reflects the profits cleared in the course of normal business or operations and is one of the most important metrics for determining a hospital's financial health. As stated earlier, almost one-third of all hospitals had negative operating margins in the most recent year of publicly available financial data. An average operating margin of between 1% and 3% is very common for most hospitals, especially larger urban ones. Smaller, rural hospitals tend to have even lower margins.

Most hospitals are able to improve their financial performance by maximizing the non-operating- or non-patient-related activities. These activities are commonly called *below the line* because they are not operating activities and are not reported in operating income. They include fundraising and donations, which can total between 5% and 10% of net income for a hospital or, based on industry-average calculations, between $250,000 for a community hospital and $10 million for a larger teaching hospital. In addition, investment and interest income is a major source of nonoperating revenue. Many hospitals have an in-house treasury or investment management professional to help direct the movement of cash, manage working capital, support bond and debt offerings, and invest in various equity markets. The role of treasury professionals in hospitals is a fairly small field, but its effect can be quite significant, adding as much as 20% to operating income. A sample hospital income statement is shown in **Table 3–1**.

Table 3–1   Hospital Income Statement

ABC Hospital

Income Statement	August 31, 2013
Inpatient revenue	$1,500,300,000
Outpatient revenue	$430,320,200
Total patient revenue	*$1,930,620,200*
Deductions, discounts, and allowances	($1,000,000,000)
Net patient revenues	$930,620,200
Total operating expenses	*($830,220,200)*
Operating income	**$100,400,000**
Other income (donations, contributions, gifts)	$5,200,500
Income from investments	$15,000,500
Government appropriations	$0
Auxiliary and nonpatient revenue	$3,000,000
Total nonpatient revenue	*$23,201,000*
Total other expenses	*($124,400,000)*
Net income or (loss)	**($799,000)**

INCOME STATEMENT RATIO ANALYSIS

Ratio analyses are important management control activities to ensure that operations are headed in the right direction and that they are competitive with other organizations. Ratios allow the details from statements to be put into common formulas that help track financial health and condition. There are several key ratios that should be monitored to assess an organization's financial condition, including profitability, liquidity, and efficiency. Specifically, ratios that measure profit margins, return on capital, labor productivity, and supply expense are vital in health care operations management.

Profit Margin Ratios

One of the most common ratios examines operating margin and total margin percentages. Operating margin is defined as:

$$\text{Operating margin} = \frac{(\text{Operating revenue} - \text{Operating cost})}{\text{Operating revenue}}$$

In the sample income statement shown in Table 3–1, total operating or net patient revenue was $930.6 million, and total operating expenses were $830.2 million. The margin was $1.4 million, or 10.8% of the operating margin percentage—which, if this were a real hospital, would be an excellent margin percentage. Total margin percentage is very similar and is calculated as:

$$\text{Total margin percentage} = \frac{(\text{Total revenue} - \text{Total cost})}{\text{Total revenue}}$$

Again using the data in Table 3–1, where total revenues were $953,821,000 and total costs were $954,620,200, the total margin in dollars was a loss of $799,000. Dividing this by the total revenue yields a 20.1% total margin percentage.

This is why it is important to understand the difference between total and operating margins. It is possible for a hospital to lose money in operations and still have positive total margins, or vice versa. Understanding this is essential to knowing which area to focus on and how cost conscious the hospital will have to be to reduce operating costs.

Return on Capital

Return on capital (ROC) is a measure of the level of financial return generated by a hospital's operations in a specific accounting period. This return produces a ratio that can be compared with all hospitals and across other industries. The higher a hospital's ROC, the better that hospital performed relative to the competition (although it is impossible to determine if a true economic profit—not accounting profit—has been earned without analyzing the cost of capital).

ROC is measured by multiplying a hospital's operating margin, expressed as a percentage, by the total asset turnover ratio. Although a more direct method of calculating ROC would be to simply divide invested capital by net income, the effects of accounting changes, depreciation methods, and financing policies tend to distort the ratio, thereby reducing reliability and accuracy. ROC combines both income statement and balance sheet variables and produces a reasonably optimal estimate of financial viability. Operating margin is calculated by subtracting operating expenses from the total operating revenue and dividing this figure by the total revenue generated. Total asset turnover is calculated by dividing total revenues by total assets, which will be discussed in the balance sheet section.

$$\text{ROC} = \frac{\text{Earnings before interest \& taxes (EBIT)}}{\text{Revenues}} \times \frac{\text{Revenues}}{\text{Invested capital}}$$

OR

$$\text{ROC} = \text{Operating margin} \times \text{Asset turnover}$$

Labor Productivity Ratios

Other key analyses using income statement data involve analyzing the labor and nursing costs. Using a combination of the personnel expense labor line plus hospital volume and activity indicators (e.g., number of discharges, number of beds, number of adjusted patient days), key staffing and productivity analyses can be conducted to see if the hospital is improving over time or relative to competition.

Consider this example. A hospital with 10,000 annual discharges incurred a labor expense of $15 million. The labor cost per discharge (or labor cost) would then be $1,500 per discharge. If the same figures were $14.7 million and 8,200 discharges a year earlier, then the ratio would be $1,793. This means that the hospital became more efficient or otherwise had lower labor intensity from one year to the next. If, however, the hospital across the street, which offers the same set of services and is relatively the same size, has a labor cost per discharge of $1,200, then there is still significantly more work to be done to reduce costs and improve overall competitiveness. The lower the figure, the better, assuming that lower-paid employees does not translate into lower-quality care or other service outcomes. Other similar ways to analyze personnel expense are to use net patient revenue divided by the number of full-time equivalent employees (FTEs) to calculate revenue per employee. An FTE is a measure of the total number of hours that an employee should work (e.g., an employee who works 40 hours is considered 1.0 FTE, while a part-time 10-hour-per-week employee is considered 0.25). Most hospitals typically average between $80,000 and $120,000. The higher the figure, the better the ratio and the more competitive the hospital.

Supply Expense Ratios

Because medical supplies and pharmaceutical expenses contribute so significantly to overall cost behaviors in hospitals, it is essential to analyze these expense categories separately (Healthcare Financial Management Association, 2005). A key metric that should be analyzed is supply cost per unit of patient activity. Typically, if a hospital were primarily inpatient based, the best denominators for all ratios would be inpatient days, number of admissions, or number of discharges.

Supply costs include the sum of all purchases of surgical supplies, general medical supplies, laboratory supplies, oxygen and gases, linens, dietary products, radiology supplies, and office supplies (Association for Healthcare Resource and Materials Management, 2005). The added costs of freight and tax, less rebates and discounts, are also included in this supply expense category.

Because supply expenses can account for 15% to 50% of a hospital's operating expenses, depending on the type of specialty and patient acuity, it is important to focus on this area. Chapters elsewhere in this text will help to focus efforts around:

- Reducing supply acquisition costs.
- Reducing costs of holding inventory and storing materials.
- Speeding up the turn rates for supplies to improve working capital and gain overall higher asset efficiencies.

To calculate supply ratios, there are several common options for the denominator, such as supply expense per discharge, supply expense per bed, supply expense as a percentage of total operating expense, and supply expense per adjusted patient discharge. Alternatively, pharmaceutical or drug expense could be divided by the same denominators.

If a hospital has a total medical supplies and drug expense of $15 million, total operating revenues of $1 million, and 15,000 annual discharges, it would have a

15% cost-to-revenue ratio and a $1,000 cost per discharge ratio. Compared with a similar hospital in the same geographic region with an $800 supply cost per discharge, the competing hospital would be seen as more efficient and probably have a greater profitability.

This all assumes, of course, that the complexity or intensity of the types of patients the hospitals serve are relatively the same. An adjustment is necessary to make these figures relative so that they can be compared across institutions. In theory, the greater the intensity, the more medical supplies that will be consumed; the lower the intensity, the fewer the supplies. A common way to adjust for patient mix differences between hospitals is to calculate a **case mix index (CMI)**. CMI is calculated by averaging the DRG weighting for all patients served over the course of an accounting period. All patients are coded with a DRG (representing the resource consumption requirements based on a patient's diagnosis, treatment, age, gender, and procedures performed), so the DRG weights are the best-known indexes to adjust for case mix. They typically are used only for Medicare reimbursement, but the calculations can be applied to all costs.

If the CMI turns out to be less than 1.0, then the supply cost per discharge would be greater than the original calculation. The formula is:

$$\text{Supply cost per discharge} = \frac{(\text{Supply expense} \div \text{Number of discharges})}{\text{CMI}}$$

For example, if supply expense per discharge was $800, as in the previous example, and the CMI for all DRGs performed was 0.77, then the total supply cost per discharge would be $1,038. If another hospital had a supply cost per discharge of $1,200 but a CMI of 1.4, then the adjusted cost would be $857. The second hospital would be considered to be more efficient in supply utilization.

BALANCE SHEET

Users of hospital financial statements cannot make informed decisions about the organization's financial condition without examining the balance sheet in addition to the income statement (Finkler & Ward, 2006). A **balance sheet** is a representation of the accounting equation:

$$\text{Assets} = \text{Liabilities} + \text{Equity}$$

Equity is often called *net assets* in government organizations. There are simply too many interrelationships among revenues, expenses, assets, and liabilities to ignore either of these statements. For example, assume that supply expenses reported on the income statement were low one month, but looking at the balance sheet you see an unusually high accounts payable balance. Accounting entries commonly balance figures between both statements. For instance, purchasing expenses can be accrued and put on the balance sheet, and supplies or pharmaceutical expenses can be held in inventory on the balance sheet. These temporary differences require users to understand and interact with both statements simultaneously.

The purpose of financial statements is to maintain a historical perspective of financial performance over time, using standards to allow for comparison purposes, which let one diagnose the strengths and weaknesses of a firm. A balance sheet, as one of the key statements, is designed to show how the assets, liabilities, and equity of the hospital are distributed at a specific point in time. It is often called the **statement of financial position**. It is usually prepared at regular intervals, such as each quarter, the end of each month, and especially at the end of an accounting year. Most hospitals are either on an academic-year (i.e., September 1 through August 31) or calendar-year basis (i.e., January 1 through December 31).

When looking at the balance sheets, assets are listed first, and they are arranged based on categories in decreasing order of liquidity, based on how quickly they can be turned into cash. Cash, therefore, is the first asset that appears under the asset section. Liabilities are listed second and are arranged in order of how soon they must be repaid or are due. Equity, or net assets, is listed third on the balance sheet. A sample balance sheet appears in **Table 3–2**.

An **asset** is anything the hospital owns that has immediate or long-term monetary value. Examples of assets are cash, marketable securities and investments, prepaid expenses, accounts receivable, inventories, fixed assets (also called *plant*, *property*, and *equipment*), and other assets. Assets can be further divided into current and long-term, or long-lived, assets. Current assets are those that will be converted into cash within 12 months or the current operating cycle, whichever is longer. Long-term assets are all those that are longer than 1 year or the current operating cycle.

Liabilities are the claims of all vendors and creditors against the assets of the business and represent all debts owed by the hospital. Current liabilities are debts that must be paid within 1 year, such as accounts payable, short-term notes payable, accrued expenses, taxes payable, and the current payment on long-term debt. Long-term liabilities are amounts owed with a maturity of more than 1 year, such as mortgages payable and long-term bank notes.

The difference between an organization's assets and its liabilities is the net assets, equity, or net worth of the business. It represents the investment of the owners, plus any profits retained, minus any losses incurred.

Table 3–2   Hospital Balance Sheet

2013 Assets	(Millions)
Current assets:	
Cash and equivalents	$325
Short-term investments	$175
Accounts receivable, net	$550
Inventories	$250
Prepaid expenses	$50
Total current assets	*$1,350*
Long-term assets:	
Land and buildings, net	$750
Property and equipment, net	$500
Investments	$200
Total long-term assets	*$1,450*
Total Assets	**$2,800**
Liabilities and Equity/Net Assets	
Current liabilities:	
Accounts payable	$360
Taxes and other payables	$40
Accrued liabilities	$80
Other short-term liabilities	$10
Total current liabilities	*$490*
Long-term liabilities:	
Long-term debt	$180
Other long-term obligations	$20
Total long-term liabilities	*$200*
Total Liabilities	**$690**
Equity/net assets	$2,110
Total Liabilities and Net Assets	**$2,800**

WORKING CAPITAL

Working capital is an important concept for operations management. Working capital is calculated by subtracting current liabilities from current assets. The excess of what will soon be converted to cash (current assets) minus the liabilities that will consume cash (current liabilities) is working capital. Conceptually, it is the funds necessary to finance the operating cycle for a hospital—from delivering services to receiving funds to paying invoices for materials used. The higher the figure, the more liquid a business is considered and the higher its ability to pay its debts.

Working capital represents the levels of inventory, cash, and accounts receivable on the books at any point in time. The current liabilities primarily represent payments to be made for accounts payable, such as supplies, materials, or services. From a supply chain perspective, both sides of the working capital equation are important because they reflect how efficiently the hospital is ordering, storing, and paying for goods and services. From a financial perspective, the amount of money in cash should be limited to as little as possible while still being able to make all required payments; the rest of the funds are held in marketable securities or accounts that have higher yielding interest and investment income. The key to working capital management is to match the amount of money needed in the short term with the amount of funds available and to keep all other assets in assets with higher returns, such as investing in a new building that will produce clinical revenue or in an equity fund.

One common working capital indicator used to measure efficiency is the number of days of working capital that a hospital holds. If a hospital has $22 million in current assets, $15 million in current liabilities, and an average monthly operating expense of about $26 million, then the calculation would be:

$$\text{Days of working capital} = \left[(CA - CL) \div \left(\frac{Op.expense}{360} \right) \right]$$

$$(\$22{,}000{,}000 - \$15{,}000{,}000) \div (\$26{,}00{,}000 \div 30)$$
$$= \$7{,}000{,}000 \div \$866{,}667 = 8.07 \text{ Days of working capital}$$

Alternatively, working capital can be measured by its separate components, such as number of days of cash on hand or number of days of inventory. Understanding which component of working capital is increasing or decreasing over a period of time, or relative to competitor hospitals, will help determine the drivers of change to working capital and focus operational management efforts.

OTHER FINANCIAL RATIOS

Common analyses performed on the balance sheet for operations management purposes include working capital indicators, debt ratio, inventory utilization, and asset management, among others.

An important measure for health care operations examines the percentage of debt that the organization maintains to sustain operations. The debt ratio examines the percentage of total assets financed by debt and is calculated as follows:

$$\text{Debt ratio} = \frac{\text{Total liabilities}}{\text{Total assets}}$$

For example, the balance sheet in Table 3–2 showed $690 million in total liabilities and $2,800 in total assets, which gives a 25% debt ratio. The lower the figure, the more equity is used to finance operations, which could suggest inefficient use of debt. On the other hand, too high a ratio suggests greater debt exposure, which tends to exaggerate earnings artificially.

Another important balance sheet ratio is the inventory turnover ratio. The simplest way to calculate inventory turns is:

$$\text{Inventory turnover ratio} = \frac{\text{Cost of goods sold}}{\text{Average inventory}}$$

Cost of goods sold is the term used to represent the cost of the materials or supplies that are stored in inventory, and average inventory is the mean value reported between two financial reports. For example, on the balance sheet in Table 3–2, the inventory was reported at $250 million. The previous year it was also $250 million, so the mean inventory is $250 million. Assuming that total cost of goods sold was $2,500, the inventory turnover ratio would be 10 ($2,500 ÷ $250).

Accounts receivable (AR) is an important component to analyze because it represents future revenue to be recognized. The faster that this can be converted into cash, the better. The most common AR calculation is called *days sales outstanding* (DSO) or *average collection period*, which defines how long on average the hospital has to wait to convert the receivables into cash. It is calculated as:

$$\text{DSO} = \frac{\text{Accounts receivable}}{\text{Revenue} \div 360}$$

Using the earlier figure, total accounts receivable is $550 million and daily revenue averages are $2,585,056 ($930,620,200 ÷ 360). Therefore, the DSO calculation is 212 days. In most modern hospitals, an average of days of AR out-standing is somewhere between 30 and 75 days.

The last common balance sheet ratio focuses on the relationship between current assets and current liabilities because it suggests how solvent or liquid the hospital is. The current ratio is calculated as:

$$\text{Current ratio} = \frac{\text{Current assets}}{\text{Current liabilities}}$$

Using the data in Table 3–2, current assets are $1,350 and current liabilities are $490 million. Therefore, the current ratio is 2.75. In general, a higher ratio indicates a larger safety margin, but it may also suggest inefficient use of assets because the higher-returning assets typically are long-term investments.

CASH FLOW STATEMENT

The third and most common financial statement is the statement of cash flows (also known as the cash flow statement or the funds statement). Cash is required to pay short-term bills, fund payroll, and finance daily operations. But monitoring the cash balance sitting in bank accounts is not sufficient to fully understand how it is being earned and used.

For public companies traded on stock exchange markets, the Securities and Exchange Commission requires disclosure and reporting of a company's cash flows. In the health care industry, which is primarily nonprofit, there is significantly less use of the statement of cash flows; even if it is not required, it should be utilized.

The **statement of cash flows** represents all of the cash inflows a hospital receives from its ongoing business activities and investments, as well as its cash outflows for expenditures, labor, and other activities. The cash flow statement shows both sources and uses of funds and reconciles both the income statement and the balance sheet back to changes in cash flow.

The cash flow statement is very useful to help analyze whether business activities are positively or negatively affecting a hospital's cash position. With most hospitals maintaining cash reserves of several days to several weeks of operations, it is important that business managers closely examine their efforts to ensure they are positively contributing to cash flows over time.

Information from this statement helps a hospital better manage its cash position, which is a critical component of working capital. It is a vital metric that hospital administrators must focus on to ensure that more cash is being "earned than burned." Knowing whether a change in cash position is due to operations (i.e., inflows and outflows related directly to services provided in the normal course of observing, diagnosing, and treating patients) or to investments or financing activities is essential to understanding a hospital's true financial position. A sample statement of cash flows is provided in **Table 3–3**.

Cash flow statements can be produced in two formats: direct and indirect. The indirect method is the most commonly used, likely because of its simplicity. The indirect method reconciles net income as the top line and makes adjustments for all entries that do not affect cash. Depreciation, for example, reduces net income, but because it is a noncash activity it will be added back to reconcile to the cash flow position. The direct method reports cash outflows and inflows only, without attempting to make reconciling adjustments back to net income. Both methods produce the same results, which is net cash used or provided by all types of operating, investing, and financing activities.

Under the operating activities, the indirect method sums all cash inflows and outflows primarily from the income statement items (e.g., net income, adjustments), but it also looks at changes in current assets and liabilities. The calculation

Table 3–3   Statement of Cash Flows

Cash Flow from Operations	
	$1,500,000
Net earnings	
Depreciation	$45,000
Decrease in accounts receivable	$15,000
Increase in taxes payable	$2,000
Less decrease in accounts payable	($25,000)
Less increase in inventory	($15,000)
Net Cash from Operations	**$1,522,000**
Cash Flow from Investing	
Equipment	($400,000)
Cash Flow from Financing	
Notes payable	$15,000
Cash Flow from FY2013, Net	**$1,137,000**

of cash flows for operating activities formula looks at the beginning and ending income statement and balance sheet and performs the following computation:

> \+ Net income
> \+ Decrease in current assets (if any)
> \+ Increase in current liabilities (if any)
> \+ Depreciation
> \+ Amortization of any intangible assets
> \+ Amortization of bond discounts
> \+ Any operating losses
> – Increase in current assets (if any)
> – Decrease in current liabilities (if any)
> – Amortization of bond premiums
> – Operating gains
>
> = Net cash provided (used) by operating activities

Similarly, a calculation for investing activities looks at both long-term assets bought or sold, as well as short- and long-term investments. Finally, a net cash flow from financing activities explores the changes in long-term liabilities; any dividends payable; and any issuing stock, treasury stock, and debt (although these are less common in most nonprofit hospitals). The net cash flow sums all three of the components to see the changes in net cash flow used or provided by operating, investing, and financing activities, and it gives a clear picture of whether the organization generated or burned cash during the period.

AUDITED FINANCIAL STATEMENTS

All of the three financial statements described in this chapter—income statement, balance sheet, and statement of cash flows—help show the overall financial health and condition of a hospital. However, obtaining these statements for benchmark comparisons with other hospitals is very difficult. For-profit, or publicly traded, firms are required to disclose their statements to the public as a condition of being listed on a stock exchange, but most hospitals are nonprofit and so are not regulated by the same rules. However, because most hospitals secure financing through debt, or the public bond market, audited financial statements are nearly always required to obtain financing through bond rating agencies. Hospital financial statements can be obtained directly from the hospital, from the Internal Revenue Service for certain charitable hospitals that file a Form 990, from an organization designated as a nationally recognized municipal securities information repository by the Securities and Exchange Commission, or from the Medicare cost report.

The best source of information to use for conducting operational analyses is audited financial statements, which are prepared or reviewed by an independent accounting firm. The independent accountant attests, based on examinations and reviews, that the statements fairly present the financial condition as of a certain period and were compiled in accordance with accounting principles. Audited financial statements give some reassurance that the overall financial statements are presented fairly, which is a potential problem for organizations that do not have to comply with generally accepted accounting principles.

DEBT IN HEALTH CARE

One of the most common ways to finance capital investments for the future is through debt. Debt is recorded on the balance sheet and can be payable in the near term (less than 1 year) or the long term (amortized over a period of greater than 1 year). There is a cost to finance the business using debt, as there is with all sources of funds, although some forms of debt are better than others. Simple forms of debt financing entail using organizational purchasing cards from banks with revolving lines of credit and an associated interest charge. Short-term working capital loans are offered by financial institutions to cover short-term imbalances in asset and liability accounts, primarily when AR is slower moving than accounts payable. Hospitals tend to use capital equipment leases for large items when vendors offer attractive terms, but for very large investments (e.g., new building, new major pieces of equipment) the use of public health care bonds is usually the desired debt vehicle.

Bonds are debt instruments issued by a health care organization to the public; the organization is obligated to repay the original principal plus interest for the period the debt was outstanding. Bonds can be very complex and often require both external legal and financial assistance in their offers. The amount of interest that organizations must repay is directly related to their credit ratings: Organizations that are the most successful, profitable, and the most creditworthy will have the best ratings and, therefore, lower interest rates. This is because the public views these organizations as being more stable and less risky; thus, they are willing to take a smaller return. Contrary to this, the more risky firms (i.e., those that have lower credit ratings) will have higher interest.

Credit ratings in health care financing are typically conducted by one of four organizations: Standard and Poor's, Moody's Investor Services, AM Best Company, and Fitch IBCA. Each of these organizations has developed separate rating schedules to evaluate the volatility and worth of those seeking credit. For example, Standard and Poor's uses AAA as the highest overall rating given to an organization, which represents the least amount of total risk, down to B2 for those that are most risky and speculative.

IMPLICATIONS FOR OPERATIONS AND LOGISTICS MANAGEMENT

All departments, functions, and managers play a role in improving the financial condition of hospitals. Understanding the effect of operational activities and how they translate into the financial statements of the hospital (which measure the changes in financial performance over time) are requirements for improving the level of competitiveness and operational effectiveness for a hospital. Operations managers, however, must take the leadership role in this effort.

The relationship between operations and working capital must be well defined and managed. When analyzing any project for a department, the working capital consumed must be calculated for that area to examine how it contributes, positively or negatively, to the institution. Similarly, operations managers must check that AR and accounts payable align and match to ensure that money is not being paid out faster than it comes in. Exploring changes in inventories for key nursing units and materials management departments is also necessary to ensure that supplies are being used properly and that there is an efficient utilization or turnover in assets.

The linkage between the revenue cycle and the supply chain must also be integrated faster and with less manual effort. There should be real-time integration between supply charges and patient medical records when dispensed so that, as new items are added to the item master, they are seamlessly integrated with the CDM, eliminating unnecessary manual steps and reviews.

Also, focusing on increasing the labor productivity for staff in support and clinical areas can mean reducing wait times for patients and lowering labor costs for the hospital. Understanding where these costs are stored in the institution's financial systems and reports is essential so that operations managers can use the right data in their analyses.

CHAPTER SUMMARY

The role that business operations managers play in improving a hospital's financial condition is a continuous and ever-increasing process. Operations managers must know where financial data reside in their hospitals—in which systems and financial reports—if they are to use them in quantitative analyses focused on operational efficiencies. A hospital's revenue is being constrained by all payers' attempts to reduce utilization of services and use competitive means to reduce reimbursement rates. This translates into lower revenues and profit margins. A hospital, therefore, has to continually focus on maximizing financial performance to ensure its survival and avoid bankruptcy and other financial distress. The financial condition of a hospital is measured through one of three key statements: the income statement, the balance sheet, and the statement of cash flows. Working capital is an important concept that focuses on operational efficiency. Ratio analyses help analyze whether the hospital is profitable, liquid, burdened with debt, or nearing bankruptcy. Analyzing the effect that operational management has on a hospital's overall performance and financial health is evident only by understanding these statements and by using ratios and metrics that show trends over time.

KEY TERMS

Accountable Care Organization (ACO)

Ambulatory Payment Classification (APC)

Asset

Balance sheet

Bonds

Capitation

Case mix index (CMI)

Case rate

Charge Description Master (CDM)

Commercial insurers

Cost of goods sold

Deductions

Diagnosis-related group (DRG)

Fee-for-service (FFS)

Income statement

Liabilities

Managed care organizations

Medicaid

Medicare

Net patient revenues

Payer

Per diems

Profit margins

Prospective payment

Reimbursements

Retrospective

Statement of cash flows

Statement of financial position

Working capital

DISCUSSION QUESTIONS

1. Why should operations managers understand financial statements?
2. What constrains a hospital's revenue?
3. Compare and contrast the incentives to health care providers under a fee-for-service reimbursement mechanism versus a prospective payment mechanism.
4. What are the three key financial statements that business managers should be aware of, and how are they related?
5. What is the logic of the order of the assets listed on the balance sheet?
6. What is a financial ratio? What value does it provide?
7. Why do organizations have their statements audited? What assurance does it provide?
8. What is the principal difference between the direct and indirect methods for preparing the cash flow statement?

EXERCISE PROBLEMS

1. A hospital has $25 million in gross revenues and $12 million in net patient revenues. What is the average deduction percentage for that period?
2. The same hospital has $40 million in current assets and $30 million in current liabilities. During a 30-day month, it incurred total operating expenses of $10 million. How many days of working capital did it maintain this period?
3. Using the income statement and balance sheet examples provided in the chapter, calculate the return on capital in 2013.

REFERENCES

American Hospital Association. (2006). *Chartbook*. Chicago, IL: Author.
American Hospital Association. (2013). *Factbook*. Chicago, IL: Author.
Association for Healthcare Resource and Materials Management. (2005). *Supply expense benchmarking study*. Chicago, IL: Author.
Centers for Disease Control and Prevention, National Center for Health Statistics. (2014). *Hospital utilization*. Retrieved from www.cdc.gov/nchs/fastats/hospital.htm
Centers for Medicare and Medicaid Services. (2013). *National health expenditures 2012 highlights*. Washington, DC: Department of Health and Human Services.

Centers for Medicare and Medicaid Services. (2014). *Hospital cost report information system*. Washington, DC: Department of Health and Human Services.

Finkler, S. A., & Ward, D. M. (2006). *Accounting fundamentals for health care management*. Sudbury, MA: Jones and Bartlett.

Healthcare Financial Management Association. (2005). *2005 supply chain benchmarking survey*. Washington, DC: Author.

Langabeer, J. R. (2006). Predicting financial distress in teaching hospitals. *Journal of Health Care Finance, 33*(2), 84–92.

Modern Healthcare. (2012). *By the Numbers: 2012–2013 Supplement*. Chicago, IL: Crain Communications.

PART II

Quality and Productivity Management

Part II of this text describes how hospitals can continue to improve their operations management capabilities through quantitative methods, improved project management, and quality management plans that will reduce waste and improve performance.

Chapter 4 concentrates on quality and process improvement efforts in operations management. The use of quality improvement practices, such as Six Sigma and Lean, are explored, and a methodology for continuous process improvement is offered. Operations management professionals should be constantly looking for ways to improve processes, through cycle time reductions, improved flow, and increased productivity.

Chapter 5 focuses on Operations Research. Operations research involves application of quantitative methods to improve management decision-making, and specifically to enhance patient and process flows. Maximizing throughput with given capacity and aligning demand with capacity are discussed in detail. An introduction to forecasting algorithms as a tool for estimating demand is presented, and sophisticated tools for de-bottlenecking wait lines are described.

Chapter 6 describes the use of productivity management. Understanding processes—their resource consumption, costs, cycle times, and outcomes—comprise a large part of a hospital's continually increasing cost structure. One of the most vital roles of operations management is to increase productivity ratios to improve operating efficiency, and the concepts of productivity and their calculations are explored. Staffing models and the use of labor optimization algorithms are explored as ways to minimize total costs. Specific use of analytical tools to manage productivity is also discussed.

Chapter 7 provides a thorough description of the key operational performance metrics used by health care operations managers. This includes a discussion of how to calculate and interpret these metrics in operational analyses. This chapter provides practical concepts that can be used immediately to measure an organization's performance against others.

Chapter 8 describes the role of project and change management and how to comprehensively develop and manage a portfolio of projects. The role of a performance improvement department in hospitals is discussed. Methods for improving rollouts of technology or process changes, including Gantt charts and project plans, are also reviewed.

Chapter 9 describes how business planning can improve operational strategy. A plan for analyzing other hospitals, the industry, and the internal environment—and for using this information to improve your own hospital—is described in significant detail. Operational planning is fundamental to understanding areas of the organization to focus on improving.

Chapter 10 describes return on investment (ROI) analyses. Operations analysts must integrate ROI models into all types of projects, especially those focused on information technology, capital equipment, and automation. To achieve a return on investment, the total benefits derived from technology and other projects must outweigh its cost. Accounting for all benefits and costs in a systematic process is important to quantify financial value, net present value, internal rates of return, and payback. Chapter 10 provides a comprehensive discussion of each of these areas and gives suggestions for maximizing return on investment during all phases of projects.

Quality Management

Central to any hospital's efforts to achieve operational excellence is a focus on continuous improvement. Improvement of processes leads to better outcomes, reduced costs, and shorter cycle times. To improve means to make something better, and it takes a process-oriented mind-set to maintain day-to-day operations while seeking opportunities for betterment. **Continuous improvement** implies a constant focus on achieving better outcomes. The use of analytical methods and tools can help hospitals achieve better results, while benchmarking allows hospitals to break down their operations into specific processes and compare these results against others to ensure that they are competitive and improving. This chapter discusses the role of process management and improvement as a component of operational management.

CHOICES FOR OPERATIONS MANAGEMENT: TOOLS AND TECHNIQUES

To make improvements in health care, it is important to use the right tool for the appropriate situation. Remember Abraham Maslow's famous quote: "If the only tool you have is a hammer, you tend to see every problem as a nail" (Maslow, 1998). In other words, you can't use a hammer to fix all problems. In the field of operations management, there is a large portfolio of quantitative tools and techniques that can be applied in the appropriate situation to solve problems involving operational efficiencies. For instance, if an emergency room is having trouble with wait lines, a combination of Pareto charts, wait line minimization or queuing models, and process analysis (all of which will be described in this chapter) may be applied. **Figure 4–1** matches the types of problems or objectives of operations with possible operational management tools and techniques. All of these are discussed throughout this text.

PROCESS

A **process** is a set of activities and tasks that are performed in sequence to achieve a specific outcome. A process can be administrative or clinical in nature and is usually called a *business process* by most quality improvement professionals.

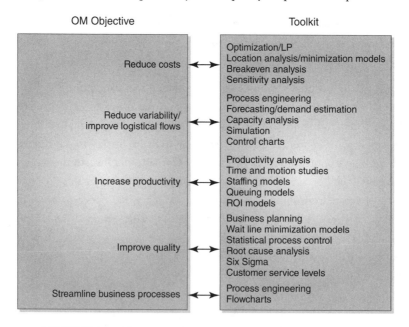

FIGURE 4–1 Operations Management—Tools and Techniques

A process typically has three high-level phases: inputs, outputs, and transformation. A process includes all activities, tasks, and steps that must be performed to complete something. Inputs are all resources to be used or consumed in a process, such as labor hours, staff, supplies, space or facilities, information systems, and other resources. Transformation is the conversion or change process, where the inputs are combined to deliver final results, which are the outputs. Outputs are the result of the transformation or conversion process.

For example, a patient schedules a visit; on the day of his appointment, he arrives at the clinic. Prior to receiving treatment or diagnosis (the output), the clinic uses its staff, systems, space, forms, and records (the inputs) to organize the patient, stage him in the appropriate locations, and allow the physician to provide treatment. **Figure 4–2** shows a sample process flowchart depicting these events.

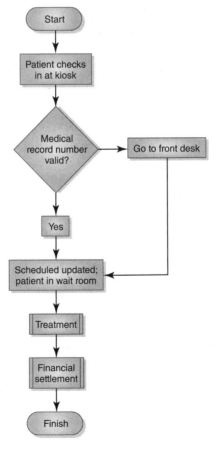

FIGURE 4–2 Example Process Maps

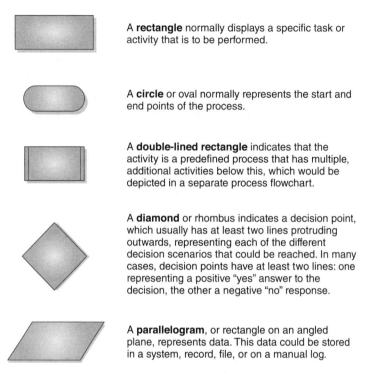

A **rectangle** normally displays a specific task or activity that is to be performed.

A **circle** or oval normally represents the start and end points of the process.

A **double-lined rectangle** indicates that the activity is a predefined process that has multiple, additional activities below this, which would be depicted in a separate process flowchart.

A **diamond** or rhombus indicates a decision point, which usually has at least two lines protruding outwards, representing each of the different decision scenarios that could be reached. In many cases, decision points have at least two lines: one representing a positive "yes" answer to the decision, the other a negative "no" response.

A **parallelogram**, or rectangle on an angled plane, represents data. This data could be stored in a system, record, file, or on a manual log.

FIGURE 4–3 Flowchart Symbols

Using the flowchart symbols presented in **Figure 4–3**, a process map or diagram can be created to show the sequence of tasks and activities from start to finish. This is called a **process flowchart**, and it depicts the flows or activity exchanges among participants and shows the sequencing of activities from start to finish. Although this is a simple example to illustrate the concepts, real process maps can be quite detailed and run across multiple pages with dozens of interactions among departments.

PROCESS MAPS

There are two major classifications of process maps: current (or as-is) and future (or to-be). An **as-is process** is a version of a process flowchart that depicts the actual, current process in place. The as-is map describes how a process really works in practice—not just in a standard operating procedure. It is normally the starting point for process improvement efforts because it shows the roles, participants, functions, and tasks involved in converting inputs into outputs.

The goal of documenting the current process is to find opportunities for reducing steps, interactions, decision points, reports, and the overall length of the process. There are three major opportunities for improving the current process:

1. Increasing the throughput, capacity, or volume that can flow through a process with little or no change in inputs. This requires an identification of the choke point, or bottleneck, that limits the capacity of a process to maximize results.

2. Reducing the costs, steps, waste, and resources utilized in the process. This requires scrutiny of individual steps that may be redundant, unnecessary, or do not add value overall.

3. Reducing the variation (or changes from the norm) in performance over time. This requires the use of statistical process control tools such as scatter diagrams and control charts.

Often, as-is maps are carefully designed and documented, yet users do not take the next steps to identify how to increase throughput or reduce resource consumption. In simple terms, the key to mapping as-is processes is to document the overall cycle time it takes to complete from start to finish; the number of touch points, or interactions, between different participants; and the total dollar amount of all inputs, especially labor. The as-is process should then be redesigned or reengineered to achieve a faster, more efficient, and more effective process flow.

Process engineering refers to the careful scrutiny of a current process to identify value creation opportunities, such as eliminating hand-offs or steps in the process, and it should attempt to find value through the three categories listed earlier (increasing capacity, reducing costs, and reducing variability). Each of the tasks in the current process that do not add value, or that could be replaced by automation or a process change that may reduce other steps, should be eliminated. The **to-be process** represents the future state, after all changes and improvements are designed into the current process.

PROCESS IMPROVEMENT METHODOLOGY

How does a hospital begin to address these process issues? It is important to follow a structured methodology so that issues can be discovered and engineered into the process (Hammer & Champy, 1993). Up to this point the discussion has focused on issues of efficiency, but health care cannot ignore the implications for quality or service. Sometimes a hospital can reduce steps and increase process speed yet still have low quality or do the wrong things. Doing the right things, or effectiveness, requires organizations to think about the broader aspects of the organization and specifically address issues such as (Harrington, Esseling, & van Nimwegen, 1997):

- Why are we using this process at all?
- What value does it add?
- Which quality improvements are necessary to improve outcomes?
- Can multiple processes be combined into a single role?
- If we make this change, will it adversely affect our service quality to patients?

It is important for hospitals to more broadly consider issues of job structure, values, and culture in the organization, as well as business process management. To accomplish this, it is necessary to follow a process improvement methodology. There are many to choose from, including the PDCA model (plan, do, check, act) or Six Sigma (George, 2003). Most of the improvement processes today are very similar in many regards. For example, most processes encourage multifunctional participation, urge planning before action, use testing or piloting of solutions before wide-scale deployment, and employ continuous and rapid measurement as feedback. **Figure 4–4** shows a suggested process improvement methodology.

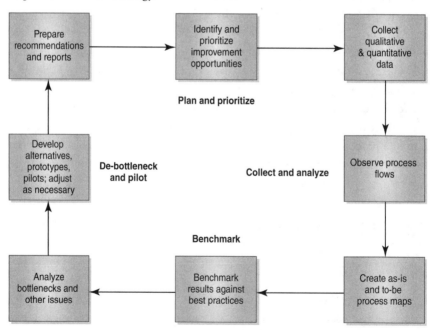

FIGURE 4–4 Process Improvement Methodology

Plan and Prioritize

The first few steps in process improvement encourage hospitals to think through all areas of the organization and then prioritize and plan the improvement efforts. Typically, prioritization should be based on potential gains in cost, quality, patient satisfaction, or some other performance category. Ranking of the various processes, based on these criteria, can help identify which process to attack first.

Once an improvement area has been targeted, a plan should be created for how to address the problem. This plan includes project schedule and time lines, team members, and project goals. The team should be cross functional, or representative of all of the major participants in the actual process. Project goals should be clearly stated, such as "Our goal is to take 40% of the cycle time out of this process" or "We will reduce at least 15% of the costs in the current process." Establishing quantitative targets helps provide a framework and eliminates one of the biggest problems in process improvement—identifying only incremental, minimal change.

Collect and Analyze

This second phase involves collecting all key data elements that need to be analyzed. A management engineer or performance improvement specialist, if available, should serve as facilitator of this process, because most data collection requires brainstorming and teamwork that is difficult to get when working with multiple personalities and individuals. Communication barriers often exist and need to be reduced as much as possible, which requires skilled facilitation.

Studying the details of the process workflow and carefully measuring start and stop times for each activity, key deliverables, reports, and interactions between individuals and departments is necessary to fully document the as-is process. Other data, such as work effort or other inputs, help provide a complete picture of the causes and effects for the current process performance. At the same time, once these current processes are diagrammed, the team begins process engineering to develop the future state process. Are there opportunities for eliminating tasks or reducing hand-offs between departments? Can automation help streamline processes? Are there ways to change this to a more exception-based process, which requires effort only if it deviates from some norm? Information on productivity, costs, quality, service levels, staffing, cycle times, number of steps and points of interaction, and key deliverables must all be collected during this phase.

Data collection also requires analyzing process performance over a broad range of time periods and dates to ensure that the sample data collected can be extrapolated and are representative of all times and dates. Consider that workflow peaks at times, and that if the process is engineered for peaks, it is not representative. Plotting the data graphically, on process control charts, helps analyze changes in inputs and outputs over time, normalize the data, and look for process deviations or variations.

The use of **Pareto charts** provides a graphic representation of the most "vital few" issues that exist in a process in a ranked order to show relative priorities. Pareto charts are based on the philosophy that 80% of the effects are caused by just 20% of the problems (also called the *80–20 principle*). The first few columns in a Pareto chart represent the categories or problems that are the highest importance or frequency, based on cumulative percentages. These first few issues are causing the majority of the effects, so they should be focused on initially. A sample Pareto chart is shown in **Figure 4–5**.

To create a Pareto chart, there are three simple steps:

1. Use a root cause analysis technique to identify the key issues. **Root cause analysis** is a process for identifying and correcting the major issues causing problems. Brainstorming, observation analysis, cause-and-effect diagrams, surveys, and many other common techniques are used to discover root causes for problems.
2. Through the use of a log or frequency chart, document the frequency of occurrence for each issue or event.

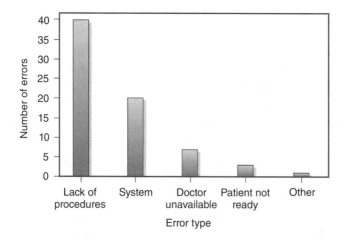

FIGURE 4–5 Causes of Errors During Patient Check-In

3. Using a graphical software tool such as PowerPoint, arrange each of the items on a bar chart, placing those with the highest occurrence in ranked order from most to least.

Surveys are often used to gather data from both employees and customers of the process. Customers may be patients, or they may be other internal departments of the hospital, as many departments exist only to serve others. Surveys may be administered through the Internet, through sites such as Qualtrics (www.qualtrics.com), SurveyMonkey (www.surveymonkey.com), or Zoomerang (www.zoomerang.com), as part of the organization's patient satisfaction surveys, or conducted as personalized interviews with random participants.

Benchmark

Once the business process is completely understood, it should be benchmarked against others. **Benchmarking** is the process of identifying best practices and comparing performance relative to others, with the intent of making improvements to your own organization. Benchmarking takes one of two forms: firsthand observations of other organizations or direct comparisons of secondary published data. Using published data is the most common way to compare against multiple organizations simultaneously, although detailed on-site benchmarking visits of other hospitals often prove invaluable.

Benchmarking involves four primary steps:

1. Select organizations for comparison.
2. Collect or observe data and processes.
3. Identify sources of differential performance.
4. Incorporate these benchmarks into performance scorecards and daily management processes.

The first step is to select the appropriate hospitals or other organizations to benchmark against. This process can use either process and performance data to compare against multiple firms or a single site for benchmarking (i.e., contact another hospital, perform a site visit, and directly compare the data).

It is more common to use external data sources for some processes, although this is very difficult in health care because there are not many clearinghouses for performance data, which is more common in private for-profit industries. One of the largest health care benchmarking firms is Truven (www.truven-health.com), which offers several tools and publications to assist in benchmarking. Other organizations, such as the American Productivity and Quality

Center (www.apqc.org) and the Hackett Group (www.thehackettgroup.com), offer benchmarking data across multiple industries. It is not necessary to focus exclusively on hospitals; some business processes are not health care specific (e.g., financial processes, such as accounting or reporting). Typically, the hospital with best practices can be discovered through write-ups in hospital news journals or by analyzing the competition's financial or quality performance.

Next, using the data collected, try to determine what makes the benchmark organization's performance different through research and interviews. It may be difficult to get competing hospitals to discuss their processes, but interviews with their patients, payers, and direct observations can all be used to evaluate what makes those hospitals' performance better. Sometimes the use of a specialized competitive intelligence firm can be employed to analyze competition. These new benchmarks should be established as targets in performance scorecards and business plans to help set goals for continual improvements. Finally, hospitals must apply this knowledge to improve performance. After discovering what makes others successful, hospitals should adapt these findings to their own unique environments and try to improve overall performance.

De-bottleneck and Deploy Pilot

There are always opportunities to de-bottleneck processes. To de-bottleneck is to eliminate constraints that limit efficient throughput in a process. Improvement teams must focus on finding ways to increase process throughput, expand productivity, reduce unnecessary steps, or otherwise improve the process being considered. One way to de-bottleneck is to use statistical process control charts to identify causes of variation. A **control chart** shows data over time, relative to both a mean (average) and control limits. Control limits work on the assumption of standard deviation, which suggest that in normal operations results should be concentrated fairly closely around a mean. **Standard deviation** refers to the spread or dispersion from the mean, defined as the square root of the sums of the distances between the observations and the mean. Deviations greater than a certain amount are considered problematic and characteristic of processes that are out of control. Typically, control limits are represented both above and below the means.

An upper control limit is typically a maximum of 13 standard deviations—represented by the Greek letter sigma (σ)—away from the mean for each observation, while the lower control limit maximum is 23σ. Tighter control around variations requires the use of upper and lower control limits that are closer to 1σ, not 3. A sample statistical control chart with 22σ upper and lower control limits is shown in **Figure 4–6**.

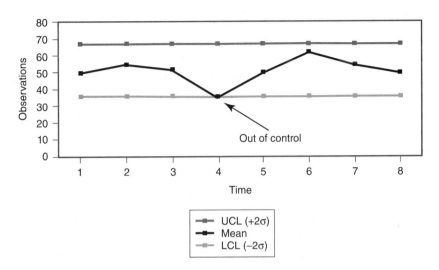

FIGURE 4–6 Statistical Process Control Charts Manage Variability

Notice in Figure 4–6 that data observations are graphed out in the control chart over time using an x–y axis, where x represents the time periods and y represents the data values or observations. A mean value of these data over time was approximately 52, and calculating 2σ variations or limits on each side kept a tight band from around 38 to 66 (38 is the lower control limit, and 66 is the upper control limit). This implies that when the process behaves normally, there will be a range of values acceptable anywhere in that band. However, in time period 4, a value of 35 occurred. This observation significantly deviates from the norm and therefore is considered to be out of control. Special investigation of this data point must occur to learn what changed during this period so that it can be prevented from reoccurring in the future. If using this statistical control chart to analyze a health care process, detailed analysis of all points out of these limits should question what created the variability. Was it:

- Changes in staffing mix or levels?
- Higher demand or patient volumes?
- System or equipment downtime or glitches?
- Modifications in supplies or resources employed?
- Different employees?
- Related to time of day or day of week?

Sources of the variation must be identified to manage and eliminate the variability.

Developing and deploying the future state in a "pilot" mode is often beneficial (Schrage, 2000). **Pilot** is an initial test of the proposed new process, under limited conditions, to help gauge issues and success in achieving the desired goals. The pilot helps identify if the future business process will help achieve the project's stated goals, and it allows for more rapid changes, if necessary, to help streamline and improve. If successful under the pilot, more full-scale deployment should be initiated.

Report and Adjust

Once process changes have been made, a summary report should be prepared that documents the changes, procedures, findings, and performance levels for the process. This should be used as an institution's "memory" to help document why changes were made and what conditions existed prior to the change.

Performance should be monitored and tracked continuously to ensure that the results achieved in the pilot and initial rollout continue, and that if any issues or problems arise they are immediately addressed. This feedback and adjustment process is necessary for at least 3 to 6 months following any process improvement initiative.

IMPROVING SERVICE QUALITY

Cost and efficiency are key outcomes of process improvement. However, a focus on efficiency sometimes comes at the expense of quality, which is unfortunate. **Quality** implies high standards, excellence, and the ability to meet and exceed customers' expectations. As hospitals continue to improve in both areas (cost and quality), they will employ improvement programs and processes focused on error reductions, process simplification, and patient satisfaction.

Quality in health care revolves around a core set of important service-level categories: patient outcomes, patient safety, financial, administrative, and patient logistics flow and facilities.

- *Patient outcomes.* Did the patient receive quality medical care? Did the patient get better during his or her visit or stay? Was the length of stay longer than it should have been? What are the facility's overall mortality or morbidity rates?
- *Patient safety.* Were there any medication errors, where pharmaceuticals or supplies were inadvertently administered to the wrong patient? Were there any other medical complications during the patient's stay? Any patient slips and falls to report?

- *Financial.* Was there a billing error or financial complication with the patient's account? Did payer type cause the discharge or reimbursement process to be slower or more painful than normal?
- *Administrative.* Were staff friendly and helpful? Did providers and staff greet the patient with a smile? Were there any issues regarding confidentiality of patient information?
- *Patient logistics flow and facilities.* Was the navigation around the organization easy? Were there excessive wait lines in any area? Did the patient endure wait times because of shortages or stock-outs of drugs or supplies? Did the patient get routed where he or she needed to go in as little time necessary? Were the patient's guests and family members comfortable in waiting rooms?

Customer service and quality cannot suffer as a result of improving health care efficiency and productivity, so metrics around each of these core quality outcome categories must be managed simultaneously. Staffing, technology, improved facility layouts, and education are all critical to improving quality service.

Six Sigma

There are several quality management programs that exist. One of the most well known is Six Sigma. **Six Sigma** is a methodology developed at Motorola, and significantly refined and advanced by General Electric, that centers its effort on improving processes and eliminating defects by focusing on sigma (or standard deviations) that cause volatility and variability of outcomes (George, 2003). Achieving a Six Sigma level implies near perfection in an operational process, with around 3.4 defects (e.g., problems, failures, or issues) per million opportunities, or 99.99966% accuracy rate. That is, the numerator is the number of errors or defects in a process, while the denominator is the total number of opportunities for error (number of encounters or output). Each sigma, or standard deviation, represents an exponential level of improvements. Five sigma represents 233 defects per million, 4 sigma represents 6,210 defects, and so on.

In health care, one patient represents literally 50 to 100 opportunities for error during each stay or visit. The moment the patient arrives through the front door is the first opportunity. The parking garage, valet, registration, financial counseling, laboratory, radiology, and clinic all represent opportunities for potential error. When documenting the error or failure rate, it is important to understand both the numerator and the denominator thoroughly if improvements are to be made.

Education on Six Sigma topics covers the concepts of process analysis, statistical tools, data collection, and control charts. Students can advance through different "belts" or learning levels, from yellow to green and then on to black. Black belt signifies complete mastery of Six Sigma to improve process and achieve results.

Six Sigma follows a process improvement methodology similar to the one described earlier, but it is typically called *DMAIC*: *define, measure, analyze, improve*, and *control*. This methodology focuses on finding sources of variation inherent in the processes through root cause analyses and eliminating them to achieve more consistent results. Once the processes are improved, their performance and behavior should be continually tracked, routinely monitoring performance using statistical process control charts and performance scorecards to ensure low levels of variability and deviations. Six Sigma methodologies, like all process improvement processes, are visually represented as a cycle or circle—because the search for perfection is never over.

Exploring Six Sigma

Six Sigma requires a comprehensive understanding of the behavior of a process. Behavior refers to the variability of the data and the relationships between inputs and outputs. A process model typically details the activity, step by step. The components of a process model include:

- *Activity*. A task occurring at a specific point in time that has a random duration and a known probability distribution function.
- *Event*. The culmination of an activity. Events can modify the state of a process.
- *Time*. The key parameter of a process, defined as the differential between the time an activity started and ended. This is usually expressed in minutes and seconds.
- *Outcomes*. The consequence, or result, of the activities and events. Outcomes are expressed in terms of a performance metric to gauge success and failure. An example of this from a cardiovascular unit's perspective might be door-to-balloon time, expressed as the minutes elapsed between arrival at a hospital door to the time a catheter is implanted.

Six Sigma is a quantitative approach to managing clinical and business processes. It requires detailed observation and monitoring of a process, as well as documentation of the precise times, events, and outcomes. Detailed logs must be kept to calculate Six Sigma metrics. For example, if a process was observing the

Table 4–1 Sample Log for Six Sigma

Activity	Cycle Time	Event	Outcome
Respiratory therapist treatment, code 99407	16 minutes, 22 seconds	Completion of 1 procedure	Successful

time a respiratory therapist spends with a patient, and the resource accessed the patient's room at 11:00 p.m. and left at 11:16 p.m. with a smoking cessation clinical procedure completed, the output matrix would look like the example provided in **Table 4–1**.

To ensure complete understanding of the process behavior, these activities would need to be monitored routinely and over a sufficient time period to ensure that they were statistically representative of typical (and not random) behavior. The process should be mapped out using the process tools discussed earlier in this chapter. Of great importance, the behavior of the activities can be statistically analyzed. This is one of the main contributions of the Six Sigma methodology.

Modeling the process time allows operations managers to understand variability in the process. **Variability** is the range of possible outcomes of a given process. It is also defined as the amount of dispersion around the mean, or the inconsistency of results. The greater the variability, the less control that exists in the process outcomes. Both standard deviation and variance are the primary statistical measures of variability, although standard deviation is probably more widely used and applied in Six Sigma. In a normally distributed set of data, +/− one standard deviation from the mean will include 68.2% of all observations, and two standard deviations represent 95% of all observations. The mean is typically represented by the Greek symbol (μ) and standard deviation by the Greek symbol sigma (σ), defined as the square root of the variance.

Looking back at the process behavior and variability in Figure 4–6, there were eight observations, with time measured in minutes. The lowest documented time (the minimum) was 35 minutes, and the maximum value was 62. The mean is approximately 51.1, and the standard deviation of these data is 7.68. Therefore, to calculate the upper control limit within 1σ deviation from the mean would be approximately 58.8 (51.1 + 7.7), and 2σ (representing the 95% confidence interval) would be 66.5 minutes. Similarly, deduct the standard deviation from the mean to calculate the lower control limits. Therefore, in 68% of the cases, these activities were completed between 43.5 and 58.8 minutes. In 95% of the cases, these activities were completed in no more than 66.5 minutes and no less than 35.8 minutes. Understanding this process behavior is key to Six Sigma management.

Defects Per Million Opportunities

Another key Six Sigma concept is DPMO, or **defects per million opportunities**. Using process behavior models, an operations manager can identify a defect. A **defect** is any instance in a process where the customer requirement has not been met (Langabeer, 2009). In the example of the respiratory therapist procedures provided earlier, the outcome was positive (i.e., the procedures were successfully completed in 16 minutes). If, however, it took 22 minutes for the procedures, and the patient was unable to have one of the three procedures completed, it would have been recorded as a defect, as it deviated from the expectation and did not meet the customer's (or patient's) expectations. Six Sigma uses DPMO to understand defect behavior for activities and processes.

To calculate the number of defects per million opportunities, follow these four steps:

1. Choose a process to evaluate, as well as the specific deliverables and outcomes resulting from the process.
2. Define what a successful outcome is and what a defect is (a defect could be a complication of a procedure, an error, or an outcome that is in any other way adverse). Then count the total number of opportunities available.
3. Model the statistical behavior of the process. Observe all tasks and activities, and gather the outcomes in a log. Then, graphically and statistically model the results, calculating the mean, standard deviation, and both upper and lower control limits. In addition, the total number of defects should be counted and recorded. For example, if you observed 500 opportunities over time and counted 75 defects (or instances that did not conform to requirements), then the DPMO would be calculated as $(75 \div 500) \times 1{,}000{,}000 = 150{,}000$.
4. Measure the sigma level. After calculating the DPMO, it is easy to calculate the sigma level to estimate the potential for quality improvement opportunities. Six Sigma actually refers to the calculation where only 3.4 defects per million are recorded, which yields a 99.99966% success rate. This yield can be calculated by subtracting from 100% the defect rate (e.g., $100\% - [3.4 \div 1{,}000{,}000] = 100 - 0.00034 = 0.99966$, or 99.9%). **Figure 4–7** allows you to graphically compare your process' defect rates against sigma and DPMO levels. Using our current example with 150,000 defects, this would equate to sigma level 2.

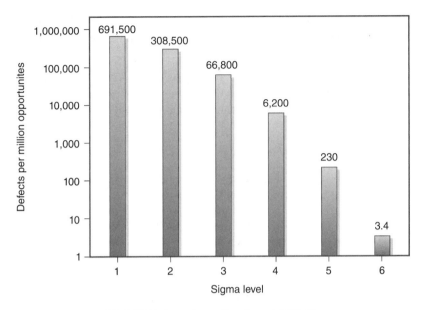

FIGURE 4–7 Sigma Levels and DPMO

Process Capability Index

One of the multiple quantitative tools that Six Sigma enables is calculation of a process capability index (often expressed as Cp). A **process capability index** is a measure for gauging the extent to which a process meets the customer's expectations. It is mathematically defined as:

$$[(\text{Upper standard limit} - \text{Lower standard limit}) \div 6\sigma]$$

A Cp > 1 suggests that the process is capable, but it does not have any relation to the performance target, nor does it suggest that the process meets the customer's expectations. To improve on this, other complementary metrics should be used, such as Cpk. Cpk is defined as the minimum of either Cpu [(USL – $\bar{x}$) ÷ 3σ] or Cpl ($\bar{x}$ – LSL) ÷ 3σ].

QUALITY AND LEAN PROCESSES

Quality management is defined as the application of quantitative and qualitative methods to ensure that health care services and products possess the characteristics necessary to completely satisfy the needs that they are designed to serve.

In recent years, the manufacturing sector has begun to use the term **lean process** to imply a quality process that focuses on improving quality while dramatically changing the operational processes to become faster and more flexible, with less waste, smaller lot sizes, and more highly customized services—all while providing the right goods or services at the specific time required. Central to lean processes are the concepts of speed and reducing cycle times.

Cycle and Transition Times

In health care processes, there are several components of time that affect an organization's ability to use speed and flexibility:

- *Process time.* This is the actual time spent performing work; it is true productive time. For example, the time that a nurse spends directly with a patient is productive process time.
- *Idle time.* This is time when patients and staff are not performing work, which could be due to system downtime or breaks.
- *Wait time.* This is time spent waiting because of lines or queues that form in parts of the facility.
- *Transit time.* This is time spent walking from one department or unit to another. For example, the time that a patient spends moving between units is transit time.
- *Transition time.* This is the time interval necessary between productive work where a conversion, cleanup, or changeover prepares a resource to switch from one state to another.

Transition time is one of the largest components of health care waste. Reducing transition time supports more rapid response and improved logistical flows. Transition time in health care is one of the largest sources of inefficiencies—and inefficiencies occur everywhere. An example of a transition in health care is when a bed is turned or changed from one patient to another. If a bed is vacated, and 45 minutes later the bed is made ready (sheets are changed, room is sterilized and cleaned), then 45 minutes of productive capacity have been lost. Losing just 45 minutes of capacity in a large hospital can be the difference between 60% and 80% occupancy rates (or utilization). Similarly, when equipment has to be temporarily taken down to ready it for the next patient (e.g., to change out films or cartridges or prepare the computed tomography equipment), this represents transition time. Reducing this transition time is essential to reduce the total cycle time and obtain greater throughput with the same capacity. This is also called *just in time.*

Quality Accreditation Programs

Accreditation of hospitals and health care organizations is a voluntary process. Many mistakenly believe that accreditation is required for reimbursement, but in fact it is voluntary and designed to help organizations in their quest for quality. There are several organizations that help to evaluate and monitor hospitals' quality improvement efforts from an accreditation perspective. The dominant one by far is The Joint Commission (www.jointcommission.org). This organization helps hospitals concentrate on process improvement, create performance standards, and manage outcomes. The Joint Commission provides an evaluation program, complete with thorough criteria and tools for evaluating the overall level of patient care (from clinical delivery of care to support services such as the condition of facilities). A relatively new accreditation organization that has emerged is DNV GL Healthcare (www.dnvglhealthcare.com). Many organizations participate in mock surveys to proactively prepare for real evaluations and continuously improve plans and processes. It is important to be familiar with all quality accreditation standards governing quality and processes. These are commonly available in a variety of texts and multimedia formats (Bryant, 2004; Taylor & Taylor, 1994).

Another quality program is available through the National Institute of Standards and Technology, which offers the Malcolm Baldrige National Quality Award. The award covers a variety of organizations, including manufacturing, services, education, and health care. The award application process encourages hospitals to evaluate their level of success in managing quality relative to other similar hospitals. The Baldrige criteria allow hospitals to either self-evaluate or participate in a formal external evaluation program. These evaluations are instrumental in helping hospitals raise awareness of quality and benchmark their programs against other organizations. In addition, it helps generate ideas and action items for improving quality. Baldrige criteria focus on process management, strategic planning, leadership, and performance, all of which are key components of business planning and process improvement.

Several hospitals and health care organizations have won the Baldrige award in recent years, including Sutter Davis Hospital in California (2013), North Mississippi Health Services (2012), Henry Ford Health System in Detroit (2012), and many others in the last 5 years (National Institute of Standards and Technology, 2014). This type of recognition affirms a hospital's plans and provides powerful branding and competitive positioning in the marketplace, both of which help generate positive publicity and, it is hoped, increased financial returns.

Table 4–2   Six Sigma Versus Lean

Dimension	Six Sigma	Lean
Goals	Conformance to customer requirements; elimination of defects (errors, re-work)	Remove non-valued-added activities; eliminate waste (errors, wait times)
Approach	Reduction of process variability	Standardization, production flow leveling
Principal tool/ method	Statistical process control, run charts, cause-and-effect diagrams	Value Stream Mapping, Kanban, 5S
Infrastructure	Through formalized structures, titles, and roles	Cultural change; "Sensei" relationships
Methodology	DMAIC (define, measure, analyze, improve, control)	PDSA (plan, do, study, act)
Performance metrics	Quantifiable, cost of quality; mapped into financial value	Not consistent; often result in new metrics

Data from Langabeer, J., DelliFraine, J., Heineke, J., and Abbass, I. (2009). Implementation of Lean and Six Sigma Quality Initiatives in Hospitals: A Goal Theoretic Perspective. *Operations Management Research, 2*(1), 13–27.

SIX SIGMA VERSUS LEAN COMPARISON

To understand the difference between Lean and Six Sigma, the goals, approaches, methodology, infrastructure, and key performance metrics can be contrasted and compared (see **Table 4–2**). Although Lean and Six Sigma are remarkably different, they are both widely used by facilities to improve quality of care. In addition, Lean Six Sigma is a combination approach that utilizes methods from both types of programs.

KEY QUESTIONS TO PROMOTE DRAMATIC CHANGES

During an improvement process, it is helpful to ensure that all aspects of the problem have been uncovered and identified. Asking the right questions of process improvement teams can help promote dramatic process changes. These questions include:

- How does the change affect our customers?
- How does the change affect organizational job structure, roles, and responsibilities?

- Can we redesign jobs and positions entirely?
- How can we focus more on "exceptions" than transactions?
- Who benefits from the change?
- What other insight or inspiration emerged from the process engineering efforts?
- Do we know the effect on cost and quality of our proposed changes?

These questions must be discussed openly within the team because the responses will help provide insight into other opportunities and may expose cultural barriers, communication issues, and even organizational politics that historically drive decision making in health care. All of these create processes that are inefficient and often ineffective.

CHAPTER SUMMARY

Improving operations requires continuous improvement of all business processes. Processes evolve over time, and without continuous scrutiny they can develop into bureaucratic, costly, and ineffective efforts. The process of analyzing processes, and modeling process behavior, encourages open dialogue, discovery, and insight into the organization. It helps raise awareness of issues and promotes change. The use of a formal process improvement methodology can help plan and prioritize efforts, analyze and collect data, benchmark, de-bottleneck and deploy, and then report and adjust as necessary. Both Six Sigma and Lean are two types of approaches to systematically improve quality in health care. Benchmarking performance against other organizations helps determine competitive processes and identify areas where improvement is most necessary. Piloting future processes helps ensure rapid feedback and identifies issues on a smaller scale so that they can be addressed quickly.

KEY TERMS

As-is process	Process capability index
Benchmarking	Process engineering
Continuous improvement	Process flowchart
Control chart	Quality
Defect	Quality management
Defects per million opportunities	Root cause analysis
Lean process	Six Sigma
Pareto charts	Standard deviation
Pilot	To-be process
Process	Variability

DISCUSSION QUESTIONS

1. In which three categories can process reengineering improve performance?
2. Define and describe the key shapes used in process flowcharting.
3. What is the difference between a Pareto chart and a control chart? When should each be used?
4. What are the major phases in the process improvement methodology?
5. What are the major types of customer or patient service-level issues that exist in health care?
6. When should hospitals benchmark against non-health-care organizations? Under which circumstances?

REFERENCES

Bryant, S. W. (2004). *JCAHO coordinator's standards*. Marblehead, MA: HCPro.

George, M. L. (2003). *Lean Six Sigma for service: How to use Lean Speed and Six Sigma quality to improve services and transactions*. New York, NY: McGraw-Hill.

Hammer, M., & Champy, J. (1993). *Reengineering the corporation: A manifesto for business revolution*. New York, NY: HarperCollins.

Harrington, H. J., Esseling, E. K. C., & and van Nimwegen, H. (1997). *Business process improvement workbook: Documentation, analysis, design, and management of business process improvement*. New York, NY: McGraw-Hill.

Langabeer, J. R. (2009). *Performance improvement in hospitals and health systems*. Chicago, IL: Healthcare Information and Management Systems.

Langabeer, J. R., DelliFraine, J. L., Heineke, J., & Abbass, I. (2009). Implementation of Lean and Six Sigma quality initiatives in hospitals: A goal theoretic perspective. *Operations Management Research, 2*(1–4), 13–27.

Maslow, A. H. (1998). *Maslow on management*. New York, NY: Wiley.

National Institute of Standards and Technology. (2014). *Baldrige award recipient information*. Retrieved from http://patapsco.nist.gov/Award_Recipients/index.cfm

Schrage, M. (2000). *Serious play: How the world's best companies simulate to innovate*. Boston, MA: Harvard Business School Press.

Taylor, R. J., & Taylor, S. B. (1994). *The AUPHA manual of health service management*. Burlington, MA: Jones and Bartlett Learning.

Operations Research Methods

Health care facilities are busy places with hundreds of people constantly coming and going. To maintain efficient operations, organizations must optimize patient and other process flows. This entails:

- Understanding patient demand.
- Aligning capacity and resources with demand.
- Using de-bottlenecking approaches to improve throughput.
- Managing patient and asset flows through tracking systems.

The use of tools and techniques such as operations research help to incorporate quantitative methods that can improve decision making. Techniques such as wait time minimization models and forecasting algorithms help to support improvements in process and patient flows. To make informed decisions about changing processes, decisions must rely on data, not just subjective gut feel. This chapter discusses these concepts in detail.

OPERATIONS RESEARCH

Throughout the years, **operations research (OR)** has been defined in many ways, often using different terms to describe the same body of knowledge and methods. In England and Europe, operations research is commonly called *operational* research, although the terms are synonymous. Similarly, the term *management science* (MS) has become popular in some schools of business, though usage is mixed. *Operations research* is still used primarily in industrial engineering departments and other schools outside of business, but for the purposes of this research, all of these terms (i.e., operational research, management science, and operations research) are considered identical and interchangeable.

The simplest definition is what the Institute for Operations Research and the Management Sciences (INFORMS, 2014b) uses today: "a discipline that deals with the application of advanced analytical methods to help make better decisions."

Generally, the operations management and management sciences can be combined using the term "OR/MS" and describe using a scientific view and quantitative methods to support managerial decision making (Hillier & Hillier, 2008; Anderson, Sweeney, Williams, & Loucks, 1999). The Operational Research Society (n.d.) defines OR as "the discipline of applying advanced analytical methods to help make better decisions"; it posits that "by using techniques such as problem structuring methods … and mathematical modelling *[sic]* to analyse *[sic]* complex situations, operational research gives executives power to make effective decisions and build more productive systems."

The three key terms used or implied in most definitions are *structured, decision making*, and *improvements*. Structured implies that techniques will focus on using rigor and sophistication. Many times this also requires a reliance on data and a mathematical or quantitative basis, although this is not always the case. Traditional methods can be classified as "hard" (i.e., relatively mathematically intense) and "soft" (i.e., rigorous but qualitative, which stresses structured problem solving for complex and messy problems that cannot be solved by traditional math models). Advanced quantitative methods, such as simulations, optimization, and mathematical models incorporating probabilities and other variables, are often tools used in this scientific process.

The focus of OR relies on improving the outcomes of decision makers through use of better methods and techniques that comprehensively and systematically produce options, scenarios, and better results (Trick, 2003). Exploring data in new ways, using new techniques, or building models that can help determine the effects of decisions so that managers and other decision makers can improve the quality of their decisions is a fundamental goal of OR.

Finally, OR is about making improvements in performance (Ackoff & Sasieni, 1968). Scientific rigor and better quality decisions should result in improved operating, financial, or strategic performance. OR is not supposed to be arbitrary or exploratory for its own sake; the results need to be better through the OR if the discipline is to grow and thrive. Thus, the new slogan for INFORMS and other OR organizations is the "science of better," focused on improving outcomes and results.

Based on its focus and intent, it is important to evaluate the scope of OR for the health care industry, both currently and its future potential.

MANAGEMENT DECISION MAKING

In a completely rational model explaining how managers "do" (descriptive models) or "should" (normative models) behave in organizations, the emphasis is placed on maximizing outcomes of the decision process. Management of any organization would identify the goals of a specific problem or situation, generate alternatives, and select the one that is optimal. In this environment, OR methods would appear to be highly complementary. OR techniques allow managers to seek alternatives; evaluate these choices using probabilities, risks, and other variables as key criteria; and then model potential outcomes. Unfortunately, managers in organizations do not always behave rationally, which has opened the decision sciences field to a much less rational approach to decision making. Due to behaviors, politics, and other potential influences, the rational model is not the norm.

OR methods play a vital role in the management decision-making process. For these purposes, **decisions** are defined as a choice between two or more alternatives, and management **decision making** is the process in an organization by which decisions are made.

Because managerial decision making occurs at higher levels of an organization and typically involves major commitments of resources or changes in strategic direction, this research seeks to understand how decision processes work in health care organizations. Understanding the unique aspects of this industry is important because they have been described as service intensive and goal ambiguous in many respects. Management theorists, such as Harrison (1987), have suggested that as the organization's environment becomes more complex, there is a higher use of "judgment" in decision making and less procedural computation, as in a rational model of decision making. Better understanding of the health care industry's organizational environment and the specifics of the decision-making process can offer greater insight into how decisions are made, which criteria are used, how the search for alternatives occurs, and the role analytical or quantitative methods can play in the evaluation of alternatives in decision making.

A BRIEF HISTORY OF OPERATIONS RESEARCH

OR seeks to apply structured analytical techniques to improve decisions made by managers. These can come in the form of qualitative (i.e., soft) techniques or the more commonly cited quantitative techniques. For this reason, it is typically described today by management theorists as being its own "school" but as a derivative of the scientific or classical school of management thought (George, 1968; Salveson, 2003), which evolved from the work of Frank and Lillian Gilbreth, Frederick Taylor, and others.

Based on most accounts, the OR discipline can be traced back to the pre–World War II 1930s and 1940s. The British government brought together several interdisciplinary teams to apply science to investigate military tactics. OR groups were used to develop the first radar system around 1941 to help the British military track and identify aircraft. This led to the use of OR for improving other communication systems, and it became instrumental in the Royal Air Force, Army, and Navy (McCloskey & Trefethen, 1954). It was due to these efforts to incorporate scientific and mathematical information into military activities that OR found its niche. Subsequently, operations researchers were deployed to numerous projects throughout all of the British armed forces. With success in England, OR began to move into U.S. military operations during the early 1940s.

During the latter part of that decade, the Massachusetts Institute of Technology developed courses in OR, and in the early 1950s a complete curriculum was developed in OR/MS by Columbia University, Case Western Reserve University, and others. Many universities in England followed suit and developed OR short courses during this time frame as well. The Operational Research Society of the UK (previously the OR Club) was formed in 1950 and is considered to be the world's oldest OR society (Symonds, 1962). The *Operational Research Quarterly* began publication in 1950, and the journal *Management Science* was launched in the

United States in 1952, both providing avenues for OR in which to publish and expand. Annual conferences soon began uniting academic researchers worldwide, and since this time the OR discipline has continued to thrive (Schrady, 2001).

Based on its military beginnings, OR quickly became known for incorporating scientific processes into decision making, and it is sometimes called a *systems* approach (Ackoff, 1971; Riggs & Inoue, 1975). A systems approach refers to how OR attempts to study the underlying behavior and structure of the systems—or interrelated set of processes, events, and activities—that define most problems and decision realms.

This systems approach recognizes that forces and relationships exist between the environment and the internal processes, and that they can be analyzed closely, modeled, and then used for predicting or simulating results. Systems can be defined formally as the "collection of activities that share in their transformation to achieve a defined purpose" (Riggs & Inoue, 1975, p. 70). When systems are modeled, they then can be manipulated in various ways to estimate the effects of changing policies or decisions. Therefore, when applied to management, OR has shown that through a variety of methods (e.g., linear programming, optimization) better or improved results can be identified.

OPERATIONS RESEARCH APPLIED TO HEALTH CARE

OR was applied to health care as early as the 1950s, with one of the first OR articles related to medicine published in the *Operational Research Quarterly* (Bailey, 1952). This early work was sponsored by a trust of the British National Health Service and led to a small collection of articles. Around the same time in the United States, the Johns Hopkins Hospital assigned a contract position (joint with the Army Operations Research) for a full-time director to assist in hospital management decisions (Flagle, 2002). From the 1960s through the early 1970s, there appeared to be a growing interest in OR, with the field gaining significant momentum around 1970.

It was then that the Operations Research Society of America (now part of INFORMS) held its first symposium on health services delivery (Young, 1969). The Health Applications Section of INFORMS was created in the early 1970s and currently has more than 500 members (INFORMS, 2014b). Subsequently, in 1975, the European Working Group on Operational Research Applied to Health Services was formed and now claims 242 members in more than 30 countries (Operational Research Applied to Health Services, 2014). The result of these societies is a much broader, global effort to apply OR to health care delivery processes. Both of these groups have conducted annual meetings and conferences to continue to encourage innovation in and research on OR topics in health care. In addition, in the late 1970s, the Society for Medical Decision Making was formed to help introduce more quantitative and sophisticated methods into health care decision processes.

Prior to this time, there were several articles published on decision methods and quantitative techniques in health care administration, but they were less focused on the unifying themes, which center on building quantitative models of systems that are stochastic in nature and ultimately patient focused.

Since this time OR has developed some momentum, although not as much as might be expected considering the size and complexity of the health delivery system. Carter (2002) described the lack of OR focus in health care when he stated in his research that only two members of the entire INFORMS membership community were professionals working in hospitals or health organizations and that fewer than 2% of the entire membership body was involved in the Health Applications Section. **Figure 5–1** shows a brief time line of the significant early events in health care OR.

About 15 books have been written that focus exclusively on health care and OR. The most significant include *Operational Research Applied to Health Services* (Boldy, 1981), *Application of Operations Research to Health Care Delivery Systems* (Fries, 1981), and *Operations Research in Health Care* (Shuman, Speas, & Young, 1975). More recently, the edited collection from Brandeau, Sainfort, and Pierskalla (2004), *Operations Research and Health Care*, provides detailed application of OR methods to health operations and clinical processes. *Health Operations Management*, edited by Vissers and Beech (2005), focuses on using

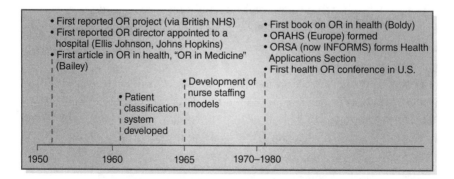

FIGURE 5–1 Time Line of Significant OR Events

OR and operations management to improve patient flows and logistics in health care organizations. It was the first book to concentrate specifically on this area and discusses basic concepts and frameworks for classifying processes in health, provides methods for analyzing supply and value chains, and offers multiple case studies on outpatient clinic scheduling, master planning, and admissions planning, among others. Other works include Blumenfield (1985), Kessler (1981), and Koza (1973). Nearly all of these books include a summary of key applications and methods used in health care, and most have focused on either clinical decisions or patient logistics.

Pierskalla and Brailer (1994) developed a bibliographic survey of OR applications in health care and describe numerous applications for OR methods. Carter (2002) maintains a database of OR research articles focused on health care, and there were more than 800 in 2002. A simple Google search shows about two million hits for the combination of "operations research" and "health care," although most of these are likely related to clinical or patient care uses of OR. It does appear, however, that OR has started to penetrate at least part of the health care field in certain areas.

OPERATIONS RESEARCH APPLICATIONS

Given the political and community concerns about health care access and costs, it is critical to use more sophisticated tools for solving problems involving variability, uncertainty, and risk. One of the key areas where OR methods can contribute is in the modeling of patient volumes and flow through organizations and health systems. Patient flow means the movement of patients from initial point of entry or service to the point when the patient exits the system. This entails understanding the key processes and transactions that patients must experience in multiple departments (such as admissions, triage, treatment room, laboratory, pharmacy, and finance) and through the network of providers. This process perspective in health care management modeling is extremely important.

Linear programming has been somewhat widely used to minimize labor costs in health care settings. **Linear programming** is a mathematical technique designed to make decisions that optimize the trade-offs necessary for resource allocation. Linear programming problems focus on maximizing (usually revenue) or minimizing (usually costs). This represents the objective function of the problem. Constraints are the restrictions that are inherent in the problem that limit the degree of change. For example, if a hospital chooses to minimize nurse labor costs but must ensure that at least one nurse is on shift at all times, this represents a constraint.

Simulation models have also been applied to labor staffing problems. A **simulation model** is a computer application that predicts the behavior or performance of a process or how something may perform in the real world. Discrete event simulation models allow for changes in resources and inputs. For instance, a model of the emergency department can show patient flow and movement if resources are changed, tasks are modified or realigned, or variability in demand occurs. Commercial software for simulation is widely available.

Revenue Cycle Management

Given today's reimbursement models, operations management in the United States is largely focused on maximizing revenues (and not just minimizing resources or expenses). Financial decisions arise from a contracting perspective with third-party payers and insurers, and it is necessary to ensure that the reimbursement from payers exceeds the operational cost in each service line. This process is called *revenue management,* or *revenue cycle management.* **Revenue cycle management** is the process of managing claims processing, setting payment practices, and generating revenue. It should be an analytical method for determining prices to achieve specific objectives, such as greater demand, higher utilization, or maximizing margins. Price (payer reimbursement) optimization models can be built that minimize risk (the variance in net profitability of a payer contract), which results in a formula such as:

$$\min\left(\text{var}\left(\sum_{j \in J} (p_j - c_j) d_j\right)\right)$$

where p_j is equal to the price of an input or patient service j, d_j is the demand, and c_j is the cost for service j. Several constraints are used (such as an equation to define minimal net margin requirements) as well as a variety of other parameters.

Risk and Financial Simulation Models

Financial simulation models were described in the early 1970s as potential OR tools for improving planning outcomes. Many large Fortune 500 corporations constructed formal models that used mathematical programming to dynamically explore changing financial policies, debt leverage, or changes in operational conditions. In essence, these tools help to create pro forma financial statements given certain assumptions and historical relationships. The models range from simple, deterministic, and top down to more complex stochastic, multivariable simulation models. Simulation models allow managers to play "what if" using many different assumptions and scenarios.

Most simulations in health care utilize **Monte Carlo simulation** analysis, which combines probability theory with random number generation and defined distribution patterns to iteratively simulate outcomes. Monte Carlo methods have been incorporated into spreadsheet solution solvers and programs such as @RISK, RiskAMP, and Crystal Ball. Software tools that incorporate Monte Carlo's statistical powers allow managers to simulate budgets and plans.

DE-BOTTLENECKING

Assume that a hospital admissions department has two full-time employees who admit patients into the hospital during the 8-hour day shift. Each employee has a computer and monitor with access to the admission system, which takes approximately 30 minutes to complete for an average new patient admission. Therefore, the maximum capacity of this process is 32 new patient admissions daily (2 employees × 8 hours × 2 patients per hour). This 400-bed hospital has a 72% occupancy rate and frees up approximately 40 rooms daily. The challenge for this hospital has always been to get more patients into the process earlier.

As described in this example, only 32 patients can be admitted based on current capacity at the entry point of the process, even though 40 is the actual demand or theoretical capacity further downstream in the process. Therefore, if more than 32 patients arrive, a bottleneck would exist (Demand > Capacity). A **bottleneck** is a choke point, or a point in a process where demand exceeds available capacity. In other words, a bottleneck can occur at any point where capacity is insufficient to meet demand due to physical or logical constraints. A bottleneck can also be a person, role, or any other barrier or obstacle to cooperation and work performance among departments.

One of the keys to increasing throughput or capacity is to remove these obstacles or bottlenecks, which is called **de-bottlenecking**. In the preceding example, potential solutions for reducing the bottleneck might be to add labor (recruit additional employees), reduce the process time below 30 minutes (invest in systems and procedures that allow for faster processing), or remove forms or tasks that are redundant. All of these should be considered. **Figure 5–2** provides an example of a bottleneck, shown visually as a funnel. In a funnel, the neck of the funnel limits volume throughput. In other words, the narrowest part of the funnel determines how quickly volume can be moved through the process, thus creating a bottleneck.

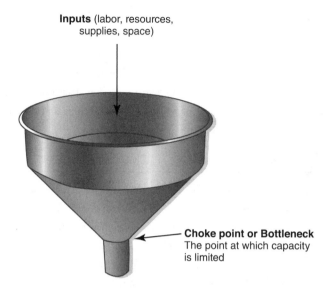

FIGURE 5–2 Process De-Bottlenecking

The key to being able to de-bottleneck is to thoroughly analyze both demand and capacity to determine where the bottleneck exists. To be successful in improving processes, it is important to determine if the bottleneck is the result of an inability to handle demand at all times, or just at a specific point in time, as well as to discover if other barriers to throughput exist.

Bottlenecks can occur at any point in the process: where a patient enters the hospital, at registration, during transition time of equipment, and at time of discharge. The earlier the bottleneck exists in the process, the fewer the number of patients (or throughput) that can be pushed through the system. Alternatively, a bottleneck at the end of the process typically results in wait times and inefficiency that can eventually affect the entire system. Eliminating a bottleneck at the beginning, only to discover that more exist in the middle or end of the system, will not help increase throughput. That is why it is important to study all processes systematically and to identify those obstacles that really limit capacity.

FORECASTING PATIENT DEMAND AND VOLUMES

Forecasting patient demand is the first step to thoroughly understanding changes in activity levels over time. Comprehensively defining patient logistic flow involves tracking volumes intraday, as well as throughout the week, using time-series data. If a hospital does not exhaustively know patient volumes and traffic levels, it cannot project volumes for individual departments and services throughout the day. Without understanding demand, it is nearly impossible to align resources and capacity with demand.

Forecasting is a collaborative process that estimates the volume of patients who will be served over a specific time period. More precisely, it is a projection of demand that will occur along three dimensions: service type, location, and time dimensions. Service type includes the specific procedures performed or the staff involved in the effort. Location includes the specific department, unit, floor, or other geographical location that performs the service types. Time refers to the hour, day, week, and month that the demand was met. Forecasts are based on time-series data. **Time series** refers to a set of values or observations at successive points in time.

Forecasting, by definition, is the practice of making a prediction or estimation about the future (Makridakis, 1996). It involves modeling the past to define the future. Demand forecasting, then, is the practice of predicting future demand to accomplish specific business goals, such as more accurately planning how many beds or clinics are needed or how much staff to hire. Performing forecasting really well allows managers to minimize unproductive wait time, maximize customer service, and in general improve operational efficiencies—the goal of operations management.

There are two major types of forecasts: qualitative and quantitative (Armstrong, 2001). Qualitative methods include mainly market research, executive opinion, or Delphi methods to make subjective or judgmental decisions about the future without relating demand to historical performance quantitatively. Qualitative methods for demand forecasting may be useful for gauging potential demand of entirely new products that have no relationship with other products and cannot be reasonably estimated statistically. Qualitative forecasts of new products that a surgeon or specialty area requires may be the best use of these types of forecasts.

In health care, forecasting should primarily be based on quantitative methods. Quantitative forecasts can be broken down into two major types: univariate and multivariate methods. **Univariate** can be defined as dependence on a single variable; univariate methods attempt to forecast demand by exploring historical data relative to a single variable, such as number of patients, procedures, or items. In standard hospital environments, all of the transactional details for patient volume are captured in the clinical scheduling or information system, such as the number of admissions or the number of surgeries. In addition to this, clinical systems also capture the date patients are admitted and discharged, which procedures were given, the drugs and supplies administered, and prices charged. Reliance on any one of these transactional data elements is a univariate method, which reflects the single variable that will be analyzed to assess historical usage levels and then, based on this analysis, used to make a projection about future values.

With univariate forecasting, there are several different statistical models that are often called on to assess patterns in the data. These include such methods as Box-Jenkins, linear trend analysis, exponential smoothing, moving averages, least squares, and many others. These models all have specific advantages and disadvantages that make them useful for single-variable forecasts. Some of these methods will be discussed in the rest of this section.

Moving Average Forecast

A moving average calculates an average historical figure for a specific time period, such as the last 3 rolling months, and then extrapolates this average forward. This is a very imprecise type of forecast because it actually lags the relevant time period. In a constantly growing environment, moving average can be too conservative, and it is underbiased in its predictions. The mathematical calculation of a moving average forecast is:

$$F = \frac{\sum (n \text{ data values})}{n}$$

The term *moving* indicates that as a new data point becomes available, the oldest data value drops off and is replaced. In other words, if you were calculating a 3-month moving average, the calculation would sum the last 3 months' actual historical data values and divide the total by 3. For example, if historical data values were 10, 20, and 30, the moving average forecast would be 20, calculated as follows:

$$F = \frac{(10 + 20 + 30)}{3} = \frac{60}{3} = 20$$

Trend Forecasting

Another type of forecasting algorithm is based on simple trend analysis. Trend analysis looks for linear upward or downward movements in data and then extrapolates them going forward. Trend models are effective when demand for a product exhibits fairly consistent demand over time. The basic formula for calculating trend forecasts uses the initial starting point or intercept and adjusts for slope (or angle of the trend) over time. This is often called *rise over run*, and it is mathematically calculated as follows, where y is the forecasted value, a is the y-axis intercept, b is the slope of the regression line, and x is the independent variable.

$$y = a + bx$$

Other Methods

Smoothing methods in demand forecasting are useful because they use a factor to weight the most recent demand observations more than in previous periods, and they help account for errors in previous periods. Smoothing, whether it is exponential (i.e., discounts previous periods with a higher magnitude as the observations age), double exponential, or third order, focuses on improving forecast accuracy by giving more weight to the most relevant historical periods.

Box-Jenkins is a slightly more complex model that uses regression or curve-fitting techniques at predefined time intervals for the single variable being analyzed. It combines single-variable linear regression with a moving average technique to achieve good results from univariate methods.

A much more comprehensive set of forecasting methods falls within the category called *multivariate*. **Multivariate** methods attempt to use more than one variable to help better explain or model the past to make more accurate forward projections about the future. Although factors such as seasonality and cyclicality (i.e., business cycles that repeat similar patterns over time) can be detected and modeled using advanced univariate methods, they are much more common in multivariate methods. Using multiple variables to help make predictions about the item being forecasted allows seasons and cycles to be combined with other causal factors (e.g., pricing, promotions, events) to model relationships with other variables and improve forecast accuracy.

The most common form of multivariate demand forecasting in large-scale causal forecasting is multiple regression. Multiple regressions use other contributing factors to help better explain the past and predict the future. For example, when forecasting demand for a downstream department (e.g., radiology), we might find a causal relationship with number of admissions, number of square feet in the hospital, patient acuity levels, case mix index, or other variables.

Excel and other spreadsheet packages can be used to create both univariate and multivariate forecasts. The Excel functions—trend, forecast, growth—and many others allow users to create forecasts with time-series data for linear trends, exponential curves, and moving averages. They are fairly simple and straightforward.

The transactional data can be organized to show the time dimension, or periods, and the corresponding item usage. Then use of Excel's "=forecast" or similar function can be implemented to point to the known dependent and independent variables, which will then plot the forecasted value. This can be shown in spreadsheet or graphical views, as **Figure 5-3** illustrates.

Similarly, analysts can use Excel to simulate multiple regressions, using the data analysis add-in package. These regressions are slightly more sophisticated than simply using linear trends because regressions attempt to fit or model the historical transaction data to predict more probable future estimates.

A	B	C
Month	Usage	Forecast
1	150	
2	135	
3	162	
4	175	
5	161	
6	191	
7	182	
8	199	
9	200	
10	185	
11	205	
12	225	
13		223
14		231
15		231
16		237
17		247
18		241

Step 1: Capture historical data for item to be forecasted, such as patient volumes or item usage (in this case, 12 months usage)

Step 2: Use built-in Excel functions (e.g., TREND or FORECAST) =FORECAST(13, B7:B18,A7:A18)

Step 3: Graph results using line charts

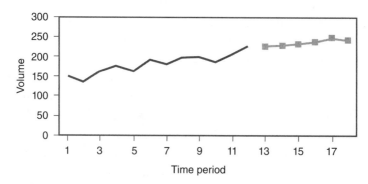

FIGURE 5-3 Forecasting Volumes in Excel

The Forecasting Process

The process of forecasting demand involves four key steps:

Identify >> Model >> Analyze >> Adapt

These steps are typically performed in a wide range of time intervals, from short range (next day or week), intermediate (next month), or long term (next year or two). For demand forecasting as it relates to patient volumes in health care, forecasting is typically done in short and intermediate time intervals. Longer-term forecasting is usually done for strategic planning purposes, such as for adding bed capacity or capital investment in new space or equipment.

The process starts with an analyst, operations manager, or planner identifying or isolating what is to be forecast; patient admissions, appointments, visits, clinic registrations, research protocols, supply usage, and pharmaceutical sales are common forecasting applications. Typically, forecasting is used to make specific business decisions, such as how many of each type of pharmaceutical to order next week or how many outpatients to expect next month. Most health care forecasts tend to focus on univariate methods, where time-series data are forecasted.

Once identified, the planner must gather all historical data for this variable. Data collection may come from a variety of systems, depending on the time-series data selected. For example:

- Appointment data reside in the organization's scheduling system.
- Admissions data come from the admission discharge transfer system.
- Pharmaceutical or supply information is stored in an enterprise resource planning or other purchasing system.

Once the system has been selected, either an interface or a download of historical data will have to be requested from the information systems group, unless the data are available for export directly. A choice of any attribute or other characteristic that describes the data values might also be collected. Time-series data, which represent values over time, are necessary for most mathematical forecasts to predict the future.

Once these data are in place, they should be incorporated into either a spreadsheet solution (for simple forecasts) or a sophisticated forecasting package. There are many excellent software solutions that can inexpensively and simply model and analyze the historical demand patterns to help understand the past and make accurate projections for the future.

The planner then needs to analyze the data to make sense of the forecast and ensure that the results seem appropriate. Closely examining the forecast and history will ensure that there were no issues with the data and that the forecast is reasonable. Finally, the analyst must continually monitor and adapt the forecast to ensure that forecast accuracy increases over time (or, alternatively, that the error rate decreases). This can be accomplished using tracking signals or by monitoring forecast errors such as mean absolute percent error. Error rates should be used in the monitoring process to adapt or refine the model to obtain better projections the next time.

It is important to focus on the data variation, whether it is random or predictable. One of the goals of demand forecasting is to reduce the uncertainty or variability that inherently exists. Ways to do this include looking at the source of the data, examining the frequency of the process, searching for patterns in volumes or demand behaviors (e.g., spikes due to purchasing increases to draw down operating budgets at year end by departments), and identifying the best level at which to forecast.

BASIC PRINCIPLES OF FORECASTING

There are some principles of forecasting that should be kept in mind to improve results. First, forecasts are always inaccurate. There is no process that will repeatedly match forecast to actual. That is why it is important to quantify the error and use it to adapt the forecasts for the future. Forecasts made at high levels (e.g., total number of inpatients weekly) are always more accurate than at the lowest levels (e.g., outpatient appointments in a specific location at a certain time). The more granular the forecast, the less precise it will be, but that is typically where the value of forecasting really can be found. Creating forecasts at the lowest levels and then grouping them accordingly for planning purposes is vital to a healthy process. Finally, it must be remembered that forecasts are only the starting point for the planning process—forecasts help provide a basis for further refinements and the selection of a most likely scenario for the future. Here are some additional guidelines and principles.

Level of Hierarchy

Decide on the level at which you wish to forecast. Forecasting at the lowest levels (typically, a patient procedure at an individual location in the hospital) provides significant levels of detail, but if this detail is not necessary it should not be used. Aggregation of the data allows for more strategic viewing, but some of the richness of the underlying data is lost. Thus, a trade-off exists between the details gained and the additional level of effort required. Forecasting attributes allow a different perspective, which may be useful during negotiations with suppliers. As much as practical, use downstream transactional data. The best source of demand is actual customer requisitions or items that have been directly issued or charged to patients, not warehouse orders or inventory movements.

Decompose the Forecast

Understand the real demand-forecasting problem first; then break it down into smaller, less complex parts. This is the principle of decomposition, which uses a general approach to drill down into more specific, narrower areas.

Time Horizon

Decide on a realistic forecasting horizon. Although the business process should dictate the forecasting horizon, shorter time horizons provide more reliable results. For most demand forecasts, forecasting out more than 3 to 6 months is not optimal.

Apply Quantitative Techniques

Utilize a mathematical or statistical forecasting application if at all possible, preferably one that is integrated with the hospital's existing information systems. More advanced tools can help to automatically isolate the effects from seasonality, pricing, operating cycles, or other causal factors and apply appropriate algorithms without significant manual intervention. Also, use combination approaches if possible. Weighting of specific statistical models based on their historical standard errors, such as the Bayesian approach, tends to generate significantly better forecasts than single-forecast methods. Some excellent solutions that are widely used in various industries include Forecast Pro (www.forecastpro.com), SAS (www.sas.com), and Logility (www.logility.com).

Simplicity First

Try forecasting in the simplest fashion possible, and add complexity only if necessary. If multiple demand patterns generate poor forecasts due to complexity or scale, look for causal relationships and better statistical models to build a more robust solution. Be careful to not "overfit" the forecasting models. In many cases, too many variables are used in multivariant forecasting. Adding this complexity does not always result in improved forecasting accuracy, so be mindful of challenging the concept that more is always better by validating each variable used in the model.

Reliable Data Sources

Utilize reliable data sources. Data coming from hospital resource planning or other clinical systems tend to be the most accurate. It is important not to use any systems or data points that are incomplete or have errors or missing data. Look for alternative sources of data that can reliably feed the demand forecasting system to generate the most valid, reliable results.

Cleanse the Data

Cleanse or scrub the data using business rules. Data coming from most hospital systems or business warehouses today tend to be inaccurate in some manner. Cleansing or scrubbing the data by applying logic and business rules (such as "do not import any history that has negative values") results in higher-quality forecasts.

Causal Relationships

Avoid making predictions on predictions. Causal relationships that are highly judgmental about the future (e.g., expected changes in interest rates or weather) tend to serve as poor causal factors because their forecast is usually inaccurate and unpredictable. Basing your product's demand forecast on these forecasts often yields unreliable results.

Exception Reporting

Make use of exception reporting to flag problem areas. Specific forecast combinations that may be problematic should be flagged based on specific business rules (e.g., where forecast error is greater than 15%).

Graphical Analysis of Trends

View forecasts graphically—visual representation of data allows users to better interpret results and identify inconsistencies. Graphical analyses allow patterns to emerge more readily than in straight tabular forms.

Apply Insight and Intuition

Never use statistical results without applying business intelligence. We know that forecasts are always wrong, so it is important to apply human business intelligence to ensure validity within the current context. For example, a statistical forecast might generate specific values, but if the models applied did not know that a clinic is closed on Mondays, the demand will be overstated.

Use Unconstrained Data

Do not forecast based on constraints. For example, if historical patient visits were down last month because of a major snowstorm that limited patient volumes, this constrained or reduced demand is artificial and biases the forecasts. Forecasting based on these artificially low figures should be explained through a causal event, by adding "pseudo" sales to account for an unrealistic month or by eliminating that period as an outlier.

Measure Errors and Accuracy Levels

Measure forecast accuracy in multiple ways. Use multiple measures of forecast accuracy or error to help remove the distortion that occurs when firms become fixated on a single measure. Use the forecasting error to improve the next forecast so that the errors generated in the last forecast are fed back into the next one to improve the quality of the forecast. Typical forecasting software or spreadsheet solutions will provide at least the mean square error rates, which is a simple statistical calculation that squares the difference between the forecast and the actual values. Another similar calculation is the **mean absolute deviation (MAD)**, which is the sum of the absolute difference between the average of the actual values and the forecast, divided by the number of observations. Mathematically, this is calculated as follows:

$$\text{MAD} = \sum_{i}^{n} \left| Fn - \bar{\chi}_n \right|$$

For example, if the time-series forecasted values were 10 in August and 8 in September, and actual values observed for those months, respectively, were 9 and 7, the MAD would be 1. The first step is to calculate the mean value of the actual data, which would be 8 in this case ([9 + 7] ÷ 2). Second, subtract the mean from the forecast value for each observation. Third, take the absolute value (the value regardless of the positive or negative sign) of the difference. In this case, that is 2. Fourth, divide this by the number of observations (2). Therefore, the MAD is 1.0, calculated as follows:

$$\text{MAD} = \left(\frac{(10 - 8) + (8 - 8)}{2} \right) = \frac{2}{2} = 1$$

Tracking the mean absolute deviation or the mean square error allows forecasters to compare how accurate their forecasts are over time to continue to refine and improve the calculations and methodologies.

CAPACITY ANALYSIS

Once demand is known, it is extremely important to understand how much capacity exists. **Capacity** refers to the amount of resources or assets that exist to serve the demand. In health care, capacity can be measured in terms of multiple resources, including:

- The number of available beds, treatment or examination rooms, and clinics.
- Labor availability of physicians, nurses, and other providers.
- Availability of key medical technologies and equipment (e.g., diagnostic imaging, x-ray).
- Supplies and other resources.
- Elevators, hallways, and other facility space.
- Cafeteria, parking, and other support services.

Capacity analysis requires detailed understanding of the organization's resources, including labor, technology, and facilities. Documentation of this capacity should be done using time-series data, similar to how demand-series data were treated, to track capacity changes over time.

For example, if a hospital has a magnetic resonance imaging (MRI) machine, the assumption may be that it could operate 24 hours per day, 7 days per week. This is called the **design capacity**, which is the maximum stated or theoretical output for a resource. However, when closely analyzing the equipment over a period of time, it would be discovered that there is necessary downtime for maintenance or repairs or other reductions to stated capacity. Therefore, the more important capacity term is *effective capacity*. **Effective capacity** adjusts the design capacity with average expected utilization rates. For example, if average operating efficiency or utilization is 75% on the MRI machine, then the effective capacity is 18 hours, calculated using the following equation, where C_e is effective capacity, C_d is design capacity, and U represents utilization rates:

$$C_e = C_d \times U$$

Consider this example. A hospital clinic has two treatment rooms and offers services that typically require 30-minute appointments. Therefore, approximately two patients can be seen each hour in each room. The daily design capacity of this system, based on an 8-hour day, is therefore 32 ($2 \times 8 \times 2$). This is the design capacity given "average" procedure types for the clinic and standard cycle times (the process for calculating normal times will be discussed later in this chapter as part of time and motion studies). However, these averages do not take into account any deviations, such as scheduling problems, patient delays, or transition times in between patients. Historically, the average clinic room utilization is 72%. Therefore, the effective capacity is really only 23 patients per day.

CAPACITY PLANNING: ALIGNING CAPACITY WITH DEMAND

Capacity planning refers to the planning process for aligning capacity with demand, analyzing whether resource constraints (shortages) or surplus (excess) exist at all points in time. If 100 hours per week of physician labor is available to a specific clinic, yet demand forecasts suggest 1,400 procedures and 120 hours of potential patient demand, there is a mismatch or lack of alignment between capacity and demand. This is very common in health care, where either demand or capacity is limited (or both). Creating a strategy for effectively dealing with this takes five key steps:

1. Forecast patient demand at detailed levels (by hour, location, etc.).
2. Using productivity estimates, translate this demand into capacity requirements (where patient flow exists; which resources will be used).
3. Analyze current level of capacity in terms of hours of labor or equipment available or numbers of other resources. Translating capacity into a per-hour basis is the most common measurement (e.g., 11 hours of equipment time available on an MRI daily, or 362 hours of nursing labor).
4. Estimate the delta (or change) between capacity and demand on a per-hour or other basis.
5. Develop a strategy for aligning capacity with demand.

Typically, this involves mapping supply and demand over time, graphically analyzing the data, and then developing plans for adding or removing capacity. The most common strategies for dealing with capacity constraints are as follows:

1. *Increase capacity*, where capital or operational dollars allow. Adding capacity suggests purchasing new capital equipment that could allow the facility to perform more procedures or operate longer hours. Organizations also add capacity by hiring more labor, adding swing beds, or increasing total square footage for new clinics or rooms. Other options include contracting with other facilities to provide additional capacity

or subcontracting certain service lines. The use of return on investment models should be utilized to ensure that the benefits of adding capacity are greater than the marginal costs to invest in the capacity expansions.

2. *De-bottleneck*, which may free capacity. The use of process engineering tools can identify bottlenecks, and targeted improvement methods can eliminate them.

3. *Reduce demand*, where possible and profitable. This may include reducing the services or procedures provided or redirecting patients to other competitor or partner facilities.

4. *Transfer capacity from other areas* (i.e., sometimes capacity exists in certain areas or departments that is often not needed, which can be used to fund capacity expansions in other areas). For example, if facilities or space is the issue, square footage can be reduced in one department and provided to another.

MINIMIZING WAIT TIMES

Typically, one of the biggest bottlenecks in health care involves the issue of wait times. **Wait time** is defined as the time interval during which there is a temporary cessation of service. Alternatively, it is the amount of time that has elapsed or has been delayed from the start point until some action occurs or until service is provided. Most of us experience wait times everywhere in our daily lives, even if they are brief—at a gas station, restaurant, convenience store, or coffee shop.

In health care, wait times are frequently a source of poor patient satisfaction and process inefficiency. In emergency rooms, for example, wait times of up to several hours are common. Some waits are more acceptable than others. Another common example of wait time is when patients arrive at a clinic but spend time waiting to get registered or checked in.

Wait lines occur in all areas of the hospital—such as patient admissions, financial services, physicians' lobbies—and are generally considered to be routine and a part of everyday business in health care. This is inaccurate. Understanding wait times is a required step to modeling process and staffing changes to improve service. Wait times are generally one of the most controllable and significant variables driving waste and inefficiency.

Wait lines form because people are seeking service faster than they can be served. There are several situations where queues typically form in health care:

1. Point of admission (entry).
2. Financial services.
3. Point of discharge (exit).

4. In the front lobby.

5. Treatment or exam rooms.

6. High-volume departments, such as emergency departments or operating rooms.

7. Point-of-use for key clinical technologies (e.g., MRI, computed tomography, position emission tomography).

8. In common clinical ancillary services (laboratory, pharmacy, blood bank).

9. Elevators, hallways, or other common spaces.

10. In the individual physician's office.

11. At supporting services (cafeteria, gift shops, social work).

Wait lines can be minimized using advanced quantitative tools. They can be modeled to improve service, align staffing with projected volumes, and control the service levels (or minutes spent in a queue). Wait line simulation models can be built around all aspects of an organization to improve service and process efficiency.

There are three key components of wait line simulation models: arrival rate, service rate, and queue structure. The speed at which patients arrive is called the *arrival rate*. Arrival rate is represented by the Greek letter lambda (λ) and is always defined as X per unit of measure (e.g., 12 patients per hour). The speed at which employees can serve them is called the *service rate*. Service rate is represented in most equations by the Greek letter mu (μ). The queue structure is defined by a few subvariables, including number of simultaneous servers or channels, which represent the employees who offer assistance to the guest or patient represented by the symbol (c), and the number of phases in the process (p). Most health care wait lines are considered to be a finite problem. Therefore, finite wait time minimization models can be defined generically as:

$$\text{Wait time} = f(\lambda, \mu, c, p)$$

There is a lot of complexity that can be built around queuing models, but for purposes of this text one primary model is discussed—that of multiple channels (or multiple servers) providing service through a single-phase process. For instance, at a clinic waiting room, there are two employees at the front desk who check in patients, register them, ensure that updated medical insurance is on file, and confirm that all other forms for registration are completed. This is represented in **Figure 5–4**.

In the example in Figure 5–4, there are currently three servers, or channels, who can provide service to the customers. All three of them are on the phone, and only one person is currently providing service to one of the waiting guests. There is a buildup of four customers in the waiting line. There is only one phase,

Doctor's Office

Multiple Channel Servers
(three employees)

Single Phase
(After check-in they enter treatment room)

Wait Line
(Four patients in the queue seeking service)

FIGURE 5–4 Wait Time Simulation Models

in that the next step after receiving service is to visit the physician. In many processes, however, there are multiple waiting rooms, or phases.

A key indicator for managing customer service is the number of minutes that a patient has to wait in the queue. This can be modeled using the following equation, where W = wait time, L = the number of customers in the system or queue, and λ represents the arrival rate, or the speed at which new patients arrive in the clinics:

$$W = \frac{L}{\lambda}$$

For example, assume that there are currently 5 people in the system, and they arrive every 2 minutes (or 30 per hour). The average wait time would be 10 minutes, solved as follows:

$$W = \frac{L}{\lambda} = \frac{5}{30}\,(60) = 0.166667 \times 60 = 10 \text{ minutes}$$

However, in practice, the number of people in the system is a complex calculation and solving for L requires several calculations that are best done in a spreadsheet solution. The formula that follows shows how to solve for L when it is not given as an assumption. In this calculation, L = total number of customers in the system, P_o = the probability that no customers are in the system, and all other variables are as defined earlier (Anderson, Sweeney, & Williams, 1997).

$$L = \frac{\lambda \mu \left(\frac{\lambda}{\mu}\right)^s}{(s-1)!\,(s\mu - \lambda)^2} P_o + \frac{\lambda}{\mu}$$

To calculate P_o, the mathematical calculation is also quite complicated:

$$P_o = \left[\sum_{n=0}^{s-1} \frac{(\lambda/\mu)^n}{n!} + \frac{(\lambda/\mu)^s}{s!} \left(\frac{1}{1-p} \right) \right]^{-1}$$

Average number of customers waiting in line is calculated as:

$$L_q = L\left(\frac{\lambda}{\mu}\right)$$

Finally, another important calculation is to define how long it takes for a patient to wait in line versus the total time spent in the system (W_q; both receiving service and waiting in the queue). This can be calculated as follows, which basically subtracts the inverse of the service rate from the total waiting time:

$$W_q = W - \left(\frac{1}{\mu}\right)$$

Wait Time Example

A patient arrives at the Solder County Hospital emergency department (ED) and finds a waiting line that is currently 60 patients long. Several negative comments are passed on to the front desk employees, which are then communicated to the ED director. When she looks out in the waiting area, she too becomes annoyed with this situation, and she makes up her mind that something must be done to help improve the situation. She decides to engage the hospital's management engineering department to study the situation and recommend possible solutions. The director wants to comprehensively understand current waiting times and determine if staffing levels are appropriate to meet these stated service levels or analyze what changes might be made.

The process has only one phase—patients are registered and then transferred back to a primary treatment or exam room (this is a simplification of course, for illustrative purposes only). The potential population or number of patients is finite and, most important, there are three employees at the front desk to handle all admissions and registration, so it is considered multichannel. The ED director has defined a service-level policy of 45 minutes, suggesting that each patient should have to wait no more than this time prior to being moved to an exam room before being seen by a triage nurse or other provider, although admittedly total cycle time or wait time has never been comprehensively monitored.

After careful analysis over a 1-week period, the management engineer assigned to the project conducted several detailed cycle time studies. He discovered that on average during the morning shift there are approximately 50 patients arriving every hour and that the front desk personnel can register a patient in approximately 3.5 minutes, or 17 patients per hour.

Using the formulas provided earlier, the probability that there are patients in the system is very high, and the P_0 (or probability of the waiting queues being completely cleared) is less than one-tenth of 1% (0.004). Therefore L (average number of customers in the system) is around 51, which is similar to the 60 that the ED director found on the day this project began. The total wait in the system is found to be a little more than 1 hour (61 minutes). Because registration time is only 3.5 minutes, the total time spent waiting in line is nearly 58 minutes (i.e., 61 − 3.5). This is significantly higher than the 45-minute service level that the director expected.

How can this situation be improved? There are some key options:

1. Streamline, or reduce, the number of checks or steps that the front-desk personnel are required to perform to increase throughput and shorten the registration time to fewer than 3.5 minutes. For example, if the process can be shortened by just 5% (to have a service rate of 18 patients per hour, or 3.33 minutes per check in), the total waiting time would fall to just 13 minutes in line!
2. Add another employee (additional capacity). Recruiting one more employee (or channel) would cause the total waiting time in the line to fall to just 2 minutes. Of course, the costs of that additional employee must be evaluated relative to the benefits of reducing the queue.

Wait Time Decision Making

Depending on the system, it may be necessary to use different optimization algorithms. The algorithms are different for each of the four types of systems:

1. Single channel, single phase.
2. Single channel, multiple phase.
3. Multiple channels, single phase.
4. Multiple channels, multiple phases.

This text covered only the third type of system. For a more comprehensive discussion of the optimization models for all four systems, consult *Introduction to Queuing Theory* (Cooper, 1981).

Wait times create poor service levels and are bottlenecks for system throughput. As much as possible, and as long as total benefits exceed costs, they should be minimized. In reality, however, there is no such thing as an optimal solution with wait lines. They can be minimized, but the total cost of adding new channels must be carefully weighed against those gains. Similarly, if a bottleneck in registration is eliminated, it may just move that bottleneck to the physician's or nurse's treatment rooms. Moving a choke point back one step in the process does not create any system benefits, so it is important that the total system wait times and process be analyzed carefully.

TIME AND MOTION STUDIES

One of the best ways to minimize wait time is to increase speed of processes through time and motion studies. All process engineering analyses require detailed understanding of the business process. Key characteristics include an estimation of the following:

- Total cycle time (D or difference between the start and stop times).
- Number of activities, tasks, or motions performed during this period.
- Details about the specific transaction or activity performed (e.g., document identifier, person performing task, time of day, day of week, number of observations).
- Analysis of inputs received and outputs delivered to the next phase.

Careful analysis of the details of each process to identify and reduce the total amount of time it takes to perform a specific procedure or achieve a deliverable, while reducing the number of motions or tasks performed, is called a **time and motion study** (or simply a *time study*).

Proper time and motion studies need two things: a stopwatch or timer and a log sheet. All of the characteristics defined earlier must be recorded in a simple log. The most critical information is to identify the specific start and stop times for an activity, but there are many other factors to consider and document.

For example, assume a nurse arrives in a patient room at 11:32:00 a.m. At 11:34:25 a.m., the vitals have been taken and recorded. At 11:38:40 a.m., an infusion pump is connected and recorded in the medical record. At 11:40:10 a.m., the nurse leaves the patient's room. What is the total cycle time for this process?

Using a stopwatch and observations, this specific process has a total cycle time of 8 minutes and 10 seconds (or 8.17 minutes). Similarly, each of the elements or subcomponents of the process can be monitored as well.

A good time and motion study follows these steps:

1. Select a random sample of participants who will perform the procedure, temporally distributed so that they are representative.

2. Observe the transactions or procedures being performed. Using the stopwatch and the log, observe all specific details of work being performed and total time for each step. Document any noticeable or unusual aspect of the environment, employee, or process that may skew results.

3. Document the procedures performed and all other details in a log.

4. Document the process activities in a flowchart, using the flowchart symbols described in the *Quality Management* chapter.

5. Plot out all observations over time on an *x–y* graph.

6. Calculate the mean for the observed cycle time and standard deviations for both upper and lower controls. Try to identify root causes or sources of any extreme values (i.e., those outside of the upper or lower controls) and determine if any outliers need to be omitted from the average calculations. Average observed cycle time can be calculated as the sum of the total times recorded for all observations, divided by the total number of cycles observed:

$$\overline{x} = \frac{\sum T}{n}$$

7. Adjust the mean, if necessary, for nonproductive times, such as breaks or work delays. Nonproductive time may require up to a 10% or 15% allowance factor to obtain a "standard time," based on all cycles and employees observed. This can be calculated as:

$$ST = \frac{\overline{x}}{1 - A}$$

For example, assume that the total observed cycle time for a procedure was 25 minutes, but the employee had an average of 85% productivity or, alternatively, a 15% allowance factor was given. This means that the standard time would be 29.4 minutes (25 ÷ 0.85).

8. If necessary, adjustments can be made for individual performance level variances, because some employees perform differently and time studies may wish to adjust for these ratings.

Common Problems in Time Studies

There are a few common pitfalls made by operations managers in time and motion studies. First, they do not observe a sufficient quantity of transactions or procedures. Simply observing the nurse performing one task, as described earlier, may not be representative of other nurses or the same nurse with other patients. Effective time studies represent the entire population, not selected individual samples. Second, time studies are highly dependent on the specific individual performing the task. Observing the same procedures for multiple providers or employees ensures statistical representation. Third, because both patient demand and provider capacity changes from hour to hour and day to day, it is necessary to observe processes over an extended time period, or on a **longitudinal basis**. Finally, all procedures or transactions performed must be verifiable—that is, they need to be recorded with an audit trail that can be referred to later.

Time and motion studies can be highly biased by several factors if they are not statistically representative, conducted over a sufficient period of time, and temporally distributed. One common bias is the **Hawthorne effect**, a phenomenon in which individuals perform differently when they know they are given attention or being observed than in other situations (Landy, 1989). Observing individuals repeatedly over extended time periods helps reduce this bias.

IMPROVING FLOWS WITH TRACKING SYSTEMS

Operations management relies heavily on advanced methods and technologies to improve operational excellence, reduce costs and waste, and improve cycle times. Doing this requires management of a variety of resources and assets, including patients, equipment, materials, and employees. Technology that can automate, simplify, and streamline business processes in these areas will help improve labor productivity and operations effectiveness.

For any resource to be closely managed, it must be observable and visible. Yet this is difficult in large hospitals, which may have 5 to 10 floors and more than 150,000 square feet. There are many places for patients and assets to hide. For example, infusion pumps are very common in hospitals (an infusion pump infuses, or administers, medications intravenously through fluids to patients). An average hospital may have 200 or more pumps, many of which are never in use. If measured in terms of utilization rates, the average utilization hovers around 35%. This is an issue of effective capacity, in that at any given point in time there are three times more pumps on hand than necessary. At several hundred dollars each, this represents significant cost and waste. Better tracking of these pumps would allow for fewer inventories on hand and higher overall utilization rates. If a pump on one unit on a floor was not being used, it could be moved to another unit where it would be used appropriately. The same holds true for all resources: emergency crash carts, IV poles, beds, and computers. To effectively use these resources, it is necessary to have tracking systems in place. **Tracking systems** are tools that monitor the position, flow, and movement of resources. Asset tracking typically involves a system that consistently allows hospitals to locate key assets. Tracking systems require two key components: software to support tracking and automatic identification of the resource by that software. To achieve the second component, it is usually necessary for items to be tagged, with a unique fingerprint.

BAR CODES

A bar code is one such fingerprint, often called a *license plate*, and it allows a resource to be tagged with key information and then monitored. Bar codes have been around for many years. The Automotive Industry Action Group used them early on for parts identification, and the retail industry uses them to track items through universal product codes. Bar codes vary by the industry they serve. Standards exist for most industries about the descriptive information that bar codes should contain, which data format should be used, and any other standards. In health care, however, because the industry is quite fragmented, standards have been slow to be adopted. In health care pharmaceuticals, the national health-related items code has been somewhat adopted by most manufacturers, although not all comply. In medical supplies, the use of a health identification number has been discussed, as well as a global location number for health care through the Uniform Code Council. The most traction for standardization is coming from the Coalition for Healthcare eStandards, which promotes the universal product number (UPN) for all medical surgical suppliers. In practice, however, many vendors set their own practices and do not follow any standards.

This makes the use of bar codes very difficult, because they rely on standardized data that are understood and used by both the sender's and the receiver's systems (e.g., vendor and hospital). A **bar code** is a single- or two-dimension machine-readable code that contains several key pieces of information. Previously, a bar code appeared as just a linear, unique serial number that was coded in an array of parallel, black-and-white bars containing keys with detailed information. A **bar code reader**, or scanning device, could then be used to scan, decode, and interpret the contents.

Consider this example. In the chapter *Operations Management in the Hospital Pharmacy* (a major expense area and priority for health care organizations), the use of national drug codes (NDCs) for pharmaceuticals is discussed. A sample drug, Merck and Company's Vytorin product, sold in 10-mg-strength bottles, could be bar coded so that, when received on hospital premises, it could be scanned and instantly logged into the hospital receiving and order fulfillment systems. Then, when the drug is dispensed to the nursing unit, it could be tracked, and finally, when administered to the patient, it could be scanned to complete the cycle. Scanning in this case ensures that the patient receives the right product and that electronic documentation of the drug administration occurs. A sample representation of that bar code is shown in **Figure 5–5**.

In addition to different standards for coding items, there are also many different bar code symbols or technologies. Different codes, such as 39, EAN, UPC, Code 128, Code 93, and many more exist, all of which are represented differently. The different standards for coding and different symbology practices cause the use of bar coding to be highly difficult. If the industry is to achieve better integration, more efficient response, shorter lead times, and improved operational efficiencies, one standard for coding and technology will have to exist. This could likely take a decade—or longer—to come to fruition. Figure 5–5 is a traditional single-dimension, or linear, bar code (Barcode Mill, 2014). A major limitation to this is that it cannot hold enough information to make it relevant enough for widespread penetration. For example, the bar code might have an NDC or UPN number on it, but it fails to show obsolescence date, price, origin, precise unit of measure, and many other pieces of information that would be useful to an organization. To hold more information, linear bar codes can expand only their widths, because the height of a bar code has no significance. As bar code widths expand, however, they cannot be easily scanned, and they often result in taking more time to be recognized than manual processes. Redundancy is built into single-dimension codes that, if they are short enough, allow for fast scanning. But as they grow longer, the

61258-0311-1

Sample bar code encoded with NDC data for
Merck's Vytorin 10mg, 30 each bottle

FIGURE 5–5 Bar Code Symbology

result is a much lower first-pass scan rate and more frustration on the part of users of bar code readers.

To improve on this weakness, modern bar code symbologies are moving toward two dimensions, where the codes no longer look like single rows of bars but more like black dots dispersed throughout a white space. These two-dimension codes can manage significantly more information and have greater overall capacity. Instead of holding 10 characters, as most linear bar codes do, the best technology can hold many times that number.

As the health care industry standardizes item nomenclature and the technologies used for stamping items, the use of bar-coding technology is one of the most efficient ways to ensure that assets are quickly scanned and monitored throughout the hospital.

RADIO FREQUENCY IDENTIFICATION

Another limitation of bar codes is that they require each item or asset to be "touched," or to have a direct line of sight, in order to be scanned. Typically, this means the reader must be within at least 1 foot of the item. If an item is going to be monitored, it has to be scanned into the system, requiring a user to scan the item and then move to another asset.

A newer technology, which does not rely on line of sight, is radio frequency identification. **Radio frequency identification (RFID)** is a technology that uses small radio transponders to read and transmit data over existing wireless standards and frequencies. Instead of relying on a direct scan through a visual pattern on a label, RFID uses electronic tags that can store data and then be used for sending and receiving.

RFID comes in two forms: active and passive. Active tags have a battery, continuously transmit data, and can store more information. They can be read and transmitted throughout the hospital, assuming ample supply of antennas and readers, and thus have the advantage of less human interaction. Passive tags do not contain a battery and can only be read when a reader calls for a signal or is nearby. Active tags are much more useful from an operations management perspective, but they come with a higher price—typically several times the cost. The costs of RFID systems are primarily in the infrastructure, with the cost of deploying wireless antennas and ensuring frequency capacity throughout the facility. The cost per chip has been decreasing significantly over the last few years (about $0.30 per chip or less at present), but prices are expected to fall to less than $0.05 per chip in the near future (Markelevich & Bell, 2006).

Uses of RFID

RFID has several very practical uses. It can be embedded in or on the packaging of certain pharmaceuticals, especially those that have a high dollar value or a high risk of abuse or theft. It can be used on expensive, durable medical equipment, such as infusion pumps or crash carts. RFID units can be placed on transportation equipment, such as beds or wheelchairs, or they can be used to help track patients themselves, embedding chips on the traditional patient wristbands. A sample RFID tag is shown in **Figure 5–6**—magnified significantly because the size of the smallest tag is measured in millimeters (or fractions of an inch).

Each of these applications of RFID helps improve utilization of resources and supports real-time tracking. Of course, these benefits will not be realized unless a hospital organizes its personnel and business processes to take advantage of the information. One way to do this is to create dashboards that can be monitored by operational personnel and used to analyze flow and movement patterns for key resources. Many hospitals fall short by implementing a simple RFID tag and then doing nothing with it. To be successful in improving asset utilization (which effectively drives up capacity), organizations need to implement RFID on patients or equipment, monitor the logistics patterns and flow, and then make

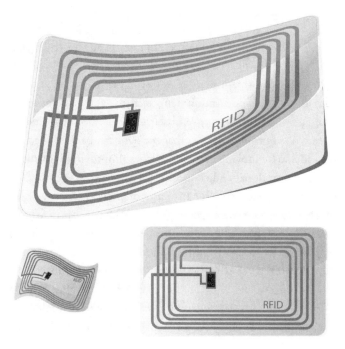

FIGURE 5–6 Radio Frequency ID Tags

© Huseyin BAS/Thinkstock

layout and process changes accordingly. This will allow increased utilization and throughput. In addition, clear performance metrics and goals should be established to determine pre- and postimplementation expectations of benefits. Defining the expected postimplementation level of performance, and then managing toward those ends, is something most hospitals do not typically do well.

RFID Infrastructure

RFID works primarily on the existing Wi-Fi, or wireless network, standards of the Institute for Electrical and Electronics Engineers, specifically, IEEE 802.11. Within this set of protocols, there are many different frequencies, data transmission rates, and ranges that are operable, including the popular 802.11a and 802.11g. The newest uses 802.11n, which can operate at frequencies of 5 GHz. When implementing RFID, it is important to conduct a radio frequency spectrum analysis. The **spectrum analysis** uses the electromagnetic spectrum to assess waves, ensure that there will be no interference from other equipment or devices, and confirm that the channels and frequencies are clear and will produce optimal results.

Walmart and RFID

Most business and logistics technologies that are in use in retail or consumer-driven industries today will eventually find their way to health care. RFID is one such technology. Today, the primary reason so much attention centers on RFID is due to the innovation and commitment to its use and value by major retailers such as Walmart. Walmart has proven itself to be the dominant player in using RFID tags to embed product data so that the data can be used for a broad range of purposes, such as removing excess inventory, improving replenishment, and understanding promotional and consumption patterns (Wailgum, 2006).

Walmart's pilot usage of RFID in many of their stores suggests that they have been able to find a way to integrate RFID tags and infrastructure to generate real business value. As a result of their efforts, the price of tags has dropped exponentially over the past decade. The health care industry will benefit enormously from these efforts. Similarly, RFID infrastructure is now using standard wireless networks, which reduces costs considerably. Still, most other organizations continue to struggle with how to use the data, deploy the technology in appropriate areas, and change roles and responsibilities to make the most of the technology.

Value from RFID

Hospitals will continue to benefit from the investment that major retailers are making in RFID technology and applications. Retail industry adoption will create cost efficiencies for the tags and help work out the issues with the technology that would otherwise be borne by the health care industry. Savings from RFID come in terms of higher capacity, higher utilization, reduced inventories, lower operating expenses, and labor savings. Considerable time reductions can be seen when employees do not have to seek out items to be scanned or replenished but can allow the systems to continuously monitor themselves. Inventories can be perpetually monitored and will not require employees to perform manual cycle counts to check inventory levels or create requisitions for new items. In summary, if used appropriately and on the right projects, RFID can save hospitals significant amounts of time and money.

Other improvements from RFID might include enhanced clinical safety and efficacy. Georgetown University Hospital is using RFID to automate the blood transfusion process as well as RFID-encoded wristbands to ensure that the right treatments are given to the right patients, thereby reducing clinical errors (Schuerenberg, 2006). Imagine if all patients had RFID-embedded wristbands— their physical movements, details about cycle time, and information about usage of resources could be monitored comprehensively. Once these data exist, it would be possible to model this and improve the alignment of capacity with demand.

In many ways, passive RFID is very similar to bar codes. While the most functional system may be passive, the benefits may not outweigh the costs at this time, but at some point in the near future the economics will shift in their favor. Currently, the primary discussion in tracking assets centers around the use of passive versus active RFID tags, as well as the use of two-dimension versus three-dimension bar codes. Regardless of the route taken, one of these methods needs to be deployed if hospitals are going to continue to improve their operations management capabilities.

CHAPTER SUMMARY

This chapter provided a brief history of OR and its initial evolution into health care. The application of OR methods is endless. At a fundamental level, there are four steps to improve patient and process flows: understand patient demand, align capacity and resources with demand, use de-bottlenecking approaches to improve throughput, and then manage patient and asset flows through tracking systems.

Each of these requires the application of quantitative techniques that use data to drive decision making. Bottlenecks cause patients to wait, resources to pile up, and operations to slow down. De-bottlenecking processes—and identifying strategies for changing demand, expanding capacity, or removing barriers—is critical to improving flows and throughput. Time and motion studies help operations managers understand the bottlenecks by breaking down processes so that cycle times can be thoroughly defined. Forecasts are essential to understand demand over time and predict changes in volumes. Demand forms the basis for aligning capacity (staffing, supplies, space, equipment) and ensures operational efficiencies. The use of wait time optimization models can help make critical decisions about how to remove one of the most common complaints in health care. Finally, asset-tracking systems help improve asset utilization, which increases effective capacity of key resources.

KEY TERMS

Bar code	Mean absolute deviation (MAD)
Bar code reader	Monte Carlo simulation
Bottleneck	Multivariate
Capacity	Operations research (OR)
Capacity planning	Radio frequency identification
De-bottlenecking	(RFID)
Decision making	Revenue cycle management
Decisions	Simulation model
Design capacity	Spectrum analysis
Effective capacity	Time and motion study
Forecasting	Time series
Hawthorne effect	Tracking systems
Linear programming	Univariate
Longitudinal basis	Wait time

DISCUSSION QUESTIONS

1. What is operations research?
2. What are the most common operations research methods used in health care?
3. Define de-bottlenecking. Does it have a role in health care, or should it be used only in industrial manufacturing settings?

4. What are four scenarios in health care where lines or queues exist?
5. How important are bar codes or radio frequency identification in tracking assets and resources?
6. What are some of the decisions that must be made prior to investing in radio frequency identification?
7. What are the key characteristics analyzed in a time and motion study? Why is it important to have a stopwatch and a written log?

EXERCISE PROBLEMS

1. Patient volumes for a radiology clinic are observed to have the following time-series data: Monday = 25, Tuesday = 28, Wednesday = 32, Thursday = 26, and Friday = 30. Using a 5-day moving average, and ignoring weekend volumes, what is the projection for the following Monday? If you used a 3-day moving average, using Wednesday through Friday values, how would the forecast change?
2. Assume that a hospital has a single-phase, multiple-channel waiting line. There are 2 employees, 10 customers currently in line, and new patients arrive at the rate of approximately 40 patients per hour. Calculate the average wait time.
3. Ten observations of cycle time were made, and the average observed cycle time was 17 minutes. Using an allowance factor of 20%, calculate the standard time for this process.

REFERENCES

Ackoff, R. L. (1971). Towards a system of systems concepts. *Management Science, 17*(11), 661–671.

Ackoff, R. L., & Sasieni, M. W. (1968). *Fundamentals of operations research.* New York, NY: Wiley.

Anderson, D. R., Sweeney, D. J., & Williams, T. A. (1997). *An introduction to management science: Quantitative approaches to decision making* (8th ed.). Mason, OH: South-Western.

Anderson, D. R., Sweeney, D. J., Williams, T. A., & Loucks, J. S. (1999). *An introduction to management science: Quantitative approaches to decision making.* Mason, OH: South-Western.

Armstrong, J. S. (Ed.). (2001). *Principles of forecasting: A handbook for researchers and practitioners.* New York, NY: Springer.

Bailey, N. T. (1952). Operational research in medicine. *Operational Research Quarterly, 3*(1), 24–29.

Barcode Mill. (2014). Home page. Retrieved from http://barcodemill.com/index.php

Blumenfield, S. (1985). *Operations research methods: A general approach in primary health care*. Chevy Chase, MD: Primary Health Care Operations Research, Center for Human Services.

Boldy, D. (1981). *Operational research applied to health services*. New York, NY: Palgrave Macmillan.

Brandeau, M. L., Sainfort, F., & Pierskalla, W. P. (Eds.). (2004). *Operations research and health care: A handbook of methods and applications*. Norwell, MA: Kluwer.

Carter, M. (2002, April). Diagnosis: Mismanagement of resources. *OR/MS Today*. Retrieved from www.orms-today.org/orms-4-02/frmismanagement.html

Cooper, R. B. (1981). *Introduction to queuing theory* (2nd ed.). New York, NY: North-Holland.

Flagle, C. D. (2002). Some origins of operations research in the health services. *Operations Research, 50*(1), 52–60.

Fries, B. E. (1981). *Applications of operations research to health care delivery systems: A complete review of periodical literature*. New York, NY: Springer-Verlag.

George, C. S. (1968). *The history of management thought*. Englewood Cliffs, NJ: Prentice Hall.

Gilbreth, F. B., & Carey, E. G. (1966). *Cheaper by the dozen*. New York, NY: Cromwell.

Harrison, E. F. (1987). *The managerial decision-making process*. Boston, MA: Houghton Mifflin.

Hillier, F. S., & Hillier, M. S. (2008). *Introduction to management science: A modeling and case studies approach with spreadsheets* (3rd ed.). New York, NY: McGraw-Hill.

Institute for Operations Research and the Management Sciences. (2014a). *Health Applications Society: Overview*. Retrieved from www.informs.org/Community/HAS

Institute for Operations Research and the Management Sciences. (2014b). *What is operations research?* Retrieved from www.informs.org/About-INFORMS/What-is-Operations-Research

Kessler, L. (1981). *Operations research and the mental health service system*. Rockville, MD: U.S. Dept. of Health and Human Services, Public Health Service, Alcohol, Drug Abuse, and Mental Health Administration, National Institute of Mental Health.

Koza, R. C. (1973). *Mathematical and operations research techniques in health administration*. Boulder: Colorado Associated University Press.

Landy, F. J. (1989). *Psychology of work behavior* (4th ed.). Pacific Grove, CA: Wadsworth.

Makridakis, S. (1996). Forecasting: Its role and value for planning and strategy. *International Journal of Forecasting, 12*(4), 513–537.

Markelevich, A., & Bell, R. (2006). RFID: The changes it will bring. *Strategic Finance, 88*(2), 46–49.

McCloskey, J. F., & Trefethen, F. N. (Eds.). (1954). *Operations research for management*. Baltimore, MD: Johns Hopkins University Press.

Operational Research Applied to Health Services. (2014). *About ORAHS*. Retrieved from http://orahs.di.unito.it/about.html

The Operational Research Society. (n.d.). *Learn about O.R.* Retrieved from www.learnaboutor.co.uk/default.htm

Pierskalla W. P., & Brailer, D. J. (1994). Applications of operations research in health care delivery. In: S. M. Pollock, M. H. Rothkopf, & A. Barnett A. (Eds.), *Handbooks in OR & MS. Vol. 6*. Amsterdam, The Netherlands: Elsevier Science.

Riggs, J. L., & Inoue, M. S. (1975). *Introduction to operations research and management science: A general systems approach.* New York, NY: McGraw-Hill.

Salveson, M. E. (2003, June). The founding father of TIMS. *Operations Research Management Science Today.* Retrieved from www.orms-today.org/orms-6-03/frtims.html

Schrady, D. (2001, February). Golden anniversary. *Operations Research Management Science Today.* Retrieved from www.orms-today.org/orms-2-01/nps.html

Schuerenberg, B. K. (2006). Bar codes versus RFID: A battle just beginning. *Health Data Management, 14*(10), 32–34, 36, 38.

Shuman, L. J., Speas, R. D., & Young, J. P. (Eds.). (1975). *Operations research in health care: A critical analysis.* Baltimore, MD: Johns Hopkins University Press.

Symonds, G. (1962, May). *Education and training in operations research in academic institutions.* Twentieth Conference on Operations Research, Operations Evaluation Group.

Trick, M. (2003, January). Best possible outcome. *Optimize Magazine*, p. 15.

Vissers, J., & Beech, R. (Eds.). (2005). *Health operations management: Patient flow logistics in health care.* New York, NY: Routledge.

Wailgum, T. (2006, September 15). RFID decision time. *CIO Magazine*, pp. 37–38.

Young, J. P. (1969). No easy solutions. In G. Chacko (Ed.), *The recognition of systems in health services: Proceedings.* Arlington, VA: Operations Research Society of America, Health Applications Section.

CHAPTER 6

Productivity and Performance Management

GOALS OF THIS CHAPTER

1. Define productivity.
2. Describe the value of tracking productivity over time.
3. Understand how to calculate capital versus labor substitutions.
4. Calculate full-time equivalent labor hours and understand their use in managing labor productivity.
5. Describe the use of a measure of inputs per unit of output for productivity.
6. Understand analytical models for staffing.
7. Create a productivity and performance scorecard.

Operations management requires efficient conversion of inputs into outputs. **Efficiency** is defined as performing tasks with minimal waste and resource consumption. Delivering health care services efficiently requires achieving the same or higher levels of output from employees, at the same quality standards, with fewer inputs over time. If a hospital requires three full-time employees to schedule 21,000 patient appointments this year and had two employees handling 18,000 appointments last year, usage of resources was 22% less efficient from one year to the next. The relationship between capacity and output is called *productivity management*. This chapter lays the framework for using health care operations management to help reduce costs and improve overall efficiencies in the utilization of labor, capital, and other resources.

THE QUEST FOR PRODUCTIVITY

Productivity is defined as the ratio of outputs to inputs or:

$$P = \frac{O}{I}$$

There are two key components of this equation: **Outputs** are the level of production or yield (of goods and services) that results from the operations management or conversion process. Outputs are the result of the work conducted through processes and automation. **Inputs** are all the time, costs, labor, materials, capital, and other resources used in the delivery of these services. For example, if a nurse can visit three patients in a 30-minute time frame, then three visits (or however many clinical procedures performed) would be the output, and the input would be 30 minutes of labor, with the associated cost equal to that time multiplied by the nurse's average hourly wage. If any supplies or other materials were given to the patients during this time frame, those would also be added to the inputs. In other words:

$$\frac{O}{I} = \frac{\Sigma(\text{Procedures, Visits, Units, Activity})}{\Sigma(\text{Time, Cost, Labor, Materials, Capital})}$$

In many industries, there is a standard measure of productivity that industry analysts, investors, and other stakeholders use to monitor changes over time. For example, in the oil and gas industry, millions of barrels of oil output are divided by total labor hours to arrive at estimated labor productivity. This figure is well known in the industry and is benchmarked by other firms to gauge the extent of technology automation and the total productivity added by each incremental employee.

Unfortunately, in hospitals this is less common. Comparisons of labor productivity among health care organizations are not widely conducted for two primary reasons: (1) lack of publications and research on the subject and (2) the perception that health care is "different" and does not lend itself to productivity monitoring. Both of these reasons will be discussed in more detail.

First, there are very few published industry reports for utilization and productivity. More than 85% of all hospitals are not publicly traded on stock markets; thus, there is no central governing body that requires financial statements to facilitate sharing within the industry. Although some organizations conduct annual surveys (such as the American Hospital Association), as with most voluntary surveys, the results are somewhat limited. They also require significant interpretation and cleansing before the data can be used reliably. For financial data, any hospital that receives Medicare reimbursement must file the Medicare Cost Report (Form CMS–2552–10) to itemize all costs, labor, and income statement accounts by major service line, as well as provide balance sheet information. Although these data are the most complete for the industry, most filings are still often incomplete and inaccurate, which can make benchmarking productivity difficult.

Second, there is a perception among many hospitals that the differences that exist, because of region or specialty, do not allow for comparisons to be made. This is an uninformed position. If not required by external or regulating bodies, then hospitals must have their own internal desire to measure productivity and see improvements over time. Operational scorecards that track productivity and performance for key business processes are needed to track performance internally over time.

MEASUREMENT ISSUES

It is possible for everything important to be quantified and measured, even if the people performing the tasks may feel that the nature of their work does not lend itself to measurement. There is a common expression that "What gets measured gets done." In other words, if productivity is measured and made important, there can be improvements over time.

In health care, physicians and researchers (in the case of academic or teaching hospitals) often feel that a measurement problem exists when it comes to health care outputs, believing that medical care services do not fit the normal definition of production of goods and services. Physicians are not typically trained in business or administrative matters, so they do not often see the usefulness in managing productivity of their time. In many cases, however, hospitals should try to look for ways to manage productivity across all areas and job categories.

Can clinician or researcher productivity be measured? Is it possible to compare one study that a cardiac surgeon is conducting to a study by an oncologist? Can hospital administrators examine a metric, such as number of procedures per day or research studies per full-time employee, to manage areas that require significant intangibles and high levels of thinking? In other words, is it only manual transactional processes that can be captured and measured? The answer is clearly no. All types of work can be broken down into outputs and inputs (even components of a more complex output such as medical care), and these component parts can be tracked to see changes in performance over time. However, it is easier to start with simple operational and transactional productivity measurements and progressively focus on the more complex measurement areas last.

Another common issue in productivity measurement is a lack of data availability. In hospitals, internal systems that measure outputs and inputs over time may not be available. Measuring productivity should be conducted frequently, which requires tracking both sides of the formula. If measuring the number of patients moved via wheelchair through the hospital, there is probably no information system in place to record these transactions. Establishing shadow or supplemental systems that can be updated daily with activity information, or summarized weekly or monthly, is a way to begin measuring such activities. A good example of this would be using data held in an electronic medical record system that would track orders for transactions such as wheelchair transports, thus allowing for the measurement of activities that previously may have been challenging to track.

Quality is often another concern with measurement. While outputs may not have changed, the level of quality of the output may have increased. For example, if a physician performs five valve reconstructions over a week, the productivity ratio is easy to calculate. However, how does the quality of the work factor into the equation? The ultimate health outcome can be measured in terms of mortality and morbidity, but that is not a factor in most productivity ratios. The same goes for all areas, whether they are clinical or operational. When managing supply inventories, it is easy to see how many requisitions were managed per employee, but if the hospital is now better equipped to offer the right products at the right location at the right time—this change in quality is not necessarily reflected in the productivity ratio without adjustments. The important part is not to ignore productivity measurement but to make sure such a measurement is balanced and represents the entire picture (e.g., quality of service, in addition to quantity).

SINGLE VERSUS MULTIPLE FACTORS

Productivity can be measured in a very basic way—using only one variable for output relative to the inputs. Alternatively, it can be measured in a more complex manner—using multiple factors, where the ratio of total outputs is applied relative to resource inputs. For example, if a hospital analyzes the movement of patients via wheelchairs, it could look at single-factor productivity using the ratio of number of patients transported as the output measure and the number of labor hours required as the inputs. If 50 patients were transported in a single day using four full-time employees (average of 8 hours per day), then the ratio would be:

$$P = \frac{50 \text{ Transports}}{(4 \text{ Employees} \times 8 \text{ Hours per day})} = 1.56$$

In other words, 1.56 patients were transported per hour in operation. How does the hospital know if this is efficient? There are only two ways to judge this: Are the number of transports per hour increasing over time, using trend analysis? Or, how does this figure compare with other hospitals? The answer to the second question is often difficult and requires external analyses or benchmarking. **Benchmarking** is the comparison of a key performance measurement relative to other organizations or the process of seeking best practices with intentions of applying those within an organization. Only by continuous measurements over time—both internally and externally—can a hospital determine if a 1.56 productivity ratio is "good" or "bad."

Now assume that the total of 50 patients is still the output, but the input included four full-time employees at an hourly rate of $8. In addition, there are two additional inputs of $25 of materials for an oxygen tank and a daily system charge of $100 (that represents amortized costs for the new transportation information system that was recently deployed). In this multifactor example, the total productivity would be equal to:

$$P = \frac{O}{\Sigma I}$$

That is, productivity is calculated as total outputs (designated by O in this equation), divided by the sum (Σ) of all inputs (I), where inputs include Labor + Supplies + Capital + Miscellaneous resources, in this example. Therefore, productivity can be calculated as:

$$P = \frac{50 \text{ Transports}}{(\$256 \text{ Labor} + \$25 \text{ Materials} + \$100 \text{ System charges})} = 0.131$$

In other words, multifactor productivity was equal to 0.131 patients per dollar spent on patient transportation. Notice that 0.131 patients per dollar is also neither good nor bad at first glance. It is impossible to tell if this result is favorable or not without benchmarking or using trend analysis to compare the same measurement internally over time. Also, keep in mind that in this example of multiple factors, all of the inputs used the same scale or unit of measure (i.e., dollars). All of the units of measure have to be consistent to sum them, which is why the 8 labor hours were converted into salary costs of $256 to keep the same units.

In most cases, multifactor productivity analysis is the most realistic and comprehensive, but it is also more complex and requires more variables and better tracking of information. To make productivity management work, the cost of productivity measurement cannot exceed the benefits derived from tracking the calculations.

COMMON HOSPITAL-WIDE PRODUCTIVITY METRICS

As stated earlier, there are very few data sources for external benchmark comparison of productivity ratios. Although productivity metrics are most useful and most actionable if they are applied to a specific business process, unit, or service line, the most common high-level metrics for analyzing hospital productivity examine one of the following:

- Number of nurses or physicians per bed.
- Hospital man hours per discharge or visit.
- Capital cost per discharge.
- Total general service cost per discharge.

Most of these metrics, however, are purely activity indicators, which are different than productivity indicators. Activity indicators merely describe the volume of work; they do not accurately capture all inputs.

It is important that all figures such as these are adjusted for both the severity of the cases served and the prevailing wage rate in the area to avoid any data biases. Case mix adjustments are necessary because patient acuity and severity of the illness dictate the intensity of the service and the amount of resources necessary to treat the patient. Similarly, wage rate fluctuations arbitrarily make certain geographic areas appear more costly, and thus less efficient, when in fact these figures are partially dependent on the prevailing local salary rates, which are outside of the hospital's control. In such cases, it may be useful to use units of input, such as labor hours, so that biases from variations in cost can be avoided.

Regardless of whether these metrics are high level and not immediately actionable, it is an initial attempt to evaluate one hospital's productivity relative to others. If a hospital evaluates its facility-wide productivity and finds that it is less productive than its peers, then the hospital will be more inclined to drill down further into each department and business process to find which area is contributing more to the productivity shortfalls and develop action plans for targeting improvements in the right departments.

Suggested data sources for benchmarking hospital-wide figures include the American Hospital Association (www.aha.org), Optum (www.optum.com), the Healthcare Financial Management Association (www.hfma.org), Becker's Hospital Review (www.beckershospitalreview.com), American Hospital Directory (www.ahd.com), and Truven Health Analytics (www.truvenhealth.com). Each of these has fee-based publications and online databases that use Medicare cost reports, surveys, and published institutional financials to allow hospitals to benchmark their productivity against others in the industry. Consulting firms also provide benchmarking services, where they use their experience with multiple organizations to benchmark the performance of their clients relative to others.

IMPROVING PRODUCTIVITY

Productivity management assumes that hospitals want to continue improving the ratios of outputs to inputs; that is, they want to become more efficient and cost-effective. Achieving this requires a plan for enhancing productivity. Productivity can improve in one of four ways:

1. Output expands with no change in inputs.
2. Output increases with a decrease in inputs.
3. Inputs are reduced, downsized, or streamlined with no change in outputs.
4. A technology or process breakthrough eliminates some inputs with no change in outputs.

The quest for productivity is to continuously find ways to improve the ratio of outputs to inputs while enhancing service levels, outcomes, and other performance metrics. Productivity management assumes that hospitals are always looking for improvements in process and performance and that maintenance of the status quo is insufficient. Given the current environment where health care provider payments are at best static and trending downward (Keckley, 2014), hospitals that maintain the status quo are in fact falling behind and likely hurting their long-term financial viability.

Technology plays a major role in improving productivity. New software and systems help automate processes and remove entire tasks and activities. In electronic commerce, systems can automate the entire purchasing and receiving process. Electronic commerce systems allow a requisition to skip the purchasing department, assuming that appropriate internal controls are developed into the system, which can eliminate several tasks and employees and may even increase the volume of outputs. The result is a change of the total productivity ratio through automation, which changes the input cost structure relative to the outputs.

The three major variables of productivity are labor, capital, and management. **Labor** is the basic element, defined as the productive work being performed by employees. Labor has many dependencies, such as the education and skill level of the employees performing the work, as well as motivation, work environment, and leadership. Typically, a change in education will have an effect on the amount of labor necessary.

Capital is the second factor of production; it represents investments in assets to offset labor or assets used to produce even more assets. Capital investment in health care is typically focused on investments in hardware, software, computer services, automation, and new equipment and devices, among others. In most well-run hospitals, investment in capital is done by performing return on investment analyses to ensure that the capital to be deployed will ultimately change the productivity ratio, either by increasing output or decreasing the level of inputs required.

Management is the final variable. Management makes the basic decisions about staffing levels and mix, compensation and motivation of employees, locations to serve, technology to put in place, and where to focus efforts. Management decides on the trade-off between capital and labor and which to invest more heavily. Utilization of capital and labor, rather than just investing in additional units of both, is one of management's key tasks. Management is both a science and an art, but it requires someone to make decisions that will help drive productivity increases.

Example

Trinity General Hospital has six cashiers in its food service operations, plus three cooks, four prep technicians, and two supervisors. The average hourly wage is $7, and each employee averages 8 hours per day, which is the total number of hours the cafeteria remains open daily. Total food supply expense is $500 per day, Monday through Friday, and averages 50% of this on both days of the weekend. Computerized food purchasing and inventory information systems were purchased last year at a cost of $100,000, and the amortized cost of this is about $500 daily. The cost of the real estate, including utilities, taxes, and lease, is about $400 daily. More than 1,400 patient and guest meals were served today. Calculate both the single- and multifactor productivity ratios for a workday. **Table 6–1** presents the results.

Using all of the productivity factors (e.g., labor, capital, materials, and other miscellaneous resources), the total multifactor productivity ratio is 0.625. This ratio is meaningless, however, without internal trend comparisons over time and external benchmarks against other leading organizations. Using a single factor, such as in this example (number of hours worked), the productivity ratio is

Table 6–1   Single- and Multifactor Productivity Example

Multifactor Productivity

Input/Resource	Number of Hours	Average Hourly Rate	Labor Cost
6 cashiers	48	$7	$336.00
3 cooks	24	$7	$168.00
4 prep technicians	32	$7	$224.00
2 supervisors	16	$7	$112.00
Total labor	120		*$840.00*
Total materials			$500.00
Total capital			$500.00
Other costs (energy, space)			$400.00
Total other costs			*$1,400.00*
Total inputs			*$2,240.00*
Total outputs (# of meals served)			*1,400*
Multifactor Productivity Ratio (meals served per dollar)			0.625
Single-Factor Productivity			
Output			1,400
Input (Number of hours worked)			120
Single-Factor Productivity Ratio (meals served per hour)			11.7

11.7 meals or guests served per hour. Both of these are useful productivity metrics to ensure that productivity increases over time.

Again, the only way to ensure that productivity is improving over time is to monitor productivity metrics relative to themselves (using trend analysis) and to external benchmarks or targets that are considered to be the best practice. **Figure 6–1** is a graphic representation of how this analysis shows that a hospital is more productive today than several months earlier, but still not as productive as the best-in-class hospitals.

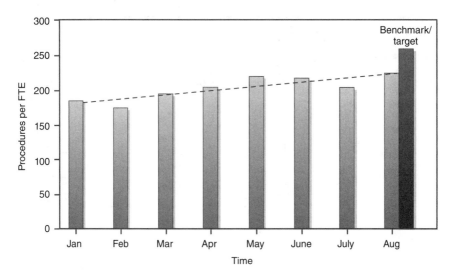

FIGURE 6–1 Trends and Benchmarks in Productivity Management

PRINCIPLES OF PRODUCTIVITY MANAGEMENT

There are five basic principles for measuring and managing productivity that must be applied. Measurement systems must be consistent, reliable, measurable, quantitative, and comprehensive.

Consistent

Consistency is a requirement in productivity management. **Consistent** means to do the same things the same way repeatedly over time. Hospitals need to measure activity (output) and resources (inputs) consistently to make trend comparisons. If a hospital measured both outputs and inputs in September, but forgot for 3 months and then picked it back up in December, the results are inconsistent and therefore problematic. Similarly, if a hospital changes the formula or basis for calculating costs, then the results are not reliable. What if December, a holiday month, skewed the output so that it could not safely be compared against September? Managing productivity means measuring consistently over time, building the tracking process into overall management workflow, and then sticking with it over time.

Consistency also means adhering to the same units of measure. Consistent use of the same definitions month after month allows comparability between numbers. If one month a department uses all factors as inputs and then the next month uses only labor costs, the numbers are not consistent and comparable and therefore cannot be relied on for meaningful results.

Reliable

Reliability is related to consistency. **Reliable** means that the productivity figures yield stable and uniform results over time. For this principle to be upheld, hospitals must ensure that systems used to generate volumes and costs do not change, are measured over the same time period (i.e., end of each week or at the month-end close), and consider all resources. For example, one hospital department measuring labor productivity chose not to count a specific supervisor's time in its calculation for inputs because, it decided, she played a large role in marketing and not as much in operations. Making the data subjective and open for interpretation creates data consistency and reliability problems, and therefore the results can easily be questioned.

Measurable

Measurable refers to how inputs and outputs are readily observed and calculated. A payroll clerk who processes paychecks clearly has measurable outputs (number of paychecks processed). A manager who oversees multiple functions, such as advertising or market research, may have less measurable work attributes. The use of tracking systems to manage all inputs and outputs is necessary. Often, payroll systems are used to track hours, general ledgers are used to track expenses, and other departmental systems are used to track outputs. Ensuring that these systems are in place, routinely printing reports with data that occurred during specific time periods, and confirming that the data are complete and accurate are vital to having measurable, reliable, and consistent results. Productivity management must ensure that the business workflow is readily measurable and can consistently be calculated.

Quantitative

Quantitative means that data and numbers are used for measurement purposes. Subjective or qualitative assessment does not translate well into productivity metrics, which require numerical expression of value to calculate ratios. There must be secondary ways to measure the quality of a service, and this is equally as important as the productivity. To remain focused on cost and efficiency, though, productivity management must adhere to quantitative calculations.

Comprehensive

Finally, productivity measurement should be simple but **comprehensive**. If multiple factors more accurately describe the cost behavior and resource consumption of a process or function, then all such data should be included in the ratios. Knowingly simplifying the calculation, at the expense of meaningful and reliable data, violates this comprehensive principle of productivity. In addition, use of scorecards that reflect quality and subjective views of performance (such as customer satisfaction, errors, or rework) must be taken into consideration to ensure a comprehensive view of performance.

RETURN ON INVESTMENT: CAPITAL VERSUS LABOR SUBSTITUTIONS

Return on investment (ROI) models are very common in most industries today. The benefit of capital (which, in many cases, is new information systems, facilities, automation, or equipment) is that it can substitute for labor (i.e., technology can often displace human effort). Use of an ROI model can help quantify the value gained for an organization when technology is substituted for labor. For example, in the household trash collection business, it used to take three employees to go on each route—one driver and two helpers to pick up the trash bags and cans and load them into the truck. Eventually, equipment and automotive manufacturers determined that an automated loading device could replace both of the helpers. Now on many routes, only a driver remains.

The same concept applies in health care. Team-based nursing allows for less specialization of labor and fewer employees. Picture archiving and communication systems have replaced several health information management professionals. Electronic commerce has streamlined the payer/provider reimbursement process, thereby increasing productivity.

The decision to undertake **capital substitution** requires careful examination to ensure that the benefits are fully realized. Most ROI models, or cost-benefit analyses, are based on a simple calculation: expected returns or benefits (B) from capital less expected costs to acquire it (C); that is, the benefits must be greater than the costs:

$$\text{ROI} = B > C$$

ROI models should detail all cost savings and avoidances, including current labor costs, and then compare these with the full benefits expected with the new capital deployed.

Example

Consider the following example. A clinic maintains three supply technicians at a total labor cost of $150,000 per year to perform basic inventory functions, such as creating requisitions for supplies as they are used, counting inventory prior to requisition, and stocking shelves. Historically, there were no supply systems in place, and all processes were manual. A vendor has submitted a proposal for an automated, inventory point-of-use dispensing system. It is estimated that this will replace 1.5 full-time equivalent positions; there will be no further need for counting products or creating 10,000 annual requisitions because these functions will be automated. The total lease payment for this system is $40,000 annually. Is this a wise decision for a capital substitution over labor? The quick calculation clearly suggests that it is, ignoring cash flow and time value of money. The calculation compares current versus future inputs, assuming outputs do not change:

$$\text{Current labor costs} = \$150,000$$
$$\text{Proposed capital and labor costs} = \$40,000 + \$75,000 \, (0.5 \times \$150,000)$$
$$= \$115,000$$
$$\text{Capital costs} < \text{Current labor costs}$$

Because the capital (or technology automation) would replace $75,000 of labor, and because total costs in the future would be $35,000 lower using a combination of factors (labor and capital), then the decision to invest in capital would be wise. Converting this into a productivity ratio, the current ratio would be 10,000 ÷ 150,000, or 0.067 requisition per dollar. After capital investment, the productivity ratio would be 10,000 ÷ 115,000, or 0.087 requisition per dollar spent. The delta or change between the before and after is 0.02, which represents about a 30% operational improvement after capital substitution for labor (i.e., 0.02 ÷ 0.067 = 29.85%).

STAFFING AND LABOR SCHEDULING MODELS

As a service organization, labor contributes between 50% and 60% of all operating expenses for an average clinical department in a large hospital. To improve the productivity of labor inputs, it is important to develop quantitative staffing models to optimize the mix of employees needed and total labor hours for each period. Most hospital departments develop schedules (sometimes called *rosters*), however, based on history and gut feel (e.g., "On Tuesdays we need more people because it is usually busier" or "We have always had 10 people in that area").

Trial and error is common in developing labor schedules, but rarely does it produce efficient or optimal labor costs. To illustrate, what happens if the patient volume is 20 on one day and 10 the next? Or, what if the hospital occupancy rate goes from an average of 65% to 90%? Does a hospital or department need to have the same level of employees regardless of output or workload? Obviously not, but that is exactly what most hospitals do—they build labor schedules based on handling either peak or average workload, and these labor budgets become fixed permanently. Any variability from the norm is difficult to manage, because capacity and demand are not forecasted sufficiently and, therefore, no flexibility exists in labor schedules. Labor is one of the most controllable costs; as operations managers continue to drive toward productivity gains, there are better ways to approach this issue. Perhaps the best way to consider managing the labor component in a health care organization is to start with an understanding of the elements that drive labor costs in these organizations. The basics of labor hour management are discussed next.

BASICS OF LABOR HOUR MANAGEMENT

In the hospital setting, productivity is usually measured by the amount of output per employee or per labor hour. The definition of an employee for purposes of productivity management is typically based on the **full-time equivalent (FTE)** metric, where productivity is usually measured by the amount of output per employee or per labor hour. The definition of an FTE employee could also change based on the time period being considered. For example, an FTE employee for a 2-week pay period would be 80 hours, as an employee who works 2 weeks at 40 hours per week totals 80 hours worked for that pay period. If that same employee worked 40 hours per week for the 52 weeks of the calendar year, then an FTE employee during a year would work 2,080 hours. Similarly, the FTE employee for a month would be the 2,080 hours worked in a year divided by 12 months, equaling 173.3 hours in a month. The annual hours divided by 12 convention is normally used in operations management rather than trying to esti- mate the amount of a work week in a given month, as there are different numbers of days per month in the calendar year. **Table 6–2** summarizes the different FTE employee definitions based on differing time periods.

If a department employed in a week, then the FTEs for that department in that week would be 1,749 hours. Similarly, the FTE employee for a month would be the 2,080 hours worked in a year divided by 12 months, calculated as 3,722 divided by 12 months, which would equate to 44.6 FTE.

Table 6–2   Full-Time Equivalent Employee Definitions by Time Period

Period	Hours	Calculation
1 week	40	8 hours per day, 5 days during a 7-day week
2 week	80	40 hours per week for 2 weeks
1 year	2,080	40 hours per week for 52 weeks in a year
1 month (1/12 of a year)	173.3	Total hours for 1 year divided by 12

It is important to differentiate between the types of labor hours used in a hospital. There are two different types of labor hours: productive and nonproductive. **Productive hours** are those that can be controlled by management and are used to directly provide patient care. Productive hours include regular paid hours, overtime and call back hours, and hours paid for training or orientation (as those hours may include delivery of patient care or facilitate the delivery of patient care). Some facilities from time to time find themselves unable to hire enough staff to meet surges in patient volume and must rely on staff from outside the organization, usually employed by staffing agencies. Staffing obtained from such outside sources is called **contract labor**. Contract labor may also be staff provided through an outsourced management arrangement, such as contracting out the dietary department, laundry, or pharmacy. Even though staff provided by an outsourced department are employees of another organization, the facility contracting for those services is using those labor inputs in the production of patient care, and so those hours should be considered when evaluating productivity. Although omission of these hours may make an organization look more productive in the short term, it is a fallacy to think that contracting out a service makes an organization more productive. Simply moving an expense line item from salaries to contract services (as would be accounted for in an outsourced labor arrangement) does not disguise the fact that a facility is devoting resources to that function. Because productivity is a measure of the number of inputs per unit of output, contract department labor must be included in the evaluation of labor productivity.

Nonproductive hours include vacation, sick time, holiday pay, and other hours paid to employees while the employees were not engaged in their normal work. Pay for additional wage premiums, such as an hourly rate for on-call obligation, shift differential, or bonus payments, should not be considered when calculating labor productivity. Most definitions of labor productivity management use only productive hours, as those are hours that directly generate outputs.

The measurements of outputs may vary depending on the type of organization involved. In a hospital, the normal unit of service is the **patient day**, which represents one patient in one hospital bed for one day. As hospitals have expanded service offerings to include care that does not require an overnight stay, other units of measure must be considered. Examples include billed tests in radiology or laboratory, treatments in physical therapy, or procedures in surgery.

Because hospitals have a multiple of outputs beyond the patient day, it is sometimes hard to evaluate the overall production of such a complex organization. This is a version of the multifactor approach described earlier. To address this challenge, some hospitals use the **adjusted patient day** as a multifactor index of hospital-wide outputs. The adjusted patient day takes the common inpatient day amount and inflates it to reflect a relative value of the other services produced by a hospital, such as outpatient lab tests, physical therapy visits, or ambulatory surgery procedures. The formula for the adjusted patient day is:

$$\frac{\text{Gross patient revenues (Inpatient + outpatient revenues)}}{\text{Inpatient revenues}} \times \text{Total inpatient day}$$

Using this formula, a manager can compare productive labor hour inputs to the overall production of the hospital, encompassing all areas of patient care production. This evaluation is usually expressed as **full-time equivalent employees per adjusted occupied bed (FTE/AOB)**. This calculation entails several steps that are detailed in the following example where, during the past year (January 1 through December 31), Mountain High Hospital reported the following results:

Inpatient revenues	$164,512,878
Outpatient revenues	69,095,409
Total patient revenues	**$233,608,287**
Inpatient days	31,534
Productive labor hours	1,487,669

Using these results, the FTE/AOB can be calculated in the following steps:

1. *Calculate productive FTE.* Because the data used here represent a 1-year period, the FTE employee works 2,080 hours. Given 1,487,669 productive hours worked in the past year, the productive FTE is calculated as:

$$\frac{1,487,669 \text{ Productive hours}}{2,080 \text{ Hours per FTE}} = 715.23 \text{ Productive FTE}$$

2. *Calculate adjusted patient days.* Using the formula presented earlier, the actual inpatient days of 31,543 are inflated by calculating the relative value of all hospital outputs as follows:

$$\frac{233{,}608{,}287 \text{ Total revenues}}{164{,}512{,}878 \text{ Inpatient revenue}} \times 31{,}534 \text{ Patient days}$$

$$= 44{,}778 \text{ Adjusted patient days}$$

3. *Calculate adjusted occupied beds.* Recall that adjusted occupied beds is equal to the average daily census in a hospital, using instead adjusted patient days rather than inpatient days. Otherwise, the calculation is expressed as adjusted patient days ÷ days in the period. Because the data used in this example are based on a full calendar year, adjusted patient days are divided by 365 days in the year to arrive at the adjusted occupied beds:

$$\frac{44{,}778 \text{ Adjusted patient days}}{365 \text{ Days per year}} = 122.68 \text{ Adjusted occuped beds}$$

4. *Calculate FTE/AOB.* Using the results from steps 1 and 3, FTE/AOB is calculated by:

$$\frac{715.23 \text{ FTE}}{122.68 \text{ AOB}} = 5.83 \text{ FTE/AOB}$$

This calculation can be valuable in determining overall labor productivity for a hospital, but as mentioned earlier, it is only valuable when trended over time or compared to a benchmark. Benchmarks for the FTE/AOB ratio are published in industry organization resources such as the Healthcare Financial Management Association (www.hfma.org) or Becker's Hospital Review (www.beckershospitalreview.com).

It is important to remember that the FTE/AOB ratio looks at the staffing level of a hospital at the highest level of labor input and patient service output. That approach can be useful for managers at the highest levels of the organization but may be difficult for managers in departments or subunits to adjust staff to such high-level output measurements. Each department or subunit has its own output measure, and using a ratio of FTE in a department per unit of output for that department can be useful in managing labor in the various parts of a hospital. In some cases, where departments turn out a large volume of outputs (such as a laboratory test), the FTE measure may end up with a small fraction that could be meaningless to a manager. In those situations, a measure of productive labor hours per unit of output may be more useful to define manageable inputs in an individual department. The challenge in measuring productivity in a hospital department is in finding a valid output measure to use, especially in those departments that may not have a specific unit of output but instead provide a service to the entire organization, such as housekeeping. **Table 6–3** provides some examples of commonly used units of measure for the work of a specific department.

Table 6–3 Commonly Used Department Workload Units

Department	Common Workload Unit
Nursing units	Inpatient days
Emergency room	Patient visits
Delivery room	Deliveries
Pharmacy	Billed medication doses
Diagnostic imaging	Billed procedures
Clinical laboratory	Billed tests
Operating room	Total surgery minutes or total surgical procedures
Recovery room	Recovery minutes
Physical therapy	Relative value units or patient treatments
EKG	Relative value units or billed tests
Respiratory therapy	Relative value units or patient treatments
Administration	Adjusted patient days or calendar days
Patient accounting	Adjusted patient days
Admitting/registration	Total patient admissions/registrations
Medical records	Adjusted patient days
Materials management	Adjusted patient days
Housekeeping	Total square feet
Maintenance	Total square feet, work orders, or adjusted patient days
Quality management	Adjusted patient days
Volunteer services	Adjusted patient days or calendar days
Human resources	Total employees, adjusted patient days, or calendar days
Medical staff office	Adjusted patient days or calendar days
Transportation services	Adjusted patient days or patients transported
Ambulatory services	Ambulatory patient visits

The types of output measures used in different departments of a hospital vary greatly, making it a challenge to derive one meaningful index of output, thus lending some utility to the notion of the adjusted patient day as a meaningful overall measure of hospital production. However, at the department level, linking labor productivity to the specific outputs of that department allows the manager to better manage labor resources. Measuring labor productivity at a department level is done in much the same way as any other productivity measurement, where the inputs are compared to measures of output. For example, the housekeeping department of Bayou City Hospital (a facility of 365,525 square feet) had 41,788 productive hours in the last fiscal year. The housekeeping manager can calculate the hours per square foot cleaned as follows:

$$\frac{365,525 \text{ Productive hours}}{41,788 \text{ Square feet}} = 8.75 \text{ Hours per square foot}$$

By using these types of ratios and tracking them over time, managers can then develop staffing plans aimed at improving labor efficiency. However, setting a targeted FTE/AOB level involves more than just calculating that ratio and using it to develop a work schedule for departments in a hospital. As mentioned earlier, workloads or outputs will vary for a variety of reasons—some controllable, some not. For example, some areas of the hospital can flex their labor hours but must maintain a minimal staff level (such as an emergency room that must have a nurse in the department at all times, 24 hours a day, 7 days a week), regardless of patient visits produced. This level of **base staffing** must be taken into consideration when developing schedules for hospital staff. Also, some departments, such as administration, may require **fixed staffing**, where labor hours may be unable to vary with outputs. Several sophisticated mathematical approaches can be used to quantify the varying labor requirements in hospitals and turn them into weekly operation schedules that can lead to an overall labor hour per output target. The challenge is to rationally predict expected volume outputs for a hospital and then align labor hour goals with those volume projections. Once labor hour targets are set, a cost per unit of output goal can be derived.

Other service industries (e.g., airlines, retail sales, and restaurants) have widely adopted the use of mathematical labor scheduling software tools. Given the right information, commercially available software can integrate with both "time and attendance" and payroll processing software to use historical information to drive optimal results. In fast-food restaurant chains, where average profit margins are less than 3%, the more sophisticated restaurant managers have statistically predicted when their busiest demand periods are, and they use this forecast to drive labor mix (i.e., cashiers, prep, cooks) and labor schedules (i.e., which specific day and time each employee is due at work). If demand is low, staffing is low, and as demand increases, labor is increased—creating an alignment between capacity and demand.

As far back as 1990, Taco Bell has employed optimization models in establishing labor requirements for each store (Godward & Swart, 1994). Similarly, Burger King used optimization techniques in labor scheduling as far back as the 1980s (Swart & Donno, 1981). Restaurant managers know that for every hour they do not have to employ an individual, the operating margin increases exponentially. An optimized labor schedule in industries such as fast food, where efficiency is required and margins are minimal, does not happen accidentally. It is well planned and mathematically generated.

There are two major types of mathematical approaches used in the labor optimization software systems available today: simulation and linear programming. Both have been used successfully. Linear programming models are probably the most common. **Linear programming** refers to an optimization technique that seeks to either maximize or minimize an objective function, given a set of variables and constraints. In staffing models, there are typically five sets of variables that drive the quantitative models:

1. Forecasted demand and patient volumes/flows (D) (e.g., 18 patients per day).
2. Per-unit labor cost (C) (e.g., $9 per hour).
3. Resource or job type and mix (R) (e.g., accountant, nurse).
4. Average transaction cycle time (T) (e.g., 17 minutes per function performed).
5. Other constraints (e.g., actual capacity constraints on the equipment or the space, base staffing levels, or fixed staffing patterns).

Each of these variables can be modeled to express the relationships between them, similar to the following equation:

$$\text{Minimize } (C_1 R_1 T_1 + C_2 R_2 T_2 + C_n R_n T_n)$$
$$\text{Subject to } D_m = X, D_t = Y, D_n = Z$$

In other words, a linear programming model would attempt to minimize total labor costs (the objective function) by using the inputs of per-hour salary expenses, labor mix by job type, and total transaction times, while using the daily demand estimates as a constraint (i.e., D_m = Patient volume demand on Monday). Many of the popular software packages have built-in algorithmic code and matrix algebra, so users only need to feed the parameters and constraints and the optimized equations are then generated and labor schedules are printed. One of the most popular optimization tools available today is IBM ILOG CPLEX (www-01.ibm.com/software/info/ilog/), which has been used widely in nearly all industries and applications.

In health care, there has been only minimal adoption of optimization techniques to date. Certain studies have reported the use of optimization models to estimate physician schedules in emergency and operating rooms (Carter & Lapierre, 2001). More commonly, nurse rosters have been developed using linear programming (Warner, 1976). Some research confirms that optimization models can save significant operating expense. In one hospital, a reduction of 16% in total labor expenses was achieved through linear program minimization models (Matthews, 2005). There just has not been wide enough deployment of optimization to make a difference yet, but this will change as health care providers continue to face greater revenue constraints.

There are other more simplistic models for staffing, which are easier to use and faster to deploy. One such approach, often called *simulation* or *activity models*, uses simpler relationships between work outputs and labor inputs.

Example

Consider the following example. A receiving department processes 500 packages per day (total demand), and each package takes 7 minutes to process (i.e., time of receipt, scan of bar code, entry into an enterprise resource planning system). The known constraints are that (1) no employee works overtime, or more than 8 hours per day, and (2) on average, each employee is utilized effectively no more than 90% of the time (which accounts for work interruptions, meetings, breaks, or other unplanned activities). Therefore, eight employees will be needed. This can be calculated in the following steps:

1. Determine the total number of working minutes daily for each employee (8 hours × 90% utilization × 60 minutes = 432 minutes each day).
2. Estimate the total number of output each individual can process (432 hours ÷ 7 minutes for each transaction = 61.7 packages per day).
3. Divide total demand or daily production by the per-person rate (500 ÷ 61.7 = 8.1 employees).

This simple model suggests that staffing based on daily volume of 500 requires approximately 8 employees. If volume was projected to increase the following week to an average of 600, then closer to 10 employees would be required (600 ÷ 61.7). One simulation tool that allows a user to change key variables and assumptions, using known mathematical relationships to estimate the effect on a dependent variable, is **sensitivity analysis**. This is often commonly called *what-if* or *scenario analysis*.

Of great importance, there must be alignment between resources and volume. Staffing for average days is never optimal because there will either be too many or too few employees on hand. Similarly, staffing for peaks or valleys creates either labor excesses or shortages. An attempt to match demand with volume is the only way to achieve optimal results.

Optimization and simulation models for generating labor schedules are slightly more complex than the traditional gut-feel approach. They require a great deal of data, and they force managers to analyze processes and volumes more thoroughly to generate the appropriate results. They require understanding of cycle times and productivity. Often, an understanding of business processes used in an organization will identify steps that do not add value to production and can be eliminated. Eliminating unnecessary steps can reduce transaction cycle times and improve productivity. All of these help improve processes and reduce costs, so the benefits of using mathematical models are much greater than these risks.

PRODUCTIVITY AND PERFORMANCE SCORECARD

Productivity is just one key of the key metrics that helps define how a department or organization is doing. Performance metrics should focus on all areas of the business, measuring financial results, customer service, competition, and operations. A balanced scorecard, unique to each hospital, is one way to develop a core set of metrics that establish the right ways to ensure progress toward a specific strategy.

While a productivity metric focuses on efficiency, other areas of performance should focus on effectiveness. Efficiency measures "doing things right," with minimal resources and waste. **Effectiveness** measures "doing the right things," which relates to strategy and planning. Both efficiency and effectiveness should be measured on a departmental or operational scorecard. A **performance scorecard** is a tool to visualize measurements of key performance indicators for an organization relative to time, targets, or another baseline. A sample scorecard for a generic department is provided in **Figure 6-2**.

Notice that the operational scorecard in Figure 6-2 has several components. First, it shows a "balanced" view, in that it is not strictly focused on a singular

Category	Key performance indicator	Target/ baseline	Current period results	Stoplight indicator
Operational focus	Cycle time, procure to pay Cycle time, room changeover Cost per unit of output (for each key process) Change in productivity ratio (output ÷ inputs) Scheduling delays/backlog Supplier performance rating (key vendors)			Green
Customer/ quality	Safety/error rates Customer/patient satisfaction scores Survey results Number of complaints/opportunities			Red
Economic	Operating margin Return on capital Days of working capital Days of inventory on hand Days of accounts receivable			Yellow

FIGURE 6–2 Operational Productivity and Performance Scorecard

dimension of performance or productivity but attempts to take a comprehensive, holistic view of the function or department (Kaplan & Norton, 1996). Second, the scorecard shows multiple indicators for each category. In general, an operational scorecard should be limited to a handful of key metrics, so as to keep it simple and useful and not overwhelm managers and employees who must use it to translate performance into action. Third, the specific metrics are generic on this scorecard, but each department should define and manage its own customized metrics for each group. Specific key performance indicators, such as number of days of accounts receivable, don't mean anything for one support service but might for another.

CHAPTER SUMMARY

Managing productivity and performance is important for operational managers to ensure that their operations are becoming more cost-effective and efficient over time. Principles of health care operations management suggest that the primary goals are to reduce costs, eliminate waste, and ensure that resources are being used efficiently. Productivity management is the ratio of outputs to inputs. Both single- and multifactor productivity ratios can be calculated to understand the relationship between outputs and inputs. Labor staffing models should be used to align volume or demand with resources. Staffing models should be calculated mathematically, not with simple heuristics or rules of thumb, employing linear programming algorithms to produce optimal results. Each department and business process can be decomposed into both outputs and inputs so that a periodic performance scorecard can track changes over time. Only by internally measuring and consistently applying these methods over the long term can hospital administrators prove that they have added value and have had a positive effect on business operations.

KEY TERMS

Adjusted patient day	Inputs
Base staffing	Labor
Benchmarking	Linear programming
Capital	Management
Capital substitution	Measurable
Comprehensive	Nonproductive hours
Consistent	Outputs
Contract labor	Patient day
Effectiveness	Performance scorecard
Efficiency	Productive hours
Fixed staffing	Productivity
Full-time equivalent (FTE)	Quantitative
Full-time equivalent employees per	Reliable
adjusted occupied bed (FTE/AOB)	Sensitivity analysis

DISCUSSION QUESTIONS

1. Why is productivity important?
2. What is the difference between productivity and other measures of performance?
3. How do single-factor and multifactor analysis differ?
4. How is a full-time equivalent calculated?
5. What is the difference between productive and nonproductive hours?
6. What are some common measurement problems?
7. Why should hospitals benchmark?
8. Is a scorecard the only tool used for improving operations?

9. How do staffing models and labor optimization algorithms contribute toward productivity?
10. How can return on investment models help the decision-making process?

EXERCISE PROBLEMS

1. Based on the following data, calculate the single-factor productivity ratio using hours of labor for a housekeeping department.
   - Number of employees = 100
   - Average hourly rate = $5.50
   - Total hours worked in September = 15,570
   - Total square feet maintained = 190,000

2. In the preceding problem, using sensitivity analysis, if the productivity ratio was 13.1 the previous month, has productivity increased or decreased? By what percentage?

3. Assume that a new piece of equipment could allow 25% of the labor force in Question 1 to be eliminated. Using a 173-hour working month for each employee, a total equipment cost of $60,000 (which has a useful life of 3 years), and ignoring the effect of cash flow and time value of money, would this be a good use of capital?

4. If a hospital reported the following results, calculate the full-time equivalent employees per adjusted occupied bed:

Inpatient revenues	$129,215,678
Outpatient revenues	44,996,104
Total patient revenues	**$174,211,782**
Inpatient days	23,926
Productive labor hours	916,882

REFERENCES

Carter, M. W., & Lapierre, S. D. (2001). Scheduling emergency room physicians. *Health Care Management Science, 4*(4), 347–360.

Godward, M., & Swart, W. (1994, Winter). An object oriented simulation model for determining labor requirements at Taco Bell. *Proceedings of the Simulation Conference* (1067–1073). San Diego, CA: Society for Computer Simulation International.

Kaplan, R. S., & Norton, D. P. (1996). *The balanced scorecard: Translating strategy into action.* Boston, MA: Harvard Business School Press.

Keckley, P. (2014, January 6). What to expect in 2014. *Hospitals & Health Networks Daily*. Retrieved from www.hhnmag.com/display/HHN-news-article.dhtml?dcrPath =%2Ftemplatedata%2FHF_Common%2FNewsArticle%2Fdata%2FHHN%2FDai ly%2F2014%2FJan%2F010614-blog-2014-outlook

Matthews, C. B. (2005). Using linear programming to minimize the cost of nurse personnel. *Journal of Health Care Finance, 32*(1), 37–49.

Swart, W., & Donno, L. (1981). Simulation modeling improves operations, planning, and productivity of fast food restaurants. *Interfaces, 11*(6), 35–47.

Warner, D. M. (1976). Scheduling nurse personnel according to nurse preference: A mathematical programming approach. *Operations Research, 24*(5), 824–856.

CHAPTER 7

Operational Metrics in Health Care Organizations

The use of ratio analysis is a common technique in financial management for interpreting values on financial statements and putting them into some context about how an organization is performing. The same approach is extremely valuable in operations management for understanding how efficiently an organization is producing services for patients. A health care provider organization operates as a production function with inputs and outputs, just as a factory does that produces goods for sale. In the case of a health care organization, the inputs are varied and examples include labor, supplies, use of outside service vendors, and capital equipment to produce multiple types of output, including a patient day, surgical procedure, diagnostic test, meals for patients or visitors, or claim for reimbursement. As with any other **production function** (P), operations management seeks to maximize the volume of **output** (O) for a given amount of **input** (I) using the ratio:

$$P = \frac{O}{I}$$

Depending on the manager's perspective, the definition of productivity, the inputs, and the outputs used in this ratio may vary. In some cases, the manager may define productivity as total cost per unit of output—one particular cost element per unit of output, such as salaries. Other perspectives may evaluate productivity as the number of inputs (such as labor hours) per unit of output. Health care management operational metrics use this same production function approach where the ratio of inputs per unit of output is measured. In this chapter, the common operational metrics and their derivation will be presented.

INPUT MEASURES FOR OPERATING METRICS

There are different ways of determining an input used in the production function just described. Depending on the organization's goal or the particular problem being addressed, multiple input measures may be useful in establishing solid operational controls. Generally, an input can be measured based on the cost of resources devoted to the production of patient care or the number of individual units of a particular resource used.

Costs of resources are often used in conjunction with evaluation of results in the organization's income statement. For example, the cost per unit of output may be used to determine the organization's performance against income statement goals when identifying if there are "good" or "bad" results in a given accounting period. Using this perspective, a good result would be defined as cost per unit of output being below a target value. Conversely, a bad result would be determined if the cost per unit of output were above that target value. Using cost per unit of output as a measure of operational effectiveness has some benefit in that it is easily derived from the organization's normally produced financial statements; therefore, data for operational analysis is readily available. Such data is also commonly understood among managers in the health care setting. However, regular variations in operating cost, such as normal inflation, changes in sources for inputs, or changes in the mix or quality of inputs, can all create routine variations from the assumptions made in determining operating cost per unit of output benchmark. Some of these issues may be beyond the operations manager's control and may limit how meaningful the cost per unit of output approach is to determining operational effectiveness. Therefore, it may be helpful to consider observed results using a cost per unit of output approach, along with the number of units of input used to generate a given level of output.

Units of input may provide a more objective view on evaluating operational performance. Examples of such units of input are labor hours; number of supply items, such as syringes or exam gloves; or the number of medications used to produce a unit of output. Units of input do not have the same price variations that a cost per unit of output would have: A labor hour used to produce a lab test may change in value if an employee gets a pay adjustment, but the time used to produce that output remains constant in its measure. Therefore, in operations management it is valuable to know the number of units used to produce patient care outputs to avoid the challenge of weighing the reasonableness of results in terms of changes in the prices of inputs. However, those items are typically not readily obtained from financial statements and require some additional work by the operations manager to gain access to the organization's statistical reports in order to track the number of units used in a given reporting period. There are multiple reports generated by the organization—often to support preparation of financial statements—that can be used to obtain counts of production inputs in a health care setting. Examples of these sources will be discussed in the next section.

When considering units of input in the hospital setting, labor units are significant because labor costs make up more than half of the hospital's operating expenses. Measuring the productivity of labor in particular can be valuable in understanding variations in the organization's financial performance. Labor productivity is typically measured by the amount of output per employee or per labor hour. The definition of an employee in the operations management field is usually based on the full-time equivalent (FTE) employee measure. Many operating metrics in the health care field use the FTE per unit of output to evaluate labor productivity. The definition of a full-time employee is 40 hours of productive work in 1 week. Because hospitals operate 24 hours a day, 7 days a week, this means 40 hours of production spread across 7 days in a calendar week. In addition, some employees may not work a full 40-hour week, yet together they equal the amount of time worked by one full-time employee. For example, if two employees both work 25 hours in a week, together they have worked 1.25 FTE (25 hours per week for employee #1 + 25 hours per week for employee #2) ÷ 40 hours for one full-time employee per week = 1.25 FTE). Additional details on other FTE calculations can be found in the *Productivity and Performance Management* chapter.

SOURCES OF DATA FOR OPERATIONAL METRICS

Usable data needed to calculate the various operational metrics can be obtained from reports that are routinely prepared within today's health care organization, including an income statement and statistical compilations. The income statement is used by the organization for external reporting and internal management purposes, along with the balance sheet and statement of cash flows. Many organizations will even prepare income statements at a department level to assist individual department managers in running a specific department. If managers are particularly interested in the costs per unit of output, then the income statement is likely the most valuable data source, especially for comparison of actual operating results with budget targets. This is particularly true when evaluating operational results within departments or subunits of an organization.

It is important for operations managers to remember that comparison to budgeted cost targets have some limitations, depending on the changes in the price of inputs used and the mix of different inputs used to generate observed results. Cost comparisons have great value in operations management due to the ease in which data can be obtained from common financial statements, but they must be used with caution to consider any changes in the price or mix of inputs that differ from the assumptions used in setting budget targets.

Routine financial statements are often supplemented with at least a basic description of the operating statistics for the organization to provide some context to the reader of the level of activity described in financial statement results. In some cases, such as the filing of government-required annual reports, certain operating statistics, such as patient days, discharges, and employee data, are mandatory. Perhaps the most common example of such mandatory reports is the Medicare Cost Report submitted to the Centers for Medicare and Medicaid Services (CMS) by hospitals, skilled nursing facilities, and other institutional providers that participate in the federal Medicare program. As a result, financial managers are likely already collecting a wide array of statistical data that is used to prepare required reports to external parties. These data can provide valuable insight into operations management in measuring the volume of inputs used to generate organizational output.

The departments within an institutional provider such as a hospital often collect operating statistics to measure activity levels for use with internal management reporting or to document patient care rendered during a given time period. These data may include manual patient logs that can be summarized or a compilation of daily transaction logs in a department. Another excellent source of data for operational inputs to the production of patient care outputs is the accounting records used to generate financial reports, such as payroll journals or inventory control reports. The labor distribution usually categorizes paid labor hours as being productive, overtime, vacation, sick, or other classifications and can be valuable for identifying productive FTE for operational analysis. Inventory control reports can describe the units of supply issued to a department for use during a specified time period and can be associated with output volumes to evaluate supply inputs to production. A list of commonly used operational data sources is presented in **Table 7–1**.

Generally speaking, health care organizations are considered to be data-intensive enterprises and so have a wealth of statistical data that often goes unused in operations management. The challenge for the operations manager is to understand which data are collected in the organization, how the data are collected, how the data can relate to the organization's operational performance, and how to obtain the data with a minimum of disruption to normal production functions. **Table 7–2** provides an example income statement with basic operational statistics for a small community hospital. Data from this table will be used to calculate the operating metric examples to follow.

Table 7–1   Examples of Sources of Operational Data

Input/Output	Source(s)
Labor Cost	Organization or departmental income statements
Supply Cost	Organization or departmental income statements
Labor Hours	Payroll journals, labor distributions
Supply Units	Inventory management journals
Emergency Room (ER) Patients Served	Department volume logs, patient accounting records with patients having ER services, medical record counts of ER patients
Tests Performed	Department volume logs, patient accounting records of tests charged
Surgical Procedures Performed	Department patient logs, medical record counts of surgical procedures

Table 7–2   Sample Income Statement and Summary Operating Statistics

Example Community Hospital Summary of Financial & Operational Data for the Year Ended 12/31/20XX

Inpatient Revenues	$66,179,014
Outpatient Revenues	24,966,033
Total Revenues	$91,145,047
Allowances & Discounts	$35,820,003
Bad Debt	1,066,397
Total Revenue Deductions	$36,886,400
Net Revenue	$54,258,647
Salaries & Wages	$27,621,506
Contract Labor	1,287,162
Benefits	7,374,942
Supplies	9,392,171
Repairs & Maintenance	1,268,733
Purchased Services	980,245
Other Operating Expenses	732,612
Total Operating Expenses	$48,657,371
Operating Margin	$5,601,276
Depreciation & Amortization	$6,169,524
Total Margin	($568,248)
Investments	$1,252,376
Donations	309,893
Total Non-Operating Income	$1,562,269
Net Income	$994,021
Beds in Operation	76
Patient Days	14,543
Discharges	2,796
Outpatient Visits	36,877
Productive Labor Hours	644,890
Non-Productive Labor Hours	77,387
Total Paid Hours	722,277

OUTPUT MEASURES

The common output measures in an institutional health care provider organization such as a hospital relate to one of two types of service: inpatient or outpatient. Inpatient volume measures have been the traditional index of output for a hospital since the history of hospital care in the United States until the mid-1980s and centered on care to patients who stayed in the hospital for a period of more than 1 day. Since then, the traditional inpatient volume measures have evolved to take into account services provided to patients who visit the hospital for care but do not stay overnight—the outpatient.

The **patient day** has been the most common measure of output for a hospital over time and represents one patient staying in the hospital's inpatient care units at midnight on a given day. The count of patient days in a hospital is based on the hospital's daily **midnight census**. For example, if Hometown Hospital has 63 patients in beds in its inpatient care units at midnight on March 3, then it has produced 63 patient days of care. Patient days are typically reported on a monthly, quarterly, or yearly basis and commonly accompany the income statement for a hospital. Because a hospital can compile patient days on a daily basis for a time period greater than 1 day, managers often look to an average number of patient days to gauge the level of inpatient activity for a certain period, or **average daily census (ADC)**. If Hometown Hospital recorded 2,105 patient days during the month of March, then its ADC for March is 67.9 (2,105 patient days during the month ÷ 31 days in March = 67.9 ADC). When considering inpatient volumes over a period of time, either the patient day or ADC is an appropriate measure of hospital output.

When a patient enters the hospital for an inpatient stay, that event is counted as an **admission** and is a common operating statistic in hospitals. Since inception of prospective payment by Medicare in the mid-1980s, hospital payments have been based on when the patient leaves the hospital, also called a **discharge**. Because discharges represent the complete occasion of care for a patient (whereas an admission represents only the start of an inpatient hospitalization), operations management uses the discharge as a measure of the number of inpatients served in a given time period. If Hometown Hospital sent five patients home after an overnight stay in the hospital on September 23, then it has recorded five discharges for that day. As with patient days, discharges are usually totaled during monthly, quarterly, and yearly time periods.

As mentioned earlier, hospitals have moved away from a focus on care to patients who stay overnight in the hospital and toward services to outpatients.

However, outpatient units of service can be counted in a myriad of ways—tests performed, procedures completed, or treatments performed. Further, a simple test in the laboratory (such as a routine urinalysis) may be less sophisticated than an outpatient MRI scan or an outpatient orthopedic surgery. It can be difficult to identify one meaningful measure of output for an organization with multiple outputs of varying sophistication or focus. Thus, the **adjusted patient day** is used as an index of a hospital's total output. It takes the inpatient days produced in the hospital for a given time period and inflates them to account for an estimate of the relative value of outpatient services provided during the same interval. The adjusted patient day is calculated using the formula:

$$\text{Adjusted patient days} = \frac{(\text{Inpatient} + \text{outpatient revenues})}{\text{Inpatient revenues}} \times \text{Inpatient days}$$

An illustration of this calculation uses data from Table 7–2. Example Community Hospital recorded 14,543 patient days, $66,179,014 in inpatient revenues, and $24,966,033 in outpatient revenues. Using these data, the adjusted patient days during the year for Example Community are calculated as:

$$\frac{(66,179,014 + 24,966,033)}{66,179,014} \times 14,543 = 20,029 \text{ Adjusted patient days}$$

The same adjustment can be applied to the hospital's count of discharges to express inpatient discharges in terms of the hospital's overall inpatient and outpatient outputs. This measure is called the **adjusted discharge** and is calculated as:

$$\text{Adjusted discharges} = \frac{(\text{Inpatient} + \text{outpatient revenues})}{\text{Inpatient revenues}} \times \text{Inpatient discharges}$$

Using the same data from Example Hospital yields the following calculation:

$$\frac{(66,179,014 + 24,966,033)}{66,179,014} \times 2,796 = 3,851 \text{ Adjusted discharges}$$

Considering the multiple types of output produced in a hospital organization, these aggregate measures of output are the most common for assessment of hospital operations. If the focus of an operational assessment is a particular department or subunit of the hospital, the department's specific output, such as tests, examinations, treatments, or procedures, may be used. Because a specific department's output will generally be the same for an inpatient or an outpatient, it is not necessary to adjust for inpatient or outpatient volumes when looking at the department's operational performance. For example, if the radiology department produced 12,000 tests for inpatients and another 3,500 for outpatients, the

15,500 total tests represent the total output for this department. If the department uses a relative value unit measure such as the College of American Pathologists (CAP) unit, the same approach would apply. If the hospital lab produced inpatient tests totaling 162,500 CAP units and outpatient tests that total another 44,000 CAP units, the lab's output can be expressed as 206,500 CAP units.

COMMON OPERATING METRICS

There are several common operating metrics used in today's hospitals. The following section will define these metrics and provide an example using data from Table 7–2.

As mentioned earlier, total patient days for a period are typically assessed using an average over a specified period of time (month, quarter, or year) and expressed as average daily census (ADC) or average occupied beds (OB). The same holds true for adjusted patient days, and a common metric to determine adjusted patient day volumes is **adjusted average daily census (AADC)** or **adjusted occupied bed (AOB)**. The AADC metric calculated using example data for the past year as well as the adjusted patient day calculation shown earlier is completed as follows:

$$\frac{\text{Adjusted patient day}}{\text{Days in the period}} = \frac{20.029}{365} = 54.87$$

Comparing the AADC calculated here with the 39.84 inpatient ADC (14,543 inpatient days ÷ 365 days in a year = 39.84) suggests that Example Hospital produced about 37.75% of the output for outpatients that it did for inpatients during the past year.

The number of patient days can be a valuable measure of how efficiently a hospital completes treatment of a patient's condition. Given that today's hospitals are typically paid a fixed prospective amount per discharge from Medicare and many managed care plans, the incentive is to minimize the number of days a patient stays before discharge. This metric is known as the **average length of stay**. An example calculation using data from Table 7–2 yields the following result:

$$\frac{\text{Patient days}}{\text{Discharges in the period}} = \frac{20,029}{2,796} = 5.20 \text{ Days}$$

This calculation tells the manager at Example Hospital that, on average, an inpatient stayed in the hospital 5.29 days before discharge. Comparing this value to a benchmark length of stay can tell the operations manager if patients are staying longer than perhaps they should, based on the experience of other facilities, and may identify a potential area of improvement for the hospital.

Management makes decisions on how much capacity to make available in a hospital, usually expressed by the number of beds available for patients to occupy. Knowing the extent to which that capacity is being used can help determine if the organization is supporting unused capacity or is operating at a high level of utilization that could result in turning business away. This metric is called the **occupancy percentage** and is calculated using data from Example Hospital as follows:

$$\frac{\text{Average daily census}}{\text{Beds in operation}} \times 100 = \frac{39.84}{76} \times 100 = 52.43\%$$

This calculation indicates that Example Hospital is operating at about 52% of its available capacity and may have the opportunity to attract additional business or perhaps reduce the available number of beds to decrease the resources expended to support unused capacity.

Labor is one of the largest resource inputs used in a hospital to produce patient care services, and the costs of labor can ruin the organization's financial results. While labor costs are important to hospital management, the management of actual labor hours can be the key to effectively controlling labor costs that appear on financial statements. This can be measured using the ratio **FTE employees per occupied bed (FTE/OB)**. The data for Example Hospital presented here is for a 1-year period, where a full-time employee would work 2,080 hours (40 hours × 52 weeks in a year). Using an annual FTE hours basis, the FTE/OB value is calculated to be:

$$\frac{(\text{Productive labor hours} \div 2,080)}{\text{Average daily census}} = \frac{(644,890 \div 2,080)}{39.84} = 7.78 \text{ FTE/OB}$$

This result shows that Example Hospital uses an average of 7.78 FTE for every inpatient served in the hospital each day.

The FTE/OB metric does not take into account the volume of outputs produced for services to outpatients. If a hospital provides a significant volume of services to outpatients, the FTE/OB metric may not fully account for a hospital's workload. To address this concern, measurement of **FTE employees per adjusted occupied bed (FTE/AOB)** may better express the ratio of labor inputs per unit of total output for the hospital. Using the AADC value for Example Hospital calculated earlier, the FTE/AOB for the past year is:

$$\frac{(\text{Productive labor hours} \div 2,080)}{\text{Adjusted average daily census}} = \frac{(644,890 \div 2,080)}{54.87} = 5.65 \text{ FTE/AOB}$$

Thus, Example Hospital used an average of 5.65 FTE in the production of 1 adjusted patient day during the past year.

If a manager wishes to evaluate the operational efficiency of a specific department, then the same relationship described in the FTE/OB or FTE/AOB metrics for productive labor hours per unit of output can be used to calculate **productive hours per unit** in a specific department. If the radiology department of Example Hospital recorded 11,463 productive hours in the past year to produce 16,772 procedures in the past year, the hours per unit are calculated as:

$$\frac{\text{Department productive labor hours}}{\text{Department units of output}} = \frac{11,463}{16,772} = 0.68 \text{ Hours per procedure}$$

This calculated result tells the radiology manager at Example Hospital that it takes about 41 minutes (0.68 hours per procedure × 60 minutes in an hour = 41) of employee labor to produce one test for a patient.

Conversely, the department manager may want to know how many procedures per employee are produced per year. Using data from the radiology department at Example Hospital, the number of **procedures per employee** is:

$$\frac{\text{Department units of output}}{(\text{Productive labor hours} \div 2,080)} = \frac{16,772}{(11,463 \div 2,080)}$$
$$= 3.043 \text{ Procedures/employee}$$

Because the productive hours in the radiology department for the year translate to 5.51 FTE, and those labor hours resulted in production of 16,772 tests, then on average one full-time employee produced 3,043 tests.

The metrics described so far look at units of output per unit of input. However, the operations manager should still review operating expenses per unit of output to evaluate the total mix of resources used in producing a unit of output. It is not feasible to calculate the different units of measure for the multiple inputs used in producing patient care services in a hospital—labor hours, units of supply, dollars of purchased services, or lease of equipment. As a result, operating cost per unit of output is the most reasonable approach to measuring the value of all inputs to producing a unit of patient care. Total **operating expense per occupied bed**, **operating expense per adjusted occupied bed**, **operating expense per discharge**, or **operating expense per adjusted discharge** are all examples of ratios used to evaluate the costs per unit of production based on the different units of production described earlier. The following example calculates operating expense per adjusted occupied bed; this same formula can also be used to calculate different units of measure:

$$\frac{\text{Total operating expense}}{\text{Units of output}}$$

The operating expense per adjusted occupied bed for Example Hospital is calculated by using the following values from Table 7–2

$$\frac{\text{Total operating expense}}{\text{Adjusted patient days}} = \frac{\$48,657,371}{20,029}$$

$$= \$2,429.35 \text{ Per adjusted occupied bed}$$

The value for operating expense per discharge is:

$$\frac{\$48,657,371}{2,796} = \$17,402.49 \text{ Per inpatient discharge}$$

Operating expense per adjusted discharge amounts to:

$$\frac{\$48,657,371}{2,796} = \$12,635.68 \text{ Per adjusted discharge}$$

Operating expense per occupied bed equals:

$$\frac{\$48,657,371}{14,543} = \$3,345.76 \text{ Per occupied bad}$$

Another perspective on the unit of output in a health care organization is to address the multiple services provided by a hospital in revenues rather than in units such as discharges or patient days. If the hospital units of output are widely varied in terms of sophistication or type of delivery (such as in a hospital that has inpatient services but also operates a skilled nursing unit or an ambulance service, then revenues may be a more appropriate overall measure of output), calculating **net revenue per FTE** can tell an operations manager the amount of net revenue that was created on average by each employee in the organization. Using values from the operating statement for Example Hospital in Table 7–2, the net revenue per FTE is calculated as:

$$\frac{\text{Net revenue}}{\text{FTE}} = \frac{\$54,258,647}{310.04} = \$175,003.44 \text{ Per FTE}$$

On average, each employee at Example Hospital in the past year completed work that resulted in net revenues for the organization of $175,003.44.

There are several other relationships that an operations manager can evaluate in assessment of operational productivity in a hospital or other health care facility. However, a critical part of using operational metrics is to compare those calculated values to industry benchmarks or trending calculated values of these metrics over time to determine if changes over time show improvement or decline in operational performance. The metrics described here can be compared to benchmarks established by health care industry organizations such as the American

Hospital Association or the Healthcare Financial Management Association. Use of industry benchmarks can be valuable for measuring how an organization compares with other organizations, but they should be used with caution. Each hospital will vary based on local labor markets, availability of resources, the payment resources of patients in the service area, and the general priorities and values of the organization's management and governing body.

OTHER OPERATIONAL METRICS

The operational metrics described so far focus primarily on the production efficiency of a health care organization, evaluating the number of inputs per output produced. Depending on the organization's strategic objectives, other metrics not described here may be considered as—or more—important. A key step in monitoring the correct operational metrics for an organization is to establish organizational goals and then link the metrics to outcomes that support such goals. For example, an organization may be performing poorly on clinical goals used to determine payment rates (such as the Value-Based Purchasing Program or "pay for performance" under the Patient Protection and Affordable Care Act of 2010). To improve performance toward those clinical care quality objectives, the organization may establish a patient safety goal and management may decide to adopt monitoring of medication transcription accuracy as a way to reduce patient medication errors. Another example would be comparison of patient treatment records against an established care plan to determine compliance with evidence-based treatment guidelines. Such an approach may be useful in organizations that incur financial losses on patients whose care is reimbursed on a prospective payment basis. Establishing a baseline treatment plan under which the organization can keep costs below reimbursed amounts, as well as monitoring compliance with the plan, can help lead the organization to improved financial results. In this way, the organization has set an overall objective and identified a metric or multiple metrics to measure performance that supports achievement of the objective. Such metrics may not have published industry standard benchmarks, but nonetheless they have value in driving organizational performance improvement. In this situation, the organization must develop its own benchmarks or at least a baseline level for use in monitoring performance.

Developing a baseline level of performance for operational metric evaluation is a multistep process:

1. Define the measurement and specific data elements to be used in calculation of the metric.

2. Establish any inclusion or exclusion criteria for data used in developing a baseline (such as excluding patients with a low hemoglobin value from counting compliance with an antithrombolytic medication guideline for patients seen in the emergency room with a suspected heart attack).

3. Define the data-gathering methodology not only for the baseline but for ongoing monitoring (such as manual chart reviews or ad hoc data queries from an electronic medical record database).

4. Establish the desired outcome to be measured by the metric, such as improving accuracy in assessing a patient's medical history to establish the presence of a community-acquired infection (which can defend against an insurer denial of payment for a suspected hospital-acquired infection).

Once these baseline development guides are established and affected parties have had the chance to buy in to the use of selected metrics in managing operational performance, the organization must gather historical data and calculate a baseline level for the metric of interest. A helpful guideline in terms of the amount of historical data to use is at least the number of months in a typical operating cycle for the organization so that seasonal variations in volume, resource availability, or other external influences on performance can be taken into account. This usually translates into a minimum of 3 to 6 months but could be as long as a year if necessary to fully account for seasonal variation (as in areas where patient census fluctuates widely due to normal phenomena such as seasonal migration of retirees). If the data have not previously been collected in the organization, it is essential that someone other than the primary data gatherer validate the data to assure accuracy in and relevance to the baseline establishment process.

Once a baseline is established, it can be used by the organization to evaluate ongoing performance with the metric. However, the baseline should be validated after a few months of use to be sure that it is relevant to actual practice in the organization (usually after 3 to 6 months) and then on a routine basis thereafter. A part of the validation process must be to track not only the chosen metric but also performance against the organizational goal to verify that the association between the selected metric and goal achievement remains reasonable. It would not make sense for an organization to track performance on an operational metric that did not lead to the desired overall result.

Assuming that the metric tracks with desired organizational outcomes, it must be integrated into the organization's routine management reporting structure and managers responsible for performance on that metric identified. Managers whose performance is measured using a new operational metric must be able to participate in development of the metric, calculate the baseline measurement, and, above all, influence performance on the metric. It is an ineffective use of organizational resources to measure performance on a metric that managers cannot influence. Moreover, holding managers accountable for performance on a metric that they cannot influence will lead to frustration, burnout, and loss of management talent to the organization.

USING OPERATIONAL METRICS

Multiple levels of managers within a health care organization can use operational metrics. However, the perspective on which metrics will be used is based on the manager's role and responsibility within the organization. In fact, the adoption of operational metrics represents a strategic decision for the organization, which must consider how the metrics will be used to manage the organization. Also, the availability of data for calculating these metrics should be considered before a management approach using these operational metrics is adopted. Finally, the organization's priorities toward financial performance, operational efficiency, or measurement of quality outcomes must be considered in developing the operational metrics used by management.

The number of metrics used by the organization should be manageable without the devotion of significant additional resources to calculating metrics or preparing routine reports on them (Ronen & Pliskin, 2006). The use of operational metrics should improve efficiency in the organization, not create a need for additional resources that do not add to the production of patient care services. Therefore, managers must balance the need for detailed evaluation of operational performance and the available resources to report on and assist in monitoring the metrics. One guideline is to use between 5 and 12 metrics in an average-size organization and no more than 20 in a large organization or multifacility system.

Reporting on the metrics should occur as frequently as is practical considering the caveat about devoting additional resources to reporting on operational metrics. Again, additional resources that are not devoted to the production of patient care outputs should be weighed against the value of detailed monitoring and reporting of operational metrics. Generally speaking, reports on operational metrics should be prepared with the same frequency as routine financial reports in the organization (Langabeer, 2009). If reports are presented to management on monthly, quarterly, and yearly bases, then reports on operational metrics should be prepared in the same time frames. The only exception to this rule would be if management felt it necessary to monitor certain high-risk or high-priority metrics on a daily basis during a time of challenging financial results. Examples of such daily monitoring metrics would be average length of stay, occupancy percentage, average daily census, adjusted average daily census, and FTE/AOB. These metrics provide a valuable overview of the organization's production efficiency, and improvement on these metrics over time should lead to enhanced financial performance.

CHAPTER SUMMARY

Operational metrics can be very useful in putting observed organizational performance into perspective, either from a production efficiency viewpoint, where the number of inputs per unit of output is monitored, or from a clinical performance angle. Be it units of input per unit of output, cost per unit of output, or percentage compliance with a clinical care plan, an operational metric can provide health care managers with a quick assessment of operational performance, especially when set against an industry benchmark or an internal baseline value. As with all management tools, operational metrics must be used with some sense of nuance and not as a unilateral measuring stick for which compliance is absolute. Buy-in from affected parties, use of rational comparative standards relevant to organizational goals, ongoing validation of the standards, and timely reporting on metrics are all a part of developing a meaningful mechanism for measuring operational performance.

KEY TERMS

Adjusted average daily census (AADC)

Adjusted discharge

Adjusted occupied bed (AOB)

Adjusted patient day

Admission

Average daily census (ADC)

Average length of stay

Discharge

Full-time equivalent employees per adjusted occupied bed (FTE/AOB)

Full-time equivalent employees per occupied bed (FTE/OB)

Input

Midnight census

Net revenue per FTE

Occupancy percentage

Operating expense per adjusted discharge

Operating expense per adjusted occupied bed

Operating expense per discharge

Operating expense per occupied bed	Procedures per employee
Output	Production function
Patient day	Productive hours per unit

DISCUSSION QUESTIONS

1. Describe the difference between a unit of input and the cost of an input, and identify the advantages and disadvantages of each for use in operational metrics.
2. Discuss why the traditional patient day does not fully account for hospital outputs, and describe how that output measure is refined to take into account the other outputs of a hospital production function.
3. What are some sources for benchmarks of the operational metrics described in this chapter? Why are they important, and what are the limitations to their use?
4. Describe the process of developing an internal operational metric.
5. Should a manager whose performance will be measured with an operational metric participate in its selection and development? Why or why not?

REFERENCES

Langabeer, J. R. (Ed.). (2009). *Performance improvement in hospitals and health systems.* Chicago, IL: Healthcare Information and Management Systems Society.

Ronen, B., & Pliskin, J. S. (2006). *Focused operations management for health services organizations.* San Francisco, CA: Jossey-Bass.

8

Basics of Project Management

GOALS OF THIS CHAPTER

1. Understand how project management contributes to project success.
2. Describe the project manager's role.
3. Understand some of the project tools that can be used.
4. Explore how change management practices influence project outcomes.

Operations management requires that hospitals continuously look for ways to achieve better outcomes. Searching for improved business processes, enhanced staff productivity, and streamlined logistics implies that organizations must continue to change. Only if activities evolve can they improve, and in hospitals there are significant opportunities for improvement. This means that projects will become much more prevalent as organizations seek to refine and improve operations. However, managing projects in hospitals is complex, given power and political tensions that can exist between business and medical staff. By understanding the role of project management and using principles of change, managers can positively achieve desired outcomes. The purpose of this chapter is to describe the tools and theories of project and change management and discuss the role that internal consulting departments play in such endeavors.

DEFINING PROJECTS

A **project** is an organized effort involving a sequence of activities that are temporarily being performed to achieve a desired outcome. Projects are temporary in that they have both a beginning and an ending, they have objectives that state their purpose and function, and they exist only to achieve a specific outcome or deliverable. The **outcome** is the result, end point, or change in performance from a project. There are many types of outcomes in health care projects that should be improved: increased patient safety, lower costs and enhanced efficiencies of clinical or administrative processes, higher quality of care, and greater patient or customer satisfaction, to name a few. A project is distinct from operations in that projects are typically centered on identifying or implementing new or changed business processes, information technology, or other enhancements. Project results typically become operational once the effort has been finalized and deployed.

The Project Management Institute, one of the largest associations devoted to enhancing the body of knowledge for project professionals, defines **project management** as "applying, tools, techniques, skills, and knowledge to a project activities in order bring about successful results and meet project requirements" (Heldman, 2013, p. 8). A **project manager** is the individual who leads the planning and daily activities to achieve the project deliverables. Some examples of health care projects for operations management include the following:

- Deployment of a pharmaceutical ordering and inventory system.
- Implementation of a new picture archiving and communication system.
- Analysis of specific patient-centric business processes.
- Design and construction of a new facility or building.
- Nursing labor optimization.
- Reengineering effort to reduce staffing levels in key areas.
- Startup of a new department, clinic, or operational process.

Although it is difficult to estimate with precision, it is likely that project work in growing hospitals can represent more than one-third of all work effort for managers and professionals. Operational managers are the beneficiaries and eventual owners of the changed or new process or system once the project has been completed, so it is important that they are fully involved in managing the project from start to finish. As such, the skills and techniques used to manage projects become extremely important. Even if a skilled facilitator or consultant exists to help support the project, operational managers must understand the basic concepts and employ the necessary tools to ensure that the project is successful.

POWER, INFLUENCE, AND PROJECT MANAGEMENT

Projects require sponsorship to secure financing approval and to ensure commitment of the right people on the project from the outset. One of the problems in hospitals, however, is centered around the well-documented struggles over political power among different factions (Rovin, 2001). Physicians and nurses have historically maintained relationships that are mutually reliant on one another for patient management, yet physicians have clearly dominated the power struggle. Similarly, physician and business leaders clash in certain decision-making processes, where physicians' dominance in the key production process (i.e., clinical care) provides influence and power over others due to their medical expertise and control of the customer (i.e., patient). In academic medical centers and teaching hospitals, struggles for control between medical and academic factions are also very common. Therefore, projects that require physician sponsorship or commitment may require additional levels of networking and "selling" to obtain support from key constituents.

In many larger hospitals, however, the power struggle that most commonly exists in business operational projects is tension among managers of different clinical or administrative units. It is not uncommon to have issues of control and influence become more important than the project itself. Tension arises from even the smallest details, such as whose name appears as sponsor and who leads the project, which can often stall projects indefinitely.

The role of formal versus informal power bases becomes important because, even if an executive sponsors the project, there may be an informal power source (at a "lower" level in the organization) that can influence the approval and direction of the project from the beginning. Other department leaders may question a project's motives, especially if it reaches beyond one department's processes, which creates uncertainty and risk for others. Achieving support, commitment, and buy-in from the outset of any project that is multifunctional or multidisciplinary is required to ensure that the project moves forward.

Cooperation and collaboration from all key stakeholders are required. Often this means that project managers must schedule appointments and personally sell the project to others. Education about the project's purpose and charter usually helps remove any uncertainty about a project. Continuous communication also helps to reinforce the concept that the project is important and that there is no hidden motive or purpose.

PROJECT SUCCESS

A hospital project is typically sponsored, or supported, by the manager or executive who has the most vested interest in the results or outcomes. As discussed earlier, the goal of a project must be to significantly alter the performance of a process or the outcome for the patient. Outcomes can be focused on efficiency, quality, safety, patient-centered service levels, or any other performance dimension for a health care organization. A project sponsor ensures that the project manager has all necessary resources and helps eliminate organizational obstacles that might arise. The project sponsor helps recruit the project manager and kicks off the project correctly, which helps ensure that the project manager gets off to a solid start.

The goal of the project manager is to successfully move the project through all phases, from start to finish, while ultimately achieving the outcomes defined at the outset. A **deliverable** is the tangible outcome that results from the project. Essentially, the deliverable represents the benefits, or the reason a project was initially undertaken. Project deliverables can include successful implementation of a new information system, a report of findings or analyses, a new facility, or a changed process. Deliverables also include customer satisfaction and quality levels, which are expected to increase as a result of the project. Financial or operational performance improvements are also deliverables for many projects. Achieving these expected deliverables represents one component of success in a project.

Project success centers on achieving optimization of four key variables: deliverables, resource investment, scope, and time lines. This is depicted in **Figure 8–1**. These variables are highly interrelated, and a change in one affects the others. For example, reducing the original amount of resources invested in the project by 50% could affect the completion date of the project, which could have a potentially negative effect on overall achievement of the project deliverables. Similarly, a large change in scope in the middle of a project could extend the overall time line, and a change in deliverables expected could affect scope and resource requirements.

Resource investment represents the budget for financial commitments, as well as staffing and other key resources. This investment level is typically defined up front, sometimes prior to or during the project planning phase. This is commonly called the *budget*, and it is expected that project managers use project resources efficiently so that the project comes in at or under budget, assuming no changes in scope occur that are outside of their control.

The scope represents the boundaries of a project. It limits the types of benefits or deliverables that are being sought, as well as defines which ones are not. Typically, scope is limited by process or organizational boundaries. For example,

FIGURE 8–1 Defining Project Success

a project may decide to examine all activities that fall within the diagnostic imaging processes or all activities undertaken by the radiology department.

Time lines represent the critical dates for major milestones. Time lines define the beginning and end point of the project, as well as the sequencing of other activities and milestones along the way. A **milestone** is a key date by which a major project deliverable should be achieved. Time lines are extremely important for projects because they help define the expectations for when activities should occur, resources will be consumed, and the project will achieve the desired outcomes. Time lines represent significant scheduling efforts, which will be described later.

KEY PHASES OF PROJECT MANAGEMENT

There are four distinct phases in project management: pre-project approval, project organization and definition, project scheduling and design, and project control and management. These phases are shown in **Figure 8–2**. Each of these stages is critical to achieving the desired outcomes for project success.

Pre-Project Approval

As described earlier, the key to achieving positive outcomes on a project is to establish reasonable estimates of the benefits and returns of a project and to ensure

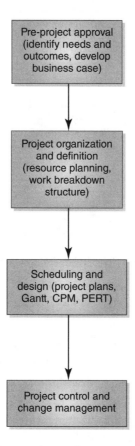

FIGURE 8-2 Phases of Project Management

that the total costs do not exceed the benefits. Some benefits may be quantifiable (e.g., increased revenues, expanded market share, reduced costs), but many benefits may be qualitative (e.g., higher quality, system end of life).

In many organizations, the process of obtaining approval for the project entails convincing management and investment committees that the benefits will be realized and are worth the risk. These two concepts—risks and realization—are key to a project's approval. **Risks** are the factors that jeopardize project success or that cause potential impairment or delay. All risks must be mitigated to achieve project success and expected benefits. A plan outlining the risks and mitigation strategies is a key project deliverable. **Realization** of these benefits is a result of how successful the organization is at mitigating the risks and adapting to changes that arise during the project.

In most hospitals, the project approval phase is quite lengthy. If a project is funded out of the normal operating budget, the approval process may be as simple as convincing department management of the benefits, approach, and costs. In more complex environments, or where capital funds are being allocated, the approval process may be more complex and could entail several levels of governance, including approvals from local management, the budget department, and separate capital investment committee approvals. In these environments, a structured business case should be used to thoroughly document all aspects of the project. Questions and issues that the business case should fully explore are shown in **Table 8–1**.

Project Organization and Definition

Once approval is obtained, the project enters an early phase called *project organization and definition*. This phase has also been called *analysis*, *planning*, or *discovery*. In this phase, the primary tasks are to document all aspects of the

Table 8–1 Elements of a Business Case

Demographics	• List project sponsor, manager, contact details
Business Challenges and Needs	• Describes the challenges faced by the process or department • Describes issues and causes of problems faced • Describe how these opportunities impact performance and contribute to the organization's vision
Business Drivers	• Describe the key performance indicators (KPIs) and how the project or technology can impact these indicators • Document benchmark figures for comparison against others to show marginal improvement to be gained
Proposed Solution	• Document the proposed solution • Describe implications on organization, policy, processes, or system architecture • Document the Risks and how they can be mitigated
Investment	• Define the proposed investment • Estimate the total costs, with annual cash flow breakdown • Model the return on investment analysis (NPV, IRR, payback) • Define recommendations for moving forward • List all key assumptions • Define the project time lines and key milestones

business process, including use of the process engineering tools described earlier. This phase should confirm and refine all of the assumptions listed in the business case and turn the high-level requirements into more detailed specifications. Understanding the specific details, specifications, and requirements for the project is essential, because they can be included in the project only if they are clearly identified and focused.

One of the key aspects of project planning is to identify the **work breakdown structure** of the project, which decomposes project activities into more detailed components to allow for better planning. This phase uses a hierarchy to organize tasks, where the top level is the highest one, and each subsequent level below the top provides more detail for the task above it. Planning typically involves allocating resources and time lines for the highest-level tasks, while the next phase (scheduling) focuses on aspects of the more detailed tasks.

This phase requires interviews with key participants, thorough documentation of the process (with aims of identifying bottlenecks and issues), and direct observations and analyses of process outcomes. This phase should be recorded thoroughly in a detailed design document that lists the key requirements and specifications. A project plan is also a key output of this process, which shows resource assignments, time lines, and milestones for each task.

Project Scheduling and Design

The project scheduling and design process takes the specifications and maps them against detailed activities and tasks. Project schedules are commonly viewed in Gantt chart form. A **Gantt chart**, named for its founder Henry Gantt, shows activities as blocks or bars over time. It is an intuitive chart used to show resources and time allocations for key tasks, and it supports monitoring of activities during the management phase.

A Gantt chart is very useful; it ensures that all activities are carefully planned for and that the total duration or activity times are considered. The use of a resource field helps isolate which person or department is responsible for the task, and the use of horizontal bars shows project activity over a time line. A sample Gantt chart is depicted in **Figure 8–3**.

A Gantt chart is often used by managers because it is fairly straightforward to understand and easy to visualize. There really is no sophistication or optimization to arrange the sequence of activities that appear on the Gantt chart, but once they are included, the chart simplifies the management and tracking process.

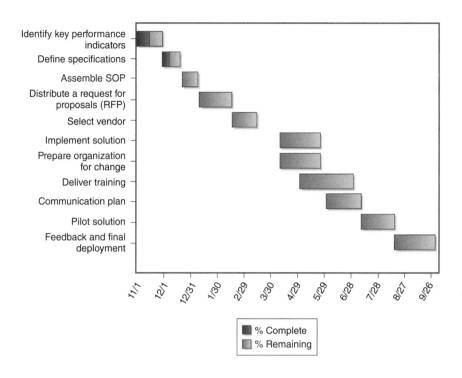

FIGURE 8–3 Scheduling Projects–Gantt Charts

Two of the more common methods to build sophistication into projects are critical path method and program evaluation and review technique. The **critical path method (CPM)** is a technique that helps identify the longest path in a project, therefore making it the most critical. If delays occur in the longest path, then a delay will occur in the overall project, while a similar delay in a noncritical path does not necessarily cause the project to be delayed. CPM attempts to determine overall time estimates for each activity and then uses predecessor (i.e., which task leads) and successor (i.e., which task follows) relationships for each node (O'Brien & Plotnick, 2006). A node is an activity or task and is connected to other nodes via lines or arcs. Using these inter-dependencies, constraints, and time estimates, it is possible to visually draw various network diagrams, such as a CPM model. Once the network diagram is constructed, it becomes the basis for the Gantt chart. Software tools such as Microsoft Project have built-in network diagramming and critical path tools that use the information the project manager provides to build the critical

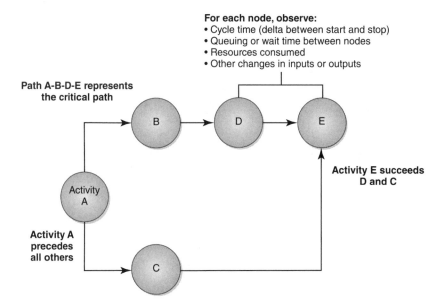

For each node, observe:
• Cycle time (delta between start and stop)
• Queuing or wait time between nodes
• Resources consumed
• Other changes in inputs or outputs

Path A-B-D-E represents the critical path

Activity A precedes all others

Activity E succeeds D and C

FIGURE 8–4 Nodes in a Network

path. A sample network diagram showing concepts of a node, critical path, and interdependencies among activities is shown in **Figure 8–4**.

A **program evaluation and review technique (PERT)** diagram is very similar, except that instead of using only a singular time estimate (e.g., task 1 takes 3 days), it requires estimates for three cases: a best case, a worst case, and a most likely case. A best case would assume no delays or issues, while a worst case assumes major resource conflicts or delays; the most likely is a conservative estimate somewhere between the worst and the best cases. PERT models use a range of estimates that are more probable and likely. Mathematically, this is calculated as follows, where T_e = expected time, O = optimistic estimate, P = pessimistic or worst-case estimate, and M = most likely time duration:

$$T_e = (O + P + 4M) \div 6$$

For example, assume that a task will most likely be completed in 5 days, but optimistically (if all goes well) it could be completed in just 2 days, and worst case it will take 10 days. The PERT calculation to use in the network diagram and Gantt charts would be 5.33 days, or

$$[2 + 10 + (4 \times 5)] \div 6 = (32 \div 6) = 5.33$$

PERT models help simulate project duration ranges that typically generate more reasonable project time lines. Both CPM and PERT are thoroughly discussed in traditional textbooks, but based on this author's research, they are not employed significantly in practice. They are useful tools, and as the level of sophistication increases in health care project management, so, too, will the use and deployment of advanced network diagrams such as these.

Project Control and Management

Once projects have been approved, defined, and designed, they enter the execution phase and require careful management to ensure tight control over time lines, costs, and scope. Two tools are useful to help improve management. The first is a Gantt chart, as discussed earlier, which helps track projects once they are underway to ensure progress against time line expectations. Another tool is a project dashboard or scorecard, which outlines all key aspects relative to the project—budgeted versus actual costs; changes in scope; estimated time lines; earned value to date, if any; project risks; and other updates on the project deliverable or progress.

The objective of project management entails finding ways to keep the project team motivated and the activities on task to achieve desired outcomes. Use of tracking tools and leading indicators helps managers foresee potential problems or risks before they arise so that prescriptive action can be taken.

CHANGE MANAGEMENT

Well-documented psychological research supports the idea that most people dislike change—or rather, dislike the uncertainty that accompanies change (Landy, 1989). Even change for the better is still change, which can cause both physical and emotional discomfort. Change disrupts people's daily activities, introduces chaos, and generally wreaks havoc for most individuals.

Projects create change. If no change or improvements were necessary, then there would be no value in establishing and managing a project. Because projects are organized and designed to change an existing process, technology, or practice, and because change is generally perceived to be negative, it is important to minimize the disruptions caused by change.

The formula for overcoming change can be shown mathematically as:

$$Y = f(m,p,a,r)$$

where

Y = successful change management

m = management and leadership skills

p = an operational plan with a vision and strategy

a = alignment of incentives with those who are sponsoring the project and those who are working on and for the project

r = adequate resources

Without all four components of this equation, change management cannot be successful. Leaving just one of these out creates uncertainty, frustration, or ambiguity for the organization.

- Management and leadership help inspire the team and set the direction.
- Plans help ensure that the vision can be executed and set strategies for achieving the results.
- Alignment of incentives helps keep the project and organization on target.
- Resources (e.g., financial, space, technology, equipment, and personnel) are necessary to ensure that the work can get done and the strategies are carried out.

One of the best ways to ensure that fear of change does not kill the project is to guarantee cooperation and collaboration up front from all central constituents. This is often called **buy-in**, where sponsors and managers craft a story or vision for their change and then obtain support from others to ensure that no organizational obstacles prevent the project's advancement. A similar concept is the use of **partnering**, or establishing mutually beneficial and cooperative relationships with others, where trust and teamwork help create synergies. Partnering with others in similar roles or adjacent departments can help pool resources and energy to achieve greater project success.

Thinking systematically about the behaviors and expectations that all key stakeholders of change desire is one way to ensure appropriate communication and change management. Understanding the key relationships that must be nurtured to build trust and support is essential to avoiding potential pitfalls.

Another way to master change is to document and obtain approval for all changes to the plan, project scope, or resource commitments. This change documentation should be supported by a business case, and modifications should be understood relative to their effect on schedule, costs, deliverables, and resource utilization.

Communication about the change is also important. Keeping communication simple and on point (or relevant) is essential. Continuous communication is also necessary. Over-communicating, as long as it follows the key message and helps to reduce ambiguity, is usually much less of a problem than under-communicating.

Besides gaining the buy-in of influential people, the participation of all of those affected by the change should be encouraged. Getting people involved and vested in the change helps reduce fears, stimulate positive morale and feedback about the project, and obtain better results. Giving people a "voice" in the change is often more important than the change itself.

A common problem is that managers focus too much on the details when communicating change. Focusing on the high-level or big picture educates people about the purposes of the change and the rationale behind it. Many are fearful of change when they suspect ulterior motives. If you expect that most people are afraid of the change—possibly because they fear they may lose their jobs or otherwise be less valuable to the organization—then address those fears early and often. You can overcome or minimize the resistance to change by keeping the communication channels open.

RAPID PROTOTYPING

In many hospitals and health care organizations, projects consume more resources and take significantly longer than a similar project in other industries. Several factors make these organizational models more complex; they also create problems for management, because delays and excessive implementation times are two of the major reasons projects fail, have budget overruns, or face significant delays.

One way to avoid these issues is to deploy rapid prototyping. **Rapid prototyping** is a concept whereby ideas and solutions can be targeted toward a very small sample to see if the solution improves results prior to wide-scale implementation. Rapid prototyping is commonly used in software development to quickly turn requirements and specifications into a solution, which can then be modified as needed. Iterative and incremental successes in projects help demonstrate success faster and can generate additional ideas for improvement. Rapid prototyping and pilots are similar in that they use small samples and attempt to demonstrate limited success prior to full deployment.

More than anything, rapid prototyping involves two factors: proven methodology and supporting culture. The methodology used to deploy projects must be established and workable to ensure that the project team does not reinvent the wheel. A methodology that is free from ambiguity is a requirement. But, more important, there has to be a supporting culture or environment in the organization that encourages risk taking and the desire for speed and flexibility—while acknowledging the potential for failure. Rapid prototyping will result in some failures, but more can be learned from failures than from many successful projects. The right culture, which supports rapid prototyping, is essential to stimulate the team to deliver—and to discover.

RISKS INVOLVED IN PROJECT MANAGEMENT

It has been suggested that the chance of a complex project surviving and achieving all of the benefits it established early on is around 50% (Lucas, 1999). In other words, one out of every two projects will have issues in some form or fashion that could jeopardize their success. It is crucial that project risks are identified early and that a plan to mitigate these risks is put in place. Any of the following factors can contribute to project failures:

- Long implementation cycles.
- Large dollar commitments.
- New, immature, or innovative technologies.
- Inexperienced employees.
- Lack of project sponsorship or management.
- Lack of formalized documentation or procedures.
- Misuse of tools and techniques for project tracking.
- Lack of training.
- Failure to launch or begin the project successfully.
- Poor communication.
- Changing priorities or scope of project.
- Lack of financial resources.
- Too many or too few people involved in the project.
- Inferior facilitation and coordination in project meetings.
- Organizational politics.
- Lack of preparation or training for a new process or system prior to implementation.
- Lack of alignment between departments.
- No pilot or prototype to prove the concept.

These risks can be mitigated if they are considered early on in the project planning phase and then proactively monitored during each of the following phases. Risks should be documented and necessary adjustments made to all Gantt and CPM diagrams.

DEPARTMENTS OF PERFORMANCE IMPROVEMENT

Many larger hospitals have created departments focused on performance improvement—sometimes called *management engineering*. The objectives of this department are to apply industrial engineering techniques to control costs and improve outcomes (Smalley, 1982). The management engineering department is often focused on implementing quality management processes, using continuous process improvement techniques, developing operational plans, administering patient satisfaction surveys, performing accreditation, and managing complex projects.

Some of the specific activities that performance improvement departments can undertake—and that are severely lacking in hospitals—include analyzing the productivity and economic effect of information technology, managing performance scorecards and benchmarking processes, and performing advanced process engineering. Rollout of Six Sigma and other continuous process techniques is also high on the list of priorities for most management engineering departments.

Training and education for management engineers in health care is lacking. This text elaborates on the concepts and techniques necessary for management engineers to be successful, because management engineers rely extensively on the operations management discipline. In addition, very few comprehensive, structured training programs exist—although this is starting to change as universities begin to recognize the need for these skills. As this evolves, the more formalized quantitative techniques prevalent in other industries will be adapted to the health care profession to provide a toolkit that is relevant to the unique challenges facing health care.

Several professional associations exist to support management engineers and to assist with networking and resource sharing. The Healthcare Information and Management Systems Society (www.himss.org) is the largest group of professionals, although it focuses primarily on the issue of information technology and to a much lesser degree on management engineering and performance improvement. Within this organization, a task force called *Management Engineering and Performance Improvement* focuses exclusively on sharing information and building educational tools and programs to advance the performance improvement profession. Another excellent association that represents operations and quantitative management professionals across all industries is the Institute for Operations Research and the Management Sciences (www.informs.org). Similarly, the Society for Health Systems (www.shsweb.org) is a valuable resource for management engineers to share information, learn new techniques, and network with other similar-minded professionals.

CHAPTER SUMMARY

A project is an organized effort involving a sequence of activities that are temporarily being performed to achieve a desired outcome. Projects in health care are becoming very extensive, as technology and process innovation are used to control costs and improve results. More sophisticated management of complex projects is necessary if health care projects are to achieve success. Projects require sponsorship to gain support, and often tension and power struggles ignite that could kill a concept before it is even begun.

Projects typically move through four phases. They start with pre-project approval, using business cases and partnering to obtain support and funding for the concept. Projects then get staffed, and a project plan assigns resources to key activities, while requirements and specifications are gathered. Project scheduling and design create network diagrams and paths that are optimized to achieve the desired time lines, while Gantt charts are used to visually track progress against plans. It is important that project managers mitigate all major risks to achieve project success, including being on time, within budget, and within scope, all while realizing the benefits that were defined at the outset.

KEY TERMS

Buy-in	Project
Critical path method (CPM)	Project management
Deliverable	Project manager
Gantt chart	Rapid prototyping
Milestone	Realization
Outcome	Risks
Partnering	Work breakdown structure
Program evaluation and review technique (PERT)	

DISCUSSION QUESTIONS

1. How does a project relate to daily operations?
2. What defines a successful outcome for a project?
3. How does a program evaluation and review technique diagram differ from a critical path method?

4. What are the components of a business case?
5. What are the four phases of project management?
6. If a project is complex, which change management techniques may be necessary?
7. Describe the four key elements necessary to master change.
8. What are some common risks in large, complex projects?
9. What is rapid prototyping?
10. What role does management engineering play in process improvement and project management?

EXERCISE PROBLEMS

1. Assume that a project has an expected total duration of 25 days, but several optimistic employees feel that it can be completed in as little as 18 days, while others expect it to take nearly 40 days. Using program evaluation and review technique calculations, what is the project duration to be used in project Gantt charts and other tracking tools?
2. If a critical path method calculation of project duration was 25 days, how does the program evaluation and review technique calculation in Question 1 compare?

REFERENCES

Heldman, K. (2013). *Project management professional exam study guide* (6th ed.). Indianapolis, IN: John Wiley & Sons.

Landy, F. J. (1989). *Psychology of work behavior.* Pacific Grove, CA: Wadsworth.

Lucas, H. C., Jr. (1999). *Information technology and the productivity paradox: Assessing the value of investing in IT.* New York, NY: Oxford University Press.

O'Brien, J. J., & Plotnick, F. L. (2006). *CPM in construction management* (6th ed.). New York, NY: McGraw-Hill.

Rovin, S. (2001). *Medicine and business: Bridging the gap.* Sudbury, MA: Jones and Bartlett.

Smalley, H. E. (1982). *Hospital management engineering: A guide to the improvement of hospital management systems.* Englewood Cliffs, NJ: Prentice Hall.

CHAPTER 9

Operational Planning

GOALS OF THIS CHAPTER

1. Understand the operational planning process.
2. Calculate breakeven analyses as part of new program or service development.
3. Describe analyses used to define the external environment.
4. Describe how operations support clinical strategies.

Creating strategy with a focus on operational excellence requires thought and planning. Rick Page (2002) coined the phrase "hope is not a strategy," which implies that the future will become reality only by carefully envisioning it, preparing for it, and then executing it. Chance and luck should not determine the effectiveness of health care organizations. Yet many hospitals and health care organizations do not carefully plan their operations; in the absence of a strategy, the results are usually less than stellar. This chapter provides an overview of how to use planning cycles to improve operations.

WHY PLAN?

Organizations plan in order to survive. It is one of the most vital management functions necessary for hospital growth, positioning, and effective execution (Zuckerman, 2005). Operational planning involves mapping the external opportunities and threats with the internal strengths and weaknesses to define strategic alternatives and stake out an appropriate competitive position. The output of planning is typically a plan that defines the specific functional strategies to employ for each dimension of business strategy.

Planning is a discovery process in which organizations define their markets, assess internal operations, and craft a course of action. However, the process of planning is more important than the product. Many people think that planning is nothing more than the "plan"—a written document that sits on a shelf, adds little value, and can be easily discarded. In fact, the plan, when written down, should be short, concise, and actionable. **Actionable** refers to the ability of an organization to execute the proposed changes and quickly address priorities. The insights gained from the planning process, however, help in many ways, as managers think about opportunities, brainstorm new services, or analyze historical performance. The process is important in that it provides the organization with shared concepts about the market, competition, changing technologies, and overall direction. The process allows for mutual discovery of information and should bring consensus among a wide variety of stakeholders. One of the more important results of strategic business planning is alignment among the hospital's administrators about where the hospital is headed and how it is going to get there, such as which product markets to invest in and focus on. This shared vision of future direction and goals is essential for success in turbulent environments.

THE PLANNING PROCESS

All health care organizations have a clinical strategy. They offer certain types of provider-based services to certain types of patients. They target their service offerings to the patients they can diagnose and treat the best; this is why some facilities focus exclusively on oncology or pediatrics. Alternatively, some larger facilities offer a broad, comprehensive clinical strategy for serving all markets through inpatient and outpatient services. Whichever clinical strategy is pursued, it is imperative that the operational plans and strategies support the clinical strategies. For example, a facility with a high Medicaid population might need an operational strategy that is based on efficiency and low cost. A 24-hour, tier 1 emergency center would need a complementary operational strategy that makes resources and supplies available around the clock. Operational strategies must support clinical priorities.

Effective operations planning processes have four primary phases: analyze operations and environment, generate strategic alternatives, deploy strategies, and measure and review. **Figure 9-1** presents a summary diagram of the planning process. Each of these stages will be discussed in more detail throughout the chapter.

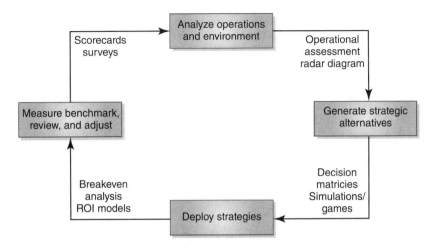

FIGURE 9-1 The Process of Crafting Operations Strategy

ANALYZE OPERATIONS AND ENVIRONMENT

The initial phase in the operations planning process is to analyze the internal operations as well as the external environment. There are multiple steps within this phase, starting with the selection process for the planning team members.

Build the Right Team

Prior to beginning the business planning process, critical issues about how to organize the planning efforts must be addressed. Choices have to be made about members of the planning team, representation from internal and external stakeholder groups, facilitation, timing and deliverable dates, and strategic analysis tools.

Choosing the planning team members wisely is critical to the success of the planning process. There are two levels of business planning: one at the strategic level and one at the clinic or unit level. For purposes of strategic planning, which involves decisions at the highest levels, hospitals should use key line managers as much as possible. Hospital planning teams may comprise the chief executive officer, chief operations officer, chief financial officer, supply chain vice president, chief nursing officer, chief marketing officer, marketing vice president, and other executives responsible for other mission-critical functional areas, such as specific centers and clinics, as well as the director of strategic planning.

Because hospitals have to satisfy multiple stakeholders, it may be prudent to include representatives from several other groups as well. For example, it may make sense to include independent physician groups, trustees, vendors, system-level management, patients, or other key participants. As hospitals become more integrated, it will be valuable to have others involved in demand and market scanning activities.

Generally, it is important that planning teams be cross functional to represent the diverse needs of the entire organization. The team's composition should be based as much on the skills the participants possess as on position. The team should contain strategic thinkers (i.e., big picture, outside the box), who are highly respected and capable of implementing cultural and directional changes within the organization. In addition, the team must include a mix of more practical and tactical representatives. Having this combination of strategic and tactical thinkers allows the team to be innovative while also ensuring that the outcomes are realistic and capable of implementation. Most of the time, planning teams should not have more than 10 members to ensure that all participants contribute and are fully engaged in the process.

In almost all situations, because of the broad mix of participants and key topics for discussion, the planning process should be facilitated. A **facilitator** guides the discussion around core themes, maintains the independence and integrity of the process, and helps remove barriers. The most important role of facilitation is to keep the team moving forward and the process on schedule. Facilitators bring the methodology to the team, provide boundaries for discussion, and ensure that all participants are engaged and active. Facilitators are trained in the use of a variety of techniques to drive sessions, such as brainstorming, flowcharting, and force field analysis. Facilitators must have the respect of the planning team members and be strong enough to bring order and consensus to the process, while also being insightful and patient enough to promote conversation from all members.

Operations planning should be continuous. Traditional planning models based on an annual frequency are not robust or dynamic enough to respond to the continual challenges of a turbulent industry environment. Instead, the process should be conducted at much shorter intervals, such as every few weeks or months. Permanent staff members who support the process, such as staff from the marketing department or the planning group, should be continually providing new data on markets and competition, and the planning team must come together routinely to evaluate and make adjustments. In addition, the planning process must have short cycle times (i.e., they must not drag on indefinitely). Typically, if the planning process is frequent enough, the process should consume no more than 2 to 4 weeks, although this varies depending on the level of resources committed and the extent of time allocated to planning daily. To ensure that the process is being conducted properly, deliverables and milestones must be established for the process. Dates for each deliverable, such as final analysis of the external environment, must be in place so that the process cycle time can remain condensed.

Planning as a process has been described as more of an art than a science. Regardless, strategies must be based on real data and information as much as possible. Information comes from using analytical tools and techniques, such as game theory, market research, competitive intelligence, and scenario models. These types of tools ensure that strategies are dynamic and sophisticated and represent an accurate view of the environment.

Sufficient staff and information resources must be devoted to the planning process. Staff resources include those functional groups devoted to capturing and analyzing data for planning purposes, such as the planning and market research groups. Information resources include a variety of published secondary statistical data on the industry markets and needs, as well as internally generated primary data from customers, payers, and other stakeholders. There should also be adequate financial resources allocated to strategic planning to allow participants to conduct benchmarking trips and acquire necessary data and reference materials.

Assess the Current Operational Effectiveness

This step should explore the organization's capabilities, including whether processes are running smoothly, goals and outcomes are being met, patients and employees have high satisfaction levels, and accreditation and other standards are being upheld. Outcome measurements are particularly important to realize gaps in target versus actual performance. The result of internal analysis should be an identification of the strengths and weaknesses, plus a better understanding of the capabilities and competencies required that allow the industry to compete more effectively. This includes exploring the capacity and demand levels that currently exist and looking for misalignment or other balance issues.

The process of internal analysis includes an exploration of all operating characteristics of the health care organization, including a review of current strategies, performance, portfolio, structure, management style, systems, and financial resources. A **radar diagram** is a graphical analysis that shows target versus actual performance in key internal areas and identifies potential problem areas. To read a radar diagram, look for the differences or gaps that exist between the two lines (one represents actual current performance of each criterion, and the other provides an ideal or expected level). **Figure 9–2** provides a sample radar diagram commonly used for this purpose.

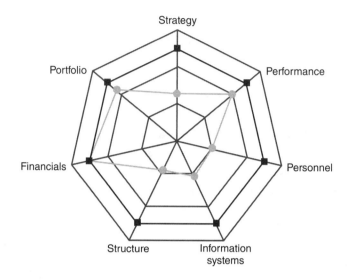

FIGURE 9–2 Analyzing Internal Operations Using Radar Diagrams

Internal analysis begins with a review of previous and current business and clinical strategies. Examining strategic initiatives and priorities provides a sense of whether the current strategy is sufficient to cope with changing competitive pressures. Questions to be addressed include:

- Is the strategy still sufficient?
- Is performance keeping pace with the industry?
- Is the strategy perceived as an industry leader or laggard?
- Do weaknesses exist that competing organizations are exploiting?
- Which issues exist that are not covered in the strategy?

Next, determine if the strategy is successful by analyzing historical and current performance in terms of quality and financial outcomes. Specific performance areas to investigate include clinical effectiveness (e.g., patient error rates, safety levels) and operational effectiveness (e.g., customer service levels, supply chain economics, average cost to perform key processes, labor productivity, margin profitability, and other key ratios). This analysis should include a comparison of performance over time to ensure that performance is improving, but it should also compare the industry's performance with other local competing organizations, as well as others considered to be exceptional organizations. Comparing an organization's performance against others helps provide a clearer picture of the strengths and weaknesses facing the industry.

In addition, performance analysis helps define the core competency for the organization. A **core competency** is an internal activity or process that the hospital performs really well relative to all other internal activities. For instance, the industry may be very good at securing research funding or implementing information systems. Performance analysis also helps define distinctive competencies for the industry. A **distinctive competency** is something the organization does really well relative to other organizations. Understanding both the core and distinctive competencies, in addition to the strengths and weaknesses, helps provide a visual map of how an organization is currently positioned to compete.

Portfolio analysis is used to help hospitals systematically assess their competitive position in each of the service lines they offer. With portfolio analysis, organizations should focus on the current profitability in each service line, the potential for market growth or demand shifts in each service line, and the capability or competencies that the industry has in each service line. Understanding where the service lines stand, both financially and in relation to the competition, will help determine if services should be added, eliminated, or pruned.

Compare Structure and Style

Typically, when reviewing internal influences on an organization, planners should consider the overall organizational structure and resulting management style that has evolved. Decisions on industry support service centralization versus decentralization, the role of a business unit manager in strategic initiatives, and how to measure business unit effectiveness are three critical issues to consider. An assessment as to whether the current structure and style complements or detracts from the strategy to be pursued is vital under this portion of internal analysis.

Strengths, Weaknesses, Opportunities, and Threats Analysis

The strengths, capabilities, and competencies of the local health care industry can be used to exploit the opportunities available in the market environment, and competitors' weaknesses exposed during the external analysis should become key components of the grand strategy. Weaknesses identified internally within an organization should be fortified or strengthened, either by investing more resources in those areas or eliminating them altogether.

A **strengths, weaknesses, opportunities, and threats (SWOT) analysis** is a thorough review of an organization's combination of these qualities. This analysis generates more questions that have to be addressed to match strategy to situation.

Issues that must be considered for opportunities include the following: Which strengths exist internally to capitalize on the opportunities in the market? Which resources will be required to pursue them? Will the organization have to increase, reduce, or maintain investments in certain product or service lines? Will, or have, any competitors already moved on these opportunities? What can be done to thwart those efforts? Issues that exist with regard to threats include addressing the following questions: Are these threats real? How can they be mitigated or avoided?

Similarly, when looking at strengths, key questions to address include: How can the organization's strengths be used to achieve a greater competitive advantage? How can any competitors' service lines or category successes be blocked by building on the strengths identified earlier in the analysis? Should these competencies be built up further by continuing investments, or should resources be invested elsewhere? Will these strengths be enough to achieve an advantage?

Finally, questions that should be addressed with regard to weaknesses include the following: How can competitors be prevented from exploiting the weaknesses identified? Can resources be invested in these areas to convert them into strengths, or at least make them neutral? Will these weaknesses prevent the organization from pursuing certain opportunities?

Assess Management and Information Systems

The planning process should assess the management and information systems in place that support the business strategies. Typically, one of the most important management systems is the pay and reward system used to provide incentives for executives and managers to achieve higher levels of productivity and effectiveness. Other key information systems to evaluate include medical informatics, pharmaceuticals, enterprise resource planning, and reporting and business intelligence systems. Questions to be addressed include: Do we have the right systems in place to inform and incentivize managers to make the right decisions? Does the current system enhance organizational effectiveness? Do current policies support organizational direction? Do changes in other systems, such as performance measurement, need to be implemented?

Evaluate Financial Resources

When comparing the internal environment of a hospital, it is extremely important to evaluate both the cost and the financial structure for departments and the overall organization. Referring to the *Health Care Finance for the Operations Manager* chapter will be helpful, as the key financial ratios and concepts it calculated and discussed should be implemented at this phase. Because every dollar of resources committed to one service line category has an opportunity cost in terms of what was given up, a cost comparison is important to determine if the level of resources committed to specific service lines is adequate and efficiently employed. Benchmark data from leading organizations about cost-effectiveness and cost structure relative to local competing organizations should be obtained in areas such as total industry volume, market share, consumer demand, and average costs.

Hospital financial position should also be thoroughly examined to ensure that the industry has sufficient funding and is efficiently employing those resources. Benchmark comparisons on debt position, financial returns, working capital, liquidity, and cash management are all important indicators of financial position and help quantify the financial implications of business strategy. Groups such as the International Benchmarking Clearinghouse and industry analysts tend to provide significant venues for benchmarking hospital performance relative to the competition.

Each of the components of internal analysis—strategy analysis, performance analysis, portfolio analysis, structure and style analysis, and financial analysis—helps shape the internal capabilities and competencies that the hospital has as part of its competitive weaponry. The strengths and weaknesses that result from these analyses form the basis for competitive strategy.

Analyze the External Environment

After carefully reviewing all aspects of the internal environment, operations managers should next analyze the external environment. The **external environment** includes all forces external to the industry that potentially influence business strategy. External analysis can be broken down into the four most significant external influences for an organization: customer, competitor, industry, and environment (Thompson & Strickland, 1998).

Strategies must be based on a thorough analysis of what the organization's current and potential customers want and need. If hospitals are to determine which products to offer and which markets to serve, the changing requirements of the customer have to be defined. In addition to the customers, an analysis of the changes in the major payer's motivation and needs must be explored.

When performing consumer or customer analysis, it is important to examine the major market segments in the industry. A market segment is best defined as a method of targeting specific customers in the market. It is possible to segment customers on the basis of their product needs, such as benefits sought. It is also possible to segment markets on any of the following demographics: geography, lifestyle, sex, age, income, usage levels, size, or application.

Customer analysis should also include a thorough analysis of the changing motivations and consumer behavior of both the industry purchasers and payers. Such demographic information helps link demand with overall market characteristics. Answers to a variety of questions could lead to changes in overall strategies:

- What motivates patients to come to this facility?
- Are customer demographics changing? How might this affect future demand?
- Which attributes of the service are important?
- Which valued-added services, options, extras, and components are desirable?
- Which objectives do customers (or patients) seek?
- Which changes in motivation are occurring or could occur?
- Are customers satisfied?
- Are there any unmet needs?

A thorough analysis of each of these aspects of the external customer analysis will yield useful insight into how to adapt the organization's strategy to better meet the changing needs of consumers. The customer value-added methodology identifies the clients who bring significant value to the hospital, which subsequently drives both customer service and supply chain business rules. This methodology should be implemented at this time. More details on the specific process are provided in the *Supply Chain Management* chapter.

Competitor Analysis

Competition should be thoroughly understood. As change or turbulence increases and financial returns continue to diminish, competitive pressures will escalate. Analyzing the competition makes your strategy more effective.

Competitive analysis requires the industry to focus on insights that influence strategy. Answers to key questions are required:

- Who are the competitors in these markets?
- How many competitors are there? How concentrated is the market?
- How strong a foothold do they have in the market?
- Why are competitors able to sustain market share?
- Which competitors should be the focus of attention? What are their strengths?
- What plans do competitors have for the short and long term?
- What do the competitors' systems and supply chain networks look like? How effective are they?

In addition, hospitals must focus on competing organizations individually and in networks. A thorough competitive assessment also includes a description of competitors' size, growth rates, and profitability. The culture of the competition should be examined, as should the competition's economics, including cost structure and margin. Finally, a review of the competitions' past and current strategies is essential to understanding potential future direction.

The success of an organization's strategies likely depends on its competitors' ability to defend their position or build a competitive advantage; thus, it is important to understand the competition's strengths and weaknesses in at least four key areas: product and service innovation, service delivery, marketing, and overall industry management.

Competitors could be strong in innovation if they have highly advanced research and development teams that continually drive new products to the marketplace. If competitors continually introduce new technology into the industry, or have high rates of commercialization or patents, they are quite innovative.

When delivering services, competitors could be strong or weak in terms of service delivery and organization, service quality level, extent of integration between competitors, and how easy they are to do business with. By examining customer retention rates, although these are often difficult to find, the strengths and weaknesses of the competition's service delivery becomes more evident.

Extensive competitor analysis includes a review of industry management. Does the competitions' management create a specific culture, or does it have loyal employees? Analysis of a competitor's turnover rates, strategic goals, and level of entrepreneurism provides a better picture of the strengths and weaknesses associated with management.

Finally, competitor analysis must focus on marketing programs. Specific insight into the brand or name recognition associated with various organizations is useful for determining the basis of competition. The focus that competing hospitals place on customers may be insightful for finding new markets or exploiting unmet needs. The current breadth and depth of competitors' product lines may highlight opportunities for new markets that might have otherwise been hidden. A review of the advertising and sales or business development strategies also helps determine the future strategic direction for each competitor.

Each of these areas of external competitor analysis is important for finding competitors' strengths and weaknesses. A summary matrix can be used to evaluate the competitions' strengths and weaknesses. A competitor's strength assessment matrix should be developed during the planning process by listing each of the key success factors that an industry must have to be successful. The planning team then critically evaluates both the subject hospital and its competing organizations. Weights are assigned to each factor, which are then multiplied by a ranking to obtain a weighted score. Weights must add to 100%. Typically, rankings from 1 to 10 are used, with a 10 indicating a very strong rating. The overall highest total ranking goes to the organization with the strongest competitive advantage—which indicates the competitor that represents the most intense rivalry. The matrix is useful for determining competitive position in local industry markets.

Successful strategies recognize competitors' strengths and find a way to mitigate them or reduce their effectiveness. Conversely, successful strategies identify a competitive weakness and exploit it by building a competitive advantage with it in mind or by building marketing programs that bring weaknesses to the attention of the market.

Analyze the Industry

The third component of external analysis is to conduct an industry analysis. Hospitals and health care organizations should continually analyze the industry structure and local market dynamics because these ultimately influence industry competitive rivalry. In addition to recognizing general trends occurring in the industry, this analysis helps organizations recognize how local markets are changing. This involves assessing new facilities that have emerged or taking note of changes in services provided.

One critical outcome of industry analysis should be definition of the key success factors for the industry. Key success factors are those activities that must be performed well if an organization is to succeed in the industry. For example, one key success factor in the industry is a conveniently located industry facility. If an industry is not physically located within the market in the right place, the industry will not succeed. Location is just one of the key success factors. Industry analysis must identify others that are important in the individual local market. Other key success factors may include brand recognition, access to qualified labor, and economies of scale.

Environmental Analysis

The final component of external analysis is to identify changes in the environment that may influence organizations. The environment includes all forces external to the industry that might influence operations. There are four primary components that need to be examined: technological, social, regulatory, and economic.

Technology effects should address new technologies that might alter productivity, breakthrough technologies that improve quality of patient care or affect service, or technologies that might give the organization an advantage over the competition.

Social factors influence the entire industry, such as demographics or change in average age or mix of patients. Understanding life-cycle trends, changes occurring in the general population, and specific implications for the hospital are all key considerations.

Regulations, laws, statutes, governmental policies, and all other requirements that are mandated or legally enforced affect what hospitals and health care organizations deliver and how they deliver it. Regulations requiring additional resources, changes in business process, reductions in reimbursement levels for procedures, or any other changes that are anticipated or known should be identified and their effect carefully assessed.

Finally, it is important to understand the changing economics of the industry, including both macro and micro issues. Macro issues for the industry economics include such grand changes as medical consumer price index changes, unemployment rates, consumer or government spending, interest rates, or currency fluctuations. Macro issues must include an examination of trends in the industry finances and potential issues and opportunities associated with these changes. Micro issues for the industry economics might include how the local city or market is changing in areas such as per capita income.

A great deal of time must be spent analyzing potential and current issues and opportunities arising out of trends and shifts in technology, society, regulations, and economics. Failure to recognize and act on these changes is one of the most probable reasons for organizational failure.

GENERATE STRATEGIC ALTERNATIVES

Once both internal and external analyses are conducted, it will be possible to identify potential choices or strategic alternatives. These alternatives can be prioritized using a combination of several tools, specifically breakeven analysis, decision matrices that use weights and probabilities to assess the most likely or valuable decisions, and simulation tools or games that help improve decision making.

Strategic alternatives in each of the three dimensions need to be explored: overall competitive approach, market orientation, and functional deployment. First, hospitals should have uncovered by this point if they are fundamentally a low-cost service provider (which most hospitals are not) or if they have a strong focus on a select group of product lines (most do not). As a result, the great majority of companies then typically attempt to fall into the broad competitive approach of a differentiation strategy (Trout & Rivkin, 2000). **Differentiation** refers to the ability of an organization to fundamentally offer different products, serve different markets, or otherwise perform differently than others in the marketplace. If the overall strategy is one of differentiation, the question of how to differentiate remains. Hospitals must search for a unique competitive position, where they are the premier providers of select products or services, where price competition is low, and where alternative providers are relatively minimal. Differentiation based on brand recognition, location, or types of service lines offered can all form the base of a differentiation strategy.

The next step in developing strategic alternatives is to review the existing operational product line portfolio strategy. Does the current portfolio of product lines make sense under new competitive conditions? Are there distinctive competencies in these service lines that can differentiate the industry from the competition? Should service offerings be removed to free up resources for investment into other service lines? Should partnerships be reevaluated? Is the organization integrated enough to compete with other networks and systems? Each of these questions needs to be answered before proceeding.

The final step in generating alternatives is to address each of the functional deployment strategies (i.e., growth, diversification, pricing, capital investment, and marketing). Do all of these strategies support the grand strategy? Do they all make economic sense given the current competitive climate and level of turbulence?

BREAKEVEN ANALYSIS

In many cases, the result of a planning process is identification of a new program or service that is not currently offered (Nauert, 2005). This might include a new support service, new clinical service line, or new medical procedures to extend current programs. All potential additions or extensions of services should be thoroughly reviewed, using feasibility analysis (How likely is this service to succeed?), competitive analysis (Will competition alter the pricing or demand structure?), and internal analysis (Does the organization have the expertise and resources to offer this at a high-quality level?). Assuming that the analyses performed support moving forward, a financial technique called *breakeven analysis* must be performed. A **breakeven analysis** analyzes

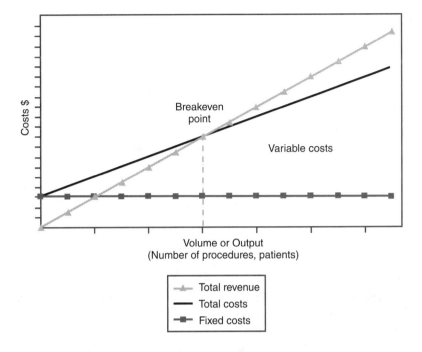

FIGURE 9–3   Breakeven Analysis

cost structures and volumes to identify at which point total returns equal total costs. This point of activity, where total revenues equal cost and thus yield a net income of zero, is called the **breakeven point**. A graphical view of the breakeven concept is shown in **Figure 9–3**.

Breakeven analysis typically focuses on how many units (the total quantity) are necessary to be sold or provided to have total revenues cover total costs. Four concepts are important to understand for this technique: fixed cost, variable cost, total cost, and price per unit. **Fixed costs** are all of the expenses necessary to deliver services, and these costs do not vary with total services provided. For example, if a hospital wants to open a new clinic to provide computed tomography scans, it will, at minimum, need capital equipment to provide these services. All of the initial setup costs for equipment, facilities, and staff are fixed. **Variable costs** are the costs that vary directly with production. In other words, as more services are delivered, additional variable costs will be required—because such costs vary with total quantities delivered. **Total costs** are the sum of both fixed and variable costs. **Price per unit** refers to the fee that will be charged to payers or customers in order to receive the service, and it is typically assumed not to vary.

Another key concept is contribution margin, which is price less variable cost. Mathematically, the breakeven point can be calculated as follows:

$$BE = \frac{FC}{(P - VC)}$$

For example, a hospital has decided to offer a new service line (a cardiology procedure that has not been offered before). After extensive analysis, the total variable cost to deliver this service (using clinical labor, administrative staff, supplies, and other direct materials) is $220 per procedure. The fixed cost of offering this service involved allocating 50,000 gross square feet of space, installing a new piece of medical equipment, and purchasing a new computer workstation; the fixed cost, then, is $100,000. Based on market analysis, the facility should be able to perform 2,500 procedures annually, and using the standard markup ratio of 25%, the expected price per procedure will be $275. This approximates the reimbursement rate expectations for these procedures from the dominant payer group in the market as well.

Using these figures, the breakeven analysis in quantity is calculated as 1,818 procedures. In other words, the first 1,817 procedures will be performed at a net loss to the hospital; when procedure 1,818 is performed, the new procedure will have broken even. All procedures delivered after this point help increase profits and operating margins for the organization. The breakeven point for this example is calculated as:

$$BE = \frac{FC}{(P - VC)} = \frac{\$100,000}{\$275 - \$220} = 1.818 \text{ units}$$

Using the figures provided, total profits for this new entity would be $37,500 if all assumptions held true. Total revenues are calculated by multiplying per unit price ($275) by the total forecasted volume (2,500), which yields $687,500 in annual revenues. Total costs are calculated by summing the variable costs ($220 × 2,500 = $550,000) and fixed costs ($100,000), which equates to $650,000. Therefore, profits are equal to $37,500 using these assumptions.

This concept of breakeven analysis is a powerful simulation tool that allows managers to play "what if" and simulate results before they actually occur. For example, holding all assumptions equal, and then varying only one assumption (e.g., somehow reducing total fixed costs by 35%, possibly by using less space or renting equipment), then the total number of procedures to be delivered would be only 1,181 [$65,000 ÷ ($275 − $220)] and total expected profit would be $72,500 [($275 × 2,500) − ($220 × 2,500) − $65,000 = $687,500 − $615,000]. This increases the "time to benefit" by speeding up cost recovery and increasing earning margins. Breakeven analysis is a useful tool when modeling programs, especially when costs and volume structures are dynamic.

Simulating a variety of different activity and cost levels helps managers determine the range of possible outcomes. If feasible, each of the strategic alternatives should be "tested" by using a game theory or scenario analysis technique. **Game theory** is an economic technique whereby the organization attempts to estimate how the competition will respond to its strategies and what the effect on performance will be. Scenarios and simulations are similar in that they help provide structure to what-if questions that might occur in the future. What if Competitor A opens a new clinic in a nearby market? What effect might that have on market demand? The use of advanced analytical tools to support these types of simulations greatly affects the speed and accuracy of the analysis.

IMPLEMENT, MEASURE, AND REVISE

The boundary between creating strategy and implementing strategy is sometimes blurred. Strategies are continuously crafted and implemented. Implementation might be done over time in phases, in pilot programs, or all at once. Once such strategies are deployed, they must be carefully measured and benchmarked to ensure that they are moving the organization in the right direction.

The use of benchmarking programs, as described in the *Quality Management* chapter, is especially useful in planning environments as well as ensuring that the strategies achieve desired results relative to the competition. The use of performance scorecards supports continuous monitoring and tracking to assess trends or shifts in performance as a result of the strategies.

Planning is a continuous process and provides a basis for routine measurement of performance and adjustments where necessary. If strategies are not successful in achieving the desired goals and objectives, it is necessary to revise the plans, reconsider additional strategic alternatives, and continuously adjust based on feedback and results. Learning from the process and making routine adjustments to the plans is critical to effective operational planning.

CHAPTER SUMMARY

Planning helps a hospital establish operations strategy and define specific actionable goals and a short-term roadmap. By understanding the key elements affecting clinical and business operations, hospitals can determine where they want to focus their efforts and how best to use their resources. Operational planning must be aligned with the facility's clinical goals and strategies. The result of these plans is a targeted list of initiatives and projects that can be undertaken to drive improved processes and financial outcomes. There are four key steps to the planning process: analyze operations and environment, generate strategic alternatives, deploy strategies, and measure and adjust. Plans focus on long-term improvements to the health care business, which ultimately drive improved financial productivity and operating results. This chapter provided a framework for beginning the operational planning process.

KEY TERMS

Actionable

Breakeven analysis

Breakeven point

Core competency

Differentiation

Distinctive competency

External environment

Facilitator

Fixed costs

Game theory

Planning

Price per unit

Radar diagram

Strengths, weaknesses, opportunities, and threats (SWOT) analysis

Total costs

Variable costs

DISCUSSION QUESTIONS

1. Why should hospitals plan? What result do plans have on operations?
2. How do operational plans support the clinical side of a health care organization?
3. What role does a radar diagram or other assessment have in assessing internal operations?
4. What does SWOT stand for?
5. What are the alternatives to a differentiation strategy?
6. What are the three components of a breakeven analysis?

EXERCISE PROBLEMS

1. Lutheran Regional Hospital uses a planning process to define a new radiology service line. The decision matrix gave it a high priority, and administrators want to evaluate its financial feasibility. Estimated fixed costs are $1 million, and the estimated net reimbursement level

is $1,500 per procedure. Physician and other provider salaries on a direct basis are $340 per procedure, and total operating expenses will add another $160 per procedure. Calculate the breakeven point for this potential new service line.

2. If Lutheran Regional discovered a way to reduce the total initial investment to $600,000, causing the average pricing level to fall to $1,200 and the other assumptions to stay the same, how many procedures would be required to break even?

3. Assuming that the hospital feels it can deliver 1,000 procedures conservatively in the first year, which option should be chosen?

REFERENCES

Nauert, R. C. (2005). Strategic business planning and development for competitive health care systems. *Journal of Health Care Finance, 32*(2), 72–94.

Page, R. (2002). *Hope is not a strategy: The six keys to winning the complex sale.* New York, NY: McGraw-Hill.

Thompson, A. A., & Strickland, A. J. (1998). *Strategic management: Concepts and cases.* Boston, MA: Irwin/McGraw-Hill.

Trout, J., & Rivkin, S. (2000). *Differentiate or die: Survival in our era of killer competition.* New York, NY: Wiley.

Zuckerman, A. M. (2005). *Healthcare strategic planning* (2nd ed.). Chicago, IL: Health Administration Press.

CHAPTER 10

Return on Investment Analysis

GOALS OF THIS CHAPTER

1. Define the complexities and challenges of return on investment analysis in health care.
2. Understand methods for cost-benefit analysis and return on investment.
3. Calculate return on investment for different scenarios.
4. Describe how a formalized capital investment approach can be implemented.

Once an operational strategy has been developed, it is usually necessary to evaluate the cost benefit of proposed and current service lines or activities. Hospitals represent significant opportunities for cost savings and operational efficiencies. This can be achieved by fixing processes, removing cost layers, and increasing the turnover or productivity ratios. One of the most common ways to improve operational efficiency is to use information and management systems and technology to automate processes and displace capital for labor. This takes careful analysis, however, to ensure that all technology benefits are captured and compared relative to the costs of acquisition and implementation. This chapter details how to analyze return on investment for technology and other projects.

LACK OF CAPITAL INVESTMENT MODELS IN HEALTH CARE

Health care organizations invest in capital programs for many reasons, but the most common is that it helps to automate, improve, or substitute capital for labor (Lucas, 1999). In many respects, the financial management of health care organizations has lagged behind other industries. Capital investment in facilities, equipment, and technology has not always utilized the traditional capital investment models; therefore, decisions are made based on other rationales besides financial viability. Following the standard of strict financial modeling techniques should be a top priority for operations managers. These financial modeling techniques will help clearly identify the expected changes in cost and revenue cash flows associated with the project through formalized discounted cash flows and net present value formulas. These models help quantify decisions and allow management to understand the bottom-line results of decisions in terms of the net economic value that is being contributed. More sophisticated health care organizations also follow return on investment models, but they are not significantly deployed throughout the industry.

Return on investment (ROI) is calculated as total amount of profits earned from a project or investment divided by the total cost of that investment. Typically, it looks at the effect of net cash flow from revenues and expenses over a specific time period, such as 3 or 5 years, using the concept of the time value of money. Formally, ROI can be defined as follows:

Return on investment = [(Total benefits – Total costs) ÷ (Total investment)] × 100

In health care, however, a large number of facility and technology investments are made for reasons unrelated to financial returns. New clinical technologies might help extend life, provide greater insight into disease that can improve diagnoses, or improve treatment success and morbidity rates. These are all potentially valid clinical outcomes and, after careful analyses, if the total nonfinancial benefit outweighs the costs, they should be considered in the capital budget. In addition, health care organizations tend to rely on the expertise of their leaders, who use heuristics and subjective gut feel to make decisions. Financial considerations have not always been the highest priority.

From an operations management perspective, however, capital budgeting processes must be driven by ROI and financial outcomes. The goal of operations management is to improve efficiency, competitiveness, and operations effectiveness, which require formalized ROI tools.

Unfortunately, because the greatest amount of a hospital's investments are in clinical equipment, facilities, and information technology (IT), the typical hospital has not required ROI projections as part of its decision-making process. In addition, the finance and budgeting departments in the average hospital are usually understaffed and not overly sophisticated. Health care must become more proactive and advanced in its capital processes to accommodate ROI analysis for all capital investments.

THE POLITICS OF CAPITAL INVESTMENT

Hospitals tend to be highly social and political organizations. Physicians hold positions of power, and culture is independent of financial condition. Therefore, capital investment processes tend to have priorities focused on non-value-maximizing attributes. Physicians and other employees with political clout and power tend to dominate investment processes in health care and can influence decisions on technology in areas where they are the most interested or involved, regardless of financial value. In addition, because physicians often believe that administrators do not understand the value or consequence of their need or request, there is a general lack of trust in allowing business managers to make critical decisions about capital budgeting.

Prioritizations in the largest hospitals are based to a great degree on qualitative, not quantitative, data, which can be highly subjective. When decisions are qualitative, they do not allow for shared understanding of the criteria used to make such decisions (Weill & Ross, 2004). This causes a lack of alignment around the importance of different systems. These political investment processes do not generally follow formalized approaches and models that help ensure investment in the right areas. This encourages the wrong behavior and eventually leads to deteriorating financial health.

RECOMMENDATIONS FOR IMPLEMENTING A CAPITAL INVESTMENT APPROACH

It is important that hospitals use ROI approaches to capital budgeting. This requires clear, well-established investment guidelines. For example, a guideline might state that a specific percentage of the largest net present value projects will be funded during a fiscal year, or that any positive net present value project will be viewed favorably, or that any projects whose internal rate of return is more than double the cost of capital will be approved. All of these represent guidelines, which help explain the financial priorities to the organization and make the decision criteria clear. There are six key recommendations for incorporating ROI analysis into daily decision-making processes:

1. Define and measure the hospital's true cost of capital.
2. Establish formalized ROI criteria.
3. Align investments with strategy.
4. Eliminate a single annual investment process.
5. Establish an IT portfolio approach.
6. Establish investment committees.

Each of these is described in the rest of this section.

Define and Measure the True Cost of Capital

Many organizations do not measure cost of capital, which makes investments very difficult. The cost of capital is the weighted average cost of all funding sources for a hospital, including both debt and equity (Patterson, 1995). The cost of capital sometimes is called the *discount*, or **hurdle rate**, which is the minimum rate of return required on projects. The cost of capital is a very important concept; unfortunately, it is not widely deployed in health care.

The **cost of capital** refers to the actual cost of money. For example, assume a hospital has no cash, stocks, or any other investments besides loans. This hospital can borrow from a bank, but it has no other sources of capital. The rate that the bank loans money to the hospital, then, is equal to its cost of capital. If the rate is equal to 6%, this means that if the hospital is to invest $500,000 in a project, it will really cost the organization $530,000 at the end of the first year ($500,000 × 6% interest charge); in other words, it will cost the organization $30,000 to borrow the funds. This cost has to be considered in the ROI equation because the total value or return from the project must now be incremented by this same amount.

Most hospitals, however, borrow money from banks over the short and long term, but they also are major issuers of debt in the form of public bonds. In addition, organizations lease or rent equipment, which has financing charges, and may even use revolving credit through organizational purchasing cards for limited working capital financing. The public for-profit hospital systems issue stock or equity through one of the stock exchanges, and more profitable hospitals tend to finance capital investments using cash or cash equivalents (through retained earnings). All of these represent sources of funds. Each source of funds has its own financing costs associated with it.

To calculate the true cost of capital for a hospital requires that the marginal costs of debt and equity be multiplied by the percentage of the market value that each represents. The comprehensive term for this is *weighted average cost of capital* (WACC). The formula for calculating WACC is:

$$\text{WACC} = [(w_d K_d (1 - T)) + (w_e K_e)]$$

where

    w = weighting factor, or percentage of market value from either debt or capital

    K = cost of equity or debt

    T = marginal tax rate

    d = debt

    e = equity, either preferred or common

In other words, WACC is based on the cost of debt in percent multiplied by the proportion of total capital that debt represents, plus the cost of equity in percent multiplied by the proportion of total capital that equity represents. Because most health care organizations do not issue stock, they have no associated costs of equity beyond that of the risk-free rate from cash equivalents or other reductions in retained earnings, which is primarily an opportunity cost. Therefore, in most organizations cost of capital is mainly a function of the cost of debt. Cost of debt can then be calculated as the cost of risk-free debt plus a risk premium.

Understanding the true blended cost of capital ensures that projects are not undertaken for purely the initial investment costs, but that they also reflect the financing effects, which can often add between 4% and 15% to a project's total marginal cost. For large hospitals, an 8% to 10% cost of capital is fairly common.

Establish Formalized ROI Criteria

Part of the difficulty in health care is due to the fact that hospitals often do not have a dominant key performance metric for financial outcomes. In other industries, the use of return on invested capital, return on equity, earnings per share, or price-earnings ratios can be used to model financial decisions. In health care, there is still limited translation of the basic measures of profitability, such as operating margin and net income. Because these are limited in their usefulness due to accounting manipulations, they are often shortsighted in nature.

Clear guidelines for hospitals should be developed to factor in the cost of capital to drive investment decisions. Prioritization of investments around projects with the highest net present values or differential between return on capital and the hurdle rate is important if hospitals are to achieve operational excellence.

Align Investments with Strategy

Hospitals also need to align their investments in IT with the hospital's strategies and initiatives (Keen & Digrius, 2003). Understanding the relationship between systems or technology and the hospital's strategy will help clarify the effect on the organization. Technology that is clearly aligned with strategy should have the higher ranking, all other things being equal.

A hospital must have strategies across all areas of the organization for alignment to occur. The use of key performance indicators (KPIs) shows the effect that technology has on a specific KPI, and this can be cascaded back to the hospital's overarching strategy and performance scorecard.

Eliminate a Single Annual Investment Process

In many organizations, capital investments can be made only once per year, at the beginning of a fiscal period. This creates a rush for funding at certain times of the year, such as January or September, which forces decisions among many projects simultaneously. This creates a competitive environment, where managers try to "game" the system rather than simply stating the benefits and facts around the investment. Annual processes discourage creative thinking year round and ultimately do nothing to improve financial results. Instead, revolving or year-round processes should be used so that as new ideas are developed—and as long as they make financial sense—they can be pursued.

Establish an IT Portfolio Approach

When investing in financial instruments, such as mutual funds or stocks, financial planners recommend taking a portfolio approach. A **portfolio** is a collection of investments grouped by different categories that are selected to help ensure a balanced and systematic approach to improving overall outcomes.

An IT portfolio balances the investments in various technologies so that they are not all concentrated around one area. For example, not all investments can be made in business systems that produce financial ROI, and not all investments can be made in clinical technologies with any direct, traceable returns. Similarly, not all capital decisions can be made around a system's end of useful life. Categories for each of the key strategies in IT could be used to create a matrix to graphically represent the portfolio and ensure balanced investments.

Another way to manage the portfolio is across the dimension of value versus risks and complexity. This suggests that even if the financial return or value is extremely high, complex projects tend to fail faster, and therefore the results may never be seen. The best case is a high-ROI and low-risk project, but those are rare. More than likely, a portfolio will include investments in all of the matrices of the portfolio. **Figure 10–1** shows a sample portfolio grid.

Establish Investment Committees

The use of an investment steering committee, which is well represented by multiple functions of the hospital, helps to systematically evaluate potential technology or facility investment decisions. Alternatively, steering teams can be used to evaluate priorities for focused areas (e.g., one team for clinical activities, one for financial, one for nursing). Each committee should be encouraged to perform planning in its area to determine strategic measures or KPIs. For example, is process efficiency the number one goal, or is enhancing revenues? Many times, KPIs are not in place, so it may be necessary to first develop strategic criteria for activities that each committee can use for evaluation purposes.

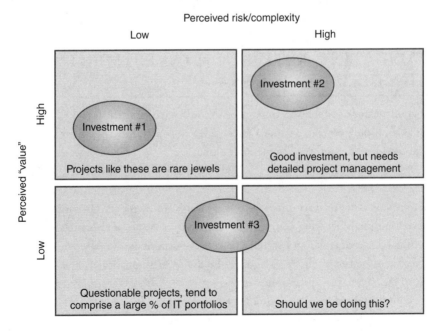

FIGURE 10–1 IT Portfolio Management

These committees should use departments such as finance or management engineering to help evaluate the business case and ROI analyses being presented for funding. ROI analysis cannot be done well by the department or individual seeking funding, because there is an inherent conflict of interest and biases may exist. The use of other departments helps ensure consistent treatment of cost of capital, as well as cash flow considerations, and helps provide independence to the process.

No two individuals share the same tolerance for risk or the same risk profile. Therefore, when asked about the level of risk in an IT project, several individuals could rate the same level of risk very differently, simply based on their risk tolerance level. To minimize this bias, committees should use standardized measures of risk and complexity to keep that part of the portfolio as quantitative as possible. For example, ratings can be created based on the number of months for the project's implementation (the greater the time, the greater the risk), total cost, the number of people or departments involved in the project, or some other quantitative guide that can help model risk fairly and consistently.

These committees should also use some form of expected value analysis, or weighted average ranking tool, for project acceptance. This tool allows the committee to evaluate the proposed IT project against key criteria and scale it based on the level of alignment around hospital-wide strategies and performance goals. Once decisions are made, they can be visually managed on a portfolio dashboard at both the committee and hospital levels.

VALIDATING RETURN ON INVESTMENT AT MULTIPLE STAGES

A sophisticated capital budgeting process should encourage the use of ROI analyses at multiple points in a project's life cycle. This includes pre-implementation, mid-deployment, and post-implementation.

Prior to an investment in new technology, many hospitals use formal or informal executive reviews to analyze the benefits of the investment, even if a formal net present value or discounted cash flow tool is not deployed. In more sophisticated hospitals, steering committee evaluations are used to estimate alignment with hospital strategies and to use quantitative criteria to evaluate and rank IT investments across multiple categories. In the most sophisticated hospitals, the use of business case justifications with extensive ROI models are employed, which are complemented by a portfolio management approach.

While in the middle of deployment or implementation, hospitals should periodically review the project to ensure that no changes have been made—either to

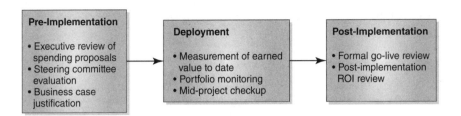

FIGURE 10–2 Multiple Points for ROI Analysis in Project Life Cycle

the conditions that necessitated the investment or to the underlying assumptions themselves (e.g., change in the cost of capital, change in implementation duration times). Mid-project reviews to assess the status and health of the project should be implemented, and the measurement of earned value recognized to date should be tracked. Earned value allows managers to compare costs incurred on a project against expected benefits of that project at the point of a certain percentage complete.

After the technology has been implemented and in production for a reasonable period of time, there should be formal follow-up reviews to evaluate if the technology is generating the ROIs that were projected during the initial business case. These post-implementation reviews compare expected results against actual results and try to find sources for the variances. For example, if expected results were to save $100,000 in operational expenses per year, but actual results show no savings, then an in-depth gap analysis should be conducted. This gap analysis should consider all of the historical assumptions for the change and identify which assumptions were ignored or invalid or if other changes mid-project resulted in the error for the initial projections. **Figure 10–2** shows the types of analyses that can be conducted along the project's life cycle.

CALCULATING RETURN ON INVESTMENT

There are three steps to measuring the ROI for a project:

Identify benefits >> Calculate costs >> Model results

Identify the Benefits

The first step in the ROI process is to identify and quantify the benefits. A **benefit** is a gain or positive change in an outcome and is often called the

cash inflow or *return*. Benefits can be categorized into five areas, shown in descending order for their ability to quantify financial results:

- Those that create revenue enhancements.
- Those that cause reductions in operational expenses.
- Those that improve or expand service lines and levels.
- Those that improve the work environment.
- Those necessary for legal, regulatory, system end of life, or other reasons.

Revenue enhancements are the easiest area to quantify, but they represent a small percentage of total projects for most hospitals. Technology projects that enhance revenue would allow for expansions in revenue-generating areas, higher prices, larger market share, or other ways to exploit new opportunities for top-line revenue growth. For example, if a hospital were to develop an online patient referral and admission process, which could potentially attract new patients and new appointments, this could generate greater revenues. Likewise, investments in technologies that improve the hospital's brand recognition could be seen as possible ways of increasing revenues.

Most projects, however, focus on reducing costs or expenses (also called *cost savings* or *cost avoidance*). Costs are defined here as all incurred costs of an investment, whether they were operationalized or capitalized, direct or indirect. Most IT project investments can be **capitalized**, or recognized as assets on the balance sheet, and the costs spread or depreciated over the time periods in which the benefits will be realized. These costs, however, should be treated the same in the ROI analysis, as shown later in this chapter. Direct expenses are those costs that directly relate to the service being provided and include labor, materials, and other such related costs. Indirect costs include space, utilities, insurance, and other costs that are necessary but not directly related to the process in question. Reducing costs due to higher productivity, improved reliability, faster cycle times, reduced manual efforts, elimination of duplicate or redundant data and systems, and overall higher efficiencies are benefits under this category.

Another benefit category includes projects that help expand or improve service lines. Improving accuracy, the quality of information provided, the level of care or service given, the access to information, and the ability to deliver more reliable or less variable performance are all areas represented in this benefit category.

Another benefit category is for projects that improve the work environment. These are difficult to measure financially, but they can have positive results. For example, ergonomic changes in a production process can allow for higher productivity due to less noise, reduced clutter, and less physical strain. Also, any projects that help generally improve the working conditions for employees can generate benefits in this category.

Finally, benefits derive by being in compliance with laws, regulations, and mandates, as well as from having current and fully supported systems. The cost of noncompliance with these areas could potentially generate penalties and legal problems that could otherwise be avoided. These areas are difficult to quantify, but they are nonetheless important considerations when making investment decisions.

Each of these benefits must be summarized. Then, calculation of estimated returns from these benefits should be prepared annually for at least 5 years, unless the technology is estimated to have a useful life less than that. Next, the cash flow impact needs to be detailed for each of the categories, defining all of the key assumptions. Finally, these benefits must be separated into annual time periods.

Consider this example. Assume a hospital is going to invest in a new technology that will bring in an additional 10 patients per month, as well as eliminate manual processes that would otherwise employ 2 full-time employees. Each employee makes approximately $30,000 annually, not including a 15% benefit package. Each new patient seen generates approximately $500 per quarter in net revenues. Calculate the total annual benefits. Ten patients generating $2,000 annually ($500 × 4 quarters) is $20,000 in revenue gains. Reduced operating expenses through cost savings are $69,000 (2 × $30,000 × 1.15), if both employees are realigned to other areas. Total benefits to be derived from this technology are $89,000 in the first year. Estimates for benefits in future years have to rely on assumptions for inflation, using the consumer price index as a gauge, as well as other changes that may occur over time. In addition, the time value of money (using cost of capital) has to be incorporated into more comprehensive analyses, as described later.

Calculate the Costs

It is important to capture all costs associated with the project. Costs represent **cash outflows** for an organization and include six primary areas: labor, hardware, software, implementation support (consulting, training), communications and infrastructure, and miscellaneous.

Labor expenses include the fully burdened personnel expenses associated with salaries, temporary labor, benefits, and training. Labor represents significant costs for most projects, and calculating these accurately at the detailed level allows for a much more comprehensive picture. The use of time and motion studies is encouraged to achieve a very detailed analysis of the actual time and effort associated with the process and/or project being considered. For example, if only 3 hours per day of total labor are connected to a specific process, it would not be accurate to show the costs for an entire employee. Instead, an average, hourly, fully burdened wage rate has to be constructed and multiplied against the actual hours used to estimate labor costs.

Hardware is another major expense area for most projects. Hardware includes all costs to purchase or lease workstations, desktops, printers, fax machines, servers, mainframes, storage devices, memory, and network devices, to name just a few. Often, new technology requires investment in new hardware, and a thorough analysis of all hardware requirements and costs must be considered.

Most technology has a software component. Software includes licensing fees, operating systems, and maintenance or support costs, which must be carefully considered. Implementation support includes the cost of consultants who will be used during the implementation period, as well as training and education costs, travel, internal resources devoted to the project, and any other costs of implementation. Communication and infrastructure fees include the cost of any telecommunications platforms or upgrades or additions to phone or data lines. Finally, a miscellaneous category can be used to capture any other project expenses that are not specifically listed in the categories given here.

Once all costs are identified, they need to be summarized by expense category and broken into the respective time period in which the expenses are actually incurred. These costs should be placed in the same spreadsheet as the benefits.

Model the Results

The final step in the ROI calculation is to model or quantify the results. This involves a direct comparison of the expected benefits less the expected costs. As stated earlier, ROI can be defined as the total amount of profits or gains earned from a project or investment divided by the total cost of that investment. Again, ROI is expressed mathematically as:

$$\text{ROI} = [(\text{Total benefits} - \text{Total costs}) \div (\text{Total investment})] \times 100$$

In simple terms, if a hospital generates $10 in benefits this year, but will expend $5 in costs to achieve those benefits, then the net gain will be $5. Expressed as a percentage, this represents

$$\text{ROI} = [(\$10 - \$5) \div \$5] \times 100 = 100\%$$

TIME VALUE OF MONEY

If investments were made today, and if the costs and benefits were only accrued today and not in the future, then the preceding method could be used to calculate ROI reasonably well. However, most large projects tend to have **payoffs** (i.e., payback on return) over several years. Some technology investments usually displace labor or manual effort forever, creating perpetual cost savings. Likewise, **software maintenance** fees (or support payments due to vendors to cover upgrades and enhancements) typically accompany many IT projects and are paid as long as the hospital wishes to remain current and continue to use the software. Capital budgeting is the process of planning asset expenditures over the long term, so a project can be evaluated by estimating the effects of multiple years of cash flows, both inflows and outflows.

As a result, the concept of time value of money is important. **Time value of money** is a financial concept: Money received in the present is worth more than the same amount received in the future. Money earns **interest**, so money received today can theoretically be placed in an investment (e.g., savings account, equities, or bonds) that can generate interest in the interim period, which would make the investment larger in the future. This concept is also referred to as compound interest theory, where interest compounds over time. Interest is the payment received by those who hold money to forgo current consumption. To calculate the true effect of interest, the use of present value is required. The **present value** of an amount is the value today of a future payment.

Consider this example. A hospital is due to receive revenue from a payer of $50. If it receives this revenue today, it is in fact worth $50. However, if it does not receive this money until next year, the hospital has lost the ability to invest it and compound the interest. Therefore, $50 next year is worth much less than $50 today. To calculate how much less, it is necessary to understand the present value formula, which can be expressed as:

$$\text{Present value of } \$1 = [1 \div (1 + i)^n]$$

where

i = interest rate, or discount rate, or cost of capital used by the hospital

n = number of years in the future that the money will be received

Going back to the earlier example, assuming a 10% discount rate (or hospital cost of capital), then $50 received next year will be worth $45. This can be calculated as

$$[\$50 \times (1 + (1.10)^1)] = \$50 \times 0.909 = \$45$$

If the hospital received the money 1 year in the future from the payer, it would essentially be forfeiting, or giving up, $5 in total returns ($50 − $45).

Alternatively, because money received today can be invested, a dollar received today has greater value in the future. This is called the **future value** of an amount. It can be calculated as:

$$\text{Future value of } \$1 = (1 + i)^n$$

If $50 is received today, that same dollar will be worth $55 next year:

$$[\$50 \times (1 + 0.10)^1] = \$50 \times 1.10 = \$55$$

In other words, in the future, the hospital would be forfeiting not just $5, as found earlier, but actually $10, or 20% of its revenue, to receive the dollar in the future ($55 − $45). This shows the significant effect of the time value of money.

CALCULATING MULTIPLE CASH FLOWS

The preceding examples are fairly easy to calculate, as long as the discount rate or cost of capital to be used in the calculation is known. Although discount rate and cost of capital are often used interchangeably, the cost of capital is the actual weighted average cost of a hospital's funding sources, which includes cost of debt (net of tax) and cost of equity. It represents the minimum required return to essentially break even on a project. The discount rate is simply the factor used in preparing present value analyses, and it may be the same as the cost of capital. Many organizations simply use the current interest rate or bond yields as proxies.

When using a stream of cash inflows and outflows, it is wise to use net present value concepts. **Net present value (NPV)** is the difference between the present value of any cash inflows (or benefits) and the present value of cash outflows (or costs), net of taxes. NPV is probably the most commonly used technique for ranking investment proposals and capital projects for most for-profit companies (Shefrin, 2006). Sophisticated hospitals use NPV, but it is not as widely understood and adopted across all hospitals. It is important to use NPV in capital rationing situations because, essentially, NPV measures the amount of economic value that is being added (or removed) from the hospital with each decision.

NPV discounts all after-tax cash flows back to the current year; it could be calculated by using the present value formula given earlier or by looking up the present value in tables that are commonly available. For example, if $50 were received in years 1, 2, and 3, the present value of those inflows would be $124.33:

$$\text{Present value} = (\$50 \times 0.9091) + (\$50 \times 0.8264) + (\$50 \times 0.7513)$$
$$= \$45.45 + \$41.32 + \$37.57 = \$124.34$$

Mathematically, NPV can be expressed as follows (Copeland, Koller, & Murrin, 1994):

$$NPV = \sum_{t=0}^{n} \frac{PCF_t}{(1+k)t}$$

where

n = number of future cash flow periods

t = time period

k = discount rate

PCF_t = periodic cash flow for period t

As long as NPV > 0, the project should be accepted because economic value is being contributed to the organization. Exceptions to this include when capital rationing, or limiting of the capital budget, exists, in which case all projects should be ranked from highest to lowest NPV, and all projects should be accepted down to the cutoff point, where cumulative investment is equal to total capital budget.

Alternatively, a spreadsheet (such as Microsoft Excel) can be used with a built-in NPV function to provide even quicker analysis over different time periods. A sample ROI analysis spreadsheet is depicted in **Figure 10–3**.

OTHER RETURN ON INVESTMENT TECHNIQUES

Besides NPV, two of the more common methods for gauging the returns on projects are payback and internal rate of return. **Payback** is the number of periods required to complete the return of the original investment and is defined as:

$$\text{Payback} = \text{Initial investment} \div \text{Expected cash flow each period}$$

For example, if a technology upgrade cost $500,000 and each year there was a net positive cash inflow of $50,000, then the payback period would be

Cash flow category	Assumptions	2011	2012	2013	2014	2015
BENEFITS						
Reduction in operational expenses		$ —	$ —	$ —	$ —	$ —
Increases in revenue		$ —	$ —	$ —	$ —	$ —
Other benefits	Define and quantify	$ —	$ —	$ —	$ —	$ —
TOTAL BENEFITS		$ —	$ —	$ —	$ —	$ —
EXPENSES						
Capital investments						
Implementation						
Hardware	(e.g., new server)	$ —	$ —	$ —	$ —	$ —
Software	(e.g., 10 concurrent)	$ —	$ —	$ —	$ —	$ —
Communication and infrastructure		$ —	$ —	$ —	$ —	$ —
Consulting, training, support						
Labor – internal and temporary		$ —	$ —	$ —	$ —	$ —
Total capital investment						
Annual recurring costs						
Labor - new position	(e.g., 1 new FTE)	$ —	$ —	$ —	$ —	$ —
Software maintenance		$ —	$ —	$ —	$ —	$ —
Server maintenance		$ —	$ —	$ —	$ —	$ —
Administration/support		$ —	$ —	$ —	$ —	$ —
Total annual costs		$ —	$ —	$ —	$ —	$ —
Contingency budget	(e.g., 15% contingency)	$ —	$ —	$ —	$ —	$ —
TOTAL PROJECT COSTS		$ —	$ —	$ —	$ —	$ —
NET CASH FLOWS		$ —	$ —	$ —	$ —	$ —
Net present value, using COC of 10%						
Internal rate of return						
Payback period, # of years						

FIGURE 10–3 ROI Analysis Tool

10 years ($500,000 ÷ $50,000). The advantage to using the payback method is its simplicity: It is intuitively easy to follow and calculate. The major disadvantage is that cash flows are not typically constant. One way around this is to cumulatively sum each year's cash flows until the total investment is reached. Another major disadvantage is that it ignores the time value of money, as well as any cash flows that might be generated after the end of the payback period.

The other common technique is internal rate of return. **Internal rate of return** is a computation in which the NPV of a project is equal to zero. Instead of the discount rate being held constant as in NPV, it becomes the dependent variable that must be solved for by setting NPV to zero and using the variable cash flows. Alternatively, a simple heuristic to determine internal rates of return is to divide 1 by the number of years of payback. For example, 1 divided by 10 years in the previous example suggests this project has a 10% internal rate of return. One major limitation to this technique is that while it provides an intuitive return percentage, it ignores the dollar value of the cash flows and therefore makes it difficult to compare investments of varying sizes.

Example

Bellingham Hospital is about to invest nearly $700,000 over the next 5 years to implement a tracking system that uses both bar code and radio frequency identification technologies; $500,000 will be paid in the first year, and the balance will be evenly split over the next 4 years. These technologies will initially be used to track two types of assets: durable medical equipment (especially infusion pumps) and transportation equipment (such as wheelchairs).

These technologies should help increase the utilization or turns associated with the equipment, which increases effective capacity. By making visible where assets are hiding, managers can better position and transport them so that they will not need to purchase as many pieces of equipment in the future. Currently, there is about a 50% utilization rate on both types of assets, suggesting that they are used only half of the time. There will be a projected cost savings of $350,000 annually in cost avoidance of future equipment expenditures for the next 3 years and then a savings of $250,000 for each of the following 2 years. However, there will be a need for one additional full-time employee to manage the systems, which will cost about $50,000 plus 15% benefits. The hospital IT department requires a 5% contingency expense in factoring all ROI analyses.

The hospital is nonprofit and therefore exempt from taxes. The existing financing is approximately 60% debt financing at a tax-free bond yield of 5%, and 40%

equity at 7% (in this example, equity returns are based on a combination of existing cash and long-term marketable securities returns). Using a much-simplified version of the WACC, the cost of capital can be calculated as

$$[(60\% \times 5\%) + (40\% \times 7\%) = 5.8\%$$

Based on this, Bellingham Hospital typically uses a 6% discount or hurdle rate in all calculations. There is also no salvage or residual value left in this technology at the end of the 5-year period, which represents the useful or economic life of these systems.

Is this a good investment for the hospital? Simply looking at the sum of all benefits over 5 years suggests that $1.55 million in benefits will result from a total capital investment of $700,000, with only $287,500 in operating expenses. Using discounted cash flows, with all of the assumptions defined, the first year net cash outflow is $235,375, which comprises cash outflows of $500,000 for the technology, $57,500 for the fully burdened staff, and $27,875 for the project contingency, for a total outflow of $585,375. Cash inflows, or benefits, amount to $350,000 in that first year. In years 2 and 3, there are positive net cash inflows of $237,125 annually. In years 4 and 5, each period had annual inflows of $137,125. At a 6% discount rate, the NPV of this project would amount to $399,000. Any NPV that is greater than zero should be accepted, assuming no capital rationing is in effect, and so this project is indeed a worthwhile financial investment.

CHAPTER SUMMARY

Investments in capital for new facilities, equipment, and technology are often good uses of cash flows if they provide a return at least equal to the costs. Benefits of these investments often include an increase in productivity, displacement of labor, cost avoidance, increased revenue, or other benefits. The costs of capital, however, can be enormous, which can change the economics of the project. It is important to thoroughly understand all aspects of expenses—hardware, software, infrastructure, implementation support, labor, and all other costs to fully model the cash flow results. Careful analysis of the benefits relative to the gains and use of a discounted cash flow approach to measuring inflows and outflows are necessary to gauge the effectiveness of each project. NPV, payback, and internal rate of return are three of the more sophisticated techniques for evaluating capital investments pre-implementation.

KEY TERMS

Benefit	Net present value (NPV)
Capitalized	Payback
Cash inflow	Payoffs
Cash outflows	Portfolio
Cost of capital	Present value
Future value	Return on investment (ROI)
Hurdle rate	Software maintenance
Interest	Time value of money
Internal rate of return	

DISCUSSION QUESTIONS

1. What are some ways that hospitals can avoid qualitative and politically based decision making around technology investments?
2. What are the advantages to taking a portfolio approach to information technology?
3. What are the six recommendations for improving capital budgeting processes?
4. Should return on investment be analyzed at multiple points during a project's life cycle? Why?
5. How does a hospital calculate its cost of capital? Which data sources are necessary?
6. Does the time value of money really affect the long-term financial outcomes for a hospital?
7. What are the limitations to net present value, payback, and internal rate of return?

EXERCISE PROBLEMS

1. Assume that a hospital has steady cash inflows of $10,000 for 3 years and cash outflows of $9,500 for this same period. At 10% cost of capital, what is the net present value of this project? Should this project be accepted, assuming there are no limits on capital?
2. Assuming that the initial project investment is $28,500 in year 0, and that $10,000 in benefits accrued annually, calculate the payback period.

REFERENCES

Copeland, T., Koller, T., & Murrin, J. (1994). *Valuation: Measuring and managing the value of companies* (2nd ed.). New York, NY: Wiley.

Keen, J. M., & Digrius, B. (2003). *Making technology investments profitable: ROI roadmap to better business cases.* New York, NY: Wiley.

Lucas, H. C., Jr. (1999). *Information technology and the productivity paradox: Assessing the value of investing in IT.* New York, NY: Oxford University Press.

Patterson, C. S. (1995). *The cost of capital: Theory and estimation.* Westport, CT: Quorum Books.

Shefrin, H. (2006). *Behavioral corporate finance.* New York, NY: McGraw-Hill.

Weill, P., & Ross, J. W. (2004). *IT governance: How top performers manage IT decision rights for superior results.* Boston, MA: Harvard Business School Press.

PART III

Supply Chain Management

Part III of this text focuses on a key area in health care operations management: supply chain management. The supply chain consumes somewhere between 20% and 50% of every dollar spent in health care, depending on the type of hospital and the scope of services offered. From an operations management perspective, this area represents significant opportunities for improving service levels, reducing costs, and increasing overall efficiencies.

Chapter 11 is an introduction to supply chain management strategy. Supply chain management is defined from several different perspectives, and its relevance to health care is explored. An explanation of supply chain management in the service sector is discussed. Details of the three key flows—physical, information, and financial—are explained. Strategies for successful supply chain management and key capabilities of hospital supply chain management are documented. The role of collaboration within the extended supply chain is discussed (focusing on organizations outside of the hospital, including distributors, manufacturers, and retailers). Collaboration is important because the chain interacts to share plans, pricing, and product information seamlessly. Successful collaboration eliminates bullwhip effects and promotes cost-efficient supply chain processes. Finally, a thorough discussion of the evolution of supply chain systems and technology is provided.

Chapter 12 explores the roles of purchasing, logistics, and materials management for hospitals. Materials management is typically the department charged with all aspects of procuring, storing, replenishing, and distributing goods and services throughout the hospital. This chapter further describes methodologies for purchasing and "spend analysis" and examines the role that group purchasing organizations play in health care materials management.

Chapter 13 is a primer on inventory management. Accounting and management of inventory is complex in health care for many reasons that are explored, and strategies for using inventory to improve operational efficiencies are defined. Inventory, and associated expenses of supplies, represent a large portion of nonlabor costs for health care, and this chapter describes what administrators need to know in this area. The basic accounting entries for receiving, issuing, and adjusting inventories based on perpetual and periodic methods are also illustrated.

Chapter 14 discusses the role of inventory management systems, which help to structure and control products or (items) in the health care supply chain. The use of item masters for classifying purchasing expenditures (spend) is also discussed. Item masters typically reside in enterprise resource planning and other supply chain management systems, and their purpose and scope in health care is described. Finally, the product life cycle and its effect on supply utilization are depicted.

The final chapter in this part describes pharmacy operations. Pharmacies by their nature are both clinical and operational. Because nearly 75% or more of all pharmacy revenues and expenses are affected by cost of goods sold, and because the primary role is to manage and move drugs to providers or patients so that they can be administered, the operational component of pharmacy administration is quite extensive. Technology and inventory management are two critical elements of operations management for the health care pharmacy.

CHAPTER 11

Supply Chain Management

GOALS OF THIS CHAPTER

1. Define supply chain management.
2. Describe the role of supply chain management in health care.
3. Describe the three key flows.
4. Articulate supply chain management strategies.
5. Learn how supply chain management collaboration improves vendor relationships.
6. Understand the capabilities required for supply chain effectiveness.

The term *supply chain* has received considerably more attention in recent years. Television advertisements showing products being moved quickly and efficiently from manufacturer to customer have given companies such as United Parcel Service (UPS) a competitive edge; UPS has moved from a relatively small shipping company to the world's fastest supply chain. Similarly, television and print ads for computer manufacturers, grocery stores, and even banks have focused on supply chain management in recent years.

DEFINING SUPPLY CHAINS

What is a supply chain and how can it help hospitals? The term is often used incorrectly or applied to only parts of the chain. A **supply chain** can be defined in multiple ways; here are just a few:

- A network of autonomous or semiautonomous business entities collectively responsible for procurement, manufacturing, and distribution activities associated with one or more families of related products. (Swaminathan, Smith, & Sadeh, 1996)
- A network of facilities that procure raw materials, transform them into intermediate goods and then final products, and deliver the products to customers through a distribution system. (Lee & Billington, 1995)
- The management of materials, information, and funds from the initial raw material supplier to the ultimate consumer. (Deloitte Consulting, 1999)
- The planning and management of all activities involved in sourcing and procurement, conversion, and all logistics management activities. Most important, it also includes coordination and collaboration with channel partners, who can be suppliers, intermediaries, third-party service providers, and customers. In essence, **supply chain management (SCM)** integrates supply and demand management within and across companies. (Council of Supply Chain Management Professionals, 2014)

The key to all definitions of SCM is that it is focused on:

- An end-to-end integration of business process and systems.
- Conversion of goods and services into a deliverable or final "product" that can be consumed or utilized.
- Integrated logistical management of materials, information, and cash.
- Processes that define boundaries and stretch beyond traditional departments, from producers to consumers.

This text often uses the terms *logistics* or *business logistics* synonymously with SCM. There is a slight difference, discussed in the *Purchasing and Materials Management* chapter, but for these purposes the words are intended to mean relatively the same thing.

The primary focus of SCM is to reduce costs through the chain, primarily through reductions in inventory holding costs, and to improve customer satisfaction downstream toward the consumers or users of goods and services. The mission of supply chains has often been characterized as providing the right goods, at the right time, to the right location, at the right price, in the right condition.

In health care, a supply chain includes several different parties: manufacturers, distributors, third-party logistics providers, transportation companies, hospital receiving and materials management departments, nursing, and finally the patient. **Figure 11−1** shows a typical health care supply chain.

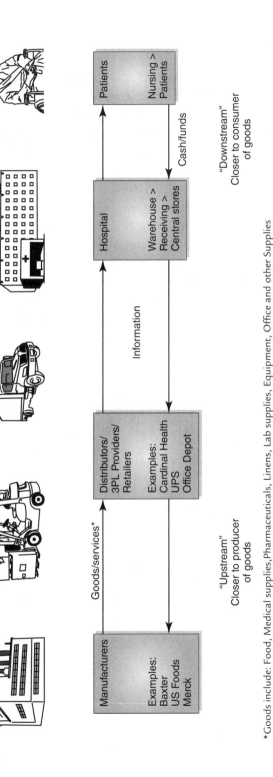

FIGURE 11–1 Health Care Supply Chain

*Goods include: Food, Medical supplies, Pharmaceuticals, Linens, Lab supplies, Equipment, Office and other Supplies

PROCESS FLOWS IN SUPPLY CHAIN

Three essential resources are depicted in Figure 11–1: information, funds or cash, and goods or services. A supply chain is typically drawn linearly to show product movement from left to right—otherwise referred to as upstream and downstream, where **upstream** is closer to the manufacturer of a good, and **downstream** is closer to final consumption or use. In other places, supply chains might be depicted as "webs," or circle diagrams, to illustrate the concept that consumer demand really drives manufacturer production, and thus it is a continuous cycle. Either way, in the illustration in Figure 11–1, goods and services are moving from manufacturers through other organizations (i.e., distributors, retailers, hospitals) and facilities (i.e., plants, warehouses, transportation vehicles) to ultimately end up in use at a hospital.

In exchange for products, cash or financial funds flow the opposite direction. As hospitals receive products, they pay the organization that sold them the goods; similarly, as distributors receive items from manufacturers, they pay their invoices as well. Financial flows are depicted by arrows moving right to left because financial flows run directly opposite the movement of products (i.e., payments are made in reverse from the sender).

The third vital resource shown in the supply chain is information. Information is every bit as critical as the product itself. Information includes data to address questions such as specific delivery location, items ordered, quantities and price paid, and location of products in the chain. Information is probably the most valuable resource, and systems and technologies are being deployed to exploit information and maximize its potential.

COMPONENTS IN THE CHAIN

There are several key components in the chain, as discussed earlier. Not all products have to pass through each facility, organization, or component of the chain. Some products move from original manufacturer directly to a hospital, others move through intermediaries, and some go through all parties in the chain. All manufacturers, distributors, retailers, and third-party logistics providers are referred to collectively as vendors. A **vendor** is any party that sells goods to others, irrespective of ownership of assets. The two most dominant players in health care are manufacturers and distributors.

Manufacturers

Manufacturers are companies that produce goods or transform raw materials and components into usable finished products. Typically, they are the beginning of the supply chain when shown linearly. Multiple manufacturers might supply products to other manufacturers as well. For example, a producer of medical infusion pumps might make circuitry, but it purchases the plastic facing and tubing from other firms. Manufacturers can create, extract, fabricate, assemble, or otherwise convert raw or semifinished goods into more consumable or usable goods.

In health care, manufacturers include firms that produce pharmaceuticals, medical supplies, medical equipment, laboratory and research supplies, office supplies, food products, building maintenance and housekeeping supplies, and much more. In many hospital enterprise resource planning systems, the vendor master can list more than 15,000 firms.

As goods are produced, they are logistically moved through one of three stages:

- They can be held in inventory. **Inventory** equals the dollar value of materials that are available for sale and represents future benefits for the firm. Because there is not always a market available for products immediately, and demand is not always predictable, inventory represents an asset on the balance sheet of the producer until such time as goods are sold and transported to the next stage in the supply chain.
- They can be transported directly to retailers, such as office supplies.
- They can be sold through distributors, or intermediaries, that aggregate supply and serve as "middlemen" between the manufacturer and retailers or consumers.

Distributors

Most medical and pharmaceutical supplies are sold through distribution channels. The largest distributors in the medical–surgical supplies business include Cardinal Health (www.cardinal.com), Owens and Minor (www.owens-minor .com), and Medline Industries (www.medline.com). Three of the largest distributors in pharmaceuticals and drug supplies are AmerisourceBergen (http: //amerisourcebergendrug.com/abcdrug/), Cardinal Health, and McKesson (www.mckesson.com). In the food products supply chain, Sysco (www.sysco .com) and U.S. Foods (http://usfoods.com) are two of the largest. See **Table 11–1** for a ranking of the top distributors in health care.

Distributors play a key role in hospital supply chains. There are four primary advantages that distributors offer:

1. They provide access and options to a larger portfolio of products and vendors. Many smaller and specialty vendors would not have an opportunity to introduce new products into the chain without distributors.

Table 11-1 The Largest Health Care Distributors

Rank	Company	Fortune 500#	Est. Revenues
1	McKesson	14	$112 billion
2	Cardinal Health	21	$102 billion
3	Amerisource Bergen	29	$80 billion
4	Owens & Minor	298	$8.7 billion
5	Henry Schein	303	$8.6 billion
6	Patterson Medical	707	$2.4 billion
7	PSS World Medical	980	$1.5 billion

Data from: Fortune 500 Rankings, *Fortune*, May 2014.

2. Distributors aggregate volume and serve as a single point of contact for hundreds or thousands of products; otherwise, a hospital would have to conduct negotiations with hundreds or thousands of different vendors, each of which requires contractual, legal, and administrative resources. This aggregation role simplifies a hospital's purchasing and inventory processes immensely.

3. Distributors reduce costs. Using concepts of economies of scale and purchasing leverage, distributors buy in bulk quantities and can often exert significantly more influence on manufacturers than a single hospital could independently. According to some studies, the average transaction cost for purchasing through distributors is only 20% of the cost to purchase directly through manufacturers (Health Industry Distributors Association, 2014).

4. Distributors hold inventory in their warehouses and therefore serve as a safety buffer that reduces bullwhip effects on the entire chain. A **bullwhip effect** is the unintended variability of demand and supply that occurs due to the lack of perfect information between parties in the chain (Lee & Billington, 1995). More specifically, they often hold enough product inventory for their customers to speed up the total order fulfillment cycle time, from initial purchase order through receipt of goods. There is, of course, a cost to holding this inventory, which ultimately is passed on to hospitals, but the offsetting advantage is better response and product availability. Distributors tend to place their warehouses centrally to accommodate their customers within a reasonable service level while maintaining maximum efficiencies.

One of the largest professional organizations that represents distributors in the health care supply chain is the Health Industry Distributors Association (2014; www.hida.org), with greater than 160 distributors in its membership and more than 450 distribution centers serving 12,000 hospitals and 125,000 physician offices.

BUSINESS PROCESSES IN THE SUPPLY CHAIN

There are four fundamental concerns in business logistics and health care supply chains—inventory, distribution, facilities, and customer service—that form the cornerstone of all business processes in SCM. Supply chain strategy is focused on maximizing return on investment, minimizing supply and inventory costs, and improving service levels, so decisions around each of the four cornerstones are crucial to performance outcomes. **Table 11–2** summarizes the four cornerstones of logistics strategy and highlights the types of decisions that fall into each category.

There are many historical processes and practices that have evolved over time to be included in SCM. When people refer to SCM in hospitals, they typically think of supply distribution or inventory management and sometimes purchasing. But SCM is much broader and includes several different functions. The historical evolution of the supply chain focuses on the following functions, because they help to manage:

- Demand forecasting.
- Purchasing.
- Inventory accounting and management.

Table 11–2   Health Care Organization SCM Strategy

Inventory	Facilities
Acquisition and order process	Network complexity
Purchase scheduling	Number of sourcing points and vendors
Forecasting right quantities	Warehouse locations and volume
Inventory levels	Space and layout design
Purchase quantities/lot sizes	Handling equipment
Storage decision	Bin and storage configuration
Distribution	**Customer Service**
Route and labor scheduling	Availability of product
Scanning and replenishment	Product quality
Mode selection	Cycle time
Equipment	Key information available
Expediting	Overall costs and pricing

- Sourcing and contracting.
- Warehousing.
- Transportation.
- Material handling and safety.
- Distribution planning.
- Order processing and fulfillment.
- Reverse logistics.
- Laundry and linen.
- Central services and sterile processing.
- Replenishment.

Many of these will be discussed in subsequent sections in this chapter.

SUPPLY CHAIN STRATEGY FOR HOSPITALS AND HEALTH CARE

Because the goal of hospital business logistics strategy is to focus on four corner-stones—inventory, distribution, facilities, and customer service—hospitals must adapt a strategy that is unique to their own situations and environments. For example, a niche specialty hospital that serves only a targeted number of service lines might require a supply chain strategy that is different from an acute care community hospital treating multiple service lines. One might emphasize product quality and availability, while the other might emphasize lower pricing and standardization.

Strategies should be developed around each of the four quadrants, or alternatively around key goals, such as financial, customer service, and suppliers. Financial strategies for hospitals should focus on:

- Creating financial value for all goods and services procured, stored, and distributed.
- Implementing a more collaborative framework for strategic sourcing.
- Optimizing working capital.
- Minimizing unproductive inventories.
- Use of electronic data interchange (EDI) and information technology (IT) to automate and streamline processes.

In areas of customer service, hospitals should focus on:

- Enhancing customer value and service.
- Ensuring timely and accurate requisition and delivery of items.

- Providing useful information systems and reports.
- Proactively developing service-level agreements with major customers that define expectations and performance requirements.

In areas of supplier or vendor management, hospitals should focus on:

- Building partnerships with key vendors through supplier relationship management processes.
- Developing collaborative relationships with key distributors and vendors.
- Establishing service-level expectations and performance requirements for suppliers and systematically monitoring them.
- Expanding EDI transactions with key vendors.
- Continuously striving for improvement in cycle times, costs, and service.

PATIENT (CUSTOMER) DEMAND DRIVES SUPPLY CHAINS

In a world where most goods and services are available 24 hours per day via Internet merchants or "e-tailers," competition for the consumer's business is becoming increasingly intense. A proliferation of competitive brick-and-mortar stores and e-businesses is changing the industry structure for virtually all market segments, from consumer goods to energy to transportation. Where competition proliferates, the market increasingly becomes a commodity, driving prices lower. As prices are reduced, manufacturers and retailers are forced to reduce costs—while maintaining product and service quality—in order to equalize profit margins. As downstream retailers cut prices to compete, upstream channel partners are forced to slash margins. This industry dynamic is a sure sign of commodity economics, where margins are always under pressure due to undifferentiated competition. As a result, organizations have no other alternative than to continually look for new markets and methods for differentiating themselves from the competition.

In many respects, the consumer really is becoming king. Consumers are demanding higher quality, better service, streamlined purchasing processes, and shorter lead times (Langabeer & Rose, 2003). Consumers want the products available and delivered immediately, and they want them offered at low prices. This same mentality carries over whether discussing a patient in a hospital or an internal customer department obtaining services from another department.

Because consumers are the focus of a firm's existence, consumer demand should be at the core of a hospital's logistics strategy. Patient demand and acuity should be used first and foremost to synchronize the planning and execution of a demand-driven supply chain, but it also drives strategy. This places immense burdens on the manufacturers, retailers, and distributors in the extended supply chain (i.e., the hospital supply chain plus channel partners external to the firm) to deliver results. Consequently, the supply chain has responded by focusing on enhanced collaboration through the various chain members to improve the overall supply chain. But this has not been enough.

Traditional SCM has focused on efficiencies, not effectiveness; on today, not tomorrow. What is needed to move forward and compete aggressively is for the supply chain to become much more in tune with the current and future needs of the marketplace—to become demand driven. Therefore, in many industries the term *demand chain* is replacing supply chain.

DEMAND CHAINS

A term that arose in other industries is *demand chain* (Ferrari, 2000). Similar to supply chain, it focuses on integrative processes and end-to-end management. But there are a few differences between supply chains and demand chains. **Demand chain** focuses primarily on revenue enhancement as opposed to the traditional supply chain emphasis on cost minimization. The ultimate goal of the demand chain is to satisfy the most profitable markets while managing service levels for the markets with less profitable demand patterns. For example, demand chains might focus on which pharmaceuticals create the highest value and have the highest prescriptions written from physicians, while a supply chain would focus specifically on replenishment levels and sourcing the items at the best possible price. The difference is primarily philosophical in nature.

In addition, the supply chain tends to "push" products based on limited knowledge of the market versus a "pull" from the consumers based on current demand. This concept of pulling demand from consumers through more targeted demand management processes is critical to reducing inventory levels that are common when products that are less in demand are pushed on the marketplace. The demand chain also blends both strategic and tactical supply chain processes (e.g., it focuses long term on changing demand behaviors but at the same time uses current demand to drive sourcing plans).

The concept of a demand chain is oriented more toward planning and strategy versus execution or transaction, because the demand chain uses key consumer and market information that is essential to the strategic planning process (Hewitt, 2001). In some respects, the concept of the demand chain is "bigger" than the supply chain, because it incorporates more departments in the hospital—such as marketing, clinical management, nursing, planning, and finance. Although the supply chain has talked about collaboration among parties in the chain, demand actually becomes the focal point for assimilating the extended organization, such as the retailers and distributors outside the company that are vital to the firm's success. Finally, while the supply chain focuses on "facilities," the demand chain centers more on "markets." This focus on markets is really what both strategic and operational management is all about.

Supply chains emphasize the efficiencies in the production and logistics processes, while demand chain emphasizes effectiveness in the business. In addition, the demand chain helps improve an organization's processes by:

- Aligning the organization and its extended units around a common plan.
- Improving coordination within the supply chain by using base forecasts and plans, thus reducing common effects of poor coordination in the supply chain, such as the bullwhip effect or inventory peaks.
- Allowing marketing and development processes to fully exploit promotional value for products by estimating consumer demand and selecting the most effective marketing promotions.

What does all of this mean for health care? First, it suggests that if hospital supply chains are to be effective, there must be a philosophical shift away from strict purchasing and replenishing when needed to using patient volume forecasts to drive the chain. Forecasting and dynamic planning for materials is just one example of this. Second, it suggests a broader role for business logistics professionals, because it will be necessary to use strategic house-wide volume indicators (such as patient days or nursing hours) to analyze values, study supply usage trends per area, and suggest process changes to more optimally align SCM resources. Finally, it encourages supply chain executives to step up and assume a leadership role in health care.

PRINCIPLES OF SUPPLY CHAIN MANAGEMENT

There are four key principles of SCM: access to information, use of advanced decision support tools, pursuit of supply chain effectiveness, and distributed intelligence.

Access to Information

As the extended supply chain moves to more complete access to patient- and provider-level information, the chain must openly share downstream data. This access to actual information—whether it is through sharing of procedural volume and usage data, bed forecasts, census data, market research, inventory levels, or transactional usage history—is vital to guarding against common effects of poorly communicated supply chains, such as the bullwhip effect.

Use of Advanced Decision Support Tools

The use of sophisticated technology can benefit most of the business processes occurring within the supply chain. Tools such as business intelligence, advanced planning systems, forecasting systems, Internet-based vendor portals, customer relationship management, and market planning systems all support supply chain strategies. As supply chains become more intelligent and require less manual manipulation, there will be a more rapid transition toward decision support systems.

Pursuit of Supply Chain Effectiveness

The supply chains of demand-driven organizations tend to focus on process optimization and overall alignment and effectiveness, rather than on other common metrics, such as average costs and staffing headcounts. Supply chain effectiveness requires a focus on all four areas of logistics strategy—not just a single dimension.

Distributed Intelligence

The goal of distributed intelligence is to allow those individuals and supply chain parties most knowledgeable about the patient or market demand to have involvement and insight into the planning processes. This distributed intelligence ensures that all parties are acting on the same information at the same time using the same set of assumptions. In addition, this creates communication feedback loops for each party in the chain to participate in improving processes and decisions.

STRATEGY AND LOGISTICS CAPABILITIES

As discussed earlier, the supply chain focuses primarily on the flow of goods, information, and funds through the distribution channel and a network of facilities. Thus, an effective supply chain strategy is one that is focused on optimizing the positioning of facilities, rationalizing and streamlining the network, and continually improving the manufacturing and logistics business processes that move products to the market (Fisher, 1997; Gattorna, 1998). A supply chain strategy must emphasize three key performance metrics: improving speed to market, minimizing throughput and total transaction costs, and simultaneously improving customer satisfaction levels.

A collaborative supply chain strategy should be developed with each of the key participants in the extended supply chain. All parties in the supply chain have the same goals and interests (i.e., improving total margins); however, it is often difficult to arrive at a consensual strategy that maximizes the total chain's performance. Suboptimization in the chain occurs more often than not, due to incomplete sharing of information between the parties, lack of true collaborative technologies, and an unwillingness to expose key business data such as prices and margins.

To achieve collaboration, the supply chain must focus on the key strategic capabilities that it seeks to develop. The five most important capabilities that supply chains should develop include (Stern & Stalk, 1998):

- *Speed* or time to bring products from design to market and from the supply chain through the demand chain.
- *Consistency* in product and service quality in all items and locations.
- *Acuity* of patient and provider demand preferences and usage patterns.
- *Agility* in the flexible sourcing and responsive distribution and logistical processes.
- *Innovativeness* in product conception and delivery.

As hospitals continue to emphasize a supply chain strategy that is built on these capabilities and is geared toward emphasizing alignment and responsiveness through the network, the supply chain strategy will continue to build demand-driven organizations.

EFFICIENT VERSUS RESPONSIVE SUPPLY CHAIN MANAGEMENT STRATEGY

There are two philosophies in SCM for hospitals: responsive (also called *just in time*) and efficiency (also called *supply to stock*). This choice of strategy reflects a continuum, with both strategies dichotomously positioned (Chopra & Meindl, 2001). Very responsive chains have resources ready to use at all times. The term **just in time (JIT)** is a concept that was inherited from the Japanese and their quality programs; it means a stockless environment where materials and resources are received when they are needed for consumption. This is also commonly referred to as lean marketing. In principle, this implies that just as a nurse is ready to pick up an item to dispense to a patient, the material arrives on site and is placed in the right location just prior to usage. In essence, JIT implies stockless; however, in reality, some degree of safety stock must always exist to guard against shortages and **stock-outs** (where inventory is 0 when demand is greater than 1).

Most hospitals compensate with a purchasing and inventory policy whereby replenishment is designed to reach a minimum level that might approximate 24 hours or more of supply.

On the opposite dichotomy is an efficient chain, which tends to buy in bulk and have fewer quantities on hand, emphasizing lower total costs. **Supply to stock (STS)** is a philosophy whereby larger quantities of materials are purchased and placed into an inventory location for storage and distribution. Typically, items are purchased in bulk quantities to take advantage of pricing discounts and economies of scale; the items are then broken down into smaller units of measure for storage internally, either in a hospital-owned warehouse or central stores. **Economies of scale** are synergies or reductions in total costs due to purchase or production of larger quantities. STS, by definition, implies higher stock levels and greater need for careful inventory management and accounting.

JIT requires a more flexible and responsive supply chain. It is more responsive because, as items are issued or consumed, they must be replenished. To make this happen, the supply chain has to be quick, responsive, and integrated between the hospital and all vendors.

STS, or bulk, is more efficient and probably cost-effective in the long term. STS requires manufacturers and distributors to focus on more economical production runs; necessitates hospitals to own finished goods inventories; and encourages hospitals to purchase in economical sizes, for both shipments and purchase quantities.

JIT is often called *lowest unit of measure*. **Lowest unit of measure (LUM)** describes the process whereby hospitals purchase and store items strictly in the unit in which they will ultimately be consumed. For example, if a hospital purchases a pallet load filled with boxes of gloves, but gloves are ultimately dispensed and possibly charged to patients by each one used, the LUM is "each." Although LUM and JIT are often used interchangeably, they are not synonymous.

JIT, as the more responsive strategy, requires hospitals to be able to quickly change over between items. If a specific type of catheter is being used today, but tomorrow it could be phased out, then a JIT environment requires quick response. **Quick response** is a process in which lead times are minimized, rapid processing of orders occurs, and changes in demand and business requirements are instantly communicated over the supply chain via collaborative information systems (Boyson & Corsi, 2001). In other words, quick response allows hospitals to, among other things:

- Update the item master with new items, costs, and attributes.
- Contact the vendors and distributors to procure new items.
- Change bar codes and bins in all inventory locations.
- Change pricing in the Charge Description Master.

Distributors play a vital role in providing flexibility and quick response, in that they have instant access to a broad portfolio of products and therefore reduce the transition time between changeovers. **Table 11–3** provides a summary of the characteristics common in both JIT and STS environments.

JIT is very difficult to implement in a rapidly changing environment and requires good information systems, collaboration with vendors, higher-level personnel, and more flexible business processes (Cox & Blackstone, 1990). It is often accompanied by premium pricing and higher transportation rates from vendors to accommodate such rapid response.

The effect on purchasing is that JIT typically results in a smaller number of line items on an individual purchase order, while STS might have many more lines and quantities per purchase order. When looking at productivity metrics for the purchasing department, the choice of JIT versus STS must be understood because the choice influences output ratios.

The effect on inventory and replenishment is quite evident. STS requires a significantly higher investment in inventory levels, which necessitates high cash outlays and higher working capital prior to material usage or consumption (Sanderson, 1985). JIT capitalizes lower inventories but requires premiums for supply expenses, because JIT is usually associated with a premium somewhere between 5% and 15% higher costs.

The relationship between service and efficiency is a well-documented trade-off (Bowersox, Closs, & Cooper, 2002). A supply chain can be highly efficient, but it might be too slow to respond to nursing's and other providers' changing needs and requirements. On the other hand, a very responsive and flexible chain might provide excellent service, but there is a premium in terms of total long-run costs.

Table 11–3   JIT versus STS

Supply to Stock (Bulk)	• Economical purchase sizes • Use of economic order quantity • Higher levels of inventory • Higher number of items per order • Fewer, lengthy orders • Lower costs
Just In Time (Quick Response)	• Rapid product change-outs • Rapid order fulfillment processes • Integrated information systems • Short lead times • More collaborative supply chain • Smaller more frequent orders • Premium prices

As is evident, total long-run costs increase as service levels and responsiveness increase. Similarly, as inventory levels increase, so, too, do total expenses. The total cost behaves similarly to other U-shaped curves, where an optimal point can be determined in this trade-off between service and efficiency. Service and responsiveness come at a cost. **Figure 11–2** presents the cost behaviors that are implicit in logistics.

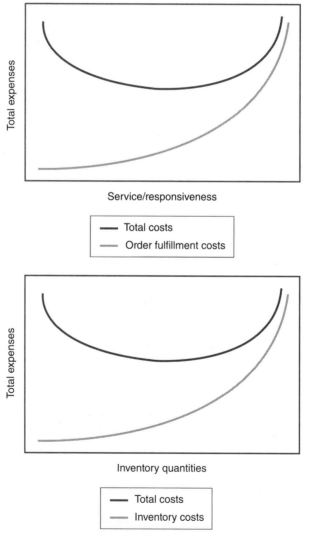

FIGURE 11–2 Cost Behaviors in Logistics

REVERSE LOGISTICS

There has not been significant research to provide exposure to the true costs of reverse logistics in health care. **Reverse logistics** is the process and methods by which hospitals reverse the physical flow of goods, returning them back internally to the originating department or all the way back up the chain to distributors and suppliers. Typically, products are reversed because they are the wrong product, they have expired, they are overflow, or for some other reason. The standard flow of products is normally better defined because it is the norm, but in some cases goods moving in the reverse direction can be quite substantial. In other industries, reverse logistics can make up as much as 25% of total supply chain costs.

In some areas of the business, such as pharmaceuticals, products are commonly distributed from the bulk pharmacy distribution area to nursing units in LUM, only to find that the patients have been discharged or moved. These items are then returned back to the primary location, and they have to be received back into the system, credits provided to the patients' electronic medical record, and inventory restocked to inventory shelves. Expired drugs are another common problem; some manufacturers or distributors accept the product back upon expiration, which requires reverse logistics processes and systems.

In other cases, inaccurate products are received and must be returned back to distributors and manufacturers. A purchase order might request one product, but another one was erroneously picked or substituted. In these cases, staging areas must be assigned, return goods authorization forms must be completed, credit memos must be applied, and careful monitoring of all accounts must occur to ensure successful completion of the transaction. Reverse logistics typically requires greater effort than normal logistics because it is the exception and, thus, no standards exist.

Hospitals are not designed to handle reverse logistics very well. While it is the exception, it may involve a significant percentage of total transactions. Reverse logistics needs to be carefully analyzed in much the same way as traditional product flows. Mapping the return process flow for key vendor groups, setting standards for the length of time items can sit in staging, defining cost thresholds at which reverse logistics fails to make economic sense, establishing physical inventory locations, and systematizing the entire transaction are necessary to treat reverse logistics properly.

SUPPLY CHAIN INFORMATION SYSTEMS

The health care supply chain is complex. It is characterized by multiple vendors, large and powerful distributors, and a disintegrated network of products and partners loosely held together by manual and people-intensive processes. Supply chain information systems are required to better manage the flow of supplies or products, information, funds, and services from all parties in the chain: from manufacturers to distributors to the point of care and consumption. This is especially difficult in health care supply chains relative to more technology-intense industries such as consumer goods or retail environments. As supplies move downstream toward hospitals and clinics, the quality and robustness of accompanying management and information systems used to manage these products deteriorate significantly. Technology that provides advanced planning, synchronization, and collaboration upstream at the large supply manufacturers and distributors is rarely in use at even the world's larger and more sophisticated hospitals.

Technology to better plan and manage the acquisition and replenishment of key resources (e.g., pharmaceuticals, supplies, equipment) in hospitals today is severely lacking relative to other industries. Driven by continual cost pressures and other operational constraints, the supply chain represents one of the largest opportunities for cost savings and value creation in the health care enterprise—if only there were a comprehensive roadmap to help get hospitals there. Data suggest that hospitals create an evolutionary path for supply chain technologies, implementing better business practices and more advanced technologies to increase vendor collaboration, optimize pricing and sourcing efforts, and improve prediction of required order quantities and inventory levels.

When most hospital executives talk about technology, typically they are referring to clinical decision support, medical informatics, or electronic records (Ball, Simborg, Albright, & Douglas, 1995). A wide range of technologies and systems is developing that bring advanced decision support to the forefront of health care practice in the "front office" (i.e., the point of care or place at which care is provided to patients) (Kreider & Haselton, 1997). In the "back office" (representing the administrative and financial functions), there has been only minimal progress. There is continued deployment of hospital resource systems, but they tend to focus primarily on those business processes generally more visible and seen as "strategic," such as human resources or financial management.

Although most of these hospital systems have procurement, inventory, and distribution capabilities, they are fairly rudimentary in scope and function—providing mainly transactional and limited reporting capabilities. This limited capability needs to be expanded to take a wider, strategic perspective on the clinical supply chain. As stated earlier, SCM is defined as the planning, organizing, and controlling of functions inside and outside a company that enable the chain to make products and provide services to the customer. All of the parties in the clinical chain (patients, providers, materials department, vendors, distributors, and manufacturers) must work together to create a chain that is effective, although in reality each is fighting to carve out a profit margin for its respective components.

The focus on the entire chain, from suppliers through delivery of care, is a relatively new concept in hospitals, and it represents a departure from the normal materials management perspective of managing internal, discrete business functions separately. It does represent major opportunities for cost savings and margin enhancements, however, as other industries have learned over the past decade. Optimizing the supply chain is very important, because pharmaceutical supply and materials expenses consume approximately 25% of hospital expenditures in most organizations. When accounting for all supply chain expenses—including the administrative cost of procuring, receiving, and administering the supply chain—total supply chain expenses can total nearly one-third of all hospital expenses. Because hospitals have employed several quick fixes that have generated savings (i.e., the "low-hanging fruit"), clinical supply chains are now primed to begin the transformation that most other consumer-based industries have undergone during the past 20 years.

This area, known as SCM technology, has yet to receive significant attention in hospitals. In the health care industry, supply chain technology has been widely used with medical supply manufacturers and with large distributors, but it has yet to trickle down the chain into hospitals and the point of care. Outside of health care, in industries such as manufacturing, automotive, and retail, there has been considerable deployment of SCM systems. Hospitals, however, have not significantly adopted the majority of these technologies, and so they remain very limited in scope and sophistication relative to virtually every other industry. A meta-search of health care information systems material published in the past decade shows very little coverage of supply chain systems, their importance, or their future. Where supply chain technology topics were covered, they were discussed in generic ways with their most common functions of automating inventory control, purchasing, and receiving. In advanced texts on SCM and technology, there is almost never any mention of the hospital industry in cases or context.

Regardless of the current state of hospital supply chain technology, the direction is clear but the pace of change is not. While the hospital industry has unique intricacies and challenges, the basic requirements remain the same in all industries. The need for predicting the right location, the right price, the right time, and the right products is consistent across all industries, which suggests that hospital SCM systems will evolve as they have in the consumer-driven and manufacturing industries. The only unknown is the timing of when individual hospitals will begin to evolve, which will partially be based on each organization's financial condition and the vision of its materials management leadership team.

EVOLUTION OF SUPPLY CHAIN TECHNOLOGY

Consumer-driven industries have led the effort to develop and deploy enterprise systems and associated supply chain technologies (Blackwell, 1997). Historically, the scope of enterprise systems has focused on automating specific transactions, such as order processing and invoice generation. The initial spotlight on automation during the 1960s through the 1980s was the period when IT was regarded as primarily a means to reduce costs and improve operational efficiencies. This early focus on internal activities, efficiencies, and execution resulted in some early success in terms of cost minimization. When enterprise resource planning systems were first introduced, they were seen as the way to handle large volumes of hospital data in terms of sales transactions, materials masters, and other manufacturing and sales data required to manage the entire business.

Since then, there has been a gradual shift away from execution toward planning processes, and new processes and technology were developed for material requirements planning (now termed *manufacturing resource planning*), which began the shift toward better planning of the production and inventory requirements necessary to manage logistical operations (now called *supply chains*). The continued evolution toward manufacturing resource planning was an extension of this focus on planning. Today, there is a much broader focus on using the Internet and e-solutions to extend the breadth and connectivity of information (Kuglin & Rosenbaum, 2001; Martin, 1999).

During the 1990s, SCM technology began focusing on planning and effectiveness versus execution and efficiency (Lowson, King, & Hunter, 1999). Business process reengineering and total quality management helped force a "process" view of the hospital; companies were urged to start looking not only at inputs but also at outputs, as well as the process used to link the two. Advanced planning systems were the first to focus on areas such as production scheduling, demand forecasting, capacity planning, and network optimization. Customer relationship management emerged and began capturing all customer data in one location to improve call center management, sales force automation, and marketing automation (Blattberg & Neslin, 1990). Now that the operational and tactical processes are addressed, SCM technology can start focusing more on what the software industry calls *demand-based systems* (predictive modeling, data mining, and business intelligence). These systems continue the evolution of more strategic planning solutions for SCM optimization, because they help focus firms on effectiveness and margin enhancement.

Hospitals cannot simply transition or evolve from manual, paper-based supply chain processes into a fully automated organization. The best approaches favor phased-in or evolutionary processes, which build on a solid foundation and continue to improve. **Figure 11–3** shows a theoretical evolutionary model of development for hospital supply chain technology. Directionally, SCM technologies focus more on becoming strategic and enhancing planning and effectiveness (i.e., moving up the *y*-axis of this model) and less on the more tactical processes of automation and efficiency. On the *x*-axis, hospital technology generally moves through three phases as it becomes more strategic.

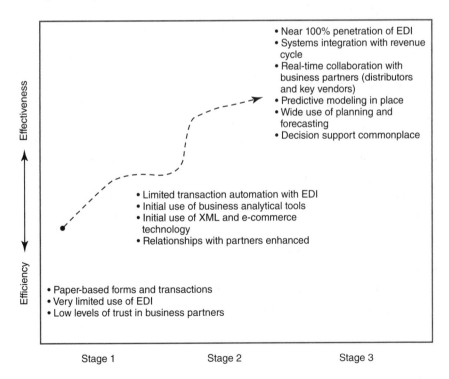

FIGURE 11–3 Evolution of SCM Systems

Most hospitals, including the largest and most advanced, are only in Phase 1 of development on this evolutionary model. During this stage, there is a strong emphasis on automating the key business processes and transactions. Ensuring that procurement staff are using electronic requisitions and purchase orders and confirming that electronic order entry is being used for supply requests from floors are examples of this focus on transaction automation. In many hospitals, paper requisitions remain the norm, but this is problematic for maturing supply chain technologies. The switch to electronic forms is a necessary step to create transaction history, which is a requirement for organizations as they move to subsequent phases and need to rely on this information for analysis and intelligence. Also in Phase 1, hospitals explore limited use of EDI with key vendors or distributors. Typically, this means that of the most common EDI transaction sets, only one or two are commonly in use (e.g., EDI 850 for purchase orders). In addition, there is a general lack of trust between hospital staff and key vendors and distributors during this early phase of development, so technology strategy is not focused on building collaboration or using electronic commerce to bridge processes. Finally, the overall technology is focused around managing and minimizing supply costs, which produces a strategy around centralization and automation. While Phase 1 produces stable results in the supply chain, there are no stellar performers.

During Phase 2, there is a significant amount of transaction history that has been captured—typically upward of 2 to 3 years. Hospitals that have reached this phase wish to put such data to use in creative ways, replacing manual, people-intensive processes with more intelligent system processes. Using advanced analytical systems, such as forecasting and predictive modeling, supply chains can make more intelligent replenishment decisions, optimize inventory levels, analyze spending patterns in key categories, and track performance metrics in significantly greater detail. Hospitals also begin to value collaboration with key suppliers and distributors and expand the use of EDI for more than one or two transaction sets. Typically, EDI progression in Phase 2 supports several transactions, such as EDI 840 (request for quotation), EDI 843 (response to a request for quotation), EDI 850 (purchase order), EDI 855 (purchase order acknowledgment), EDI 856 (advanced shipment notice), EDI 870 (order status report), and EDI 810 (electronic invoice). In addition, hospital supply chains in this phase start to explore the use of broader e-commerce tools, such as e-procurement or other Web technologies. The initial use of XML in collaborative planning and forecasting processes, for example, and Internet-enabled e-procurement and online catalogs for suppliers are ways in which hospitals can move beyond

EDI toward more scalable, flexible Internet technology (Cross, 2000). Overall, the technology strategy in this phase focuses hospital management systems on optimization.

As hospitals progress to Phase 3 in this model, there is a much higher concentration on collaboration and integration—both on internal business processes and with external parties in the supply chain. While during the first two phases the supply chains tend to be inward looking at supply costs and efficiencies, during this phase there is a heightened focus on alignment with the revenue cycle. Ensuring seamless integration of supply chain and revenue cycle is vital during this phase to obtain higher effectiveness. Tracking a supply's history into the chain, ultimately ending at consumption or point of use to a specific patient, is necessary to align revenue and supply processes as well as reduce system redundancies.

In Phase 3, hospitals and suppliers become integrated through systematic processes and technology. For example, consider an environment in which a facility's patient acuity or procedural case mix changes. Analytics would automatically suggest different buying and replenishment plans, and key suppliers would be instantly alerted to this change. Plans are adjusted, causing fewer inventories to be held in the chain, thus reducing expenses and ensuring strong collaboration with all parties. While such systems seem distant, they are in use today in many food and beverage and other consumer goods industries.

Technology used during this phase helps support many advanced decisions that are seen today as unpredictable. For example, a hospital will have an instant ability to determine how many items to purchase, how and where it should store the product, key timing in the chain, which vendor it should use, what the patient chargeable price should be, and what the overall financial margin result will be on the chain. Many of these questions go unanswered in most hospitals that remain in the first two phases.

Potential obstacles that stand in the way of the development and delivery of this integrated SCM system are numerous and well documented. There are literally dozens, including lack of financial resources, lack of physician sponsorship, too many competing interests, low prioritization from chief information officers and staffs, and lack of leadership and vision from SCM. But the two most significant, yet manageable, are trust and discipline. The most obvious of these roadblocks is trust—trust internally among the various functions in the hospital, but more than that, trust that allows the hospital to share information openly with external vendors and distributors. The movement toward e-procurement and other Internet-enabled processes linking multiple parties requires significant trust with key business partners. Hospital supply chain managers have historically lacked this trust. In addition, lack of disciplined strategic thinking in materials management has limited SCM technology deployment. The lack of disciplined thought to create a technology plan, build required business cases, explore new technologies and bring them into health care, and take a disciplined approach to implementation and follow through has contributed to the quality and robustness chasm that exists between hospital SCM technology and those of other industries.

As previously stated, most of the 6,000 hospitals in the United States today are in Phase 1 of this evolutionary model. Many hospitals have not focused their limited IT resources toward the supply chain, but that will begin to change as hospitals start using their supply chains as a competitive tool.

RECOMMENDATIONS FOR SUPPLY CHAIN MANAGEMENT TECHNOLOGY

Hospitals lag significantly behind other industries in the deployment of advanced management systems to drive supply chain optimization. First, hospitals must begin to value the supply chain as a potential tool for competitive advantage and focus on management systems in this area if they are to catch up or make progress. Second, hospitals need to shift their internal information systems technology strategy to focus more resources and vision toward the supply chain. Chief information officers and their staff must become more engaged in defining SCM business processes and performance metrics and align the SCM technology strategy and respective roadmap accordingly. Third, an integrated portfolio of management systems will have to be deployed to achieve the vision of an optimal SCM system, because it is highly probable that a single vendor will not be able to provide advanced functionality in each of the areas specific to the hospital industry. This integrated approach requires prioritization of functionality and establishment of a single supply chain technology strategy, knowing which areas will add the highest value for each individual hospital. Finally, this integrated SCM system must focus on collaboration, optimization, planning, and effectiveness. Opportunities exist for significant cost reductions and revenue enhancements, as they do in other non-healthcare industries, if they are pursued ambitiously and with vision and discipline. If executed appropriately, based on experiences from implementations in multiple industries, hospitals can expect significant improvements in performance, such as a 15% to 20% decrease in inventories, several percentage point improvement in revenues, 10% reduction in returns, and significant declines in cost of goods sold.

SUPPLY CHAIN COLLABORATION

At its core, SCM is highly collaborative in nature. **Collaboration**, defined as working jointly with others in an endeavor to accomplish similar goals, is fundamental to effective operations and SCM. Improving relationships, processes, and systems for key vendors and distributors is essential to SCM for pharmaceutical, medical, food, and other suppliers. There are two collaborative planning processes that have the potential to significantly improve distributor and manufacturer planning processes, and, if used properly, they will help hospitals substantially achieve better results. These two processes are sales and operations planning and collaborative planning, forecasting, and replenishment.

Hospitals and providers do not use these two processes today, but other components of the upstream supply chain do. It is important for operations managers to know the processes involved in the rest of the chain to help reduce bullwhip effects and improve supply chain operations, as well as to understand the processes that vendors utilize daily.

Although there are other business processes in existence that are also collaborative, such as quick response and efficient consumer response, they are variations on the two processes described here. In general, these processes are effective tools because they use demand to drive alignment through the supply chain, promote the use of a single set of numbers to produce departmental and company plans, and focus on improving results through streamlined business process management.

SALES AND OPERATIONS PLANNING

Sales and operations planning (S&OP) is a specific process that helps firms focus on one thing: making the best choices of where and how to fulfill demand. Distributors and manufacturers in health care widely use S&OP because of the huge array of stock-keeping units in multiple distribution locations. Therefore, the demand side of the equation is difficult to predict and thoroughly understand. On the supply side, manufacturing plant capacities are often limited, and many constraints exist that complicate the ability to fulfill demand (such as distribution, lead time, manpower, and other resource constraints). Couple these constraints with the fact that the demand strategy for successful organizations is to serve demand with the highest customer economics first, and the process becomes even more complex.

The S&OP process is about matching demand with supply at aggregate levels. It involves managing these constraints to identify the demand that the firm seeks and fulfill this demand in the most responsive and efficient means possible. Balancing demand with supply to make profit-maximizing decisions (in all parts of the business) is the basic mission of S&OP.

S&OP is a collaborative process, and thus it is interconnected with other key business processes in the organization. The difference is that S&OP helps integrate the strategic aspects of the company (i.e., Where is the market heading?) with the tactical aspects (i.e., In which product families might we have supply problems?). In addition, S&OP focuses on:

- A long-term view (e.g., next month or next quarter).
- Aggregated views at the higher product levels, such as categories or families.
- Fulfillment of key areas of market demand (e.g., satisfying the profitable demand).
- Finding key constraints in balancing demand and supply (e.g., such as targeting capacity issues and finding alternative sources of production).
- Achieving consensus among senior levels of management cross functionally.

OBJECTIVES OF SALES AND OPERATIONS PLANNING

While the overarching purpose of S&OP is to provide aggregate demand and supply management, the objectives are clearly much more complicated. S&OP allows for the organization as a whole to collaborate around one of the most important business processes for the hospital. The collaborative S&OP process has four key objectives:

1. *Provide a common base of information around the immediate market dynamics.* Driven by senior managers from the marketing/commercial side of the business, in conjunction with supply chain managers, the S&OP process helps all parties gain a common understanding of how the market is changing and the effect this will have on demand and supply. A common understanding and implication of pricing, base demand, trends, competitive maneuvers, and market research findings

all have an effect on the demand and supply chains. Therefore, the sales and operations process becomes extremely important in the overall planning process to drive alignment and share common assumptions about the future.

2. *Manage the performance of the supply chain.* The S&OP process is the appropriate forum to discuss strategic aspects of the most recent supply and demand chain performance. This includes analyzing metrics such as target versus actual customer service levels, inventory days on hand (i.e., retailer inventory or similar measure), order fulfillment cycle time, and manufacturing yields versus plans. In addition, other relevant demand chain indicators, such as an analysis of promotion and assortment effectiveness, should also be explored.

3. *Collaboratively manage product portfolios.* Plans for immediate or future development of new-product launches/introductions, product line extensions, product phase-outs, and other changes in product families can be jointly discussed in terms of their effect on all areas of the extended hospital.

4. *Create shared business plans and scenarios.* The end result of the S&OP meetings can be summarized as better decisions and execution. S&OP processes help manufacturing, supply chains, demand chains, sales, marketing, and other departments make better decisions than they otherwise would have made. At the same time, each department can execute against a plan that is shared by all other parties in the chain. Both better decisions and more effective execution are the two principal outputs in creating shared business plans and scenarios.

THE BASIC SALES AND OPERATIONS PLANNING PROCESS

The basic S&OP process is highly meticulous and collaborative and occurs cross functionally from senior management, supply chain, manufacturing, sales, marketing, and finance. The process can be broken down into five major phases:

Business planning >> Demand analysis >> Supply analysis
>> Balancing >> Decisions

Each of these steps has many more activities and subprocesses. These steps will be defined at a high level in the rest of this section.

Business Planning

The purpose of business planning is to define the key strategic aspects of the business. This includes an analysis of sales, market share, profits, and expected return on investment. At this stage, the sales and marketing groups are responsible for providing general direction to the hospital in terms of managing the product portfolio. The business plan should guide decisions on manufacturing capacities, logistics requirements, and retail distribution strategies.

The next few steps have to be undertaken within the context of optimizing the primary business goals for the firm, such as improving the profit and loss position and increasing market share by market segment and category.

Demand Analysis

In the demand analysis phase, companies must focus on obtaining a collaborative, unconstrained plan that can be expressed quantitatively by a single forecast for demand by product category. It is more accurate and productive to plan a chain around a single forecast than a range of expectations, so the focus should center around a single view of the future. Specifically, this includes the following tasks or subprocesses:

- Run statistical forecasts on historical demand (based on combinations of historical sales, confirmed or booked orders, and committed customer schedules).
- Share these preliminary forecast figures.
- Obtain collaborative business intelligence on volume sales plans, retailer or supplier promotions, and planned price increases.
- Gain collaborative input on other key events that may occur during the period.
- Perform sensitivity or simulation analysis.
- Secure a common demand scenario.
- Publish the final unconstrained demand plan.

In addition, during this phase it is important to look at demand not only for current products in the portfolio but also for product line extensions, new display or bonus packs, and completely new items. Every product must undergo a thorough demand analysis to identify and validate its phase of the product life cycle to finalize the demand plans. New items to be introduced or utilized should be a part of this process.

In general, it is the primary role of the sales and marketing team to obtain field input on all demand factors to establish the most accurate demand plan. It is important to remember the following equation for a good demand plan:

$$\text{Demand plan} = \text{Statistical forecast} + \text{Business intelligence} + \text{Collaboration} + \text{Action}$$

The output of the demand analysis phase is typically a report or system view that outlines at the product family level the following information: sales history analysis, target inventory levels (based on the cycle inventory policy), customer service levels (e.g., order backlogs, out of stocks, fill rates), and all demand assumptions taken.

Supply Analysis

During the supply analysis phase, the key inputs are the reports prepared during the demand analysis phase that define demand for each product family. The supply planners use this information to review and refine the operations plan to determine if sufficient supply exists to meet expected demand. The available supply equation is fairly easy to define:

$$\text{Supply} = (\text{Capacity} \times \text{Utilization}) + \text{Inventory on hand} + \text{Goods purchased for resale}$$

Given this, supply planners must explore the assumptions taken during the planning period (i.e., next month or quarter) and analyze if capacity additions have occurred (e.g., new plants coming on line), capacity reductions have occurred (e.g., plants have been transitioned to other families or have been closed entirely), plant utilization or yield rates have changed (e.g., due to maintenance), or any other supply factors have a bearing on supply. For example, obtaining adequate supply of components or raw materials in certain industries, such as the chip fabrication sector, often creates frustrations for planners in their attempt to balance supply with demand.

The end result of this phase is a rough-cut capacity plan that details the planned available inventory levels and supply positions at the family level, as well as a list of issues that are the source of the supply constraints (such as manufacturing line bottlenecks, resource limitations, and upstream supply chain or vendor-related problems). Following this rough-cut capacity analysis, summary reports should be distributed to key members of the full sales and operations planning team to begin their analysis.

Balancing

At this point, the key input is the combined demand/supply rough-cut planning report. This report details the potential problem areas for the company so that the group can focus on attacking the exceptions (those areas where demand and supply are seriously misaligned). The balancing process typically takes place in two parts: an informal pre-S&OP discussion and a formal S&OP meeting. The pre-S&OP discussion among the key members of the team focuses on making some recommendations on how to balance demand and supply, including many demand or supply management decisions. For example, if demand exceeds supply, such actions may include:

- Increasing prices temporarily to reduce demand.
- Allocating available supply to only key retail or downstream locations.
- Adding new capacity or resources, such as people, shifts, equipment, or plants.
- Purchasing product for resale from other collaborating companies.
- Establishing customer priorities (based on customer service-level expectations, customer value added, and ABC rankings) to determine which demand will not be immediately fulfilled.

If supply exceeds demand, some appropriate actions that may be recommended include:

- Decreasing prices temporarily (i.e., **temporary price reductions**) to generate additional demand.
- Adding additional promotions, such as premiums or rebates.
- Scaling back on the production plans, which might result in short-term labor and resource savings.
- Building or "loading" inventory, especially if demand is increasing and the cost of shutting down production is greater than the cost of capital attached to finished goods inventory.
- Adjusting other constraints that might affect the balance.

In the process of deciding on these demand and supply strategies for balancing, there should be an aggregated view of all product families in the business units to roll up the financial or top-line business effects of all decisions and assumptions. Once completed, the planning process is ready for senior-level decisions.

Decisions

The high-level view of the plans at this point should be summarized and presented in the monthly formal sales and operations meeting. This meeting should summarize and review the key elements of the business plan, the current financial climate, the supply chain performance metrics, the family-level rough-cut plans, and the summary of key decisions that need to be made to balance demand and supply. At this point, the S&OP process must be focused on aligning the business (i.e., manufacturing, logistics, extended supply chain) around a core S&OP business scenario, so decisions have to be made quickly and must be fully supported. Consensus in the multifunctional meetings must be achieved, because the goal of S&OP is to create a common, collaborative scenario for how to best manage the combined hospital.

In summary, S&OP is an effective collaborative business process for managing demand and supply activities in large distribution and manufacturing organizations. While hospitals and providers are historically less involved, an understanding of this process helps drive alignment with the upstream supply chain. Benefits from the S&OP process include better cross-functional alignment, gap analysis, more efficient resource planning, and more effective use of promotional resources. This process is essential to synchronizing the demand and supply chains with shared scenarios that can streamline operations, reduce demand variability, and create consistent actions and strategies for all parts of the extended hospital.

COLLABORATIVE PLANNING, FORECASTING, AND REPLENISHMENT

Collaborative planning, forecasting, and replenishment (CPFR) is the name for the process that seeks to improve the relationship or partnership between retailers and suppliers. The intent of this process is to achieve full collaboration and improve the sharing of information around consumer point-of-sale data through the retail supply chain to enhance overall chain performance.

OBJECTIVES OF COLLABORATIVE PLANNING, FORECASTING, AND REPLENISHMENT

While the primary objective of CPFR is to improve relationships within the other parties in the supply chain, there are many other objectives:

- Alignment of the chain around a common process, common formats for data exchange, common systems, and common performance metrics.
- Sharing of one common forecast and demand plan, based on downstream sales and usage data, that ensures that suppliers, manufacturers, distributors, and hospitals all share common business and supply chain plans.

- Communication of issues around meeting demand, prioritizing demand, and managing supply allocations within a collaborative framework.
- Advanced notification of pricing or promotions to more adequately plan future months without experiencing the bullwhip effect.
- Better visibility of demand, inventory, and shipment data through the supply chain by sharing common technology and messaging formats among parties in the chain.

Each of these objectives translates into maximizing collaboration in the planning process to streamline operations and increase the effectiveness of the entire chain—not just components within the chain.

COLLABORATIVE PLANNING, FORECASTING, AND REPLENISHMENT GUIDELINES

Fifteen years ago, the **Voluntary Interindustry Commerce Standards (VICS)** Association was created by industry executives who brainstormed how to collectively improve the supply chain coordination in the retail industry among retailers, manufacturers, and suppliers. The objective of the VICS Association at the time was to use better demand information to drive alignment through the supply chain by creating voluntary standards within the industry that all parties would use to share data in a consistent manner (Schenck, 1998). Today,

> VICS' overall global objective is to improve product availability to the consumer by providing leadership and encouragement in the identification, development, and implementation of volunteer standards, protocols, guidelines, and other mechanisms that, . . . when properly utilized, are expected to lead to better anticipation of, and reaction to, changes in consumer demand for these products with the subsequent optimization of production and carrying costs. (VICS, 2001, p. 3)

The VICS Association has been the driving force behind the creation of a CPFR process and standards within the consumer packaged goods and retail industries. VICS has not yet had much influence on the health care industry, although many of the manufacturers that sell through retail chains are currently participating, such as Johnson & Johnson and GlaxoSmithKline. It has been a slow process, but it has been well received by the world's leading firms, such as Procter & Gamble, Hewlett-Packard, Walmart, Nabisco, and JCPenney. Other firms, although interested in the concept and excited about the opportunities, have been slow to embrace the actual CPFR standards.

The guidelines for CPFR allow for the creation of a common trading framework. Specifically, this means common language, common process models, and common data standards (Cross, 2000; Hoque, 2000). Of these, the most important is to share a common philosophy or paradigm with all parties in the CPFR framework. This shared philosophy is carried out with the use of common vocabulary and language within the process. Both business and technology terminologies and definitions must be designed to support a common base of understanding among all participants. Achieving this common base is essential for multiple retailers and suppliers to interact and improve relationships.

Second, the business process used must be very well defined and detailed. In successful firms using CPFR, the process models describe exactly which elements of the relationship need to be documented, which key aspects of the combined business plan must be shared, which categories will be emphasized and which strategies will be used, which steps will be used to provide a sales forecast, how to handle exceptions in the process, and how to evaluate performance. The use of a very detailed process model enables maximum returns.

Third, these process models and common terminologies must be translated into specific and common data standards. In fast, flexible supply chains, the CPFR process has to allow for quick and accurate exchange of data among parties. As such, the datasets must be standardized across all parties to ensure that the parties are translating and interpreting the data the same way. Specifically, this means creating IT standards for data structures, data interfaces, data integrity, and security.

COLLABORATION PERFORMANCE METRICS

The outcomes of CPFR processes should focus on the creation of system-wide performance improvements through completely collaborative business processes. Hospitals and health systems, as downstream members of the chain, need to focus on critical metrics that affect the reliability and cost of the goods and services they procure. The performance metrics that CPFR seeks to affect include improved forecasting accuracy, enhanced customer service levels or fill rates to providers, increased product line availability, reduction of inventory levels, and generally better financial cash flows.

CHAPTER SUMMARY

The supply chain is a key component of operations management. SCM entails the integrated management of resources, finances, and information among the various parties that produce, distribute, sell, and consume. Health care SCM must consider the role of information and intelligence in several key processes from procurement to inventory management. Supply chain strategy should be built around four key cornerstones: inventory, distribution, facilities, and customer service. Responsive supply chains are quicker, more agile, and react faster to different patient and provider needs, but they come at premium pricing. Efficient supply chains are more cost-effective but are typically slower in responding, require greater in-house labor and storage space, and provide lower levels of customer service. The concept of JIT helps improve speed and cycle time and has a key role in many hospital supply chains. Technology has now evolved substantially for supply chains in other industries, and gradually hospitals are beginning to adopt these technologies and incorporate them into daily operations. These technologies will make health care significantly more operationally effective.

The health care industry has an extended supply chain that spans manufacturers, distributors, providers, and patients. This chain is very fragmented, and significantly greater collaboration is needed among the parties. Two of the most common collaborative business processes are S&OP and CPFR. Although today's hospitals and providers do not have much of a role in these processes, it is important to understand and use them to promote improved communication and collaboration and to begin utilizing similar processes in health care to improve relationships and build better supply chains.

SCM collaboration processes attempt to link systems, business plans, and processes to achieve a tighter integration of information and products among parties in the chain. Aligning patient and provider demand all the way upstream to manufacturers in a collaborative planning environment will be useful when the industry is ready. The goal of improved collaboration within the extended supply chain focuses on reducing inventories and improving overall cycle time and responsiveness. The use of highly collaborative planning processes between multiple parties internally and externally will help drive improved overall supply chain economics.

KEY TERMS

Bullwhip effect	**Economies of scale**
Collaboration	**Inventory**
Collaborative planning, forecasting,	**Just in time (JIT)**
and replenishment (CPFR)	**Lowest unit of measure (LUM)**
Demand chain	**Manufacturers**
Distributors	**Quick response**
Downstream	**Reverse logistics**

Sales and operations planning
   (S&OP)
Stock-outs
Supply chain
Supply chain management (SCM)
Supply to stock (STS)

Temporary price reductions
Upstream
Vendor
Voluntary Interindustry Commerce
Standards (VICS)

DISCUSSION QUESTIONS

1. What is a comprehensive definition of supply chain management for health care organizations?
2. What is the primary focus of supply chain management?
3. There are four cornerstones to supply chain management. Describe them and provide the key components of each.
4. What does upstream mean?
5. Name three reasons distributors add value to a hospital's supply chain network.
6. Demand should be aligned with supply to optimize the chain. What does demand mean for health care?
7. A stock-out is common when supplies are distributed throughout all areas of the hospital. What are some ways to reduce stock-outs?
8. Are the concepts of lowest unit of measure and just in time the same? Why or why not?
9. What role does reverse logistics play in supply chain management?
10. In what specific ways can hospitals improve their collaboration with key vendors, such as the large distributors in food services, pharmacy, and medical supplies? Which type of data could be shared that would help improve the overall supply chain?
11. Have the Voluntary Inderindustry Commerce Standards had much of an effect on health care? On which part of the chain?
12. Sales and operations planning is a process adapted from industrial and manufacturing settings. How can it be applied to hospitals?

REFERENCES

Ball, M. J., Simborg, D. W., Albright, J. W., & Douglas, J. V. (Eds.). (1995). *Healthcare information management systems: A practical guide* (2nd ed.). New York, NY: Springer-Verlag.

Blackwell, R. (1997). *From mind to market: Reinventing the retail supply chain.* New York, NY: HarperCollins.

Blattberg, R. C., & Neslin, S. A. (1990). *Sales promotion: Concepts, methods, and strategies.* Englewood Cliffs, NJ: Prentice Hall.

Bowersox, D. J., Closs, D. J., & Cooper, M. B. (2002). *Supply chain logistics management.* New York, NY: McGraw-Hill.

Boyson, S., & Corsi, T. (2001). The real-time supply chain. *Supply Chain Management Review, 5*(1), 44–50.

Chopra, S., & Meindl, P. (2001). *Supply chain management: Strategy, planning, and operation.* Upper Saddle River, NJ: Prentice Hall.

Council of Supply Chain Management Professionals. (2014). *CSCMP supply chain management.* Retrieved from http://cscmp.org/about-us /supply-chain-management-definitions

Cox, J. F., & Blackstone, J. H. (1990). *APICS dictionary* (9th ed.). Alexandria, VA: APICS.

Cross, G. J. (2000). How e-business is transforming supply chain management. *Journal of Business Strategy, 21*(2), 36–39.

Deloitte Consulting. (1999). *Energizing the supply chain.* Quebec, Canada: Author.

Ferrari, R. (2000). *The report on supply chain management: Demand planning and management will leverage the Web.* Boston, MA: AMR Research.

Fisher, M. L. (1997, March–April). What is the right supply chain for your product? *Harvard Business Review*, 105–116.

Fortune. (2014). *Fortune 500 2014.* Retrieved from http://fortune.com/fortune500/

Gattorna, J. (Ed.). (1998). *Strategic supply chain alignment: Best practice in supply chain management.* Hampshire, UK: Gower.

Health Industry Distributors Association. (2014). *HIDA fact sheet.* Alexandria, VA: Author.

Hewitt, F. (2001). After supply chains, think demand pipelines. *Supply Chain Management Review, 5*(3), 28–38.

Hoque, F. (2000). *e-Enterprise: Business models, architecture, and components.* New York, NY: Cambridge University Press.

Kreider, N. A., & Haselton, B. J. (1997). *The systems challenge: Getting the clinical information support you need to improve patient care.* Chicago, IL: American Hospital Association.

Kuglin, F. A., & Rosenbaum, B. A. (2001). *The supply chain network @ Internet speed: Preparing your company for the e-commerce revolution.* New York, NY: AMACOM.

Langabeer, J. R., & Rose, J. (2003). *Creating demand driven supply chains: Concepts, economics, and strategies for demand driven organizations.* Oxford, UK: Spiro Press.

Lee, H. L., & Billington, C. (1995). The evolution of supply-chain-management models and practice at Hewlett-Packard. *Interfaces, 25*(5), 42–63.

Lowson, B., King, R., & Hunter, A. (1999). *Quick response: Managing the supply chain to meet consumer demand.* New York, NY: Wiley.

Martin, C. (1999). *Net future: The seven cybertrends that will drive your business, create new wealth, and define your future.* New York, NY: McGraw-Hill.

Sanderson, E. D. (1985). *Effective hospital materiel management.* Rockville, MD: Aspen.

Schenck, J. (1998). CPFR: Stitching together the partnership. *Apparel Industry Magazine, 59*(8), 72–73.

Stern, C. W., & Stalk, G., Jr. (Eds.). (1998). *Perspectives on strategy from the Boston Consulting Group*. New York, NY: Wiley.

Swaminathan, J. M., Smith, S. F., & Sadeh, N. M. (1996). A multi-agent framework for modeling supply chain dynamics. *Proceedings of the AI and manufacturing research planning workshop* (pp. 210–218).

Voluntary Interindustry Commerce Standards. (2001). *Voluntary guidelines for direct to consumer commerce*. Lawrenceville, NJ: Author.

12

Purchasing and Materials Management

GOALS OF THIS CHAPTER

1. Describe materials management.
2. Understand the effect that facility design has on logistics.
3. Describe the basic approach to cost minimization or optimization models.
4. Describe the basic purchasing methodology.
5. Understand the role of group purchasing organizations.
6. Describe key elements of customer service and service-level agreements.

In health care, departments called *materials management* are responsible for directing the supply chain. Materials managers control significant resources. Total spending for materials and supplies can be nearly 50% of a hospital's budget. Sourcing new and better methods and implementing value analysis in the handling of materials can help health care create financial value for the entire organization. Materials management departments have a broad scope of responsibilities; many of these roles are discussed in this chapter.

MATERIALS MANAGEMENT ORGANIZATION

In hospitals, the common name for departments that focus on acquiring, storing, distributing, and replenishing materials and supplies is **materials management**. Other names include storeroom, distribution, central stores, purchasing, patient supply, receiving, inventory, procurement, acquisition, and many more. In recent years, larger hospitals and systems have started to name departments either supply chain management or logistics, a positive trend that will continue. However, this currently is the exception—most hospitals refer to their operational support department for the supply function as materials management.

The basic mission of materials management in the hospital setting is to direct and control the movement of goods in an efficient manner through the organization. In health care, materials management performs supply and resource logistics. Logistics management is

> that part of supply chain management that plans, implements, and controls the efficient, effective forward and reverse flow and storage of goods, services and related information between the point of origin and the point of consumption in order to meet customers' requirements.
>
> Logistics management activities typically include inbound and outbound transportation management, fleet management, warehousing, materials handling, order fulfillment, logistics network design, inventory management, supply/demand planning, and management of third-party logistics services providers. (Council of Supply Chain Management Professionals, 2014)

Materials management directs the health care supply chain by coordinating the flow of goods from manufacturers, through distributors or other suppliers, through hospital receiving docks, to the point of ultimate use or consumption for patient care. Centralized coordination of the chain relieves clinical departments and nursing from the intricacies involved in ordering products, negotiating and managing vendors, and performing other nonclinical tasks.

Materials management means different things at different hospitals. Ordinarily, in most community hospitals, it is an umbrella department that includes many other functions:

- Purchasing.
- Inventory management.
- Supply distribution and replenishment.
- Central stores and warehousing.
- Revenue charge capture for supplies and equipment.
- Sterile processing.
- Laundry and linen operations.
- Mail and courier services.
- Patient transportation.

In smaller hospitals, these functions can be performed by a handful of people, but in larger ones, materials management can encompass hundreds of employees. A fairly typical organizational structure for large hospitals is depicted in **Figure 12–1**.

To successfully manage hospital supply chains, there has to be a solid foundation of skills around customer service, logistics, human resources, finance, and business analysis. However, many times the succession to management in this area of the hospital is the result of tenure within the department, rather than academic or formal preparation. One of the major problems in today's hospital supply chain is the lack of specialized skills and training that would prepare administrators to better manage the multiple demands of this function.

In other industries, it is a job prerequisite that logistics professionals receive undergraduate or graduate degrees in logistics and supply chain management. Schools such as the University of Tennessee, Michigan State University, Massachusetts Institute of Technology, and Arizona State University all have well-established logistics management programs that teach the fundamentals of what hospital supply chain executives need to know, from inventory optimization to customer service. In health care, such job prerequisites are not commonly required for leading the materials management function, although they should be.

CULTURE OF MATERIALS MANAGEMENT

In many hospitals, materials management departments are considered very tactical and relatively unimportant, much like housekeeping or plant maintenance. There are similarities: The activities in these departments are actually quite operational and managed in a tactical manner, focusing primarily on supply procurement and distribution. These efforts influence downstream departments and patient satisfaction, are labor-intensive processes, and often draw from the same labor talent pool as housekeeping and maintenance. But, the comparisons should stop there. Materials management has control over the routine expenditure of millions of dollars (Kowalski-Dickow Associates, Inc. & American Society for Healthcare Resources and Materials Management, 1994). These responsibilities require complex accounting skills to manage inventories and revenues associated with medical supplies. Materials management departments are also quite large in terms of number of employees, size of operating budget, and overall scale and complexity. In short, materials management is a challenging and complex environment.

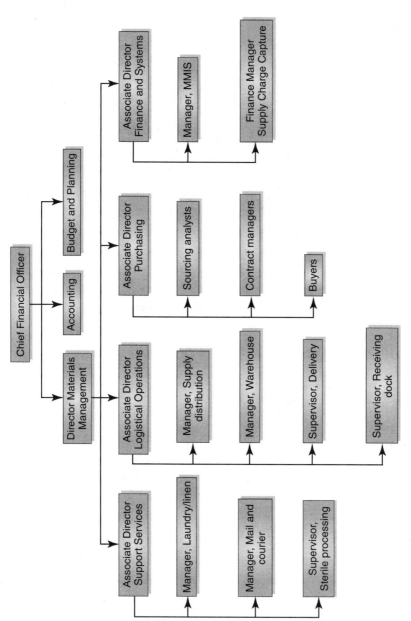

FIGURE 12–1 Materials Management Organizational Structure

Historically, the culture of most materials management departments is not typically associated with such significant responsibility. Owing to the similarity with housekeeping and maintenance mentioned earlier, salaries are often lower than in other professional areas of a hospital. Despite the significant responsibility and challenging tasks, these professionals receive very little publicity or recognition for their efforts. Materials management is typically housed in basements or remote locations away from the hospital, giving materials managers a feeling of remoteness or isolation from the more mainstream functions of the organization. Finally, most chiefs or directors over materials management were not (until recently) high-ranking hospital officers. They typically report to a chief financial officer, controller, or other senior officer who does not have the operational appreciation for the value or challenges of the materials management function.

This prior norm in hospitals is starting to change. With significantly more technology being deployed in materials management, the level and type of professionals who find themselves in this function are starting to positively shift the hospital culture. Professional certification in the field might help as well. The Association for Healthcare Resource and Materials Management offers the Certified Materials and Resource Professional certification, which helps provide specialized knowledge about health care logistics. As materials managers are viewed more as professionals, equal to those in accounting or patient care, the culture and image of the department will continue to improve.

REVENUE GENERATION IN MATERIALS MANAGEMENT

The materials management department can be organized as either a cost center or a profit center. A **profit center** is a business unit in which managers have the responsibility and authority to make decisions that affect both revenues and expenses, while a cost center simply serves as a support function for profit centers and focuses on operating expenses. This operational view of materials management is dependent on several factors, such as the reimbursement strategy of the hospital overall, the significance of the level of potential supply revenue as a percentage of total revenues, and the role that service lines or business units play throughout the hospital. Some hospitals choose to have all revenues roll up to departments or service lines, such as the operating room or cardiology. In this case, all professional services (i.e., physician fees, room charges, and drugs and supplies) would be credited to that department.

In a great majority of hospitals, materials management departments serve as profit centers and are responsible not only for managing inventories but also for generating revenues from supplies used in patient care services. In this case, a different skill mix of employees is required because revenue management necessitates several skills that do not exist in traditional procurement and inventory functions. These skills include pricing, sensitivity analysis, some "marketing" efforts, an understanding of product life cycles and patterns, and knowledge of medical reimbursement programs.

With respect to medical reimbursement, the materials manager holds great sway in billing and collection for services. Most hospital supplies today are billed to payers using a total of the prices of all supply items used for a patient under a group of specific classifications on a hospital bill known as a **revenue code**. Examples of hospital revenue codes are:

- 270 – Medical/surgical supplies
- 271 – Nonsterile supplies
- 272 – Sterile supplies
- 273 – Take-home supplies
- 274 – Prosthetic/orthotic devices
- 275 – Pacemaker
- 276 – Intraocular lens
- 277 – Take-home oxygen
- 278 – Other implants
- 279 – Other medical/surgical supplies

Products outside of routine supplies (such as syringes, sutures, or surgical packs), and services not included in the Current Procedural Terminology-4 codes, such as ambulance services and durable medical equipment, prosthetics, orthotics, and supplies, also fall under the control of the materials manager and are billed using the **Healthcare Common Procedure Coding System (HCPCS)**, which allows uniform coding and reporting of medical supplies, durable medical equipment, pharmaceuticals, and procedures (American Medical Association, 2001). **Durable medical equipment** is equipment that is used repeatedly for multiple patients, used for a medical necessity, appropriate for use outside of the hospital, and not of beneficial use to patients if or when they return to good health.

HCPCS is Level II of a three-level coding system. Level I is called **Current Procedural Terminology (CPT)** and was developed by the American Medical Association for reporting services performed by providers. CPT has been in existence for nearly 50 years and continues to be modified and improved. Prior to this uniform code, each payer had its own standards, and hospitals were responsible for managing thousands of codes for each payer. HCPCS is officially required for Medicare and Medicaid reimbursement but is used for many other commercial payers and managed care organizations because of its simplicity and widespread adoption.

Level II of the system is the HCPCS, and it is used primarily for medical supplies and pharmaceuticals, as well as durable medical equipment. HCPCS uses a five-digit alphanumeric code, with the first digit being alphabetic followed by four numbers. For example, C1753 is a specific type of catheter (intravascular ultrasound) that can be used for outpatient services only, and A4570 is a splint. In these examples, the first alpha digit, A, defines the supply as a medical/surgical category, and the C tells the user it is a temporary outpatient code.

HCPCS is a complex coding system for the following reasons:

- Many of these codes appear nearly identical, and it takes careful examination to determine which ones can be used for specific types of patients.
- There is regional variation to these codes; in some regions a code may be reimbursable, and in others it may not.
- The codes are constantly changing. New codes are added, and old ones are changed and deleted all the time. Updates and careful analysis are required on a continuous basis.

Materials managers in the hospital setting therefore must be able to track supplies by these various classifications and then be able to identify revenues associated with those supplies in order to support the correct billing of services to insurers. Errors in associating supplies with the correct revenue code can result in delayed or lost reimbursements to a hospital. Consequently, the materials management function serves a critical role in the hospital revenue cycle where supplies are concerned. This further raises the professional profile of materials management above the past perception of only a support role. Consequently, there are multiple, critical questions for materials departments to address in meeting the increased responsibility for generating revenues, including:

- Which items are **chargeable** or reimbursable? In other words, which items can be separately billed to patients in addition to other hospital professional and provider charges?
- How can these items be tagged appropriately in the purchasing and inventory system, as well as the Charge Description Master?

- How can a systematic process to review all charges be built and integrated? How can minimal lost charges be ensured?
- Which items are included in procedural or room charges and should not be charged separately?
- Under which conditions are they chargeable? Which codes are appropriate for the item?
- Which pricing levels, or markup strategy, should be used?
- What is the process for entering the item in all systems (enterprise resource planning, Charge Description Master)?

Based on the answers to each of these questions, it is highly advisable that materials and logistics professionals collaborate with their counterparts in finance and reimbursement to help build processes and procedures to address these questions uniformly, especially because reimbursement has both legal and regulatory consequences.

In general, a markup formula will have to be applied for each supply that is introduced into the hospital. **Markup** is the difference between the invoice cost and the price charged to patients and is used to cover the reasonable costs of doing business; markup is typically expressed as a percentage. Markup ratios on supplies and drugs are normally set to cover costs plus a reasonable return or profit margin. However, because a hospital's overall pricing strategy is also reflective of losses that occur in some parts of the business, and because those losses must be offset in other areas, supply markup ratios can range anywhere from 10% to 300%, depending on the pricing strategy for hospitals, geographic location, and other factors.

There is no single acceptable markup percentage. Markup ratios must be created comprehensively by understanding required profit levels, analyzing historical deduction rates, and modeling supply usage patterns. Again, the distinction between gross charges and the net revenue collected must be well understood. Hospitals can charge $10 to all payers for a $0.50 item, but they may only collect $1 from each payer. In this case, while $10 is the gross patient revenue, the net patient revenue is only $1. Selecting a pricing markup strategy that does not artificially inflate gross revenues, and subsequently have huge deductions, is a more practical and effective strategy.

The act of issuing or dispensing items to patients generates revenue. Typically the inventory flow is as follows:

Materials >> Nursing unit supply room
>> Exam or treatment room >> Patient

In this flow, the material exchanges custody from materials management to the patient caregiver at the nursing supply room, which is then relocated (when required) to the examination or treatment room, and then finally issued to patients. When the issue of a supply to the patient occurs, it is documented in the medical record, whether in paper or electronic form. The **medical record** is the formal, auditable account and history of a patient's encounter in the hospital, including description of illnesses, procedures performed, supplies provided, notes, and discharge procedures. At the point that a supply issue to the patient is documented in the patient record, if that supply is deemed chargeable, then revenue for that item has been earned and should be recorded on the patient's account.

In many hospitals, a removable "sticker," which essentially is a bar-coded tag identifying the type of supply, is placed on a manual charge form that can then be keyed into the patient billing system, when collected. This manual process of using stickers is quite common, even though it is inefficient, time consuming, and subject to error. It also places the burden of charging for supplies on nurses, taking their time away from delivery of patient care to a role better handled by the materials management staff.

Alternatively, the use of automated technologies, or **point-of-use systems**, can help streamline this process. A point-of-use system is similar to a vending machine in that it allows automation to drive replenishment, charge supplies to a patient account, and inventory calculations. Two of the most common types of these systems in place today are provided by Cardinal Health's Pyxis and Omnicell.

As mentioned earlier, charges are applied against the patient's account as supplies are issued or administered, which generates revenue—assuming, of course, that the hospital's pricing policy bills supplies separately and does not embed them in the overall procedure codes for the diagnosis-related group or CPT. An example of this would be the use of gloves and a bandage for a simple laceration closure. These items are relatively inexpensive and not usually tracked as individual items in the inventory but rather as part of a larger unit of measure such as a box. In this case, the items would simply be considered part of the fee for the simple laceration closure procedure and not billed as individual items. Based on this common type of situation, proper inventory management must be used to track actual cost of goods sold so that a realistic estimate of operating margins from supplies can be calculated.

OPTIMIZING FACILITY LAYOUT AND DESIGN

Ideally, hospitals should be designed with supply and logistics operations in mind. In the retail business, stores are laid out and designed with one goal—moving customers through aisles in a particular fashion to ensure high traffic flow, extended routes through multiple aisles, and higher receipts per customer. In hospitals, the design goal should be moving patients and resources efficiently through the units and floors to minimize wait and transport times. The fact that the average hospital is several decades old, and that in the design process there is usually a higher focus on nursing and clinical space layout than operational efficiency, creates logistics problems.

Operations management must spearhead efforts during facility expansion and construction phases to raise visibility of the importance of layout and traffic flow and their effect on operational efficiencies. There are five important principles for improving productivity and efficiency in hospital logistics.

Keep Distribution Cycle Times and Productivity in Mind

Analyze the length of time it will take to move staff, supplies, and other resources from point A to point B. Variations in the amount of time required by staff to move resources between locations can affect the amount of staff needed to carry out supply chain functions. Therefore, it is critical to analyze the staffing and productivity levels required for one design over another. Time and motion studies should be used to observe movement patterns, volumes, distance traveled, time required, and costs incurred. The productivity results from different scenarios should also be modeled using scenario analysis or simulation tools.

Separate Patient Traffic Flows from Staff Traffic Flows

The Disney model developed at Disneyland and Disney World does not allow guests to see back-office operations. Disney has high guest satisfaction levels, which should be a primary driver for hospitals as well. This model should be applied significantly more in health care, where patient and staff traffic flows are separated for a variety of reasons, including efficient movement of staff and protecting patients from contact with materials used for the care of other patients. In an environment where patients may be treated for infectious diseases, separating patients from supplies can promote good patient care and greater efficiency while improving patient satisfaction. In most hospitals, however, patients routinely vie for space in hallways and elevators with replenishment carts and personnel, creating crowded corridors, confusion, and delays. Use of separate elevators and especially dedicated supply or resource corridors is essential to improving patient satisfaction and operational efficiency.

Focus on the Interdepartmental Process Flows on Each Floor

Consider workflow and movement around each unit and floor. Pathways should be developed with the most direct travel paths between interdependent units or departments in mind. Ensure that costs and utilization are fully understood during the design process. Creating a matrix of interdepartmental movements and activities ensures that interactions, staging points, volumes, and trigger points for transactions and supply transfers are all documented and considered.

Use a Hub-and-Spoke Model

A hub-and-spoke model concentrates space and supplies in a central hub (similar to airline distribution models) and distributes goods to service departments at the ends of multiple spokes radiating from the hub. Placement of procedural carts, key resources (e.g., medical supplies, linen, and durable medical equipment), and geographic proximity to patient examination or treatment rooms must be carefully understood to minimize total number of trips, total distance traveled, and total overall cost.

Use Optimization to Minimize Costs

It is important to balance the two competing sides of the service–cost equation. On the service side, there is a need for higher utilization of products brought to patient caregivers, better access, higher patient satisfaction, facility flexibility, and improved staff morale. For example, wider walkways allow faster throughput and generally easier access. On the cost side of the equation, there are design and construction costs and constraints. Increased walkways are costly, and they reduce the revenue that can be gained if the same space were used for beds or treatment rooms. Both sides of the equation (improved flow and handling), with costs and space constraints, are important and need to be considered when designing floor layouts. Focusing strictly on clinical needs, without carefully analyzing the operational effects, results in higher operational expenses in future years.

Optimization is a mathematical approach to solving a problem in which an optimal (or best) solution can be reached given the constraints and parameters defined. Optimization is typically used to maximize a dependent variable (such as revenues, profits, or units of service for nonrevenue departments) or minimize outputs (such as costs or resource usage).

A sample floor layout should be built for optimal results, using several important parameters and considerations such as space constraints, distance, and costs. A sample floor layout is depicted in **Figure 12–2**.

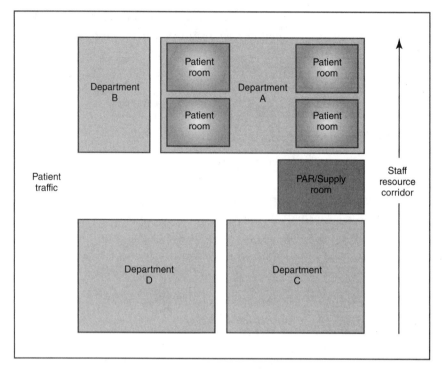

Considerations:

• Location of key resources (linen, supplies) using the cost minimization model
• When movement occurs most frequently between areas, they should be placed contiguously
• Distance traveled between all points fully documented and minimized
• Patient satisfaction and staff interaction
• Space capacity constraints
• Productivity of employees
• Cost, design, and operational space utilization

FIGURE 12–2 Layout Impact Costs and Throughput

COST MINIMIZATION MODELS

It is important to construct analytical models that provide various scenarios and show operational results on overall utilization, costs, and cycle times. There are several process-oriented mathematical and optimization models that can be used to help build optimal designs for operational efficiencies. Software such as Arena (www.arenasimulation.com), SIMUL8 (www.simul8.com), and ProSim (www.prosim.net) offer simulation tools that can help solve these types of problems.

Other models can be constructed that focus on queuing and staging supplies and patients to better understand human and product traffic flows. One such approach has been used to model patient movements between floors and units in hospitals (Heizer & Render, 2004). A general assignment or cost minimization model can be expressed as:

$$\sum_{i=1}^{n} \sum_{j=1}^{n} X_{ij} C_{ij}$$

where

n = total number of departments in the model
i, j = specific individual departments
X_{ij} = number of patients moving between each department
C_{ij} = distance traveled or cost incurred

Using a model such as this to help manage layout decisions has proven to minimize costs in layout decision-making processes. To apply this cost minimization model, it is necessary to construct a matrix showing product movement, as well as associated volumes and costs, from department i to department j. Using simple matrix algebra, it is possible to solve for several different combinations and select the one with the lowest overall cost.

Use of this cost minimization model is fairly straightforward. Consider this example. Look back at Figure 12–2, which has four departments on the floor. A hospital wishes to optimize the positioning of these departments, based on minimizing costs of logistics (which would include reducing cycle time, because the longer it takes to get from one location to the next, the greater the labor effort, and therefore the cost). The general process for solving this problem requires six steps:

1. Determine the maximum number of potential layout options that exist (i.e., number of observations $\times$ [n]) $\times n - 1$, until $n = 1$. This is calculated as the factorial of n, or $n!$, which is the product of the number n with all of the other numbers less than n. In this example, there are 24 potential layout options (i.e., 4!, or $4 \times 3 \times 2 \times 1 = 24$).
2. Estimate the total traffic flow between each unit or department. For example, observe or estimate the number of times a patient or staff member moves from department A to department B.
3. Construct a matrix diagram that shows each of the four locations in a table (see **Table 12–1**), and place the count from Step 2 in the appropriate matrix.
4. Estimate the costs for contiguous and noncontiguous placements. This would require a detailed analysis of how long it takes to move between each

Table 12-1   Cost Minimization Layout Model 1

	Department A	Department B	Department C	Department D
Department A	—	10	50	20
Department B	—	—	30	40
Department C	—	—	—	15
Department D	—	—	—	—

location, multiplied by an average salary rate for the type of employee per-forming the task. For this example—and to keep things simple—assume $10 for nodes A → B, B → C, and C → D that are considered adjacent for these purposes for their close proximity, while all other nodes are not con-sidered adjacent and therefore cost $20 each move because it takes more steps for distance traveled, which requires greater labor. For instance, in **Figure 12–3**, departments A and B are contiguous, while A and D are not.

5. Using a network diagram, model the current results. In this case, the total current costs are $2,350 and would be calculated as follows:

   a. A → B = 10 moves, and because this is considered adjacent, it costs $10 per move. Total costs are $100.
   b. A → C = 50 moves × $20 = $1,000
   c. A → D = 20 × $20 = $400
   d. B → C = 30 × $10 = $300
   e. B → D = 40 × $10 = $400
   f. C → D = 15 × $10 = $150

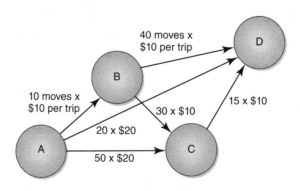

FIGURE 12–3 Cost Minimization Layout Models Step #2: Construct Node Diagrams and Assess Costs

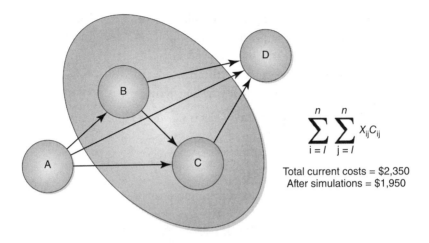

$$\sum_{i=l}^{n} \sum_{j=l}^{n} x_{ij} C_{ij}$$

Total current costs = $2,350
After simulations = $1,950

Repositioning C and B saves $400 in total costs

FIGURE 12–4 Cost Minimization Layout Models Step #3: Apply Minimization Formula and Simulate

6. Iteratively, reposition the locations to achieve improved results. For example, it is clear that the highest volume movements occur between locations A → C and B → D. If these two locations could be placed contiguously, swapping, for instance, the lower-movement areas such as A → B, then total costs can be minimized. The use of sensitivity analysis or repeated iterative calculations can help identify more optimal cases. For instance, if C is positioned in the place of B in this layout, it could change the diagram and reduce total costs to $1,950. This comprehensive modeling process can be seen in **Figure 12–4**.

The uses of a general assignment or cost optimization model are limitless. They can determine the order in which nursing floors or units are resupplied, position nursing stations, locate par linen and supply rooms, install pharmacy dispensing cabinets, or improve process layout for all departments relative to those in newer buildings.

PURCHASING

The purchasing function represents a significant source of potential financial value for hospitals. The primary role of purchasing is threefold:

1. To find sources of supply for various types of goods and services that the hospital requires.

2. To manage the sourcing process for soliciting vendors and obtaining competitive responses that provide lower product price as well as lowest cost of acquisition (primarily shipping and storage).
3. To engage in purchase contracts that minimize total costs (price, shipping, procurement, and storage) over the long term.

The purchasing process or methodology is shown in **Figure 12–5**.

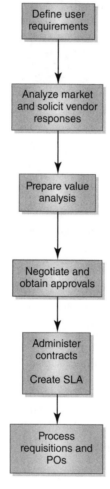

Special focus on:
• Internal controls and audit trails
• Ensuring ethical purchasing practices
• Creating long-term financial value through economies of scale and standardization
• Reducing order fulfillment cycle time

FIGURE 12–5 Standard Purchasing Methodology

In many hospitals, however, purchasing is seen as an administrative function: processing purchase orders (POs), handling supply inquiries, and pushing paperwork. Manual POs are paper based, often maintained in large file cabinets (or in large piles on desks), and require routing from one department to another. When executives and other managers view this morass of paper to acquire supplies, it does not help change this perspective, so it is important that purchasing departments transform themselves into more automated, value-focused functions.

In hospitals, the purchasing department does not develop product needs or specifications, but it does document them and provide assistance to hospital departments to conduct detailed assessments of those specifications to help meet the needs of those departments. For instance, the need for a new medical device is based on physician preference or procedure, but documenting these specifications allows purchasing to complete a sourcing analysis to study the market, find vendors, and solicit pricing information to help obtain the new device in such a way that can meet patient care needs while minimizing cost to the hospital. Such assistance should be viewed as a core function for the purchasing department.

Competitive bidding is a formalized process that engages multiple vendors simultaneously to ensure a competitive marketplace, improve economies of scale, and possibly lower total cost of ownership for products. Competitive bidding also ensures that a contract is not entered into without exploring all reasonable options. A competitive bid process works on the "perfect competition" theory, which suggests that rationality, free flow of information, and a competitive marketplace with multiple suppliers will reward those firms that offer the best products at the best prices.

The bid process typically starts with a formal **request for information (RFI)**, used by a potential buyer to obtain information on vendors that can be used to compile a list of qualified vendors for a purchase or procurement. The RFI can help the hospital narrow down a list of potential vendors based on their responses—in fact, some vendors may ask to remove themselves from consideration based on the questions or qualifications presented in the RFI. As many as 50% of potential vendors can be eliminated through an RFI process, simply by setting standards for vendor capabilities, financial capacity, and product specifications. Generally, the RFI will consist of the following basic elements:

- *Title of project or procurement.* A description of the item(s) to be procured.
- *Needs statement.* A short description of the procurement goals.
- *Hospital background.* A brief description of the background of the organization conducting the procurement.

- *Vendor qualifications.* Any minimum qualifications that a vendor must meet to participate in the bid process.
- *Product information.* Information needed to select a vendor for the product or contract.
- *Decision criteria.* A description of the decision process and criteria used to select a vendor.
- *Time for response.* A deadline by which the vendor must respond to the RFI and the time frame for which a formal bid process will be conducted.

Once the hospital has some data on vendors that may participate in a bid process through the RFI solicitation, these data can be reviewed and used to prepare the next formal bidding document, the **request for proposal (RFP)**. While the RFI is sometimes seen as an informal information-gathering process, the RFP is a more formal process used to solicit binding bids from vendors for a specific purchase or contract. Handling of a formal RFP and bid process is a critical skill for purchasing staff and hospital senior operations managers. Although the solicitation and evaluation of bids obtained through an RFP may seem a tedious process, it can be very valuable to the hospital by:

- Identifying vendors that are unable to meet hospital needs for terms, conditions, or product quality specifications.
- Helping to objectively define the procurement, selection criteria, and important elements of the procurement for the hospital.
- Forcing vendors to compete on a standard set of product specifications to obtain the lowest price and most favorable terms for the hospital.

Vendor selection is an inexact process. However, by creating a systematic review framework to evaluate proposals submitted by vendors in response to the RFP, the hospital can usually arrive at a supportable decision aimed at the best interests of the hospital and its stakeholders. The review should be conducted with measurable criteria as appropriate to eliminate as much subjective judgment from the evaluation as possible. Once proposals have been received from vendors solicited by the RFP, the evaluation criteria defined in the RFI and RFP preparation processes should be objectively applied to the proposals. This process, if done objectively, could eliminate between 25% and 50% of submissions based on a failure to meet all specifications set out in the RFP. This alone can make the bid process much easier for the hospital and purchasing staff by allowing them to focus only on qualified vendors offering products appropriate to the hospital's needs.

Evaluating bid proposals should ultimately come down to only a few low bidders offering comparable products at comparable prices. It is here that some subjectivity may introduce itself into the process, especially if there is not an easy one-to-one comparison between proposals. In some cases, it may be necessary to interview final bidders to clarify proposals and establish which proposal will best meet the hospital's needs. It is important that, in any interview process, the questions are the same for all bidders and that responses be analyzed based on hospital need and not some subjective characteristic of the bidder.

As the competitive bids are reviewed, it is advisable to utilize an evaluation scorecard. A **scorecard** is an evaluation tool that lists the key attributes or decision criteria and applies a quantitative approach to evaluating responses. Having all internal parties, or those individuals primarily affected by the decision, rate each vendor in several areas ensures collaboration and feedback from multiple sources. Keeping the bid process as objective as possible helps the hospital best meet its needs and avoid potential grievances from bidders that were not selected. It can also serve to promote the equitable access of vendors to hospital contracts, ensure transparency in the purchasing process, and increase competition among vendors. Moreover, it confirms that the process is fair, competitive, and focused on multiple criteria, not solely price. A sample evaluation scorecard is shown in **Figure 12–6**.

Once the requirements are defined and supplier research and competitive bidding is completed, negotiations are conducted with the vendors that are most competitive. A thorough valuation analysis should be conducted at this point to examine baseline costs, given current pricing and quantities, and compared with the competitive responses. Negotiations conclude with contract management, where legal terms and conditions and all performance and service levels are defined. It is also important to consider price protection, or price escalation, for future periods.

Defining and including service-level expectations into contracts for each vendor are also necessary to continuously improve performance (Lambert, 1999). Excluding these performance expectations creates problems because both parties are more focused on execution postcontract, and many vendors adhere to only the most minimal service levels required to keep them in good contractual standing. Buyers have the most leverage prior to the initial award and contract. Defining minimal performance, penalty clauses for inferior performance, and even performance rewards or gain sharing for exceptional service should be part of all major vendor agreements. During the sourcing and contracting phase, it is important to remember the cost–quality relationship and ensure that the right vendor is selected to create an optimal balance between lowest price and best service. This is sometimes called *best value*.

	Decision criteria	Weight	Competitive options		
			Supplier #1	Supplier #2	Supplier #3
1	Proximity of regional warehouse	10%			
2	Total annual costs	20%			
3	Perceived product or service quality	30%			
4	Meets all product requirements	20%			
5	Number of referenceable customers	5%			
6	Product ease of use	10%			
7	Expected ability to meet service standards	5%			
	Average				

Instructions:
• Evaluate each vendor against all criteria
• Use a 5- or 10-point rating scale
• Multiply rating times weight
• Sum results

FIGURE 12–6 Supplier Evaluation Scorecard

In many cases, the use of bundled contracts can be explored. Some of the larger medical supply vendors have dozens of product lines and hundreds of items. Handling each of these items separately, with different competitive bidding events, can be cumbersome.

Once contracts are finalized and the executive and legal approvals are obtained, contracts must be administered. This includes ensuring that the vendor's products are updated in the hospital's item master of the enterprise resource planning system or the materials management information system. Current prices and all vendor details (e.g., bank account information, addresses) must be input as well into the accounts payable and ordering systems.

In some cases, the product in question may be a commodity that is widely available in the marketplace with little differentiation between products offered by different suppliers. In this case, purchasing may employ a simpler process known as a **request for quotation (RFQ)**. Under this type of sourcing approach, purchasing sends a simple RFQ to suppliers known to offer a specified product, spelling out particular specifications (size, volume, or type) and minimum terms and conditions required in the purchasing transaction. Negotiation with vendors on additional conditions may encompass shipping terms, order and delivery schedules, or minimum lot sizes. At this point, requests or requisitions from user departments can be taken for purchases. A central processing group is typically assigned to convert requisitions into completed POs. This represents the transaction order processing phase of purchasing.

PURCHASING INTERNAL CONTROLS

There are several inherent risks in the hospital purchasing process. First, there are a limited number of vendors in certain vendor categories, which creates a lack of perfect competition. These environments introduce ethical dilemmas where vendors might offer gifts, trips, and other potentially negative inducements to purchasing agents in exchange for increased purchasing volumes. Developing policies and procedures that limit gifts and encourage ethical behaviors will reduce bribery and other negative outcomes.

Second, it is critical to maintain a complete audit trail or history for all vendor negotiations, PO transactions, and pricing adjustments (e.g., rebates, credits, discounts). The key concern is that an unethical buyer might agree to purchase from a specific vendor without going through a competitive process or, more commonly, to pay a fictitious vendor (i.e., one that does not exist but is artificially created by the buyer to redirect funds to itself or to other people working in concert with the buyer). There have been multiple hospital audits in which rogue purchasing agents have been found to fabricate companies, create fictitious purchases, and then direct purchases and payments to themselves.

Historically, one of the most basic ways of limiting this risk is to ensure a **three-way match**, meaning that the three key documents in the procure-to-pay process are performed by different individuals, therefore segregating duties and responsibilities. These documents include:

Purchase order >> Receipt or proof of delivery
>> Invoice processing and payment

If a PO is generated by one person, and confirmation of the receipt is given by a second individual, and then payment processed by a third party, unethical behavior would require participation or collusion by at least three individuals—making it that much more difficult to commit fraud or theft. A continuous review process of vendors and items purchased, as well as careful examination of vendor listings in both purchasing and the accounts payable areas (known as the **vendor master**) for incomplete and suspicious information, is essential to improving internal controls.

One problem with the use of a three-way match is that it is manual, requires storage and movement of lots of paper, and is generally slow. Technology has matured greatly over the past 20 years, which has significantly automated this process. As hospitals continue to use further automation and electronic commerce in operations, such as electronic data interchange (EDI), auto-mated routing from vendors to hospitals will completely eliminate redundant paperwork and forms. While automation offers many benefits, it does require different internal controls and policies because paper trails are eliminated. Hos-pitals using two- and three-part carbon forms, which can be detached and routed through various departments, are decades behind in streamlining their operations for efficiency.

The same segregation of duties can be accomplished with use of electronic pur-chasing, inventory, and accounts payable systems. Instead of moving paper among multiple persons, the same verification transactions can be accomplished by the same persons using specifically defined roles in computer systems that prohibit other members of the purchasing process from handling other steps in the process. For example, the purchasing agent may issue a PO for items but cannot note the items as received or process the payment for those items within the hospital infor-mation system. Similarly, an inventory clerk cannot process an order for goods or submit a payment to accounts payable for those same items. Of course, using the same role-based approach to segregating duties in the purchasing process, the accounts payable clerk could only process payment in the accounts payable system for items noted as received by the inventory clerk in the inventory system against an authorized PO created by the purchasing agent in the purchasing system.

Ideally, the systems associated with all three steps are interoperable, allowing transaction data to seamlessly move from purchasing to receiving to accounts payable. This interoperability can be expected when the hospital information system comes from the same vendor, such as Epic (www.epic.com), McKesson (www.mckesson.com), or MEDITECH (www.meditech.com). If the systems are purchased from different vendors (perhaps inventory management from McKesson and accounts payable from another vendor such as Great Plains), then custom software interfaces must be installed to allow these different vendor systems to communicate. Otherwise, a manual matching process cannot be avoided.

Another control that can be implemented in an automated matching process is the use of sampling techniques that pull transactions for auditing either randomly or through exception-based management (where a transaction involves a specific higher risk type of transaction, dollar volume, or type of vendor) to be separately verified before processing. In any case, information systems used to process purchasing must include the ability to maintain details on all transactions processed (known as an **audit trail**). This allows management and auditors to randomly test transactions for accuracy and appropriateness in the absence of paper forms for concurrent or retrospective review.

SPEND OR VALUE ANALYSIS

Once an item, its classification, its phase in a life cycle, and its usage patterns are understood, what happens with all the data? First, a simple spend analysis can be performed. **Spend analysis** is an in-depth, comprehensive analysis of a hospital's expenditures (primarily routine operating expenses) focused on what, how, and with whom an organization spends dollars. Typically, spend analyses focus on which vendors are being paid, how many transactions or POs are being issued, which commodity types and item categories are purchased, the types of items most commonly used, and how items are used to identify opportunities for cost savings and improved contractual negotiation. Understanding the source of spending allows procurement managers to selectively isolate contracts and vendors that can create financial value for the hospital. Spend or value analysis typically involves three steps, as shown in **Figure 12–7**. The three phases in this figure represent the process for getting started in spend analysis processes: automate, analyze and forecast, and measure and reinforce.

Automate

Automating items is the first phase, and there are multiple steps:

1. Automate all item master data and ensure that there is limited use of manual, paper-based purchase requisitions and orders.
2. Capture and add all item attributes in the required database field in the enterprise resource planning system.
3. Institute a formalized item classification system, such as the United Nations Standard Products and Services Code (UNSPSC), Universal Product Classification (UPC), or a similar scheme, and ensure its full use and rollout across all items and PO transactions.

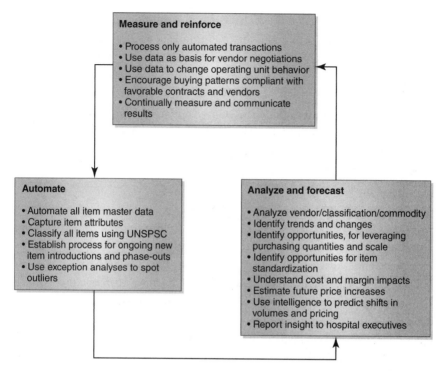

FIGURE 12-7 Value/Spend Analysis

4. Establish a process for ongoing new-item introductions and phase-outs so that, as new items are introduced, they also are automated and classified appropriately.
5. Use exception analyses to spot outliers and act appropriately.

Analyze and Forecast

The second phase focuses on analyzing and forecasting. There will be a need for analytical skills during this phase, using tools such as spreadsheets, databases, online financial analyses, and comparison and benchmarking tools to understand spending and cost behaviors. At a minimum, this phase involves the following tasks:

- Analyze transactional spending data across several attributes and levels, such as spending by vendor, a certain family or segment classification, and commodity type.
- Challenge the concept of physician preference behavior. **Physician preferences** in this context reflects a situation in which a provider chooses established vendors and known products based on existing comfort level

and a possible reluctance to change. These preferences do not always represent the best value or economical choice. The introduction of additional vendors and products encourages collaboration with clinical staff, offers a broader portfolio, and instills discipline in spending processes.

- Identify trends and changes over time, such as a shift in usage from one vendor to another or from one item to another. Look for exceptions and large spending categories that are not actively covered with negotiated contracts.
- Identify opportunities for leveraging purchasing quantities and scale. Ensure that all high-volume areas have contracts, either through the group purchasing organization procedure or a direct contract negotiated with a vendor internally (this concept is described in the next section). Identify areas where the last contract review date was greater than 12 months.
- Identify opportunities to review pricing against any published benchmarks, if available. Such comparisons can ensure that the hospital is fully leveraging its existing group purchasing organization contracts.
- Identify opportunities for item standardization. Find areas where small orders of similar products are frequently ordered from multiple low-volume vendors. If a single item can be identified that meets the need previously addressed with multiple items (a good example is surgical gloves), the hospital may be able to consolidate all such purchases with one vendor to trade larger order volumes for lower purchase prices while reducing order frequency and purchasing transaction costs.
- Understand cost and margin effects from all analyses and recommendations.
- Estimate future price increases, if known, to model in spend analyses and budget preparations for the following periods.
- Use business intelligence systems to predict shifts in volumes and pricing.
- Report insights gained in this analytical process to hospital executives.

Measure and Reinforce

The last phase of the spend analysis process involves measuring and reinforcing. This phase ensures that all analyses and recommendations—for vendor or item changes, future contract negotiations, standardization, and other purchasing practices—are systematically measured and buying behaviors are reinforced. This phase requires that hospital materials managers:

- Process only automated transactions. Eliminating manual, paper-based forms is one of the first steps to ensuring that the sourcing opportunities analyzed become a reality.

- Use data as the basis for vendor negotiations. Continually measure performance and transactional usage data with vendors at all meetings. Create service-level agreements on pricing, usage, supply fill rates, and other performance areas to ensure that vendors uphold their end of the deal and that spend savings are realized.
- Use data to change operating unit behavior. Presenting requesting departments with data supporting recommendations and analyses for operational savings will be necessary to ensure that requestors commit to and follow through with desired purchasing behaviors.
- Encourage buying patterns compliant with favorable contracts and vendors.
- Continually measure and communicate results to all parties.

Spend analyses are valuable tools for generating operational efficiencies in the hospital. They must be used as part of a comprehensive toolkit, however, if operational managers are to succeed in the mission of reducing costs, eliminating inefficiencies, improving productivity, and shrinking overall process cycle times.

GROUP PURCHASING ORGANIZATIONS

A **group purchasing organization (GPO)** is a collaborative arrangement in which multiple parties unite for the purpose of increasing their collective bargaining power with vendors. If a hospital purchases 1,000 oxygen tanks per year from a vendor, it might be able to purchase each item for $65; however, if 20 hospitals collectively contract with the same vendor, they might be able to buy each item for $40 or less. GPOs are similar in concept to unions, which collectively bargain and determine ground rules for employees.

GPOs can change the competitive dynamics of a marketplace by encouraging suppliers to reduce costs to secure additional business. GPOs are avid proponents of the competitive bidding process, where multiple vendors are given the same opportunity and business requirements but may offer a variety of different cost–quality combinations in an attempt to win the business. In doing so, GPOs have been known to drive down collective costs of many items, especially in the commodity product lines that have many suppliers and limited buyers. They work less well in places where only a handful of vendors offer differentiated, specialized, highly expensive, and customized products, like in the medical technology category. A GPO collectively sources, negotiates, and contracts with vendors to achieve economies of scale and lower total costs for its members.

GPOs offer their members a portfolio of products that their member hospitals utilize. **Penetration** represents the percentage of usage or purchases against a specific contract. The higher the penetration, the more likely the supplier will continue to offer attractive prices to the GPO for future periods. Lower penetration rates represent three potential issues for GPOs:

1. They have a sourced product that is not well received or desired by their member hospitals.
2. They made poor vendor selections, and their members are not interested in obtaining goods and services from those vendors.
3. The hospital could directly negotiate better local rates than the GPO.

Most GPOs claim that they can reduce supply costs by 1% to 15% or more, although such claims are difficult to confirm and measure, depending on the type of items procured and any seasonal variations in product use.

GPOs are viewed by suppliers as a collaborative partner or customer, as well as a potential competitor. Of course, any organized attempt to reduce pricing and exert greater influence is not typically welcomed by powerful suppliers. Less mature companies, or those that might have difficulty gaining market share without an introduction by a large GPO, would, however, find GPOs quite appealing because they offer a faster potential growth strategy. Although there has not been any conclusive academic research about GPO economics, evidence suggests that many suppliers view GPOs as one of several entrances to hospitals, and therefore they selectively choose which products to offer to the GPO and which to retain for direct sales to hospitals.

Many suppliers use the GPO channel to market loss leaders and gain entry into an organization so that they can offer exposure and opportunity to sell other more profitable products. A **loss leader** is an item that is sold by a vendor at a loss to attract customers to buy other premium items. Loss leaders are usually early-stage or late-stage items, have poor growth prospects under normal conditions, or might not otherwise sell well. Loss leaders allow suppliers to protect pricing for their premium products by not disclosing prices or destroying price points through a competitive bidding process, while still showing some participation on a GPO's contract lists. This will help them get in the door of most hospital purchasing departments, where they can then directly attempt to sell other higher-margin products.

The largest GPOs in the U.S. health care market are Premier, Novation, and MedAssets:

- *Premier,* www.premierinc.com. Based in North Carolina with approximately $59 billion in member purchases, Premier is generally considered to be the largest and possibly most successful GPO.

- *Novation*, www.novationco.com. Based in Texas with more than $49 billion in purchases and 2,500 members in the University HealthSystem Consortium and the Voluntary Hospitals of America, Novation also represents many of the largest academic teaching hospitals.
- *MedAssets*, www.medassets.com. Based in Georgia with nearly $50 billion in volume, MedAssets is now one of the larger competitors in the GPO arena.

Collectively, the top nine GPOs account for nearly $500 billion in purchasing volume (Healthcare Purchasing News, 2013).

TRENDS IN HOSPITAL PURCHASING

There are several trends developing in most health care facilities, including smaller, value-focused teams; implementation of e-procurement and electronic commerce systems; standardization; and postponement.

Purchasing teams are getting smaller, more focused, and more analytical. With expected annual GPO savings representing anywhere from 1% to 15%, many administrators are questioning the role of large, extensive purchasing organizations internal to the hospital when GPOs can serve the sourcing, negotiating, contracting, and performance monitoring functions for hospitals for seemingly less money. Designing smaller, more focused purchasing teams that help to manage vendor relationships, administer and participate in the GPO contracting process, and use advanced analytics to perform value analysis are the new roles of purchasing professionals.

Another key trend is the continued use of EDI; automated requisitioning and supply chain systems are reducing cycle time and streamlining the procurement process. Electronic procurement systems are being used to simplify the purchasing process and offer punch-out capabilities to supplier product lines, in addition to standard electronic commerce functionality. E-commerce typically focuses on improving the level of EDI penetration rates, while simplifying the purchasing system's ease of use. This translates into higher productivity levels and significantly reduced staffing.

Standardization drives another trend in health care—value focus. Aggregating purchase volumes from multiple departments, and standardizing them around the same goods and services from a limited number of vendors, allows purchasing departments to source higher quantities and volumes, which helps drive efficiencies into operations. Focusing on value is primarily visible through two structural mechanisms: the spend analysis process, which was described earlier, and the use of what many hospitals call the *clinical supply evaluation committee*, or materials use evaluation. This group is an ad hoc interdisciplinary team of physicians, nurses, materials managers, and administrators who assemble to evaluate the introduction of new materials into the supply chain. The role of these groups should be threefold, but rarely do they perform all three functions well.

- The first objective is to control access of vendors' products into the organization, which allows some standardization over the types of items used by physicians and in procedures.
- The second objective is to evaluate the economic impact of these new-item introductions into the organization. If surgery begins using a new medical/surgical supply, what will this do to overall surgery costs? The role of this committee should be to explore the economic effect and determine if the improved outcomes or clinical efficacy are greater than the increased product costs, if any.
- The third objective of this group is to communicate findings and analyses to all units and floors about the product changes so that it is not left solely to purchasing and materials managers.

Typical problems related to these committees are that they tend to make easy decisions (i.e., adopt a new product) but do not address the implementation of the decisions or the more difficult questions (e.g., eliminate the older product, standardize usage among all units, and decline adoption of products where costs are greater than proposed benefits).

Postponement is another emerging trend. **Postponement** refers to making decisions about purchasing until the latest possible point in the process, which reduces inventory levels and encourages rapid response on the part of vendors. Postponement is especially useful in reducing transactional purchasing costs because they can be aggregated and submitted only when necessary. Also, losses from stale or obsolete inventory should decrease because purchases will not be made until the latest possible time, thus maximizing the potential shelf life of purchased goods added to the hospital inventory. Postponement is a concept related to quick response and just in time.

Internal value processes will move purchasing from order takers to internal consultants. Using principles of aggregation and standardization, purchasing professionals can help large departments such as the operating room and radiology understand their consumption patterns and change utilization behaviors. This type of role is significantly different from that of a traditional purchasing agent and requires different skills and techniques.

RESOURCES FOR MATERIALS PROFESSIONALS

Very few resources are dedicated to materials and supply chain management for health care. The Association for Healthcare Resource and Materials Management facilitates knowledge transfer and networking among materials managers in health care and provides education, publications, and conferences to materials managers. Another group, the American Society for Healthcare Central Service Professionals, is more focused on central supply and sterile processing, but it is another good resource for education and networking. Both groups are governed by the American Hospital Association.

Outside the health care industry, other professional associations exist that offer knowledge and networking for supply chain management in general. Many such organizations include membership from the hospital industry and maintain interest groups for hospital-affiliated individuals. These associations can provide materials managers with a large group of organizations with which to network and become affiliated, as well as to provide exposure to new supply chain and logistics practices from other industries that could be applied in the hospital setting. While the products and networks in health care might be different, a supply chain is a supply chain. Individuals who want to learn about inventory management, transportation, supply distribution, network management, and purchasing have a whole list of professional associations available to them, even though most of these are quite foreign to the typical hospital manager. Many of these have very respectable journal publications; professional certifications that emphasize tools, concepts, and techniques; and a wide multi-industry focus. Here is a list of well-known and respected professional associations:

- American Society for Healthcare Central Service Professionals (www .ashcsp.org)
- American Society of Transportation and Logistics (www.astl.org)
- Association for Healthcare Resource and Materials Management (www .ahrmm.org)
- Association for Operations Management (www.apics.org)
- Council of Supply Chain Management Professionals (www.cscmp.org)
- Institute for Supply Management (www.ism.ws)
- Institute of Management Accountants (www.imanet.org)
- International Warehouse Logistics Association (www.iwla.com)
- Materials Handling and Management Society (www.mhia.org)

CUSTOMER SERVICE IN MATERIALS MANAGEMENT

Customer service can generically be defined as the means by which a provider attempts to keep customers happy and loyal while differentiating itself from others (Wayland & Cole, 1997). Because materials management is a service provider, it needs to be especially focused on customer service levels and trends in performance.

Materials management and the supply chain serve two major groups of customers—those internal to the organization and those external. Internal customers include nurses, technicians on the floors and units, physicians, and other health care providers. Any department that orders, receives, or uses goods and services is a customer. External customers include hospital patients and their families and friends. Patients are very important, but they are usually customers of nursing or unit personnel and only indirectly served by materials management. Although external, vendors represent a different type of stakeholder and are not necessarily customers. Similarly, employees in the chain are important, but they are different than customers. Customers represent buyers or consumers of goods.

Internal customers can be very demanding on materials management. The key criteria for customer satisfaction in nursing and other clinical divisions is product availability and service reliability. If products are available and usable when needed, with minimal paperwork and effort, clinical departments are usually satisfied. As items become out of stock or unavailable, or if the process to procure and receive these items is bureaucratic and lengthy, then customer service will be considered poor.

When designing a materials management customer service program, it is essential to focus on those factors that are most important in supply chain management—namely, reliability (accuracy), speed (responsiveness, timeliness), customer acuity (intelligence, foresight about customer needs), and accountability (Boyson & Corsi, 2001). Materials management departments should focus their efforts on process and system improvements with these outcomes in mind.

An essential aspect of customer service is a proactive system that records and triages process breakdowns as they occur. A complaint or issue tracking system, with resolution processes, will help managers not only record problems but analyze the sources of the problems. By understanding the sources of variability in the outcomes (i.e., reliability, speed), then the outcomes can be measured and improved.

Another essential aspect of customer care is to document performance-level expectations with end users through a service-level agreement. A **service-level agreement** is a formal agreement that clearly communicates the types of services to be offered, performance expectations, hours services are provided, inputs or resources to be committed, and payments, if any. A service-level agreement can also allow for history to be kept about new service lines or commitments, as well as establish a standard for measuring performance of the materials management department.

For example, if an operating room department creates a new program where it opens for surgical cases 2 hours earlier than before, there will be a significant downstream effect on materials management. Employees' schedules might have to change, vendor delivery schedules might be affected, increased usage and storage of supplies might be required, and more resources will be consumed. Any time a new program is developed, or as existing ones change, an opportunity is created for a lack of clarity about the actual customer needs and business requirements. During these times, service-level satisfaction typically dips, as customers get frustrated with the inability for materials to respond appropriately. If a service-level agreement were created in advance, the exact inputs and outputs would have been discussed openly and agreed to, which would minimize the margin of error.

In addition to service-level agreements, customer surveys and other monitoring tools should be used to remain connected to the customer's pulse and satisfaction. Interviews with key customers should be conducted periodically to establish benchmarks in each of the performance areas. Critical areas of surveys and interviews would be cost, quality, cycle time, and interactions with personnel, in addition to reliability, responsiveness, and accountability. Most complaints about service in hospitals can be categorized as late deliveries, missing or unfilled items, or damaged or expired products. These three areas represent the significant majority of customer issues.

A performance scorecard should be created and monitored to track customer service performance over time. The specific metrics could include:

1. The number of telephone calls coming into the department.
2. The volume of complaints and concerns.
3. Product availability (or "on-shelf" fill rate percentages versus out-of-stocks).
4. On-time deliveries.
5. Total order cycle time.
6. Delivered cost.

A scorecard should be created using these metrics on a continuous basis (i.e., monthly, quarterly) and disseminated to employees, managers, and customers. This scorecard should define future plans and strategies because it highlights gaps and deficiencies in current performance.

LAUNDRY AND LINEN

In smaller hospitals, laundry operations are often considered part of materials management. In larger hospitals, laundry management is a separate function from materials management and requires hundreds of employees processing millions of pounds of laundry per year. Either way, laundry and linen management is essential to the proper operation of a hospital. Without clean linens, hospitals would not be able to offer the same high-quality care environment that patients expect and that is required by regulations and quality guidelines.

Laundry operations can either be managed internally or outsourced. Surveys suggest that 50% of all hospitals outsource their laundry processing to third parties or engage in "cooperatives" with other hospitals through shared service contracts to process their laundry (Hospital and Health Networks, 2001).

Laundry operations are subject to strict quality control guidelines, due to the high risk of disease transmission from patient to patient. The Centers for Disease Control and Prevention and The Joint Commission are two groups that have created guidelines for proper handling of laundry. There are several specific guidelines governing design and construction of new hospital laundries or operations of existing ones, including the following (Healthcare Purchasing News, 2004):

- U.S. Department of Health and Human Services: "Guidelines for Construction and Equipment of Hospital and Medical Facilities"
- Office of Health and Safety, Centers for Disease Control and Prevention: "Guidelines for Laundry in Healthcare Facilities"

These guidelines primarily emphasize the control of infection and reduction of disease transmission. Some specific recommendations include the use of hot water (greater than 160 °F for most linens for periods equal to or greater than 25 minutes) or the use of specific chemicals if lower-temperature washing is used. Safe handling of linens requires that transportation methods and devices should not contaminate clean linens and that soiled linen collection must be in bags that are leak resistant (Centers for Disease Control and Prevention, 2003).

Laundry management is defined as the process of collecting, processing (washing, drying, assembling, staging), transporting, and replenishing linens during the linen life cycle, from acquisition to final ragout or disposition. **Linens** are fabrics used for health care purposes and include scrubs, pillows and cases, sheets, blankets, towels, lab coats, rags, and protective gear and gowns. Some of the largest linen or textile manufacturers specific to health care include Standard Textile (www.standardtextile.com) and Medline Industries (www.medline.com).

In larger hospitals, collecting **soiled linen** (i.e., dirty or used) is usually performed by the housekeeping, laundry, or materials management department on a prearranged pickup schedule. In smaller hospitals, nursing collects the linens and uses automated chutes or moveable soiled linen hampers to move linens back to lower floors of the hospital to be picked up by laundry personnel. Either way, the movement of soiled linens is a resource-intensive, manual process. Soiled linen on average weighs approximately 10% more than clean linen (and if soaked with liquid can be more than double the weight of clean linen), and carts full of linen can weigh several hundred pounds or more.

Most laundry operations use **par levels** to manage inventories of clean linen on each floor or unit, very similar to the concepts used for medical supplies or pharmaceuticals. A par is an inventory location that holds a specific product mix with minimum quantities that will cover the unit for a predetermined number of hours or days and defines which type and how many linen items are required for each location. In many hospitals, a par refers to either a physical location (e.g., the par in pediatrics) or inventory levels and mix (e.g., the par for sheets is 20). Pars exist for medical supplies and pharmaceuticals, as well as for linens. Smaller hospitals might have a dozen or fewer pars, while larger hospitals can have several hundred pars. A typical par will have a breakdown of items required for the period (e.g., 12 towels, 15 sheets, and 20 rags).

Pars can be replenished by use of either exchange or bulk replenishment carts. **Exchange carts** are large moveable steel structures, and new items on a cart are swapped entirely for the existing cart. In this replenishment process, one cart is always redundant and is used solely to provide fast exchange of all items on the par. **Bulk replenishment** occurs when items are simply augmented to the existing cart. If 10 towels are on the par, but only 3 exist, 7 more would be added from bulk stock. Neither exchange nor bulk replenishment is necessarily a better method than the other. They both have advantages and disadvantages that must be considered in each hospital's unique circumstances. Bulk is often much more economical for washing but less efficient for replenishment, while an exchange cart is faster and usually has higher service levels. A careful analysis of the economics and service levels for each should be conducted for each location.

Laundry is processed or cleaned at a production facility that uses commercial laundry equipment. One of the major pieces of equipment is a tunnel washer, which is a modular machine where batches of linen move through phases or modules during the process. Tunnel washers are typically called *continuous batch washers* because they operate as a production process. Washers are some of the more expensive pieces of equipment and can process 1,000 pounds or more of linen per hour.

In addition to washers, hospital laundries must have commercial dryers, extractors, ironers, folders, and other similar equipment. Other technology, such as conveyor belts, help push linen through the assembly-line production process, as follows:

Sort >> Wash/extract >> Dry >> Iron or fold >> Assembly >> Transportation

The cost of new laundries must factor into the capital equipment as well as the land and building costs. Total costs, then, can be $10 to $20 million for new laundry facility construction (Lees, 2001). The total cost of laundry and linen for a hospital is a component of four factors:

1. Acquisition and replacement cost of linens.
2. Cost of processing (washing, drying, folding).
3. Cost of collecting and distributing linens.
4. Consumption and utilization patterns.

Together, these four components significantly add to the cost structure for a hospital. In many larger hospitals, total costs can amount to several millions of dollars annually. On an adjusted per-patient per-day basis, the total cost of linen can range from $7 to $20, which is quite significant. More common metrics are recorded on a per-pound basis and typically range from $0.50 to $1, based on overall economies of scale and other efficiencies.

To continually improve service levels to nursing while reducing laundry and linen expenses requires careful oversight. Laundry operations must focus on managing nursing utilization patterns to ensure that the right linens are being used for the right task and that excessive amounts are not being used for any one task. **Utilization** refers to the usage patterns of linens; thus, linen use must be carefully monitored to ensure stable or declining utilization over time. Managing staff productivity for distribution and collections is also important, which requires careful scheduling and monitoring of employees during routes. The use of automation and workflow (including chutes, belts, and automated guided vehicles) can also reduce labor expenses, so their use should be encouraged when cost effective. Finally, ensuring that the right levels of inventory are on hand at all times (i.e., not too many, not too few) is extremely important, so the use of economic order quantities, safety stock calculations, and proper replenishment practices covered in the *Inventory Management and Accounting* chapter are extremely relevant for laundry management. Excessive safety inventory is evident when linens are stockpiled in nursing supply or patient treatment rooms, and this results in excessive costs to the linen system.

CHAPTER SUMMARY

The materials management organization in large hospitals plays a key role in operations management. Materials management typically includes oversight of purchasing, strategic sourcing, inventory replenishment, laundry and linen, patient transportation, and sterile processing, in addition to revenue responsibilities for medical supplies and equipment. A comprehensive purchasing process focuses on the use of GPOs and strategic sourcing methodologies to lower total costs and increase financial value. Internal controls are important in this process because materials management has a fiduciary responsibility to prevent loss, reduce waste, and provide sound oversight to the use of operating funds. The management of laundry and linen is just one of the areas with large customer and patient consequences in a hospital, and it should be managed appropriately.

KEY TERMS

Audit trail
Bulk replenishment
Chargeable
Competitive bidding
Current Procedural Terminology (CPT)
Customer service
Durable medical equipment
Exchange carts
Group purchasing organization (GPO)
Healthcare Common Procedure Coding System (HCPCS)
Laundry management
Linens
Loss leader
Markup
Materials management
Medical record

Optimization
Par levels
Penetration
Physician preferences
Point-of-use systems
Postponement
Profit center
Request for information (RFI)
Request for proposal (RFP)
Request for quotation (RFQ)
Revenue code
Scorecard
Service-level agreement
Soiled linen
Spend analysis
Three-way match
Utilization
Vendor master

DISCUSSION QUESTIONS

1. What role does materials management play in health care?
2. What are the key functions and processes of materials management?
3. How does the layout of a hospital floor or unit affect operational efficiency?
4. Discuss the concept of cost minimization models. When can they be applied, and what are the steps to follow when using them?
5. Differentiate between a request for information, request for proposal, and request for quotation, and describe the utility of each in the hospital purchasing process.
6. What is a group purchasing organization? What value can it bring?
7. Why does a hospital need both a group purchasing organization and a purchasing department?
8. Which types of technologies are involved in laundry management?

REFERENCES

American Medical Association. (2001). *Healthcare common procedure coding system 2002.* Atlanta, GA: Author.

Boyson, S., & Corsi, T. (2001). The real-time supply chain. *Supply Chain Management Review, 5*(1), 44–50.

Centers for Disease Control and Prevention, Office of Health and Safety. (2003). *Guidelines for laundry in health care facilities.* Atlanta, GA: Author.

Council of Supply Chain Management Professionals. (2014). *CSCMP supply chain management.* Retrieved from http://cscmp.org/about-us/supply-chain-management-definitions

Healthcare Purchasing News. (2004). *OSHA guidelines for laundry in healthcare facilities.* Sarasota, FL: Author.

Healthcare Purchasing News. (2013). *2012 group purchasing survey.* Sarasota, FL: Author.

Heizer, J., & Render, B. (2004). *Operations management* (7th ed.). Englewood Cliffs, NJ: Prentice Hall.

Hospital and Health Networks. (2001). *Contract management survey.* Chicago, IL: American Hospital Association.

Kowalski-Dickow Associates, Inc., & American Society for Healthcare Materials Management. (1994). *Managing hospital materials management.* Chicago, IL: American Hospital Association.

Lambert, D. (1999). *Strategic logistics management.* New York, NY: McGraw-Hill.

Lees, K. (2001, July 20). New facility takes laundry high-tech. *Duke Today.* Retrieved from http://today.duke.edu/2001/07/laundry720.html

Wayland, R. E., & Cole, P. M. (1997). *Customer connections: New strategies for growth.* Boston, MA: Harvard Business School Press.

13

Inventory Management and Accounting

GOALS OF THIS CHAPTER

1. Define inventory.
2. Understand the pros and cons of maintaining inventory.
3. Understand the difference between perpetual and periodic methods.
4. Explain common accounting entries for inventory management.
5. Calculate common inventory ratios.

Inventory is a complicated subject in most industries, and it is even less understood in health care. **Inventory** represents the acquisition and storage of materials that will not be consumed today (and thus have some value in the future) and that will be used within the normal operating cycle. It is therefore treated financially as a current asset, and proper treatment requires capitalizing it and recording a value on the balance sheet.

However, in most hospitals inventory is geographically dispersed and of relatively small financial value in disaggregated form (i.e., hospital inventory usually sits in treatment and exam rooms, surgical suites, and supply closets). When aggregated, these supplies can represent millions or even tens of millions of dollars for most hospitals. This chapter discusses the basics of inventory accounting and management in health care.

INVENTORY AND ITS ROLE IN HEALTH CARE

Inventory can be defined from an accounting or operations perspective. From an accounting view, inventory includes those assets that are used to generate revenue and that will be converted to cash in the short term. They are assets (e.g., supplies) that are held for sale. In the case of hospitals, medical supplies and pharmaceuticals are directly or indirectly charged back to patients—through direct charges from the Healthcare Common Procedure Coding System or other procedural charges—or they are reimbursed as part of per-diem, diagnosis-related group, room, or other service procedure codes. This depends on the specific hospital, the types of services they typically receive reimbursement for, and the specific payer mix. Regardless, most medical supplies and drugs are reimbursed either directly or indirectly, and therefore they represent costs incurred that will deliver future benefits.

From an operations perspective, inventory represents a margin of safety to protect the business from unpredictable levels of demand. Without inventory, hospitals could purchase just enough products to sustain normal operations, but if one more incremental unit was used or consumed, then the entire supply chain would be thrown into chaos due to a lack of supplies needed to provide services (known as **stock-outs**), reduced service levels, and a potential inability to fully treat a patient. In operations terms, inventory is a buffer against demand variability.

Operationally, inventory serves a multitude of other functions:

- Inventory improves customer service by making products available immediately.
- Inventory allows for economies of scale, as it encourages aggregation of production, purchase, and transportation to achieve reduced costs.
- Inventory allows for batching of orders, which creates economies of scale for purchasing. Larger orders usually are associated with pricing discounts. In addition, batching allows staff doing purchasing to process fewer total transactions, thus reducing costs for the purchasing function.
- Inventory takes advantage of pricing discounts for large quantities. For most manufacturers and distributors, it is significantly easier to work in larger volumes or batches than in smaller quantities (e.g., "each" or individual items). Because manufacturers produce in large batches to reduce production costs, and distributors receive quantity discounts for buying in volume, they are often able to pass significant savings on to hospitals if they can purchase in larger volumes. Unfortunately, many hospitals have

very little warehouse or storage space and must work on a just-in-time basis.

- Inventory allows for transport economies from larger shipment sizes. Smaller orders have a very high transportation cost, especially relative to the unit cost. For example, assume a $2 surgical procedure kit was ordered and shipped with transportation costs of $3 minimum for overnight delivery. The transportation cost, then, is 150% of the product cost. Assume 10 items could be purchased and shipped using this same $3 minimum shipping (the weight of 10 items falls under the weight restrictions), then shipping costs per unit would be only 15% of the total cost (i.e., $3 ÷ 10 items = $0.30 per item; $0.30 ÷ $2 = 15%).

- Inventory hedges against price changes. If a supply cost is increasing at a greater rate than the average consumer price inflation of 3%, it is sometimes beneficial to hold larger volumes of inventory as a hedge against the risk of rising prices.

- Inventory allows purchasing to take place under most favorable price terms.

- Inventory protects against uncertainties in demand and lead times for receipt of ordered goods.

- Inventory helps accurately report financial results, because the timing of the supply expense must be associated with the period in which revenues are generated. If material is on hand but not actually used and patients have not been charged, then it is proper not to record payment for those items as an expense. Therefore, inventory serves a valuable purpose in the accurate statement of operations.

- Inventory protects against demand volatility. When demand is less than certain, or variable, inventory helps protect against this variability. For instance, if 100 packs of bandages are used fairly consistently, but a large incident might create demand for another 50, inventory would help provide some measure of protection or margin of safety to keep operations running when demand levels and lead times cannot be known for sure.

- Inventory provides buffers against tragic events and other disruptions in supply. When the major hurricanes of 2005 hit the Gulf Coast of the United States, supply lines were essentially cut off completely—highways were jammed and many vendors and distributors were closed down. In the event that a hospital was forced to continue operations, it likely did so because of inventories that were built up prior to the storm.

Thus, there are many positive reasons a hospital would want to hold inventory, but there are also some negative and financial reasons not to do so. The biggest reason not to hold excessive inventories is that they consume cash and capital resources that might be put to better use elsewhere. Inventories represent prepaid supplies—cash spent on supplies that once spent cannot be used for other purposes. If a hospital does not need an item until some period in the future, the most optimal case is that that item is not procured or delivered until as close to point of need or consumption as possible. This is called **postponement**. For example, if a hospital paid for $1 million of pharmaceutical supplies 2 weeks earlier than they were needed, at a 5% cost of capital or interest forfeited that could have been invested elsewhere, the hospital forfeited $1,923 unnecessarily. This loss is calculated as $1,000,000 paid × 5% cost of capital × (2 weeks early ÷ 52 weeks in a year) = $1,923. Also important in this case of the lost use of investable cash is that this calculation does not include the additional holding cost of inventory (i.e., cost of storage and handling of items while at the hospital).

Of course, this is not always possible, as discussed earlier. But from a cash flow perspective, the timing of the receipt and payment of goods should be as late as possible to allow cash to be invested in other higher-returning areas, such as new buildings, investments, or other capital programs.

Another reason not to hold inventories is that they often hide problems. Inventory serves as a buffer, and as such, operational problems that exist might go unnoticed for many periods. For example, if a nursing unit forgets to accurately record supply usage or administration against a patient's medical records in a timely manner, then there could be potential for lost charges. If hospitals do not build inventory, it is much easier to discover this omission. Otherwise, days or weeks worth of inventory sits onsite and might only be discovered during periodic physical counts of inventory on hand (known as **cycle counts**). Also, in systems that are not working properly, lower utilization rates, slow cycle times, and otherwise unproductive processes are often masked by inventory.

THE COSTS OF SUPPLIES AND INVENTORY

The purchase costs of pharmaceuticals and medical supplies are anywhere from 13% to 17% of a hospital's total operating expenses, depending on the size of the organization (Healthcare Financial Management Association, 2013). But this is only a small part of the total supply cost. Most hospitals are nonprofit and therefore prepare financials differently than a public firm would (especially in the manufacturing or retail industries); calculating the true cost of goods sold is not ordinarily performed. If it were, the cost of converting or transforming these products into revenue would include all salaries for time spent by nursing and materials personnel moving supplies toward point of consumption, inventories, logistics, information technology, and other associated carrying expenses. Based on this author's previous research, the true cost of supplies is somewhere between 25% and 35% of total operating expenses.

In smaller organizations, supply costs can range from $3.2 million for a hospital with a $25 million annual expense budget to $170 million for a $1 billion organization. Add the costs of materials management departments, the salaries of technicians and nursing staff who touch supplies, warehouse and other facility expenses, the cost of systems time, and the expense for managing these items, and total costs only get bigger.

Because most hospitals are nonprofit and do not necessarily follow **generally accepted accounting principles (GAAP)** to accurately record expenses and inventory values (GAAP represents the accounting principles required for use by public companies), there is little consistency in how supplies are expensed and inventory is capitalized. A few findings from this author's research of published hospital annual reports and Medicare cost reports for nonprofits suggest that these accounting practices are not used correctly in most cases. For instance, most published financials for hospitals tend to show a very small inventory balance and lump supply expenses under a large group called *operational expenses*. Very little detail below this aggregated value is publicly available. Where the data are available, they are inconsistent with actual practice and should be approached with caution.

The best way to understand the true costs of inventory and supplies, in an environment that is probably more cost conscious and that is required to use GAAP accounting, is to examine the publicly traded, for-profit hospital systems. Examining the inventory balances of several of the largest for-profit hospital chains shows the following patterns:

- Average inventory for medium-size hospitals is around $3 million to $4 million per hospital.
- Inventory represents approximately 5% to 15% of current assets.
- Investments in inventory constitute about 2% to 4% of total assets and net revenues.
- Inventory represents the largest portion of working capital requirements.

The bottom line is that inventories are a significant investment for hospitals and should be treated accordingly.

DIFFERENCES BETWEEN SUPPLY EXPENSE AND INVENTORY

What is the difference between supply and inventory, and is there really a distinction between the two? The answer is yes—but the distinction can be described in just two words: *timing* and *chargeable*.

Timing represents the difference between when a supply is purchased and when it is consumed. If it is purchased and consumed in the same period, it is treated as a supply expense and presented on the income statement with all other expenses. For example, if $1,000 of suture packages were purchased during the month of April and all of those sutures were used in the same month, a $1,000 supply expense would be recorded in that month. If that same amount of sutures were purchased in April but half were not used as of the end of that month, then the remaining unused portion of that purchase is shown on the balance sheet as capitalized inventory.

Chargeable means that if the purpose of the material is to charge it back, directly or indirectly (through room or procedure fees) to patients, and if it is not consumed by the end of the period, it is held as inventory. If the items have no role in reimbursement (e.g., office supplies for administrative purposes), then the cost of those items, whether or not they are used in that period, is probably expensed. (Note: If there is a significant amount of monies represented, these could be capitalized as prepaid assets, but they would not be considered "inventory.")

EFFECT OF TIMING ON EXPENSES

Consider this example. A large hospital purchases $5 million of pharmaceuticals in preparation for a category 4 hurricane that is heading toward the city. The distributor delivers 1,200 tote boxes of medications, which are put in a back room for use if needed. The date is July 29. The hospital continues operations; fortunately, the storm never reaches the city, and all operations continue as normal. The medications remain unused but the payment for them is recorded as an expense when paid. The general ledger then officially closes for the month, and the hospital finds itself with a $3 million loss—a direct result of the recorded purchase of the medications as a precaution against an emergency need. This is fairly standard accounting treatment for most hospitals.

The quality and maturity of information systems used in most health care settings for managing supplies, inventory, and the supply chain are generally poor in comparison to other industries. In retail, manufacturing, and consumer goods industries, sophisticated enterprise resource planning (ERP) tools are used to manage the movement of goods through all parts of the organization with extreme precision. In health care, however, most of the larger hospitals and systems use some form of ERP, but the configurations were not originally designed to bring the hospital systems up to the same level of functionality. As hospitals realize the potential savings of ERP usage, they are moving to increase their technical sophistication in this area beyond simple inventory count ledgers and online purchase order applications currently in wide use in the industry.

The hospital described in the earlier example did not use or consume the $5 million of drugs purchased in the period in question. An entry should have been made to record this as inventory because it is prepaying a future expense and it is used for items generating revenue. If the hospital had booked this as inventory, no net effect on operating expenses for that month would have been noted and the hospital would have shown a $2 million profit for the period. Current assets would have increased by $5 million and, more than likely, accounts payable (i.e., a short-term liability) would have increased by the same amount. The net effect on cash flow would remain unchanged during that month.

This is not an accounting scheme or game. Instead, it represents matching expenses to the appropriate period in which the revenue was incurred, as is called for under the matching principle of accounting. Because the hospital did not use or charge a patient for the pharmaceuticals, the expense should not be recorded, and the future benefit of the current asset should be offset by an expense at a future date.

IMPORTANT FACTS ABOUT INVENTORY

Inventory on most hospitals' books is severely undervalued. If all hospitals complied with GAAP and Financial Accounting Standards Board pronouncements, there would be a much broader emphasis on comprehensively counting and valuing hospital inventories. For this reason, however, benchmark comparisons about inventory levels with most hospitals will not yield fruitful results due to the undervaluation and lack of consistency in treating supply expense versus inventory.

The cost of inventory is directly related to the relative severity of patients served by a hospital, as described by its case mix index. **Case mix index** is calculated based on classification schemes such as diagnosis-related groups where each group is assigned a relative value of severity, with a higher value representing a more severe case. Therefore, a hospital that has more intense, complicated, and resource-intensive procedures (and so a higher case mix index) will likely see a higher percentage of its operating budget being spent on supplies and inventory.

The larger the hospital, in terms of beds and procedures performed, the higher the associated supply expenses. Inventory, however, reflects efficiency in utilization and planning and may not be directly related. A hospital that employs quantitative planning and inventory techniques and attempts to model inventory using economic order quantities or forecasting practices would likely have less inventory than a similar hospital, even though current-period supply expenses might be comparable.

It is very difficult to explore utilization of supplies and inventory on a per-procedure basis, especially in larger hospitals, given the current state of information systems used for inventory management in hospitals. Implementing an activity-based costing approach to service-line management in clinical settings would be highly advantageous to track actual quantities of items utilized relative to patient reimbursements.

In most industries there are three classifications of inventory: raw materials, work in process, and finished goods. Most hospitals deal with only finished goods inventory, which refers to items that are complete and ready for sale (i.e., there is no conversion or manufacturing that must be done to make them usable).

There are two other types of inventory. **Consignment out** reflects the hospital's inventory that is placed elsewhere for sale. This type of consignment might be where a hospital provides certain supplies to other facilities or even retail stores for them to resell. Consignment-out inventory must be recorded on the hospital's books and routinely counted to ensure that the recorded value is correct, because that inventory is usually not under the hospital's direct control. The opposite of this, **consignment in**, measures someone else's inventory (i.e., some type of vendor, either the manufacturer or the distributor) that is being held or stored on the hospital's facility at no charge until sold. Examples of this are orthopedic implants (such as an artificial hip), stents, and other expensive cardiology or operating room supplies where a vendor will place them onsite until they are consumed. At the point of usage, the vendor is paid, expenses are increased, and the vendor's inventory is decreased. The hospital does not own inventory that is consigned in, so it does not include it on its balance sheet.

CRITERIA FOR INVENTORY

To capitalize the value of materials on the balance sheet, there have to be criteria that determine materiality (i.e., what dollar threshold should be placed on inventory that is capitalized versus expensed) and what makes inventory unique to each hospital. Without criteria in place, and without complying with GAAP accounting requirements, organizations would immediately expense all items that were purchased, which, of course, does not properly reflect timing and matching principles in accounting (Bragg, 2006).

Criteria should be defined so that each department and location purchasing and storing materials would check the following:

- Are the items held for sale to patients directly (i.e., through the Healthcare Common Procedure Coding System) or indirectly (i.e., through bundled hospital room or procedure charges)?
- Are the items consumable?
- Are they greater than the dollar amount defined as "material" or significant to the hospital's financial records? (This must be defined based on the size and unique situation of each hospital because no standard material threshold exists.)
- Are the materials owned by the institution and not leased, rented, or otherwise consigned to the hospital?
- Are the materials used in permanent and ongoing service lines? (That is, they are not to be used in a special one-time situation.)

The capitalization criteria defined should be consistent across all areas of the hospital and should identify each unit, floor, and nursing station that holds inventory and then apply the criteria comprehensively. Any inventories that meet this test should be physically counted, valued, and recorded in the general ledger on the balance sheet (this assumes, of course, that the items are not already in a perpetual inventory system, which will be discussed later). Even when a perpetual inventory system is in use, counts shown in that system must be periodically verified with cycle counts.

VALUATION METHODS

One of the most important decisions to be made in inventory management is the choice of accounting valuation methods. **Valuation** is an assessment of the financial value of an asset (Muller, 2002). This is an important decision and has broad financial implications, but in the health care industry it is not well understood even by accountants—especially if they do not come from other, more inventory-intensive industries.

Accounting Research Bulletin 43, Chapter 4, is the official pronouncement with the highest-level authority in GAAP, and it lays out the inventory pricing conventions. There are a multitude of valuation methods in use, but the three most common are first in, first out; last in, first out; and weighted average. Other less common methods are dollar-value last in, first out; retail method; specific identification (used for high-dollar items, such as airplanes, where specific units are recorded); and moving average. Choosing a method can have different effects on the financial statements, especially if prices are continually changing. These differences will be illustrated using the example of Hypothetical Hospital where, during its fiscal year beginning July 1, 20×4, it recorded the following purchases of intravenous (IV) solution bags as shown in **Table 13–1**.

First in, first out (FIFO) is likely the most common valuation method in health care. It assumes that the first unit purchased is the first unit sold, and therefore the units that are remaining in inventory are the last units purchased.

Using the example of Hypothetical Hospital from Table 13–1, the FIFO valuation of inventory would be completed like this: The hospital had 400 bags of IV solution on hand, so a price must be assigned to the on-hand units of stock to record a value of that inventory on the balance sheet. Because FIFO assumes the first items received are the first ones used, the ending inventory is valued based on the latest purchases—in this case, from purchases in March and May of 20×5. The process works in reverse where the May purchases of 100 bags are

Table 13–1   Example Purchase and Inventory Data for Hypothetical Hospital

	Units	Price/Unit	Total $
Beginning inventory balance, July 1, 20X4	200	$5.25	$1,050
Purchases September 1, 20X4	200	$6.09	$1,218
Purchases November 1, 20X4	200	$6.44	$1,288
Purchases January 1, 20X5	300	$7.00	$2,100
Purchases March 1, 20X5	300	$7.63	$2,289
Purchases May 1, 20X5	100	$8.03	$803
Total	1,300		$8,748
Ending inventory balance, June 30, 20X5	300		

assumed to be among the 300 bags still on hand at the end of the fiscal year. The remaining 200 bags of solution are then assumed to be from the purchases made on March 1, 20×5. The 200 bags from the March purchase and the 100 bags from the May purchase are then combined to create a cost per unit for the 300 bags on hand on June 30, 20×5. The average cost for the 300 bags using this method is $7.76 per bag, and that amount is multiplied by the 300 bags on hand to estimate the ending inventory value at the end of the fiscal year:

March 1 purchases	200	$7.63	$1,526
May 1 purchases (applied to 100 units)	100	$8.03	$803
	300		$2,329

Cost/unit for inventory valuation	$7.76
Total inventory value on June 30, 20X5	$2,329.00

In an environment where prices are rising, FIFO expenses the lower-costing items first, which causes net income to be higher than other methods and leaves higher-cost items as on-the-shelf inventory at the end of the accounting period (this will be discussed in more detail later).

Using the **last in, first out (LIFO)** method, the premise is that the last unit purchased is the first unit sold. Alternatively, the oldest item in the inventory would be the first item purchased. This method assumes that sales are made from the most recently acquired units and that ending inventory comprises the oldest available goods. This method is generally problematic in health care in that it does not reflect the true physical flow of goods, where most medical supplies and drugs have expiration dates that require earlier products to be sold first. It does have an advantage in that it matches the most current cost against current revenues, but the balance sheet appears undervalued relative to current market or replacement costs. The net result is that net income under the LIFO method would be lower in this period, as long as quantities remain constant or increase.

Using the same data for Hypothetical Hospital in Table 13–1, the ending inventory valued using the LIFO method is calculated using costs from the beginning of the fiscal year to calculate an average cost for the 300 bags still on hand on June 30, 20×5. Because LIFO assumes the items in inventory are the oldest, the calculation starts with the 200 bags on hand at the beginning of the year and the remaining 100 bags (to get to the total of 300 bags on hand). The average cost of $5.53 is calculated as $[(200 \times 5.25) + (100 \times 6.09)] \div 300 = \$5.53$, and that amount is multiplied by the 300 bags on hand to arrive at the $1,659 estimated value of inventory on hand on June 30, 20×5, as follows:

July 1 cost	200	$5.25	$1,050
September 1, 20X4, purchases (applied to 100 units)	100	$6.09	$609
	300		$1,659

Cost/unit for inventory valuation	$5.53
Total inventory value on June 30, 20X5	$1,659.00

Another common valuation method used in health care is weighted average. **Weighted average** assumes that the cost should reflect the averages of all items purchased over time. Using the data for Hypothetical Hospital in Table 13–1, the weighted average method would result in an ending inventory balance of $2,018.77 using the following calculations:

$$\frac{\text{Weighted average Total \$ purchases}}{\text{Total items purchased}} \quad \frac{\$8,748}{1,300} \quad = \quad \$6.73$$

Total inventory value on June 30, 20X5 $2,018.77

Thus, the total inventory value at June 30, 20X5 using the weighted average method is calculated using the $6.73 weighted average cost per unit × 300 units on hand = $2,018.77.

The net effect on the financial statements using the weighted average method would be lower net income than FIFO but higher than LIFO. Comparisons of the expense amounts and ending inventory balances for Hypothetical Hospital under each of the three methods described here is shown in **Table 13–2**.

Most hospitals choose to use either FIFO or weighted average for their valuation methods. Most information systems can support either of these, and it is acceptable to use a combination of several methods, as long as they can be supported. The most important thing is to select one of these methods and stick with it. This consistency principle is essential so that comparisons can be made over time.

Table 13–2 Comparison of Expense Recorded and Ending Inventory Values

Method	Expense	Ending Inventory
First in, first out	$6,419	$2,329
Last in, first out	$7,089	$1,659
Weighted average	$6,729	$2,019

LOWER OF COST OR MARKET

Regardless of the inventory costing method chosen, the value has to follow the "conservative" principle of accounting, which states that inventory should be valued at the **lower of cost or market (LCM)**. The complexity in this is to understand what is meant by "cost." Determining market cost can be complex, as described next, but market typically refers to the current replacement cost or cost to purchase a new unit.

The first step is to determine the market cost. Hospitals should use the concept of a "ceiling" and a "floor." A ceiling is the upper limit, defined as selling price minus all cost to sell the items, which also is called the **net realizable value**. Next, look at the floor, which is defined as the ceiling minus the normal expected profit margin. The result is two numbers, a ceiling and a floor, and the market price will fall somewhere in that range. Now, compare the current replacement costs for that item to the range. In general, hospitals use the replacement cost if the replacement cost fits between the ceiling and the floor. If the replacement cost is below the floor, use the floor. The second step is to compare the historical cost to the market figure calculated earlier. Hospitals report the lower (or more conservative) of the two figures.

Consider this example. A drug is purchased for $200, which reflects the original purchase cost. The average markup is 30% on this type of item, and therefore the sales price is $260. Additional selling costs are estimated at 10% of cost on all pharmaceuticals, and so the net realizable value is:

$$(\$200 \times 1.3) - (\$200 \times 0.10) = \$240$$

Thus, $240 is the ceiling price. The floor is defined as the ceiling less normal profit margin, which is $60 in this example, or ($260 − $60) = $200. The current replacement cost for that same item is $225. Because this replacement cost falls inside the relevant range, the replacement cost of $225 will be used for inventory valuation purposes.

In practice, most hospitals have thousands of items to manage, so it is impossible to calculate an LCM on each item. The principle is important but, in practice, very difficult to manage without good systems. The real distinction that most hospitals make is whether to book at historical cost or replacement cost (which is captured in the earlier discussion of LIFO, FIFO, and weighted average).

PERIODIC VERSUS PERPETUAL SYSTEMS

Another choice to be made with regard to inventory is whether to manage items on a periodic or a perpetual basis. Periodic inventory in general is easier to manage. **Periodic inventory** does not keep a running record of items that are sold or purchased, so a real-time balance of inventory on hand is never available. Periodic inventory relies heavily on physical counting and observation of goods because no system is used to track balances.

Perpetual inventory, on the other hand, keeps a running record of the inventory balance on hand at all times. Perpetual inventory is very common in retail and manufacturing industries, where having a precise idea of inventory on hand is very important. In health care, it is used less, although the trend is to incorporate more perpetual systems throughout the industry as reimbursements cause hospitals to be more judicious in the amount of money they can invest in inventories.

In central stores and the warehouse, perpetual systems are commonly used for several reasons:

- A person usually works the location and is responsible for closely guarding the inventory.
- A system at this point can be used to enter requisitions from units (or issues against inventory) as well as receipts or additions to inventory.
- They are usually smaller, more controlled environments where all ins and outs can be monitored.

Perpetual systems can best be used in situations involving a small number of locations with a high dollar unit value, whereas periodic systems are often used in situations that are low cost and high volume. In decentralized storage areas of the hospital (sometimes referred to as a par or supply room), there is typically no centralized control or monitoring of supplies coming in and out. Multiple people over several shifts come in and out of these areas to retrieve items for patients, and in these cases a perpetual system is not necessarily appropriate or cost-effective (the use of supply automation that enables perpetual monitoring even in decentralized locations is discussed later).

In a periodic inventory, a physical count is taken at least once at the end of the fiscal period. Receipts or purchases from vendors are typically incremented to separate purchases or expense accounts. A physical count of inventory at the end of the next period yields a figure, and the difference between the beginning and the ending inventory is adjusted to find the true **cost of goods sold (COGS)**. COGS becomes the supply expense for the period, which reflects actual usage of items, or the delta between beginning and ending period positions. Alternatively, items could be expensed as procured, and then an adjustment is made for any differences at the end of the period. When using periodic inventory, the ending inventory in units is multiplied by the FIFO or weighted average values to determine an inventory balance.

A perpetual inventory system, however, recalculates based on each transaction occurrence. If beginning inventory is five items, and three items are purchased the next month, the total goods available for sale is eight. Subtract the issues to patients or floors to get the ending inventory balance. Automated ERPs and materials management information systems allow for real-time entry of receipts as supplies come through the receiving dock and issues as they are charged out to patients or patient care units.

The real advantage to a perpetual system is that it provides valuable information about supply expenses and inventory values throughout the year. If a hospital is only interested in its end-of-year financial position, then either method will yield the same result. Because most hospitals today are encouraging sound financial practices and continuous performance measurements, intraperiod inventory balances are extremely important for monitoring operational and financial performance. In addition, this same perpetual information will drive improved inventory replenishment plans, because transaction histories are associated with the actual months in which they occurred—which is vital to predicting demand and generating usage forecasts for the future.

Another advantage to perpetual systems is that they help materials managers avoid excessive inventory levels throughout the year. Working capital, the net current resources necessary to sustain operations, should be held as minimally as possible so that investments in more productive assets can be made. Inventory is one of the key components driving increases in working capital, so a more detailed, real-time understanding of inventory will lower working capital requirements.

Perpetual inventory systems also allow for the use of automated replenishment versus manual ordering and replenishment processes. Automated replenishment is less people intense, more efficient, and less expensive in the long run, but it is also faster and ensures fewer stock-outs (i.e., having zero items on a shelf when an item is needed). Two ways these perpetual systems can automate the replenishment process are:

- Forecasting an order based on transactional usage history, which will generate an automatic order based on previous consumption patterns.
- Using predetermined minimum and maximum levels (discussed in more detail later). If current inventory falls below the minimum required on hand, an automated order is placed for the difference between the minimum and the current quantity.

At most hospitals there will be a combination of both perpetual and periodic systems. The perpetual system is preferred, as long as the cost of using such a system does not exceed the benefits derived (avoided costs of stock-outs or holding of excessive inventories). However, a perpetual system may not be practical in all locations, especially in small organizations with a fairly narrow range of products used in few storage locations. For that reason, an understanding of the accounting treatment for both periodic and perpetual inventory is important. Under either scenario, periodic physical inventory counts (cycle counts) must be conducted to verify the accuracy of the perpetual inventory or accounting records.

ACCOUNTING ENTRIES FOR SUPPLY AND INVENTORY

Accounting treatment is different depending on whether the hospital or department is working in the perpetual or the periodic environment. Starting first with perpetual inventories, the basic calculation of inventory is:

$$BI + P - COGS = EI$$

where

BI = beginning inventory, in units and dollar value
P = cost of the units purchased
$COGS$ = the cost of goods sold for issues to departments and patients
EI = ending inventory

For example, assume that there is $500,000 in beginning inventory on January 1. Inventory has a debit balance on the balance sheet and reads $500,000 under current assets. (Note: Recording of debits in the following examples will be referred to using the abbreviation DR, while credits will be CR.) During January there were total purchases of $1,000,000. The entry to record, assuming that the invoice was not paid immediately from a cash account, would be:

DR inventory	$1,000,000
CR accounts payable	$1,000,000

In other words, a liability is created, and there is an offsetting asset for the same amount. Assume that there were sales or issues of $1,750,000 for charges to be reimbursed by payers for supplies that were given to the nursing units or floors for direct dispensing to patients. The entry to record this transaction would be:

> DR accounts receivable $1,750,000
> CR revenue $1,750,000

When the actual payment is made to the manufacturer or distributor, based on the contractual invoice terms, an entry would be made to reduce cash and liability, as follows:

> DR accounts payable $1,000,000
> CR cash $1,000,000

Next, an entry will have to be made to record the cost or expense of the items that were sold. Using FIFO and ensuring the LCM, the hospital determined that $900,000 in inventory expenses was consumed. The entry would be:

> DR supply expense (COGS) $900,000
> CR inventory $900,000

The net result of this is shown in **Table 13–3**. Thus, the net effect is a $100,000 increase in inventories on the balance sheet. The effect on the income statement, for these transactions only, shows a positive operating margin of $850,000 (or $1,750,000 in sales less $900,000 in COGS).

Under periodic inventory accounting, the treatment is somewhat different. Beginning inventory stays the same, at $500,000, but instead of booking the items purchased into inventory, they are recorded to a separate, temporary purchases or expense account that will be closed at the end of each period. Inventory maintains the same balance until the end of the period, when it would be physically counted again. If the count reveals only $400,000 worth

Table 13–3   Inventory Accounting

INVENTORY

Beginning inventory	$500,000
Issues/cost of goods sold	($900,000)
Purchases	$1,000,000
Ending inventory	$600,000

of inventory on hand, the calculation would be made as follows, assuming the same level of sales:

Beginning inventory	$500,000
+ Purchases	$1,000,000
− COGS	XX
= Ending inventory	$400,000

Solving for the COGS shows that it would have to be $1,100,000. The transactions would be as follows:

DR purchases	$1,000,000
CR accounts payable	$1,000,000

Notice that these purchases are not recorded into inventory as under the perpetual method. Also, the entry to record the revenue and accounts receivable would remain the same:

DR accounts receivable	$1,750,000
CR revenue	$1,750,000

The entry to record the payment to the vendor is the same as the previous entry for perpetual:

DR accounts payable	$1,000,000
CR cash	$1,000,000

Because beginning inventory ($500,000) plus purchases ($1,000,000) equals cost of goods available for sale of $1,500,000 and the ending inventory was observed and counted to be $400,000, the COGS would be $1,100,000, as shown earlier. The entry then has to be made to net out the temporary purchases account and book this to COGS:

DR COGS/supply expense	$1,100,000
CR purchases	$1,000,000
CR inventory	$100,000

This brings the inventory account down to $400,000 as counted, closes out the purchasing account, and moves all COGS to a supply expense.

The net result on the financial statements using periodic accounting methods is net operating margin of $650,000, versus $850,000 in the earlier example. This is just coincidental, however, because both methods will yield the same results over time, assuming that perpetual is capturing all transactions and that periodic counts are conducted.

In addition, under both the periodic and perpetual methods, entries must be made to reflect any adjustments to inventory. Adjustments are made when a comparison of the general ledger to actual observed quantities shows material variances. For example, if a cycle count was performed in a perpetual environment, and the count showed $100,000 worth of items but the general ledger reported $122,000, an adjusting journal entry would have to be made to record an additional $22,000 of expense and reduce the general ledger balance to the new correct level. This adjustment would be recorded as:

> DR COGS/supply expense $22,000
> CR inventory $22,000

This adjustment would be called **shrinkage**, or loss, which can arise as a result of several reasons:

- Failure to charge out properly to patients as items were dispensed or utilized.
- Misplacement or overuse of drugs or supplies.
- Items that have passed the expiration date or are obsolete and therefore have no value.
- Loss due to theft.
- Pricing or value decreases.
- Any other general loss.

INVENTORY ERRORS

Hospital supplies are dispersed geographically and decentralized throughout the hospital in multiple rooms, closets, and other storage areas. A physical count of the inventory results in a figure being recorded on the balance sheet as inventory. It is quite common to have errors in the counts, to have pricing discrepancies due to a large item master and complex pricing structure, or to overlook certain pockets of supply, which might understate or overstate the balance sheet.

One concern already noted is the effect that inventory errors have on reported earnings, especially as inventory plays a role in determining current-period operating margins. For tax-exempt or nonprofit organizations, the relative size of earnings may not matter, but in for-profit hospitals there has to be careful consideration of the inventory effects on earnings. Here are some facts to keep in mind about inventory:

- Overstating EI leads to understating COGS and therefore overstating gross operating margin.

- Understanding EI overstates COGS and therefore understates gross margins.
- The EI of one period becomes the beginning inventory of the next period.
- An error in one period carries over to the next period, having the opposite effect on gross margin.

Inventory errors generally "correct" themselves at the end of the second period and are commonly referred to as a **counterbalancing error**. This is one of the positive facts about inventory: Eventually, all errors self-correct over time. If inventory is not counted one year, resulting in undervalued inventory and higher supply expense on the income statement, it will be caught and fixed in the second year when an additional count discovers the error and makes an adjustment. By the third period, all inventory errors have self-corrected. This may happen with other line items on the balance sheet, such as in the valuation of discounts on receivables, for much the same reason—an error in estimate in one period can be offset by an error of the same magnitude in the opposite direction.

INVENTORY RATIOS

It is important to track inventory ratios and statistics over time, gauge the health of the business, monitor utilization, look for trends, and ensure internal controls. The key is to look for consistency of the ratios, and if a ratio is far outside of the normal range or published benchmarks, then additional research and analysis can be conducted.

One of the key ratios used in hospitals is days of inventory on hand, which alternatively can be called *days of supply* or DIO. This metric measures the amount of inventory on hand relative to an average daily usage. The calculation can be made for either quantities or dollar values, assuming pricing is relatively stable. The calculation for days of supply is:

DIO = Total number of units on hand ÷ Average daily units used

For example, if there were 1,000 syringes on hand, and on an average day 100 were used, there would be 10 days of supply on hand. This is simple enough when looking at each item, but when there are thousands of items and a materials manager wants to measure the portfolio as a whole, it requires conversion to currency. In that case, the calculation would be total dollar value of inventory on hand divided by average daily COGS. From the earlier example, assume an average usage or COGS of $1,000,000 monthly in a 30-day month and an average inventory of $450,000 [($500,000 + $400,000) ÷ 2]. It is possible to calculate this ratio using just EI values as well, but average inventory is more common. In this case:

$$DIO = \$450,000 \div \$33,334 = 13.5 \text{ days}$$

Another useful metric for inventory management is inventory turnover. This metric is often used to measure liquidity; because it shows how efficiently the organization is turning or converting supplies into cash. The metric is similar to the earlier definition of days of supply, but it provides another way of looking at it. The calculation of inventory turnover is:

$$\text{Inventory turnover} = COGS \div \text{Average inventory}$$

In the earlier example, COGS was $1,000,000 and average inventory value was $450,000, so the inventory turnover is 2.22 days.

Another useful metric is gross margin percentage. This ratio allows tracking of the relative importance of supply cost on a hospital's supply revenue; alternatively, it can estimate the gross markup on supplies. This figure differs from the actual markup used in the Charge Description Master, of course, which is based on gross revenues and purchase cost, not actual usage or COGS. The definition for gross margin percentage is:

$$\text{Gross margin percentage} = (\text{Net supply revenue} - COGS)$$
$$\div \text{Net supply revenue}$$

Assume a hospital generated $500,000 net in supply revenue (i.e., gross revenues less contractual adjustment and discounts for the supplies, provided that the entire net amount is collectible), and cost of goods was $210,000. The gross margin percentage would be calculated as 58%:

$$(\$500,000 - \$210,000) \div \$500,000 = \$290,000 \div \$500,000 = 58\%$$

If materials management departments fully charge for all hospital supplies, another useful metric is return on inventory. This metric examines the net income effect of inventory and is calculated as:

$$\text{Return on inventory} = \text{Net income} \div \text{Inventory}$$

If net income (or operating margin, after subtracting labor, supplies, and other costs from net revenues) is $50,000 and the total inventory balance at the end of the period is $500,000, then the return on inventory would be 10%. Analyzing this figure over time helps managers find useful patterns and remain focused on supply profitability.

Finally, a shrinkage calculation can be performed. Shrinkage can exist for a multitude of reasons, including theft, lack of internal controls, date expiration of supplies or drugs, and many other factors, as explained earlier. Shrinkage or loss calculations can be defined in terms of percentage of total inventories. For example, shrinkage percentage would be calculated as:

$$\text{Shrinkage} = (\text{Total book value} - \text{Observed value}) \div \text{Inventory}$$

OTHER INVENTORY CALCULATIONS

There are several other important inventory calculations that can be used to monitor asset utilization and improve operational efficiencies. These analytical calculations include safety stock, customer service level, economic order quantity, and cycle inventory.

Safety Stock

The basic purpose of **safety stock** is to carry additional inventory to satisfy unexpected demand (i.e., demand that exceeds the amount expected to be used or forecasted). This unexpected demand or variability can be predicted using the calculated standard errors from the forecast and incorporating them into a final version of a forecast. For instance, if the demand plan showed 12 units being sold in a specific department in a certain period, and the actual demand was 15, a shortage or stock-out would have occurred. To counter the effects of demand variability in the planning process, safety stock calculations are used to counter the uncertainty in the supply chain. Although there are multiple ways to calculate safety stock, the most common is to use service levels as the parameter (it is also possible to use fill rates and replenishment policies to calculate safety inventory):

$$\text{Safety stock} = sz(p)$$

where

s = standard deviation of a sample of errors from the sales and forecast history

p = desired customer service levels

$z(p)$ = z-value or number of standard deviations from the mean on a normal distribution curve for a specific service level. The higher the z-value, the lower the risk of stocking out.

Thus, safety stock builds in previous forecast errors and the desired service levels to create inventory buffers.

Customer Service Level

The **customer service level** is a measure of the probability that product will be available when the internal customer demands it. It can be measured in multiple ways, including product fill rates or stock-out percentages, but here is the most common method:

$$\text{Customer service level} = [Q - E(z)] \div 100$$

where

$$Q = \text{order quantity}$$
$$E(z) = \text{expected number of units short}$$
$$z = \text{number of standard deviations of safety stock}$$

$E(z)$ can either be calculated with an equation that examines annual demand, orders placed, and orders short, or it can be estimated. For example, suppose monthly demand is 100 units and standard deviation is 10 units. If there is half a standard deviation, or $z = 0.5$, then using a z-value table finds that $z = 0.198$. Therefore, to solve for customer service level:

$$[100 - (0.198)(10)] \div 100 = 98\%$$

Alternatively, and to maintain simplicity, fill rates are used to measure customer service level. Fill rate is the percentage of orders that are filled completely and accurately. Mathematically, fill rates are calculated as:

$$\text{Fill rate} = R/O$$

where

$$R = \text{number of purchase orders or lines actually replenished}$$
$$O = \text{the total number of orders requested or submitted}$$

Economic Order Quantity

The **economic order quantity (EOQ)** is one of the most basic calculations used to help firms improve the balancing between demand and supply. This calculation represents the "best" solution to the offsetting priorities of minimizing the amount of inventory on hand, the costs of ordering goods, and the carrying costs of inventory. EOQ affects order lot sizes, which represent the average size in units that a firm should procure at a given time to take advantage of economies of scale. Because many hospitals use a just-in-time basis of replenishment and have no inventory outside of the distributor, this formula may not be useful for them.

For hospitals that own their own inventory or buy in bulk and break down and distribute that inventory to the nursing units and floors when required, this formula will be helpful. Using the EOQ formula, hospitals can define the optimal amount of inventory to reduce overall inventory carrying costs and reduce working capital while maintaining adequate service levels. The formula is as follows:

$$\text{EOQ} = \sqrt{\frac{2(\text{Annual usage in units}) \times \text{Cost for one order}}{\text{Annual carrying cost for one unit}}}$$

The annual supply usage is in units, the order cost (i.e., purchase or setup costs) is the total costs each time an item is ordered, and the annual carrying cost is the total cost of keeping inventory on hand (e.g., warehouse or storage costs, taxes, insurance). Carrying cost is usually stated as a percentage of the total dollar amount spent on products. For example, Bayou Medical Center wants to calculate the EOQ for surgical packs given these facts:

- Annual usage: 844
- Cost per order: 26
- Annual carrying cost/pack: 1.25
- Average lead time for delivery: 1 week

The EOQ in this situation is calculated by:

$$\sqrt{\frac{2(844) \times 26}{1.25}} = 187 \text{ packs}$$

In reality, the EOQ is extremely valuable, but it is rarely used in practice because of the difficulties in implementing it and capturing the required data elements. It works best when demand is fairly stable or certain and when quantity discounts are minimized. That is not to say that EOQ calculations cannot be adapted to take into account the costs and consequences of variability in demand, if the costs of carrying too much inventory (known as an overstock) and of a stock-out can be estimated, and there is some understanding of the frequency distribution of actual demand. Using the EOQ calculation for the earlier example from Bayou Medical Center, assume that management has determined the following additional facts:

- Cost of a stock-out per occurrence: $9.25
- Cost of an overstock: $1.25
- Calculated EOQ: 187 packs

- Probability of demand of packs per week:
  - 177 packs: 10%
  - 182 packs: 25%
  - 187 packs: 30%
  - 192 packs: 25%
  - 197 packs: 10%

The EOQ calculation can be modified to take into account the costs of overstocks and stock-outs, weighted for the probability of demand in this manner:

	Potential demand (packs)					
	177	182	187	192	197	
Probability	10%	25%	30%	25%	10%	
Reorder point			Cost ($)			
177		$0.00	$11.56	$27.75	$34.69	$18.50	$92.50
182		1.38	0.00	13.88	23.13	13.88	52.25
187	EOQ	2.75	3.44	0.00	11.56	9.25	27.00
192		4.13	6.88	4.13	0.00	4.63	19.75
197		5.50	10.31	8.25	3.44	0.00	27.50

In this situation, the user should look for the reorder point that has the lowest total cost, which occurs at 192 packs because the $19.75 cost of overstock/stockouts is minimized at that level. In this situation, management at Bayou Medical Center may elect to adjust its calculated EOQ up to 192 packs to account for the uncertainty in demand. This sort of adjustment may introduce a degree of "reality" to address the limitations of the traditional EOQ calculation noted earlier.

Cycle Inventory

The calculation of **cycle inventory** is used to manage the effects of lot sizes that cannot be matched precisely to actual demand (e.g., if a hospital needs to produce 100 units to balance demand with supply but the required lot size is 200, the difference—averaged over time—is the cycle inventory). The calculation is fairly straightforward as follows:

$$\text{Cycle inventory} = \text{Lot size} \div 2$$

LIMITATIONS OF INVENTORY RATIOS

There are four limitations to the use of inventory ratios in health care. First, all ratios are meaningless unless they are tracked and measured over time. An inventory ratio equal to 2.2, without understanding the context and specific department, is meaningless by itself. This ratio must have points of comparison, such as looking at other departments of similar scope and structure. Most important, it has to be tracked consistently over time to see if the metric is improving, stable, or declining.

Second, there have to be average values and standard deviations that are expected for each metric. Tracking the ratio monthly relative to the average and minimum–maximum standard deviations provides very useful information that allows application of exception management and looks for red alerts and potential problems.

Third, ratios have to be tracked relative to other hospitals in the industry. A 2.2 turnover ratio in the health care industry means nothing by itself. Attempting to benchmark turns in health care against other industries is irrelevant. Average turns in the publishing business might be 50, while the grocery industry might be 20, because the industry has expected demand variability that drives unique inventory behaviors.

Fourth and most important, if inventory is not consistently and comprehensively measured in each location, it is impossible to produce valuable statistics. Comparison of inventory benchmarks is fairly impractical in the nonprofit hospital structure at this time due to the variety of different treatments that inventories and supplies are given. If one hospital expenses all of its items as purchased and does not count any inventory except possibly what is stored in a central warehouse, then the inventory would be significantly undervalued and the COGS would appear overstated. A ratio for this type of hospital cannot be compared equitably against a hospital that comprehensively values inventory for all locations. The key is to select the benchmark hospitals carefully—such as from the for-profit hospital sector that is more methodical about the use of GAAP and proper valuation techniques.

INVENTORY POLICIES AND PROCEDURES

A hospital needs to have a policy in place to ensure that it is comprehensively and completely valuing and managing its inventories. At a minimum, all of the components described earlier need to be in this policy (e.g., valuation method), but the policy should contain all of the following as well:

- *Inventory capitalization criteria.* This policy should focus on which inventories to **capitalize** (to hold as an asset on the balance sheet), thresholds for "materiality," and general expense versus capitalization procedures.
- *Scope and purpose of inventory.* This policy should detail the extent of coverage and the role of internal auditing in inventory management and should generally provide the framework for concepts of inventory accounting.

- *Periodic versus perpetual.* This section, if not detailed in other policies, should focus on the method of accounting for inventories—either perpetual or periodic—and discuss which is appropriate, preferred, and allowable.
- *Definition of supply versus inventory.* This policy is likely a subset of a policy listed earlier, but it should clearly define when to expense supplies versus capitalize them.
- *Inventory reporting requirements.* This policy should describe the timing and nature of management reporting, as well as define acceptable metrics and baselines.
- *Instructions for cycle counts.* This policy should provide details around cycle counts, if used in a perpetual or periodic method, and describe how they should be administered, which precount instructions are required, which level of documentation is acceptable, and how to report time lines back to the general ledger.
- *Instructions for other periodic physical inventory counts.* This policy is the same as that defined earlier, only for other more comprehensive periodic counts, such as the end of the fiscal year.
- *Treatment of obsolete inventory.* This policy should clearly define how to account for obsolete inventories. **Obsolete** means that the useful life of the product has expired. This policy should establish which accounting treatments will be given, how to physically dispose of inventory, and instructions for reverse flow logistics.
- *Calculation of period end inventories.* This policy describes how the final accounting entry will be determined for a fiscal period, given the observed inventory count plus adding all receipts and netting all issues out.
- *Management of consignment inventories.* This policy should describe physical location of consignment inventories, procedures for notes or entries into nongeneral ledger systems, and general segregation of owned versus consigned inventories.
- *Use of systems, radio frequency identification, and bar codes.* This policy should lay foundations for deployment of systems that meet key criteria of automation; use standard coding technologies; and allow for real-time, perpetual management of inventories.
- *Receiving of materials into inventory.* This policy governs how materials are systematically received into a hospital resource system and describes the accounting entries necessary to increment inventory, plus how to track and manage inventory once it has been received.

- *Treating shrinkage and suspected inventory losses.* This policy discusses the accounting entries necessary to support shrinkage and loss, as well as the documentation required in the event of theft. Loss prevention procedures should also be reported here.
- *Inventory measurements and metrics.* This policy sets the required inventory calculations that must be managed by each inventory location, including a description of the metric, a definition, and acceptable data sources.
- *Approved inventory valuation methods.* This policy outlines which GAAP requirements are allowable for each hospital, whether they are LIFO, FIFO, weighted average, retail method, or some other method.
- *Inventory records retention.* This policy governs the retention period (i.e., length of time a document must be maintained by regulatory bodies) for inventory records, including systems transaction history.
- *Internal pricing and charging.* This policy outlines how internal pricing, cost transfers, or other chargeback processes work for supply cost allocation to floors and units.

INVENTORY PLANNING

Planning and managing inventory are vital to effective inventory management, sales and operations planning, and collaborative planning forecasting and replenishment (both of which will be described later). The purpose of inventory is to buffer the variability inherent in both supply and demand environments. In a perfect world, where demand is constant and manufacturers or distributors supply the exact amounts in the plan, no inventory is necessary. However, in real life, this variability or fluctuation in the market is inevitable, and effective business processes have to be put in place to plan and manage accordingly.

The key aspects of inventory planning include:

1. Establishing safety and cycle inventory policy levels.
2. Obtaining the right amount of items just at the point of need or consumption.
3. Evaluating demand and planning inventory positioning accordingly.
4. Building effective replenishment processes based on collaborative demand plans and inventory policies.

The first of these, developing inventory policies, should be consistent with the **ABC classification** schemes for the key internal customers. ABC analysis assigns priorities based on volumes, margins, turnover, required service levels, or other relevant metric that shows relative importance compared to others across key dimensions.

They should be statistically based (e.g., using previous forecasting errors and real demand forecasts) and should be continually updated with new assumptions, such as lead times. Finding an optimal safety stock level, for example, should not be taken lightly. In many companies, the safety stock levels are established by setting vague and general rules, such as "15 days on hand for all products." These types of policies have devastating results for firm economics. If an average hospital changes its blanket policy of 30 days on hand at all locations to a statistically based demand estimate, it could possibly reduce total inventories by nearly 25%—with no service effect on operations. However, attempting to manage the multiple items in a hospital storeroom can prove daunting, and setting priorities for the most relevant items may help to address customer satisfaction and minimize the costs of managing inventories.

Applying the ABC model to priority setting in inventories will assist managers in focusing on the parts of the inventory that can have the most favorable effect on the organization. Typically, an ABC system groups inventory into three classifications: A for the 20% of items that have the highest proportion of the organization's inventory, B for the next 30% of items, and C for the remaining 50% of items. This type of classification can be illustrated using the example of Hometown Hospital, where the 10 items in the hospital inventory identified by stock-keeping unit number are listed in **Table 13–4**.

The inventory list should be sorted from high to low in terms of dollar volume (the rightmost column in Table 13–4) to assign the highest dollar values at the top of the list, as shown in Table 13–5.

Table 13–4   Listing of Items in the Inventory at Hometown Hospital

Item SKU #	Annual Usage	Cost/Unit	Volume in $
12750	8,000	$14.24	$113,920
21599	225	$201.98	$45,446
44084	6,000	$12.76	$76,560
70140	10,000	$6.00	$60,000
77824	3,250	$16.01	$52,033
82183	2,350	$14.98	$35,203
86449	200,000	$2.13	$426,000
87159	600	$144.56	$86,736
99243	140	$600.00	$84,000
99503	24,000	$9.07	$217,680
Total			$1,197,577

Table 13–5 Inventory Listing Sorted by Annual Usage

Item SKU #	Annual Usage	Cost/Unit	Volume in $	Cumulative % Volume in $	Cumulative % SKU#
86449	200,000	2.13	426,000	35.6%	10%
99503	24,000	9.07	217,680	53.7%	20%
12750	8,000	14.24	113,920	63.3%	30%
87159	600	144.56	86,736	70.5%	40%
99243	140	600.00	84,000	77.5%	50%
44084	6,000	12.76	76,560	83.9%	60%
70140	10,000	6.00	60,000	88.9%	70%
77824	3,250	16.01	52,033	93.3%	80%
21599	225	201.98	45,446	97.1%	90%
82183	2,350	14.98	35,203	100.0%	100%
Total			$1,197,577		

The ABC classification is based on the column at the far right of Table 13-6, where the top 20% of stock-keeping units are placed in category A, the next 30% in category B, and the remaining 50% in category C, as depicted in Table 13–6.

By assigning inventory to these three broad categories, management can achieve in detail 20% of the items in inventory, but effect 53.7% of the inventory value. Another 23.8% of the inventory can be managed with further

Table 13–6 Assignment of ABC Classifications

Item SKU #	Cumulative % SKU Volume	Cumulative % Volume in $	Classification
86449	10%	35.6%	A
99503	20%	53.7%	A
12750	30%	63.3%	B
87159	40%	70.5%	B
99243	50%	77.5%	B
44084	60%	83.9%	C
70140	70%	88.9%	C
77824	80%	93.3%	C
21599	90%	97.1%	C
82183	100%	100.0%	C

attention to an additional 30% of items. In this example, managers can focus on 50% of the items in the inventory, but effect almost 78% of the entire inventory value.

In addition to setting priorities to focus on managing specific items of inventory, hospitals must adopt some of the best practices for inventory management, such as:

- Continually updating business rules and assumptions.
- Using advanced statistical engines to calculate accurate inventory levels based on rough-cut demand–supply balances.
- Building safety policies around specific customer groups or product categories.
- Managing lead times, usage, and overall safety stocks held at each location.
- Using an ABC customer classification scheme to drive inventory business rules.
- Building and continually improving demand forecasts.
- Collaborating on schedules and changes in customer operations that might affect inventory (e.g., new operating room suite opening five additional beds).

One way to improve inventory planning is to utilize vendor-managed inventory. **Vendor-managed inventory** is a process whereby a supplier manages the inventory stock levels for its customers based on forecasted usage or demand. The largest health care distributors have vendor-managed inventory programs in place with many of their largest accounts. The process is designed to be proactive by the supplier, which controls the distribution plans and sends out orders with minimal involvement from the customer. This process essentially places the control around inventory planning, and the risks of inventory levels, in the hands of the supplier, which can be very beneficial from a cost perspective.

INVENTORY AUDIT

Internal and external auditors routinely **audit** (i.e., examine, verify) inventories in most hospitals. The primary role of an audit function is twofold: financial and operational. Financial audits typically focus on ensuring four things:

1. The existence and completeness of inventory in terms of knowing which items are in the hospital and included in inventories and which controls exist over inventories to ensure that they are protected from loss and used only for their intended purpose.
2. That valuations on the books are materially correct and use appropriate pricing methods.

3. That the presentation and disclosure of inventory balances on the published financial statements are accurate.
4. That ownership of all inventories has been established.

Operational audits tend to focus on whether hospitals are utilizing resources in the most appropriate manner; therefore, they concentrate on issues of effectiveness, efficiency, and compliance.

The following is a sample inventory audit program that may be similar to one used in a hospital. It is important that operational managers understand how they may be reviewed, so that appropriate policies, procedures, staffing, systems, and other management systems can be developed to ensure operational excellence.

A. Audit Overview, Purpose, and Scope

Audit guidelines exist to identify the specific financial controls and business procedures to be assessed as part of the inventory review and audit process. This includes existing cycle count procedures and controls over picking, packing, staging, and distribution of both inbound and outbound inventory. The objectives of this review are to:

- Confirm and test the accuracy of the ledger or subledger (i.e., book) to physical inventory balances in total and in all locations (existence, completeness, ownership).
- Ensure that inventories are properly stated at the LCM determined by a specific method, such as FIFO (valuation).
- Assess the effectiveness of these processes in ensuring, recording, and documenting the accuracy of the inventory balances (presentation, disclosure).
- Assess the effectiveness of the area's inventory cycle count process in identifying shortages, shrinkage, and other errors in balance or counts (effectiveness, compliance).
- Observe and document the processes affecting inventory, such as shipping and receiving (efficiency, accuracy).

B. Planning and Initial Review

During this phase of an audit, the auditors will:

1. Obtain and review prior working papers and historical audits, if any.
2. Send a copy of the prior audit cycle and periodic count programs, including documentation around ABC classifications or procedures, to the materials manager or inventory manager.

3. Discuss the scope of the audit and background information with management.

4. Request copies of any information required by warehouse or inventory location, including current organizational chart, business procedures and inventory policies, cycle and periodic count procedures, and ratio analyses conducted year to date.

5. Request a current book values or stock status (stock on hand) report for the facility.

6. Request copies of reconciliations from general ledger balances against perpetual reconciliations, as well as general ledger versus physical inventories (cycle counts).

7. Review the custody chain and organizational structure. Meet the management team and become familiar with the department layout and staff. Ensure existence and location of all inventory sites to be included in the count process.

C. Observation and Documentation

During this phase of the audit, operations managers can expect the auditors to do the following:

1. Confirm the results of the last inventory audit and follow up on any solutions or action items that should have been implemented.

2. Discuss the organization. Specifically, identify the individuals responsible for the cycle count program, including those employees responsible for counting, reconciling, and reporting. Determine if there were any recent, significant organizational changes (e.g., terminations, resignations) of warehouse or inventory staff, specifically any management or senior-level changes. Document accordingly.

3. Inquire about any major systems changes at the facility or any major changes in the cycle count process since the last audit. Thoroughly review the documentation from the last audit, and document any changes.

4. Review the last audit of inventory counts. Review the ABC classification scheme for inventory. Select three of each item in each classification for review. Count quantity on hand for each of these items, and document next to the stock status report from inventory or the ERP system. Document any reason for discrepancy or variance.

5. Review reported results for the year, including a focus on:

   • Inventory turn ratios and loss calculations.
   • Adjustments that were conducted.
   • General ledger entries not related to receipts and issues.

6. Document the process for making, reviewing, and approving adjustments into the hospital resource planning or inventory systems. Document cutoff times. Document if any adjustments were made for deleting inventory or changing entries once they were recorded. Document results of discrepancy.

7. Document any variances between the general ledger and inventory systems. Document if either system excludes quantities due to different status (e.g., consignment) or other locations (e.g., distributed par locations, patient rooms).

8. Observe the picking and packing process. Are there manual forms for tracking picking during the count process (so as not to affect book values)? Are there appropriate levels of documentation? How does the distribution manifest get into the ERP or inventory system? What happens to a product in the ERP or inventory system if a product is picked but not shipped or distributed? Do exception reports appear?

9. Inquire into the usage and status of systems. Are the ERP or inventory systems working properly? Do they appropriately decrement and increment inventory as materials are issued and received? Is there utilization of bar-coding or other automated systems for tracking movements? Is there a data flow diagram available for the systems that shows information flows?

10. Observe the process of receiving inventory into the ERP or inventory system. Are purchase orders properly loaded? Compare system versus paperwork from manufacturer or distributor against system. Are receipts properly processed against the purchase order? Are they processed against the proper line number on the purchase order? Document the process for receiving goods. Select one receipt and observe processing into inventory.

11. Inquire into any expired products. Are they medical supplies or pharmaceuticals? If pharmaceuticals, were they controlled properly based on the control level of drug per the Drug Enforcement Agency? Were all adjustments out of inventory handled properly? Where do the items physically move to after inventory (e.g., donated to a distribution company that delivers them to countries in need)?

D. Reporting and Presentation

1. Summarize audit findings and discuss with local management on the last day of fieldwork. Develop and agree to proposed solutions with local management. Draft an audit report.

2. Submit draft audit report to inventory or materials managers for review and comments. Include these comments in the final report. Finalize and distribute the report.

INVENTORY MANAGEMENT EXPECTATIONS

Inventory ratios are metrics that gauge how well inventory is being utilized or managed over time. The expectation of materials managers is not only to continuously improve these metrics but to also focus on inventory utilization, order fulfillment efficiency, revenue generation, and operational efficiency.

Inventory Utilization

This performance indicator measures how efficient the group is in delivering and managing overall inventories for the organization. The metric is defined as both the total inventory values, as well as the DIO, which is a better metric for measuring inventory when patient volumes are growing. Tracking current DIO, setting a targeted level, and then managing toward that goal improves inventory utilization.

Order Fulfillment Efficiency

This measures the efficiency of a department's picking, packing, and handling process. It should be measured as both the overall cycle time for fulfilling orders as well as the number of items picked per hour, plus any number of other metrics available. Similarly, fill rates can be used.

Revenue Management

Inventory is responsible for maximizing revenue sources, such as for pharmaceutical items, medical supplies, or durable medical equipment. Capturing 100% of the potential revenues and minimizing the associated expenses is the goal. Tracking the return on inventory, as calculated earlier, ensures that inventory is successfully generating revenues for the organization.

Operational Effectiveness

This metric measures the extent to which a department is effectively performing a variety of activities necessary to continually improve, including:

- Setting optimal inventory levels, including the creation of forecasts and plans with key vendors and distributors.

- Monitoring product mix and key item usage, including the development of ABC inventory classifications.
- Ensuring 100% customer service levels.
- Ensuring inventory accuracy through cycle counts and systematic tracking of issues and receipts.
- Continually improving staff productivity and eliminating redundancies.

Focusing inventory management efforts around each of these four areas, and developing the right set of metrics and ratios for inclusion in a scorecard, will improve the overall management and utilization of hospital inventories.

CHAPTER SUMMARY

Inventory represents supplies that have been purchased but not yet consumed or utilized. Inventory in health care is very disaggregated throughout hundreds of rooms, clinics, and storage areas. Managing and accounting for inventories represent a very complex subject that is common in the manufacturing or retail industries but not very well understood in health care, given its focus on managing COGS.

Several important accounting entries must be understood by the operations manager, because these entries form the basis for the financial statements. The uses of financial ratios are very important in providing internal controls over inventory because they allow analysts to understand typical inventory utilization behavior and look for exceptions and deviations. Other techniques and ratios use analytical strategies to minimize costs and continuously review asset utilization. Inventory audits are focused on reducing risks of loss and maintaining adequate controls over these expensive resources. Incorporating audit concepts into daily inventory management improves operational effectiveness immensely.

KEY TERMS

ABC classification	Cost of goods sold (COGS)
Audit	Counterbalancing error
Capitalize	Customer service level
Case mix index	Cycle counts
Chargeable	Cycle inventory
Consignment in	Economic order quantity (EOQ)
Consignment out	First in, first out (FIFO)

Generally accepted accounting
   principles (GAAP)
Inventory
Last in, first out (LIFO)
Lower of cost or market (LCM)
Net realizable value
Obsolete
Periodic inventory
Perpetual inventory

Postponement
Safety stock
Shrinkage
Stock-outs
Timing
Valuation
Vendor-managed inventory
Weighted average

DISCUSSION QUESTIONS

1. What is inventory?
2. What distinguishes inventory from a supply?
3. What are five benefits to having inventory in a health care supply chain?
4. What are two reasons not to hold inventory?
5. Why do generally accepted accounting principles help ensure accurate financial accounting of inventory?
6. Should consigned inventory be counted on the balance sheet for a hospital?
7. Does inventory normally have a debit or a credit balance?
8. Compare the basic differences among the last in, first out; first in, first out; and weighted average valuation methods.
9. Why is perpetual inventory so important?
10. What does days of supply measure?
11. Describe vendor-managed inventory.
12. Define shrinkage and possible sources of loss.
13. Describe the ABC classification system and its utility in managing inventories.
14. Why is it important to understand the elements of an inventory audit?

EXERCISE PROBLEMS

1. A community hospital in Pennsylvania has a 15% supply expense ratio. If total operating expenses are $1 million this month, what is the total annual cost of supplies?

2. A hospital buys certain supplies for $50 each. The average markup is 100%. Additional selling costs are 25% of the total cost. What is the net realizable value?

3. Assume this same product has a current replacement cost of $40. What is the lower of cost or market?

4. An organization discovers in a physical inventory count that the actual inventory on hand is $50,000 less than the value on the books. Write the accounting entry to record this shrinkage transaction.

5. Miami Trinity Health Care has an average inventory balance of $2 million. The total annual supply expense is $10 million. Using a 360-day year, calculate the days of supply.

6. A product has total usage of 1,000 over the course of the year. Each item costs $20. The transactional order cost from procurement is $50 each transaction, and the annual carrying cost is 10% of the total annual cost. Calculate the economic order quantity.

REFERENCES

Bragg, S. M. (2006). *Inventory accounting: A comprehensive guide*. New York, NY: Wiley.

Healthcare Financial Management Association. (2013). *Value project benchmarking report*. Washington, DC: Author.

Muller, M. (2002). *Essentials of inventory management*. New York, NY: AMACOM.

CHAPTER 14

Forecasting and Supply Chain Management Systems

GOALS OF THIS CHAPTER

1. Define items.
2. Describe data classification and the United Nations Standard Products and Services Code.
3. Understand the role of hospital resource systems.
4. Understand the role of forecasting for new-item purchases.

A supply chain manages three key flows—information (data), finances (cash), and products (items). This chapter focuses on two of these: information and items. Specifically, the role of managing data quality and item structure is detailed because this is necessary to drive efficient procurement, replenishment, and inventory of goods. This chapter provides a definition of the term *item*, explains the rationale behind data classification schemes, describes the role that enterprise resource planning and information systems play in managing item masters, and introduces a process for understanding data patterns that can help improve product forecasting and replenishment.

ITEMS AND ATTRIBUTES

Several chapters in this text have focused on the management of products, or goods, through a hospital's supply chain. These goods are also called *items*. For some, an item is inherently understood and needs no definition. For many others, an item is complex and needs further clarification.

An **item** is any physical good that is procured for ultimate use or consumption, whether in its current form or following some degree of processing or transformation. An item has physical characteristics—that is, it can be touched, weighed, moved, and stored—and it has quantitative characteristics—these include dimensions, such as size, weight, density, firmness, color, and the like. Contrary to services, such as health care service delivery that involves delivery of procedures or other qualitative characteristics, items are physical goods.

An item that is in its final form for consumption or utilization is called a **finished good**. A finished good will not be further processed, mixed, blended, processed, or otherwise transformed. Most of the goods purchased in hospital supply chains are finished goods. A finished item can be a syringe, a chair, or a loaf of bread.

Items that need further processing or transformation are called *raw materials* or **intermediate goods**. Intravenous injection, or IV bags, which might require additional processing with other injectable solutions, are intermediate goods. Hospital pharmacies that compound or mix their own drugs also manage intermediate goods. In pharmacies, the process of combining multiple fluids is called **admixture**, while the breakdown of tablets or solid substances is called **compounding**. These types of items are somewhat more complex, because they require an understanding of bills of materials, or multiple items that comprise each finished goods item. A **bill of material** is a listing or recipe that defines the specific raw materials or components and the quantities required to create a finished good. For example, if 5% dextrose and 1% iodine are the two key components a pharmacy uses to blend with an IV bag, then these two items are the raw materials on the bill of material.

Thus, items have quantitative and sometimes qualitative characteristics. These characteristics uniquely define each item and make it somewhat distinct. Walking down the bread aisle in the grocery store, you will see many loaves of bread, which can be described by their taste or weight attributes. For example, bread might be wheat, thinly sliced, honey flavored, one pound, oval shaped, artisan, or split top.

Each of these defining characteristics of an item can therefore be called its *attributes*. **Attributes** are nothing more than the quantitative and qualitative characteristics that help to explain and define an item. These attributes are useful for three primary reasons:

1. They describe an item and allow categorization and classification to occur. Without classification, it would be impossible to purchase and manage thousands of items for a hospital's supply chain.

2. They facilitate electronic transaction processing among manufacturers, distributors, and hospitals, using common language, which expedites purchasing and logistical processes and streamlines commerce. Coding of each item, in a standardized system, can allow buyers and sellers to exchange data faster and more efficiently, which ultimately results in lower inventories and quicker response.

3. They allow sophisticated operations managers to analyze patterns and trends that otherwise would not be evident. By "slicing and dicing" data using attributes, and not just looking at discriminate analysis at the lowest levels, it is possible to find exceptions and patterns to improve overall results.

All of these are described in more detail later in this chapter.

DATA HIERARCHIES

A **hierarchy** is a classification system that organizes data around common attributes. These attributes as they are aggregated are called *categories* in supply chain and marketing terminology. A hierarchy helps analyze data from a different level and allows groupings to make sense of data more readily. For example, a hospital might use 20 × 20 bandages and then replace them with 1.50 × 20 bandages. The first bandage might be made and purchased from three vendors, and the second from two vendors. Therefore, at the lowest level for these items, there would be five distinct stock-keeping units. A **stock-keeping unit (SKU)** is a specific item at a specific unit of measure. SKUs represent the lowest level in an item hierarchy, as shown in **Figure 14–1**. Notice in this figure that one type of medical supply is a glove. A glove **category** can be decomposed by multiple attributes: latex versus nitrile, powder versus powder free, a variety of different colors and scents, sterile and nonsterile, all sizes, and a variety of manufacturers. Exploding, or decomposing, each of these individual hierarchies shows different levels of details and attributes.

In terms of an item or product hierarchy, products are classified according to a standard set of attributes, uses, and characteristics. An aggregation of items that share similar attributes creates different categories, and these categories roll up to others. Aggregating items up to higher levels allows decisions to be made that might not be evident if items were managed only at the lowest level of detail.

A non-healthcare example might make this clearer. When consumers walk into a grocery store wanting to purchase toothpaste, they walk into that aisle and see multiple brands, flavors, and sizes—each offering slightly different benefits. A specific tube of toothpaste is an individual SKU, but this can be aggregated up

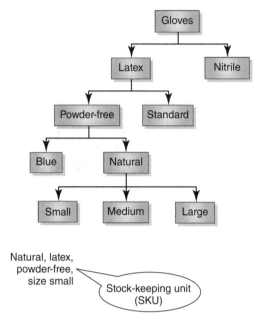

FIGURE 14-1 Item Hierarchy

by brands: Crest, Colgate, Aquafresh, and so on. Each of these brands can then be aggregated based on other categories. If the grocery store wanted to determine which item was making the most profit so that it could market that item a little differently (e.g., to position on an end-cap display or to adjust pricing), it would be impossible given that an average large-scale store has more than 200 different toothpaste SKUs. But, if the store could slice that data differently among all 200 SKUs, it might find that a certain size, brand, or flavor dominated sales. What if the new strawberry mint toothpaste had 45% of sales in the last month, spread among 40 individual items? The store never would have noticed the trend if it had not captured the attributes in the hierarchy.

In hospitals, the most commonly purchased items are in the general category called *medical supplies and equipment*. This category can further be described in multiple ways, depending on the hospital. The next lower level could be organized by specialty, such as surgical or cardiology, or by major type of use.

THE NEED FOR STANDARDS

Most hospitals create their own categories, which are usually limited and not very robust. It has been said that the average hospital has only about 25% of its items properly classified in a hierarchical categorical system. And, because health care distributors and manufacturers have not combined to create standards, each hospital has historically done its own thing.

Several companies and organizations have attempted to create a comprehensive standard for classifying items in health care. Unlike the retail and consumer goods industries, however, which are closely integrated and aligned, the health care supply chain is fragmented and segmented. In consumer goods, all manufacturers, distributors, and retailers use common coding and classification systems, and they share information routinely and often to help facilitate faster transactions and lower total costs. Organizations such as the Uniform Code Council and the Voluntary Interindustry Commerce Standards Association help promote commerce across the globe and across many industries. Health care, however, has been slow to adopt such standards and has not rapidly joined forces with overwhelming participation.

The health care industry lags behind other industries for the following reasons:

- *Late adopters.* Historically, hospitals and health care are always late adopters of new tools and technology when they relate to business operations instead of medical technology.
- *Fragmentation.* The health care supply chain is fragmented by groups that focus on nursing, medical, pharmacy, imaging, and other specialties. Vendors tend to follow their specialty groups and not act as one with other vendors. Similarly, medical supply distributors are fragmented and highly competitive and have not historically collaborated well to create industry-wide improvements. Neither have manufacturers, except for those that also serve retail chains with consumer-based medical supplies. Finally, hospitals are fragmented.
- *Lack of resources.* Hospitals especially are plagued by low operating margins, which typically encourages operations management to allocate resources to pressing issues affecting them today, not those that can help improve their processes tomorrow.
- *Education.* In other industries, management is keenly aware of the gains that can be made from improving commerce flow among vendors. In hospitals, however, there is a lack of education about these types of issues; hospital management tends to be more concerned with patient and clinical issues and is simply not aware of the role standards can play in improving overall competitive advantage, reducing costs, and increasing productivity.

During the last decade, however, the health care industry has slowly started to work toward adoption of standards. Many health care organizations, such as the Healthcare Information and Management Systems Society and the American

Hospital Association, are pushing for legislation, regulation, or other standards that unite the industry more comprehensively. This participation will not come easy, given the reasons listed earlier.

Three organizations are positioning themselves to help create standards in the industry: the Health Industry Business Communications Council, the Coalition for Healthcare eStandards, and the United Nations Development Programme. The Health Industry Business Communications Council focuses on standards for communicating electronically using electronic data interchange and advocates for standards for unique hospital identification numbers, as well as standards for bar coding and universal product numbers. The Coalition for Healthcare eStandards has also been pushing for standards around customer and product identification. For purposes of standards around items, the United Nations Development Programme has been the lead organization for product classification and coding.

UNITED NATIONS STANDARD PRODUCTS AND SERVICES CODE

The **United Nations Standard Products and Services Code (UNSPSC)** is a coding system that can be used across all industries, for all types of goods and services. It is a classification system that has evolved over many years, and it was originally developed by the United Nations Development Programme and Dun & Bradstreet Corporation in 1998 (UNSPSC, 2014).

UNSPSC classifies item-level data into a hierarchy that is organized as follows:

Segment >> Family >> Class >> Commodity >> Business function

A segment is the highest-level category, and the business function is the lowest. The code can be up to 10 digits long, with 2 digits representing each of the five levels of the hierarchy, although the standard code is usually 8 digits long.

For example, look back to the gloves example in Figure 14–1. Gloves overall fit into the highest segment called *medical equipment, accessories, and supplies* in the UNSPSC schema. This is segment 42. Within segment 42, there are 20 different families, such as veterinary supplies, surgical products, nutrition, and many more. Gloves fit into family 13, *medical apparel and textiles*. In this family, there are three classes—surgical textiles, housekeeping textiles, and medical gloves, which is class 22. At this point, the class can be broken down into another five commodities, including glove boxes, finger cots, and surgical gloves. Assuming that the gloves in the figure are medical, general-purpose gloves, they are categorized as commodity 03. The complete eight-digit code for these gloves would therefore be 42-13-22-03.

How can this code be useful? This code helps hospitals improve their overall operating efficiency. If the supply chain can standardize this coding, then, as hospitals purchase items from distributors, they can use this as a common code. Each party in the chain has its own fragmented system, so a distributor might code this same product 123, a manufacturer might code the product ABC, and a hospital might code it XYZ. For hospitals to streamline their procedures, they need to use automated purchasing processes, sharing the right item numbers collaboratively among all parties. This code can then be shared with distributors during the ordering process automatically; with no manual intervention, then, the order can be filled and shipped.

Today, each party maintains a cross-reference table that links a hospital's item number against its own item master, or the party requires the hospital to disregard its own item numbers and use the vendor's. Either way, it takes multiple cross references, duplicate entries, manual effort, and careful oversight of each item procured. This is a complex and lengthy process, which guarantees a high level of returns and lower productivity.

ITEM MASTERS IN THE ENTERPRISE RESOURCE PLANNING SYSTEM

Aligning the supply chain with a common product identification system will improve operational efficiencies, if adopted by the industry as a whole. In preparation, hospitals must ensure that the enterprise resource planning system, or other procurement and replenishment systems in use, have robust and complete item master data. An **item master** stores item-level data. These data include important attribute fields necessary for both transactional processing and analytical reporting. **Table 14–1** shows the optimal attributes for an item master in a hospital.

There are likely significantly more attributes that a hospital might want to manage if it used advanced analyses and planning, but those shown in Table 14–1 are some of the most relevant ones for successful item master management. These attributes must be maintained in database fields, which can be sorted and searched independently of the item. Many hospitals use one large comment field to capture free-form text and possibly significant attributes. This is a big mistake, however, because text fields are not searchable and therefore are of little value in terms of analysis, reporting, and managing items.

Table 14–1   Item Master Attributes

Attribute	Purpose
Item number	Order fulfillment
United Nations Standard Products and Services Code	Electronic commerce
Segment	Spend analysis
Family	Spend analysis
Class	Spend analysis
Commodity	Spend analysis
Color	Spend analysis
Size	Spend analysis
Weight	Spend analysis
Unit of measure	Spend analysis
Manufacturer	Contract negotiation
Contract/group purchasing organization number	Contract negotiation
Cost	Spend analysis and contract negotiation
Chargeable flag	Revenue generation
Chargeable price	Revenue generation
ABC classification	Inventory management
Life-cycle stage	Forecasting

Thus, attributes are important because they allow users to separately sort them, report on different types of aggregation, and analyze patterns and trends. The term **slice and dice** is used to describe the process of breaking data down into component parts, using different angles or perspectives. If a hospital is negotiating a contract for sterile gloves, and all of the information it has is at the lowest level, it loses significant bargaining power. If it walks into negotiations understanding all of the buying behavior, such as type, color, and size, as well as trends and forecasts for the future, its analysis will likely yield significant cost savings.

The concepts of rollup and drilldown are also important. A **rollup** is an aggregation in the hierarchy. Rolling up all gloves into higher-level families and segments provides useful reporting and analyses. Similarly, **drilldown** allows users to continuously drive data deeper by moving lower within the hierarchy, thus helping further refine, understand, and analyze data at more descriptive levels using narrowly defined attributes. Drilldowns are useful when the analyses need to move from general to more specific.

ENTERPRISE RESOURCE PLANNING SYSTEMS

In addition to storing item-level data, enterprise resource planning systems are essential to integrate the activities of an organization, including financial, human resources, quality, procurement, and inventory management. In most industries, the **enterprise resource planning (ERP) system** is the primary "system of record" to track products or services provided, costs, customers, and cash associated with the entire operation. In health care, the ERP plays an important, but somewhat reduced, role.

ERP systems originated in the manufacturing sector and evolved from the need to understand all aspects of goods manufactured—from the time they were procured until the time they were sold. ERPs were designed to integrate, or consolidate, all data and processes to eliminate redundant technology and business processes, decrease double keying of information into multiple information systems, and ensure a comprehensive view of the entire operation. Questions about the business—such as "What is the true cost of goods sold for a specific product?" or "What is the real profit margin for a certain product line?"—could be addressed more accurately with one primary system.

Without integration of systems into a single ERP, manufacturing industries found that they did not have complete information and were often unable to make intelligent decisions (O'Brien, 1996). ERPs then became the repository for managing human resources and payrolls (because they play a critical cost and quality role in manufacturing goods); quality management (tracking returns, defects); production planning (which plant produces specific products at targeted production levels); procurement, inventory, general ledger, and financial reporting; customer relationship management (tracking all details about customers, such as their locations, pricing, and usage patterns); and many other important activities. An ERP is very prevalent now in most industries. The primary roles of an ERP system are outlined in **Figure 14–2**.

In hospitals, ERPs play a somewhat reduced role. In Figure 14–2, those functions highlighted are hospital specific, while the others represent the range of functionality offered in other industries. The reduced functionality is primarily

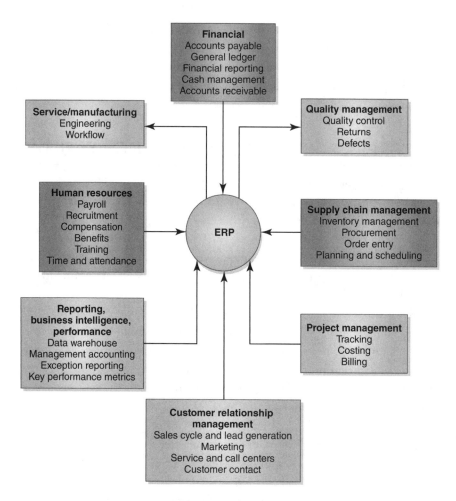

FIGURE 14–2 The Scope of ERP Systems

because hospitals are service intensive and do not have a manufacturing or finished goods conversion process. Management of service lines (e.g., radiology) often requires its own discrete specialized systems, like picture archiving and communication systems, which are not part of a typical ERP.

The role of a hospital ERP tends to focus primarily on the financial, human resources, and supply chain components. If best practices are used—such as streamlining processes prior to the system implementation, eliminating paper-based reports, and validating organizational roles and responsibilities for the new processes—then ERPs can make a significant contribution to a hospital's financial performance.

The largest ERP systems are offered by vendors such as SAP (www.sap.com) and Oracle (www.oracle.com), which provide solutions across multiple industries. For health care systems and hospitals, one of the larger ERP players is Infor (www.infor.com). There has been significant consolidation recently in enterprise systems, and many of the other large players, such as PeopleSoft, JD Edwards, and Baan, have all been acquired by one of these larger, more dominant vendors.

Advantages of an ERP

One of the primary advantages of an ERP is that it helps integrate all data and processes across the enterprise. For hospitals, if a stand-alone system is used for procurement and a separate system for inventory, then significant duplicate entry would be required to manage item masters, pricing, and product utilization. Similarly, if accounts payable does not leverage the same system as purchasing, then it would require extensive manual effort to confirm receipts of items purchased prior to payment. A single system helps integrate the business process, which helps improve overall internal business controls.

Another key advantage is that it helps eliminate redundant or duplicate systems. If each department or process used its own systems, there would literally be dozens or hundreds of small systems in existence. Each system requires specialized knowledge, training, and support, which is very expensive from an information technology investment perspective. ERP also helps eliminate paper; it provides formal electronic records for all aspects of a business process, thus eliminating the need for printing and filing each transaction (such as an order or invoice).

Most important, ERPs help provide full revenue cycle integration for patients—from point of invoice to point of cash receipt. If used properly in health care, it helps eliminate valuable cycle time and allows posting of charges on patients' bills at the time of administration, rather than batching hours or even days later.

THE ITEM LIFE CYCLE

As hospitals begin to use items, hierarchies, and item masters to improve the management of their data, it is important to understand the usage, or demand patterns, for each item. In health care, innovation continuously brings new technologies, equipment, and supplies to market that help physicians and providers improve the quality of care. These new items replace older ones and have their own sets of attributes and economics. Behavioral and structural change in usage and demand determines the stage of the life cycle that the product occupies. For example, while a certain type of catheter might be on its way out, a new one is being introduced to replace it.

Therefore, all items move through a standard life cycle (Onkvisit & Shaw, 1989). This life cycle comprises six phases: prelaunch conceptual design, new-product introduction, growth, maturity, decline, and phase-out. A product that currently resides in a specific stage of the cycle has an entirely different demand pattern than a product in another stage (as discussed in the next section), and this demand pattern requires different ordering patterns and replenishment practices. The duration and magnitude of the pattern determine the overall shape of the demand pattern. **Figure 14-3** presents a standard, bell-shaped, product life-cycle curve highlighting each of these phases.

Although Figure 14-3 represents the life cycle as a bell-shaped curve, where a smooth predictable usage pattern exists in each phase, the actual shape of the curve is based on the specific item type, the competitive intensity of the manu-facturers for that item, and the level of investment the industry is conducting for research and development. For instance, cardiology and oncology products are classic examples of industries in which items are continuously improving and evolving, while some other items, such as the syringe, have very few changes over time. As new items evolve, others must be phased out. Each of the phases is described in the rest of this section.

Prelaunch Conceptual Design

Prior to any item ever generating usage or sales, it must be designed and launched. The prelaunch phase of the life cycle has no demand, but it is characterized by

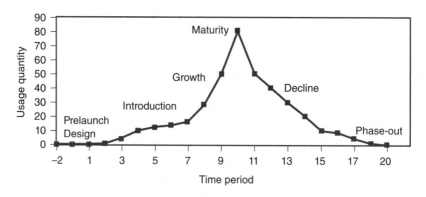

FIGURE 14-3 Phases in an Item's Life Cycle

heavy investment in market and consumer research, prepositioning of brands, test market deployment, product research and development, and extensive advertising. It is critical to focus on making planning decisions about retail outlets and channel positioning at this phase. Brand and product managers use their preliminary qualitative and quantitative figures to estimate potential demand for the product and to make a "go–no go" decision on whether to move forward with the product. Estimates of market share, prices, competitive maneuvers, and expected sales are all outcomes of this phase in the process. An estimate of the duration and magnitude of the life cycle is required. In addition, time and speed are of the essence in this phase, because plans are continually revisited and adapted on an hourly basis.

New-Product Introduction

During the new-product introduction phase of the life cycle, demand can exhibit multiple patterns. In some cases, sales for well-known brand or product extensions can soar instantly, such as in high-tech industries or certain food lines. Other times, the pattern is less defined, and the slope of the demand curve is gradual. At this point, demand is very uncertain, making planning more difficult. Margins can be high, depending on the specific industry—such as pharmaceuticals, which tends to start with premium pricing that declines over time. Management of demand should be based on either association of similar patterns experienced for other new products introduced historically or on market research estimates. Demand association involves taking a product that is being phased out and associating its demand with the new product to be introduced. For example, if a 25-gram hypodermic needle is being replaced with a 27-gram needle, the historical usage must be associated with the new item to ensure that future ordering plans, contracts, and inventory plans do not use zero history and usage as the baseline. Manufacturers' tendency to use promotions during this phase can distort the true demand picture, making planning even more complex as it moves to the next phase; from their perspective, however, it is essential to ensuring "mindshare" early to gain some successes. Decisions about inventory placement and location must be made during this phase. For innovative products, there is little competition, allowing for strong margins during the introduction phase.

Growth

As products reach this phase, demand becomes more stable and predictable. Supply chain and operational managers can use trends and statistics to accurately define the pattern and can use these figures to improve ordering patterns, as well as levels of inventories. Marketing promotions, such as manufacturers' rebates and pricing discounts, are still important but play a lesser role in generating new business; it is more critical to capture others' market share. Competition has escalated rapidly, forcing smaller margins at this stage.

Maturity

Usage and demand during the maturity phase are quite stable. Competition also tends to be intense because the industry's structural characteristics are well known, and most competitors have entered the market by this time. As a consequence, profit margins remain fairly low. During this phase, it is imperative to introduce new products to begin balancing the portfolio and planning for the impending decline. Supply chains must focus on cost minimization and maintaining high customer service levels because it is extremely important not to lose any customers at this stage.

Decline

If an item is experiencing declining usage (e.g., down from 100 per month of a specific item to less than 10 per month), the item has entered the next phase of the product life cycle. If a hospital continues to order based on minimum thresholds that are not updated continuously, significant amounts of inventory will be built that will never be consumed, which is very costly and inefficient. However, predicting demand during the decline phase is often extremely difficult. The slope, intensity, and timing of the decline make it hard to understand the demand pattern. The best way to analyze the item's decline is to explore the company's historical product declines and associate a similar timing and intensity evidenced in other products and categories. During the decline phase, prices tend to be at historical lows, and no promotions are utilized, thus simplifying the planning process somewhat.

Phase-Out

At this stage, the product has been phased out. All demand that existed has either been transferred to a complementary or replacement item or has been moved to another product. It is important that the transition to the replacement or extension item was handled smoothly to associate or chain this product demand to the replacement.

In summary, each phase of the life cycle results in changes to the demand pattern and likewise requires a different type of technique to analyze and manage supply and demand. Where the early stages rely on judgmental demand tools, such as market research, consumer profiling, test marketing, and demand association (or product chaining), the later stages rely heavily on trend analysis and statistical forecasting. The use of collaboration internally and externally within the supply chain is essential during all phases of the life cycle to achieve improved plans and forecasts (Campbell, 2000).

Example

Consider this example. A hospital purchases 500 central venous catheter trays per week of Model A. These trays cost approximately $25 each; the weekly cost, therefore, is $12,500. The usage patterns dictated an automated replenishment program: A once-weekly order is placed with the distributor for 500 trays, to be delivered on Monday mornings. At some point, Model B has been introduced by a manufacturer's sales representative, and a few physicians are starting to explore its efficacy. Model B was introduced to the hospital's material use evaluation committee and accepted. Materials management began to purchase a few of the new-model trays, based on initial requests of 10 each week, at a cost of $40 each, or $400 total. During week 3, all physicians began using Model B.

Model A just moved from maturity to phase-out; it skipped the decline phase entirely, which is quite probable. Meanwhile, materials management continues to use its heuristic rule of once-a-week ordering patterns and realizes—more than 3 weeks later—that more than 1,700 items have amassed in inventory, at a cost of $42,500. At the same time, after repeated service-level issues and physician complaints, materials management decided that it needed 2 weeks of safety stock inventory on hand for Model A to offset the problems it was encountering with Model B, so $40,000 of safety inventory was also being housed in central stores. The clinics, seeing their physicians continuously being without the proper supplies, have also horded Model A in various examination rooms and closets. In effect, then, a total of $75,000 of inventory has been stockpiled!

The distributor sees that the new product is taking off and simultaneously builds up inventories of Model B but, because it studies usage trends more proactively, has already realized a decline of Model A and holds only 50% of the normal cycle inventory.

What happens in this case?

1. The hospital has increased its inventories by 600%.
2. The distributor has also incurred additional stock and will have to find alternative ways to sell its products, or it will ultimately charge back the hospital through higher pricing later.

3. While volumes have now increased, because orders are being placed for both items, the real productivity of procurement and materials employees has declined significantly because they are all busy working on items that do not serve a purpose.

The mission of "right goods, right time, right location, right price, and right condition" has obviously been neglected.

An item master that is robust and supports tracking of items by attributes and phases of the life cycle—where analysts continuously scrutinize the data looking for exceptions and outliers—could have prevented this from occurring.

PRODUCT USAGE PATTERNS

The stage that an item occupies in the product life cycle greatly affects the slope and shape of the usage and demand curve in the long run. However, in the short term, as planners focus on narrower time horizons, a variety of patterns can be seen. In general, there are nine types of usage, or utilization, patterns that products can exhibit:

1. Increasing trend
2. Decreasing trend
3. Seasonal demand
4. Random patterns
5. Intermittent or lumpy
6. Cyclical
7. Transient or irregular
8. Horizontal, even, or constant
9. Auto-correlated patterns

Because the goal of effective item management is to ensure optimal purchasing, replenishment, and inventory of the right products in the right quantities, understanding the key usage patterns is essential to predicting the right levels.

For example, if an item is showing signs of increasing trends, but the procurement department orders as if it were continuous usage, shortages or stock-outs will occur. Similarly, if an item is declining, a purchasing strategy that adds 10% each week to historical usage patterns is not a good business practice. **Figure 14–4** shows some of the more common item usage patterns.

The first two patterns are fairly straightforward: A product is exhibiting either **increasing demand** or **decreasing demand**. Increases or decreases can be detected if the **slope**, which is the tilt or angle of the rise or fall over the run, or the absolute

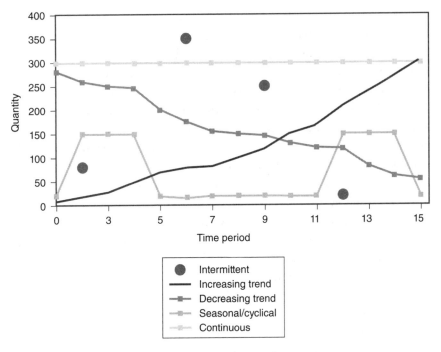

FIGURE 14–4 Common Item Utilization Patterns

value, increases continuously over time. This change in usage is captured in most sophisticated ERP packages, or it can be extracted and calculated through spreadsheets. Mathematically, it can be calculated using the following basic formula:

$$y = a + bx$$

where

y = total usage
a = intercept or the point of the initial value
b = slope of the line
x = the time period

Consider this example. If an item has only two points of usage of 10 items in Period 1 and 15 items used in Period 2, the calculation of the slope represents a 50% increasing trend, calculated as follows:

$$y = a + bx$$
$$y = 10 + 5(1)$$
$$b = 50\% \text{ increase or slope}$$

This same formula can be used with additional data points to confirm trends, both increasing and decreasing, but it becomes significantly simpler to rely on advanced planning technologies or even spreadsheets.

Depending on the time frame analyzed, the increasing trend might indicate a product in the introductory or growth phase, while the decreasing trend might indicate the decline phase. A third pattern indicates strong **seasonal demand**— spikes in the Christmas months for toys, the sale of chocolate at Easter time, or even seasonal patterns when events are repetitive and periodic in nature (holidays, timing of specific promotions, and climate or weather). Another item usage pattern might be completely random, where no observed pattern can be found. This is especially evident when no systematic or constant patterns exist.

Another type of demand is called *lumpy* or **intermittent demand**. This is characterized by demand that is not dispersed evenly over time but tends to occur only at specific periods in batches or lumps. This might be caused by order batching (i.e., when customers tend to order in large lot sizes infrequently), by forward buying (i.e., when customers buy product earlier than is required for consumption purposes due to special pricing or to take advantage of financial reporting irregularities), or for some other reason entirely. As described earlier, **cyclical demand** can be seen when naturally occurring cycles tend to result in a predictable ebb and flow in the demand. Irregular or transient demand is one of the least predictable of all because it has no apparent pattern except that it emerges for a specific period or two and then disappears.

The most predictable and regular of all demand patterns is the horizontal, or **continuous demand**, which refers to evenly dispersed usage throughout all time periods. Another demand pattern that exists (although it is not pictured in the graph) is the **auto-correlated demand** pattern, where the value of demand in one period is related to the demand for itself in previous periods. This type of demand pattern tends to be visible in areas in which trends and seasons are highly influential. Demand is a function influenced by many factors, such as trends, seasons, levels, causal factors, events, and other factors. The combination of any of these factors with the product's stage in the life cycle gives a very clear picture of the overall long-term behavior and pattern of the product.

CHAPTER SUMMARY

An item is any physical good that is procured for ultimate use or consumption. Items move through a chain—from manufacturers to vendors and on to customers. Understanding how items are being utilized (or "moving") is essential to being able to purchase an efficient quantity of items at the right time and avoid having either too much or too little inventory on hand. The UNSPSC is a highly structured categorization system that could be adopted by health care organizations to help understand the huge volumes of item data. Understanding the data requires knowledge of the phase of the product life cycle that the item currently occupies. Sophisticated purchasing managers can use both volume and pricing data to conduct a sourcing spend analysis to identify where value opportunities exist. The use of ERP systems helps support robust item masters, but ERPs also play a much larger role in supply chain and business management for health care. Forecasting item usage by quantitative techniques allows materials executives to become more efficient in the purchasing and replenishment processes. Tracking forecast accuracy and error rates is essential to understanding how forecasts compare with reality so that future adjustments can be made in both methodology and process.

KEY TERMS

Admixture	Hierarchy
Attributes	Increasing demand
Auto-correlated demand	Intermediate goods
Bill of material	Intermittent demand
Category	Item
Compounding	Item master
Continuous demand	Rollup
Cyclical demand	Seasonal demand
Decreasing demand	Slice and dice
Drilldown	Slope
Enterprise resource planning (ERP) system	Stock-keeping unit (SKU)
	United Nations Standard Products
Finished good	and Services Code (UNSPSC)

DISCUSSION QUESTIONS

1. How can attributes be used to improve the management of items?
2. What are the six steps of a product life cycle?
3. What is an item master, and which key attributes should it hold?
4. What is an enterprise resource planning system? What are three advantages to this system?

5. What are the reasons for the lack of standards in the medical supplies industry?

6. What role is the United Nations Development Programme playing in the creation of standards?

EXERCISE PROBLEMS

1. Assume the following time series data:

January	100
February	200
March	300
April	400

   Is there a trend you can observe in the data? What is it called?

2. If a product has utilization of 50 in Period 0 and a slope of 10 each subsequent period, what is the expected forecasted value in Period 2?

REFERENCES

Campbell, M. (2000). A spirit of collaboration takes over. *RetailTech Magazine*, pp. 23–24.

O'Brien, J. A. (1996). *Management information systems* (3rd ed.). Chicago, IL: Times Mirror.

Onkvisit, S., & Shaw, J. J. (1989). *Product life cycles and product management*. Westport, CT: Praeger.

United Nations Standard Product and Services Code. (2014). *Frequently asked questions: What is the UNSPSC?* Retrieved from www.unspsc.org/faqs

CHAPTER 15

Operations Management in the Hospital Pharmacy

GOALS OF THIS CHAPTER

1. Define a pharmacy.
2. Describe the role a pharmacy plays in both clinical and operations management.
3. Understand the national drug codes.
4. Describe key trends affecting pharmacy administration.

There are many departments and functions throughout the hospital that are primarily defined as operations management. Besides materials management, departments such as pharmacy, operating room, laundry and linen, food services, admissions, asset management, housekeeping, and many more are all business support services that rely on operations management to convert resources efficiently into outputs. Because of the significance of the pharmacy in terms of both resources consumed and revenue generated, a separate discussion of operational management for the pharmacy department will be provided in this chapter.

THE MODERN PHARMACY

The pharmacy is often one of the largest and most profitable departments in a hospital. A **pharmacy** is a facility that exists to fill and dispense drugs and medications that are prescribed by physicians or other caregivers. Pharmacists and pharmacies are active participants in the health delivery process (along with physicians and nurses) and are often structurally organized within the clinical care or clinical support services divisions (Griffith, 1992). They play a partnership role with physicians and other providers in evaluating the overall efficacy, safety, and quality of medications on patient outcomes.

The purpose of this chapter is to describe the modern pharmacy from an operational perspective, so any discussion of the clinical role in patient healing and health has been purposely omitted here. There are several characteristics about pharmacies that make them primarily operational and logistical in structure. In many respects, pharmacy management is similar to operating a retail establishment. For example, pharmacies actively "sell" goods, whose cost can represent 50% to 90% of the total expenses of the department. There are typically two components of expense, similar to retail: labor (for filling, dispensing, and compounding orders and drugs) and cost of goods sold. Lastly, pharmacies also provide service to customers or patients and are responsible for ordering, replenishing, storing, and providing controls over drugs.

A **drug** is a substance or article that is "intended for use in the diagnosis, cure, mitigation, treatment, or prevention of disease in man or other animals" and "intended to affect the structure or any function of the body of man or other animals" (Food and Drug Administration [FDA], 2004). Drugs are formally recognized through the FDA, as well as the National Formulary and the U.S. Pharmacopoeia.

Pharmacies can be quite complex in their operations. They are required to be staffed and managed primarily by pharmacists because state and national boards require all dispensing of drugs and medications to be performed by registered pharmacists licensed in that state. There are many laws and regulations, such as those set in place by the U.S. Drug Enforcement Agency, the FDA, the National Association of State Boards of Pharmacy, and several others. Pharmacies must maintain strict management controls over certain drugs, such as those classified as narcotics or other controlled substances.

Controlled drugs (also known as **scheduled drugs**) are those that are tightly monitored around usage and distribution because of potential for misuse and abuse. The Drug Enforcement Agency, through the Controlled Substances Act (Title 21, Chapter 13, Drug Abuse Prevention and Control) has outlined specific guidelines for safe registration, handling, and documentation requirements for drugs that have high potentials for abuse. These drugs are placed in a schedule, which is organized C-I through C-V. C-I (or Schedule I) represents those drugs with the highest risks and potential for abuse, such as heroin or marijuana, with very little medical value. The others are organized by descending risk levels (C-II through C-V) and are all drugs that typical hospital pharmacies might dispense. Accordingly, there is a need for stricter controls around all business processes for

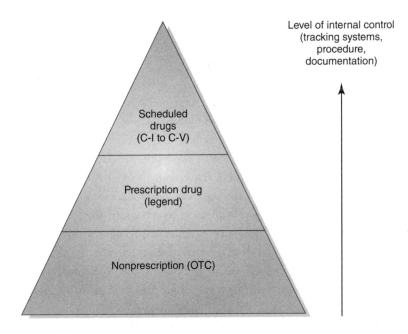

FIGURE 15-1 Pharmaceutical Goods Control Hierarchy

pharmacy inventory management than in other areas in the hospital—for both inbound and outbound flows of product. **Figure 15-1** depicts the hierarchy of items, from those that require a degree of control similar to other medical/surgical supplies to those that require very strict management processes.

Information systems, business policies and procedures, and the level of documentation and internal controls must be directly related to the item type managed in a pharmacy. For example, although a pneumatic tubing system might be used to quickly send certain products to a floor, it cannot be used for any scheduled drugs because the chain of custody cannot be directly established and the drug could end up being administered to the wrong patient. **Chain of custody** refers to the handling audit trail, which details who handled specific items and when and where the transfers of physical products occurred. This is necessary to maintain integrity in the process and to ensure comprehensive management of the life cycle of an item, from initial acquisition to final disposition.

THE PHARMACEUTICAL SUPPLY CHAIN

In smaller hospitals, a pharmacy might be defined as one finite, centralized geographic facility. In these environments, the pharmacy has higher intrinsic control because direct oversight takes place in one location, where drugs are both received and dispensed. In more complex and larger hospitals, however, a pharmacy department might have dozens or even hundreds of distributed locations. In the most complex pharmacies, there are both inpatient and retail pharmacies. Within each of these categories, there could be multiple locations and technologies and literally hundreds of employees.

Most of the largest pharmacy manufacturers do not deal directly with hospital or retail pharmacies, primarily because of the highly fragmented and competitive nature of the manufacturing industry. Hundreds of pharmaceutical suppliers might have to contract with thousands of hospitals, so an intermediary or middleman role has developed to help procure, transport, store, and replenish in a much simpler manner. Firms such as Amerisource Bergen, McKesson, and Cardinal Health distribute products from thousands of suppliers to thousands of providers, simplifying the network significantly. These large **distributors** have also taken on other roles to help provide value and extend their competitive influence in the chain, such as delivering systems and technology to providers, offering outsourced labor and services, and even manufacturing generic supplies.

The pharmaceutical supply chain tends to move through several phases, beginning with a concept for a biologic or chemical reaction that has potential; to eventual manufacture and commercialization; to full-scale production, distribution, and sale through either a retail or hospital pharmacy. **Figure 15–2** shows the health care value chain, describing both the new-product development chain and the operational supply chain.

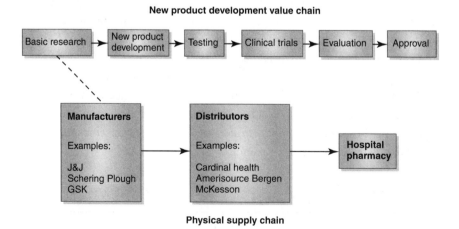

FIGURE 15–2 Pharmaceutical Value Chain

The pharmaceutical manufacturer or biotechnology firm is responsible for new-product development. This process is expensive, time consuming, and requires extensive testing and trials over multiple years and phases. It has high risks, multiple failures that require restarting or changes to medications, and high levels of regulation from the FDA and others. As such, the highest level of risk and investment is performed early in the supply chain, significantly prior to the commercialization and full-scale production and distribution.

As this happens, there is a constant struggle for power and financial value in the pharmaceutical network. Hospitals typically lose this struggle. Manufacturers are dominated by some very large firms, including Johnson & Johnson, Pfizer, Merck, GlaxoSmithKline, and Eli Lilly, although there are hundreds of smaller pharmaceutical and biotechnology firms located throughout the world.

The major pharmaceutical manufacturers in 2005 earned an average profit of about 15%. The largest pharmaceutical distributors averaged less than 2%, while leading retail pharmacy chains (such as Walgreen's and CVS) averaged around 3%. Meanwhile, hospitals averaged only about a 4% profit margin (see **Figure 15–3**).

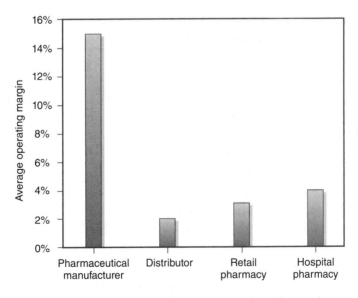

FIGURE 15–3 Manufacturers Winning the Value Battle

Data from Hoovers (A D&B Company), 2006; Author's analyses.

MANAGING ITEMS USING THE NATIONAL DRUG CODE

Pharmacies represent multiple operations management challenges, including inventory, personnel management, technology and automation, management controls, location analysis and selection, procurement, and network distribution. The most difficult is that of managing the movement of these drugs, which accounts for the largest percentage of expenses for hospital pharmacies.

The primary purpose of a pharmacy is to dispense medications; thus, pharmacies ultimately are "physical" supply chains, managing the physical flow of goods both inbound and outbound. The management of drugs acquired for replenishment to each physical location requires careful control over stock-keeping units and item categories, much the same way as materials management departments manage general-purpose medical supplies. Pharmacies are somewhat different, in that most items are stamped or coded with a proprietary pharmacy-industry coding system called a *national drug code*. The **National Drug Code (NDC)** is an industry identifier created in 1969 by the FDA to provide a comprehensive listing of all approved drugs. The NDC is a 10-digit identification number assigned by the FDA to all commercialized products, which helps uniquely identify the manufacturer or labeler of the product, the specific product, and the packaging type.

The first segment of the NDC (the labeler) is either a four- or a five-digit number that identifies the firm that manufactured, packaged, or labeled the product. For example, the GlaxoSmithKline labeler identifier is 00173, and Merck has been assigned 61258.

The second segment of the 10-digit code is the product identifier. This can either be a three- or a four-digit number, which uniquely identifies the specific product. For example, Vytorin product in tablet form is 0311.

The third segment of the code is the packaging type. This is either a one- or a two-digit code that defines the base unit of measure and specific packaging size (i.e., vial, bottle, cartridge). **Figure 15–4** shows the NDC coding structure for Merck's Vytorin medication in a bottle with 30 tablets.

There are some exceptions and issues to the NDC coding system. In any of these NDC numbers, 0s can cause problems because they can be scanned by barcoding technology or information systems as either null values (i.e., no entries or blanks) or actual zeros. In some cases, asterisks (*) are used to identify digits. In addition, many government agencies use an 11-digit NDC identifier, which creates comparison problems for the same unique drugs. All labelers, products,

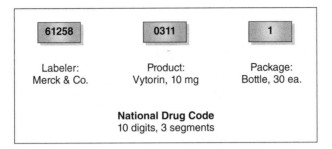

FIGURE 15–4 Pharmacy National Drug Codes
Data from FDA Database, www.fda.gov.

and packaging types can be queried on the Internet at the FDA website at this address: www.accessdata.fda.gov/scripts/cder/ndc/default.cfm.

With the NDC number, a bar code can be applied, which allows tracking of items into the hospital and then through the dispensing and administration process. A bar code has also been called a *license plate*, but it is basically a label that is placed on a product to provide visual representation through a set of identifiers that contain useful information about the product. When you walk into a grocery store, the common label used in retail is the universal product number code. In health care, although there are many standards, the most common are the National Health Related Items Code (NHRIC), the Universal Product Code (UPC), and several more.

Using NDC and bar-code technology, it then becomes possible to monitor the physical movements of drugs, ensure proper internal controls around the inventory, and confirm proper charging of the medications to patients using bedside scanning at the time of administration of the drug by the provider.

PROCESS WORKFLOW AND AUTOMATION IN THE PHARMACY

The process of providing drugs and medications to patients requires a licensed health care provider to write a script, or prescription. A **prescription** is a doctor's written order for medication or other course of treatment. This script then has to be filled, which is the primary role of pharmacies. In large, modern hospitals, this script might be entered directly into a computerized physician order entry (CPOE) system. This allows the physician to enter the treatment and medication information for patients directly into an information system, which captures that information, routes it to the appropriate person in the workflow process (i.e., pharmacies for filling orders, nursing for delivering other services), applies any number of business rules to further promote patient safety, and ensures that the right patient receives the right medications. While this process can be very manual and labor-intensive, technology is being deployed quite extensively in pharmacies to automate much of the process. In less sophisticated hospitals, these prescriptions are given to nursing, and that department then either faxes or manually transports these forms to the nearest pharmacy site, which might be located in a nearby nursing supply room or pod or on a centralized floor somewhere else. Typically, these orders are scanned into an imaging system and routed to a pharmacy technician for entry into the pharmacy order entry system. There are a large number of information systems that exist to enter and fill pharmacy orders, such as those offered by Siemens, General Electric Healthcare, McKesson, and many others.

Once entered into a system, the items have to be picked, packed, and distributed back to the point of care. Items are picked manually off shelves by automated pickers, often with **robots** and **carousels**. This equipment uses technology and large mechanized systems to help select single- and small-dose packages, label them, and store them in the right location. Robots and carousels work together with other ordering and dispensing systems to automate the storage and retrieval of goods. Automation helps reduce manual labor, decrease error rates, minimize patient waiting times, and generally increase the number of orders filled with the same staffing level—all key goals of operations management. Several specialized pharmacy technologists, including ScriptPro, McKesson, and Swisslog (three of the largest competitors in this arena), offer this technology.

Forward positioning of inventory is often used in pharmacies. **Forward positioning** refers to the placement of medications near the point of use, prior to their actual usage, based on forecasted needs. For example, if three doses of a specific drug are needed today at 5:00 p.m., instead of the pharmacy waiting for the order to appear; entering it; and then picking, packing, and dispensing the order, the drug could be staged in a forward position nearer the unit or floor on which it will be used.

The use of automated dispensing solutions, from vendors such as Pyxis, Omnicell, and McKesson, allow forward positioning. These medication-dispensing systems are very similar in concept to vending machines, which require a form of consideration (e.g., cash) that, when supplied, renders appropriate products (e.g., soft drinks). In pharmacies, however, the consideration is a secure identification (through badge, employee identification entry, or biometric means) that appropriately identifies the person as an authorized user who should be granted access to the appropriate medications and drugs. **Biometric methods** are newer security systems that use physiological characteristic, such as fingerprints or retinal scans, to uniquely identify an individual. Dispensing systems use these various types of security measures to ensure that the right provider enters the right product information to be dispensed to the right patient, thus providing controls and safety for the patient.

Medication-dispensing systems allow for much tighter controls over inventory, especially where required for scheduled or controlled drugs. If a nurse scans his or her badge, enters the patient medical record number, and selects a product, and if all three entries meet established controls and security, then a drawer or cabinet is opened that grants access. Simultaneously, inventory controls are checked as nurses are prompted for a count of remaining items in the bin.

Finally, once dispensed, the drugs are taken to a patient's room for administration. The administration phase should be the trigger for charging patients, because this is the point of true consumption. The provider should record the administration in the medical record (whether paper or electronic), and this information becomes the formal written record of consumption.

KEY OPERATIONS MANAGEMENT TRENDS FOR PHARMACIES

Some of the key trends in pharmacy management toward achieving operational excellence include the following: perpetual inventory, strategic pricing analysis, systems integration, and location and network optimization.

Perpetual Inventory

Many large hospital pharmacies are now pursuing perpetual inventory. As the dollar value of most large pharmacy inventories continues to climb into the multimillion-dollar range, there is a much stronger need for higher levels of internal controls over these resources, as well as the ability to monitor for theft, shrinkage, and other forms of loss. **Perpetual inventory** denotes the expansion of the use of information systems to ensure real-time, continuous tracking of inventory through the purchasing, receiving, distribution, dispensing, and medication administration workflow. **Perpetual** refers to the ability to know, at all points in time, actual balances through continuous tracking of receipts and issues.

Strategic Pricing Analysis

Strategic pricing analysis refers to the application of differential pricing mark-ups to each drug based on its potential for reimbursement, usage, the item's history and life cycle, payer mix, and other factors. Strategic pricing suggests that some drugs will have higher margins than others, but the net result will be larger net revenues for the pharmacy as a whole. As pharmacies closely monitor the usage of medications, and the associated reimbursement levels from payers, continuous analysis of price points must be conducted.

System Integration

Most pharmacies have dozens of systems: robots that pick, cabinets that dispense, procurement systems that order, carousels that store, pricing systems, retail charging systems, and many more. Integrating all of these pharmacy systems, from the point of order through administration, including synchronization of other major systems, from computerized physician order entry systems to electronic medical records to patient billing, is required to ensure that all information flows quickly and accurately between systems. Such **system integration** also ensures higher levels of internal controls because there are reduced opportunities for manual error or abuse.

Location and Network Optimization

One of the biggest elements of large-hospital pharmacy strategy centers around the dichotomy of distributed versus central (often called *bulk*) pharmacies. Larger hospitals tend to have multiple pharmacy locations distributed throughout hospital floors, units, and clinics, in addition to dispensing cabinets positioned in dozens of locations. In other hospitals, a centralized pharmacy is used to buy and store items, and a greater number of pharmacy technicians are employed to provide frequent distribution and replenishment of orders as they come in from providers on each floor. The strategy with optimal economic results typically is one or the other; however, most hospitals utilize a mixed strategy, which seems like it offers many positives but in reality guarantees higher inventories and more personnel providing distribution services, both of which create excessive cost infrastructures.

Careful analysis of strategy and locations ensures efficient operations. These analyses should be based on profitability of existing transportation, stocking, and other process costs—in order to ensure that the right network of pharmacies exists. In general, more locations translate into higher numbers of items held and greater investment in inventory. Similarly, more locations suggest higher service levels. Finding the right trade-off, or optimization point, is essential. To illustrate this point, consider the square root law of consolidation. The **square root law of inventory** suggests that the total costs will increase dramatically as the number of stocking points increases. This can be written as the following equation:

$$I_t = I_i \sqrt{n}$$

where

I_t = amount of inventory at one location
I_i = amount of inventory at each of n locations
n = number of stocking points

Consider the following example. A pharmacy has three physical locations on different floors. Each location has $200,000 worth of inventory, so the total inventory is currently $600,000. If this hospital were to consolidate from three locations down to one central location, the result would be a 30% reduction in inventory, calculated as follows: The square root of 3 is 1.732051, multiplied by the average inventory in each location ($200,000) is $346,410. If all three locations were collapsed into one, then a savings of nearly $154,000 in inventory investment would be realized. This is equivalent to a 30% reduction in inventory levels:

$$\sqrt{3} \times \$200,000 = \$346,410$$
$$\$500,000 - \$346,000 = \$154,000$$
$$\$154,000 \div \$500,000 = 30\%$$

As this illustrates, even ignoring the costs of staffing and replenishing, there is a large benefit to be gained from closely monitoring the number and location of pharmacy sites.

EFFECT ON PHARMACY PERFORMANCE

Hospital administrators evaluate a pharmacy's performance in several ways: These can be clinical (effect on patient safety and effectiveness), organizational (collaboration with other health care providers), operational (ability to satisfy demand at high quality and service), and financial (ability to earn reasonable returns on drug expenditures). Strategic effectiveness ensures that pharmacies cover all four of these dimensions, which can be summarized as providing the medication most likely to safely address the patient's condition, with the knowledge of all involved caregivers, at the lowest cost per unit of effect. If compounding or mixing is occurring, the outcomes of these medications must be monitored to ensure that the pharmacy augments the clinical care process.

In addition, most pharmacies have financial expectations and are considered profit centers. **Profit centers** are organizational units that generate revenues, and they are required to earn reasonable returns on those revenues, after considering all costs of operation. Achievement of expected pharmacy operating margins is another strategic performance indicator.

From an operations management perspective, however, there are many more key performance indicators that are critical:

- *Cycle time*, from order request through order fulfillment. Cycle time represents the service level given to both providers and patients and is expected to continuously decrease.
- *Cost per dose or order filled.* This figure should be tracked continuously to ensure that the operational labor costs decrease over time.
- *Percent of inaccurate orders or doses.* This metric, which is defined as the number of errors (wrong dose, wrong location) over the total number of orders filled, represents a quality metric for pharmacies. A similar metric, percent of items returned, measures how many items are being sent back to the central or bulk pharmacy locations for any reason.
- *Total days of inventory on hand.* Calculated as the average inventory balance divided by the average daily pharmacy operating expense, this metric describes how efficient the pharmacy is, the level of safety inventory being held, and how quickly items are being turned. Average figures for hospital pharmacies are 10 to 12 turns per year, or 30 days of inventory on hand.

Together, these metrics help continuously improve the operations of a pharmacy.

SPOTLIGHT ON McKESSON

One of the biggest health care technology and distribution firms is McKesson. McKesson operates as the largest pharmaceutical distributor, but the scope and vision of the company portfolio encompasses more than just drug distribution. As a Fortune 15 firm with more than $80 billion in revenues, McKesson operates three business units focused on several complex health care problems, including the largest health care technology business in the United States.

In an interview, I had an opportunity to discuss McKesson's strategy and the health care industry with one of its top executives—Marc Owen. Owen is president of McKesson Specialty Health, and he is responsible for oncology services, vaccine distribution, manufacturer services, and many more multispecialty offerings. Owen has many years of strategy and technology experience, following an extensive consulting background with McKinsey Consulting.

McKesson's business strategy is to "attack $300 billion in operational administrative inefficiencies" in the health care system, coupled with interrelated safety and quality issues. These challenges are complex and unique to this industry, and McKesson is uniquely situated to help address these issues for all aspects of the health care value chain, from providers to payers. McKesson's strategy combines four critical success factors that differentiate the service offerings: deep clinical expertise, process knowledge, technology capabilities, and scale. In fact, more than 10% of McKesson's company is clinically trained, and the solutions reach more than 50% of U.S. hospitals today.

According to Owen, "Some hospitals have a stronger process mind-set than others, but most attack processes one at a time." He sees a "cause for hope" in that certain hospitals are achieving dramatic results in some areas, like an 80% to 90% drop in medical error rates or a double-digit improvement in revenue cycle metrics. McKesson's focus on pharmacy distribution, pharmacy automation, and health care decision support and technology allows the key challenges in all major areas of the health care business to be addressed.

Interestingly, Owen points out that one of the primary reasons health care lags behind other industries in technology is because of the focus on mobile computing. "Health care involves mobility of people and resources, which are not stationary as in other industries." He sees these technologies receiving a lot of interest and being adopted fairly quickly.

Finally, Owen offers some prudent advice to health care professionals: "Start slowly on process improvement, and continue to improve and build on it. It is not necessary to have revolutionary or breakthrough change all at once."

Interview with Marc Owen, 2006; *Fortune*, April, 2006.

CHAPTER SUMMARY

The pharmacy is essential to hospitals and health care. Modern hospital pharmacies play a key role in providing clinical care as well as improving operational efficiencies. Understanding the pharmacy's business challenges, from use of standardized NDC codes to automation of the prescription order process, is necessary for operations managers. Multiple key performance metrics can be established and monitored to ensure continuous improvement in this area. The role of technology, including the use of robots, carousels, and other automation, helps make the pharmacy much more operationally efficient than other parts of the hospital.

KEY TERMS

Biometric methods	Perpetual inventory
Carousels	Pharmacy
Chain of custody	Prescription
Controlled drugs	Profit centers
Distributors	Robots
Drug	Scheduled drugs
Forward positioning	Square root law of inventory
National Drug Code (NDC)	Strategic pricing analysis
Perpetual	System integration

DISCUSSION QUESTIONS

1. What role does a pharmacy play in operations management?
2. Should controlled drugs be given the same level of oversight as prescription drugs?
3. How are systems and technology streamlining pharmacy operations?

REFERENCES

Food and Drug Administration. (2004). Federal Food, Drug, and Cosmetic Act. Chapter II, Section 201. United States Code Title 21, Chapter 9.

Fortune. (2006). *McKesson: Fortune 500 2006*. Retrieved from http://archive.fortune.com/magazines/fortune/fortune500/snapshots/850.html

Griffith, J. R. (1992). *The well-managed community hospital* (2nd ed.). Ann Arbor, MI: Health Administration Press.

PART IV

Summary

Operations management in health care is complex. It also affects the clinical and business sides of the health care industry. Chapter 16 illustrates how integrative operations management is in the hospital setting and presents some examples of how benchmarking and operations analysis should be used in day-to-day management. Chapter 17 offers final thoughts on the trends and best practices for operations management; recommendations are summarized to provide a launching point for deploying improved health care operations management.

CHAPTER 16

Operations Analysis and Benchmarking

GOALS OF THIS CHAPTER

1. Describe the elements of operations analysis and review examples of such analyses.
2. Define benchmarking.
3. Review the use of mathematical tools for benchmarking performance.
4. Apply an example of benchmarking operational performance in a hospital department.

In this text, readers have been introduced to several different concepts to be employed in improving operational performance in a hospital, including use of operational metrics, clearing up bottlenecks, and managing labor hour efficiency. However, how do you analyze operational performance and determine how well you are doing in performance improvement? What is the measurement scale used to know if management interventions are truly working to improve performance, increase efficiency, and deliver better patient care? Typically, this measurement is achieved through comparison to some standard that is developed to be relevant for the organization and the operational problem capturing management's attention. A valuable way to make this measurement is known as benchmarking. **Benchmarking** is the comparison of key performance measures relative to the competition or other leading organizations, with the clear intention of applying these best practices internally. This chapter will explore operations analysis and benchmarking in greater detail and apply benchmarking to a common operations management challenge in a hospital.

OPERATIONS ANALYSIS

Ultimately, a hospital (or any other health care organization) has strategic objectives to achieve: profit, community health promotion, and serving the poor, for example. Operations management supports the organization's pursuit of those objectives. Thus, **operations analysis** represents a valuable tool to management in measuring progress toward strategic objectives and identifying ways to improve performance that meets those objectives. Operations management in many respects works to determine how to express strategic objectives in measurable terms, measure performance against those objectives, identify gaps between actual and expected performance, and understand what may be causing those differences and develop corrective actions as needed.

The first step in operations analysis is to establish operational metrics that are aligned with the organization's strategic objectives. Using metrics such as those outlined in the *Operational Metrics in Health Care Organization* chapter offers a way to begin defining what is measured. Because an organization needs to generate at least a nominal margin to sustain its operations, monitoring profitability using a profit margin calculation is an overall target. The value for that ratio must end up above zero to indicate that surpluses are being generated to fund the ongoing operation of the organization. Beyond that, the analysis can be much more nuanced, based on variations in the individual circumstances of the organization. As the analysis is set up, it is essential to recall this rule of thumb: monitor between 5 and 12 metrics. As long as the metrics align with the organization's objectives, then the analysis will help move the organization forward and improve desired performance.

When defining an operational analysis, it is also important to focus on those metrics that can be influenced by management action. Following along with the example of a strategic objective of profitability, perhaps an organization is constrained by limited payments due to reliance on government program payments. In a situation where the revenues are not controllable through actions such as a price increase (something perhaps more easily accomplished in a retail setting or an airline), then operating expense is probably something that is controllable by management. Keeping expenses within an externally imposed (and not controllable) constraint is a reasonable approach for analysis. This is a common situation for hospitals that serve a large proportion of Medicare, Medicaid, and indigent patients. Consequently, operations analysis in the hospital setting often focuses on producing the maximum number of outputs per unit of input to work within a revenue constraint. Wasted motions or wasted steps in production of hospital services might not be identified unless an operating metric determines a shortfall in performance and it is investigated. Thus, the analysis must start with an evaluation of performance metrics that are important to the achievement of organizational objectives.

The time frame for monitoring operational performance will vary based on the needs of the organization. Looking at data across a full year is a good start to get an idea of the organization's overall performance . A full 12 months of data allows the analysis to take into account possible seasonal variations in volume and availability of resources that may affect observed results over a shorter period of time. This big-picture approach can help to set a backdrop of what is "normal" for the organization across a full-year time period. This is not to say that looking at the same metric for a month or a quarter is not useful; it can be helpful as long as management takes possible seasonal variations into consideration when evaluating analysis conducted in a shorter time frame. In one sense, the 12-month view of operations can help to establish a sort of average that can be used to add some context to monthly or quarterly analysis where seasonal variation can have a material effect.

Often, hospital managers will conduct an operational analysis of selected operating metrics for a year to establish a baseline but use measurements for periods of a month, the fiscal year to date, and the same month a year ago for ongoing routine performance analysis reporting. Fiscal year-to-date values can provide an idea of how the organization is progressing toward a full-year target. Comparison with the same month in a prior year provides valuable context for seasonal variations in observed results because the same seasonal variation in a given month would be expected to repeat itself at the same time each year. A good example of this variation would be inpatient census for a hospital, where volumes are expected to be higher in the winter (especially in areas with large numbers of winter retiree visitors such as Florida or Arizona) and lower in the summer. An example of such a report format is included in **Table 16–1**.

Considering the example results shown in Table 16–1, the analysis might lead management to conclude that results in the current month were good on most areas evaluated. While occupancy percentage in the current month appears lower than the same month in the prior year, it is a small variance and the year-to-date comparison shows a slight increase over the prior year. In an environment where fixed prospective payments for inpatient services do not vary with patient days,

Table 16–1   Example Operational Analysis Report Format

Metric	Current Month	Current Month Prior Year	Fiscal Year to Date	Prior Fiscal Year to Date
Profit margin %	3.2%	2.9%	2.8%	2.7%
Occupancy %	82%	83%	71%	70%
Salary expense % of revenue	51.5%	52.9%	52.5%	53.0%
Full-time equivalent/ adjusted occupied bed	5.41	5.52	5.65	5.72
Operating expense/ adjusted occupied bed	$5,232.17	$5,115.92	$5,351.76	$5,298.56

and patient days affect occupancy percentage, a slight decrease in this metric may indeed be favorable. Profit margin percentage for the month was higher than the same month in the prior year and is also better than results for the fiscal year to date. Salary expense (as a percent of revenue) and the full-time equivalent (FTE) per adjusted occupied bed were also improved over this period. Only the operating expense per adjusted occupied bed metric shows what appears to be an unfavorable increase over the prior year for both the current month and fiscal year-to-date calculations. However, if the manager takes inflation into account, then perhaps these results are also favorable. The increase in the current month operating expense per adjusted occupied bed from the same month in the prior year was 2.27%, calculated as:

$$\left[\left(\frac{\$5,232.17}{\$5,115.92}\right) - 1\right] \times 100$$

The increase when comparing year-to-date periods is 1%, calculated in the same manner as the current month values as:

$$\left[\left(\frac{\$5,351.76}{\$5,298.56}\right) - 1\right] \times 100$$

If price inflation for inputs (such as hourly pay rates) used by this hospital over the past year amounted to 3%, then the observed results in Table 16–1 would also reflect favorably on management's efforts to improve operational performance over the past year. Despite a 3% increase in the average rate paid per hour of work, the hospital used fewer labor hours, which resulted in an overall increase in costs that was less than the overall inflation of prices. This conclusion would be borne out in the results shown in Table 16–1, where the FTE per adjusted occupied bed in fact decreased from year to year.

While a concern in managing operating expenses is important considering that revenue for hospitals and other health care organizations is not increasing at the same rate as inflation for operating expenses, cost per unit should not be the only focus of an operations analysis. In some situations where labor markets are competitive, it may not be possible for management to have a significant effect on the price per hour paid for employees. In that case, operations analysis must take into account both the cost per unit of output and the units of the input per unit of output. The example in Table 16–1 uses such a mixed approach including both unit and cost measurements. Mixing unit and cost metrics allows management to get a much better perspective of the overall operational performance for the organization because a singular focus on either cost or units of input could mask other things happening in the operational picture, as was illustrated in this example.

Just because a report such as that shown in Table 16–1 has been prepared and perhaps understood for macro-level results, such as seasonal variation or reductions in total FTE inputs, it should not be the only analysis of operations undertaken in a hospital. Instead, managers should use observations in such a report to guide efforts to dig deeper into operational data to understand the causes of these observed results. Analyses like Table 16–1 serve as a valuable guide to set priorities on where to place initial focus in a detailed operations analysis.

Using the example discussed so far, the first impression is that profitability is higher than in prior months, which appears to be a result of fairly normal utilization levels (based on the occupancy percentage metric) and better expense control (see the salary expense % of revenue and the operating expense/adjusted occupied bed metrics in Table 16–1). It would be easy to conclude that the improved profitability was based on well-controlled expenses, and that may be a key factor. However, the operations analysis must provide greater insight into observed results. Despite the higher profit, was there also a change in revenues that needs to be taken into account? The operations analysis should look at the factors driving revenues as well as understand if there was a change in patient characteristics (lower-paying insurers or lower-acuity patients, for example). Examination of patient characteristics using data from the electronic medical record or the patient accounting information systems would provide valuable insight into the revenues earned in those different time periods. Considering that patient volumes were higher year to date and expenses were lower, one might surmise that patient acuity was lower and that examination of medical record data would reveal any such changes. Another possible conclusion might be that profit was higher on flat utilization when comparing the current month with the same month last year. Review of patient accounting data would help understand if the increased profit was related to lower average length of stay for patients with a fixed diagnosis-related group payment. If the slightly lower occupancy percentage happened with the same number of patient discharges, then profitability would increase based on the same payment per discharge and lower costs related to fewer patient days.

Looking at the salary and FTE metrics, the observations are that salaries as a percent of revenue dropped for the current month and the year-to-date comparisons. The operations analysis here may also rely on the same data examined for understanding profitability. Depending on changes in patient acuity between the two periods, the lower FTE input levels could be a result of lower labor hour needs due to lower patient acuity. Other explanations could be found in analysis of payroll data. Perhaps the improvement in salary expense and FTE usage could be attributed to decreased use of high-cost, low-efficiency contract labor; a change in skill mix of staff to increase the number of lower-cost nursing staff (licensed vocational nurses or nurse aides); or a decrease in higher-cost managerial staffing (which makes less direct contributions to direct patient care). Comparing details from payroll records in the current month and the same month in the prior year, and then compiling that data for the fiscal year, will provide those needed insights.

Finally, the change in operating expense per adjusted occupied bed could be significantly influenced by the favorable change in labor costs just discussed. However, the analysis should not stop there. Examination of the hospital inventory and accounts payable records will help the analysis determine if there were also changes in the volume of supplies or drugs used. Perhaps there were favorable changes to the hospital supply chain that reduced supply costs between the periods. Linking data from inventory and accounts payable to clinical data from the electronic medical record could also reveal the extent to which patient acuity influenced changes in supply expenses and therefore any nonlabor expense changes in the operating expense per adjusted occupied bed metric.

A focus on operations at the department level would likely lead an analysis to track metrics such as operating expense per test or supply cost per procedure. When taking an operational analysis to the department level, it is important to consider the use of a measure of output that is relevant to the department, such as that referenced in Table 6–3 in the *Productivity and Performance Management* chapter. Output measures such as adjusted patient days or adjusted discharges will not be useful in understanding the operations of a hospital pharmacy or cardiopulmonary care department. The operations analysis must consider metrics that are controllable by department management. Decisions on the number of FTE worked or supplies used are made by the department manager and define how the department performed from an operational perspective. Therefore, the analysis at a department level must evaluate those metrics influenced by the decisions of a department manager. Also, in some situations—such as with analysis of an operating unit or department within the organization—fewer metrics may be useful in an operational analysis at that level.

The example discussed here based on data in Table 16–1 demonstrated an overall favorable change in the operating metrics used in a hypothetical operations analysis. However, this same approach could be useful in the opposite situation where changes between periods are not favorable. If profitability decreased with increased expenses, the same evaluation of patient acuity from the electronic medical record or patient revenues from the patient accounting systems would help understand if unfavorable changes in profitability came from changes in revenues. Similarly, an increase in FTE per unit of output or an increase in salary expense per unit of output could be understood through analysis of payroll data to determine if skill mix, pay rate changes, or use of contract labor influenced that change. Correlating data from payroll records with data from the electronic medical record can help to identify if changes in labor utilization were caused by changes in patient acuity. Finally, a review of inventory and purchasing data— again, correlated to patient acuity data—can reveal the causes of adverse changes in metrics such as the operating expense/adjusted occupied bed.

Explanation of variances between time periods can provide insight into operational performance based on evaluating what changed in the hospital's production function between periods. However, that approach identifies differences between two end points of a specific time period. It does not consider what may have happened month by month during that period. A trend analysis for operational metrics can produce a useful analysis of changes in operational performance over time. An example of a trend analysis of operational metrics is shown in **Table 16–2**. This table expands the current fiscal year data used in Table 16–1.

The trended analysis in Table 16–2 shows some seasonal variation in observed values of selected operating metrics in this hospital that started its fiscal year on July 1 of the current year. Through the first 6 months of the fiscal year, lower volumes and profitability were noted during the summer months, when utilization tends to be lower. This can happen due to a tendency for people to put off elective care to take summer vacations. The hospital shows lower utilization and

Table 16–2   Example Trended Operational Analysis Format

Metric	July	August	September	October	November	December	Year to Date
Profit margin %	2.5%	2.6%	3.1%	3.0%	3.0%	3.2%	2.9%
Occupancy %	80%	80%	94%	81%	81%	82%	83%
Salary expense % of revenue	53.9%	54.2%	51.0%	52.8%	54.0%	51.5%	52.9%
Full-time equivalent/adjusted occupied bed	5.65	5.57	5.42	5.52	5.54	5.41	5.52
Operating expense/ adjusted occupied bed	$5,124.22	$5,111.87	$5,002.84	$5,001.17	$5,223.27	$5,232.17	$5,115.92

profitability during these "down" times but sees an increase in volumes in September and October when vacations are over and utilization tends more toward a "normal" state. Patient volumes can also increase during this time due to seasonal increases in obstetrical volumes and increases in pediatric illnesses from return to school for many children. Details to confirm this hypothesis in an operations analysis would be obtained from data in the hospital's electronic medical record, where a summary of utilization classified by diagnosis-related group or unit of the hospital would reveal any characteristic changes in patient volumes from month to month. Managers who have a grasp on variations through the year can then take proactive measures to preserve profitability in low-volume periods by reducing variable staff, decreasing supply orders and using up inventory, or performing outreach to referral sources to perhaps bolster volumes during these seasonal decline periods.

With increases in volume come decreases in the salary expense as a percent of revenue and the FTE per adjusted occupied bed metrics. This seems reasonable as there are fixed elements of staffing in a hospital for administrators, the business office, and base levels of staffing in the obstetrical and emergency room areas where the number of FTE does not vary with patient volumes. With increased patient volumes, one should expect to see a decrease in these labor-related metrics as fixed staffing is spread over more units of output and more collected revenues. This sort of conclusion would be supported by review of payroll records for each month of the fiscal year to note any changes in FTE or pay levels among the various departments in a hospital. Again, with some insight into the trends up or down in volumes throughout the year, a manager may be able to take proactive steps to maintain operational performance through reducing inputs to better align with expected downturns in hospital utilization.

While use of productivity standards can help to mitigate adverse variances in labor when volumes decline, the fixed element of hospital staffing will keep labor-related operational metrics high at low volumes. An operations analysis will usually see some degree of inverse variation between volumes and labor metrics.

Operating expense per adjusted patient day can also have some element of fixed cost in that it can bring this metric lower as volumes increase. Expenses for maintenance contracts, prepaid insurance, information systems support, and utilities are all examples of items that will not vary much with increased patient volumes and so will tend to keep operating expense per unit of output higher at lower volume levels. However, as volumes increase in patient care areas, this metric could vary upward if patient acuity increases and higher cost supplies are needed to treat a patient's condition. During the winter, an increase in orthopedic injuries could occur when people slip and fall and break bones. Orthopedic prostheses (artificial joints, fracture plates, and bone screws) are relatively expensive supply items that are necessary to treat these injuries. An increase in such injuries in the winter can precipitate an increase in operating expense per adjusted patient day as these conditions are much more resource intensive than conditions such as gastrointestinal disorders or simple abdominal surgeries. That appears to be the case with the trended report in Table 16–2, where expense per adjusted patient day was higher in December than in prior months. The winter months also tend to bring with them an increase in respiratory illnesses that may require additional lab testing and antibiotic therapy. Depending on the age of the patient and the type of pathogen causing an illness, the costs of antibiotics can be significant on a per-patient basis, thereby increasing expense per adjusted patient day.

A review of data from the electronic medical record can provide valuable insight into the severity of patient illnesses treated during each month in the analysis period. An operations analysis using a trend across months of a year would take into account the types of conditions treated in each month, the relative severity of each, and then identify month-to-month changes in that measurement. Once the relative change month to month is understood, the analysis can then look at labor and supply data to correlate changes in these inputs with changes in the intensity of treatments provided to patients across the analysis period.

In general, an effective operations analysis follows this progression of steps:

1. Identify a few (5–12) operational metrics that align with strategic objectives for the organization (and for which data can be readily obtained).

2. Determine the time frame for which the analysis should be undertaken. Using data for an entire year takes into account seasonal variations in the operation but may be limited in its utility to management unless compared to prior periods. Conversely, looking at a smaller time period (month or quarter) gives more real-time feedback to management on performance but may be skewed based on any normal seasonal fluctuations in the organization's business cycle. It may make sense for the analysis to use multiple periods such as a current month to the same month last year comparison, a year-to-year comparison, or even a month-to-month trend in order for the analysis to yield meaningful guidance to managers on where opportunities to improve performance may occur.

3. Once relevant metrics are calculated for the selected time periods, the analysis then focuses on understanding observed changes and should rely on clinical, patient, payroll, inventory, and general ledger accounting data to explain the underlying causes of the observed metric values.

4. Use the explanations derived from Step 3 to identify opportunities to improve performance on the metrics in the analysis.

5. Repeat the analysis on a routine basis to provide real-time feedback to managers on the effects of any changes made (such as implementation of staffing standards or changes in supply chain management).

A common question that arises when evaluating the information provided in an operations analysis is "What is a good value for that metric?" There are as many answers to this question as there are different metrics to calculate in an operations analysis. Perhaps the best way to determine what is "best" is to understand which result drives the organization toward its strategic objectives. If the organization serves the poor and uninsured (such as in a county "safety net" hospital) and strives to increase patient access to care, then a patient visit perday metric would be useful to measure performance in this area. Seemingly, the "goodness" of an observation for this metric would be determined by the simple adage of "bigger is better." In the absence of any problems with quality of care or ability to retain staff that is continually busy, that assessment may make sense. However, if the visit perday observation is not taken in the context of the hospital's actual capacity, then at some point more visits could be bad for the hospital and its patients. Continual operation of the hospital at levels above 80% capacity may result in long-term problems through staff turnover, lowered quality of care due to hurrying, excess wear and tear on equipment, and potential excessive waits for patients to obtain care. Understanding the context of an operating metric's value can help set the stage for determining if the observation is "good" or "bad."

The organization will usually prepare a budget each year and, in some sense, the budget should align with the organization's strategic goals (Gapenski, 2013). Deriving operational metric targets based on budget values can be useful in operations analysis. However, many organizations build budgets based on historical performance. If an organization has inherently inefficient production of health care services or has not identified areas where performance—though acceptable—could be improved, then using the budget as a source of guidelines for an operational analysis may promote continual lost opportunities to do better. As resources become more and more constrained for hospitals, the successful manager is one who not only maintains good operations performance but continually seeks out opportunities to improve it. Using only an internal view may leave opportunities unrealized for management. That is where developing other bases of comparison can become an invaluable tool in the operations management area. Benchmarking is the way that operations managers can gain these useful insights into improving operational performance.

BENCHMARKING

Health care makes extensive use of benchmarking for applications ranging from occupancy percentages to case management protocols to clinical pathways in patient care. The problem being considered by management often will determine just how a benchmark for comparison is developed. The Internet offers a variety of sources of data points reported to government agencies (such as the Medicare Cost Report, the IRS Form 990, or state agency annual reports) or industry trade associations (e.g., the American Hospital Association, the Healthcare Financial Management Association, and the Healthcare Information and Management Systems Society). Journals published by these organizations often provide articles on latest best practices used in the field and can be used to help brainstorm ways to improve performance in other organizations. Clinical journals or publications by organizations such as the Institute for Healthcare Improvement or The Joint Commission may offer ideas on improving clinical practices that can yield improvements for patient care outcomes. However, those sorts of clinical best practices and pathways are beyond the scope of this text and the remainder of this discussion will focus on benchmarking quantitative measures of operational performance in hospitals.

An Introduction to Benchmarking

Benchmarking in its simplest sense is comparing a measurement of operational performance to some objective standard (Gott, 2010). Others consider benchmarking to be the identification of best practices in the field and assimilating them into the organization to the extent possible (Tweet & Gavin-Marciano, 1997). This is a common practice in business where competing organizations attempt to learn from the positive results of other organizations and then refine their practices in order to do better than the competition. Benchmarking started with the Xerox Corporation in the 1980s as a means of finding best practices in the industry and using those practices to improve their products and production efficiency. Included in this process was the establishment of operational ratio targets (such as cost per unit) that reflected the results of industry best practices. It is this type of benchmarking that can be most effective in guiding operational performance improvement.

A benchmark is established based on objective data obtained from comparison with peer organizations (an **external benchmark**) or from historical performance data in the organization's internal records (an **internal benchmark**). External benchmark sources can be used to make comparisons on objective measures such as cost per unit of output with peer hospitals. Large databases that encompass all U.S. hospitals can be valuable in creating benchmarks for comparison with peer hospitals in the local market area as well as other hospitals across the nation. Cost data from hospitals in other states or cities should be used with great caution in benchmarking performance, as there are wide variations in the costs paid for the same inputs across the country. For example, a review of average hourly rates for hospitals in the 2012 Medicare Cost Report Database revealed a low of $9.68 and a high of $41.38 per hour. An effective benchmark using data sources from across the country may be better crafted using units of input rather than costs. However, local market conditions generally keep costs among hospitals in a finite geographic area in a narrow enough distribution to make cost comparisons within smaller units of analysis. The key point to remember when using external benchmarks is to be cognizant of market conditions and look for facilities with similar characteristics when gathering external data for benchmarking: ownership, bed size, case mix index, and similar mix of services. Failing to consider the differences between hospitals in different areas or with significantly different characteristics could lead to an analysis based on flawed and irrelevant benchmarks. Some examples of data sources for external benchmarks are shown in **Table 16–3**.

Internal benchmarks can be useful when some consideration is given to the point raised earlier where using internal data may mask relative inefficiencies as

Table 16–3 Examples of External Benchmark Sources

Source	Examples of Data Available	Potential Use
American Hospital Association, Annual Survey of Hospitals	Revenues, bed size, volumes by department, case mix index, full-time equivalent by discipline	Comparison of labor inputs per unit of output at department level
Healthcare Financial Management Association	Financial ratios for all U.S. hospitals	Comparison of financial metrics with peer hospitals
Centers for Medicare and Medicaid Services, Medicare Cost Report Database	Revenues, bed size, volumes by department, salary and nonsalary expenses by department, case mix index, full-time equivalent in total and by some disciplines	Comparison of labor and nonlabor inputs per unit of output at department level

"normal." Comparisons between similar departments in a hospital (such as medical/surgical nursing units, intensive care areas, or ambulatory clinics) may yield some useful benchmarks to share within the organization. Internal benchmarking may cause the hospital to lose opportunities to improve by studying other organizations and learning how their operational results may guide improvements. Also, the amount of comparative data usable for a hospital or hospital department may be very limited. Internal benchmarks may make sense within a large multihospital system where operational results could be benchmarked between peer facilities. However, from the perspective of a single hospital within a multihospital system, the benchmark would still be external. Thus, for quantitative measures of operational performance, use of external benchmarks is recommended.

When used with a good understanding of the operational entity being measured (entire hospital versus a hospital department) and of the data used, benchmarking can be a powerful tool to guide management in identifying the steps needed to improve operational performance. An important first step in benchmarking operational performance is to identify what to measure and ensure that what is being measured is actually relevant to the desired operational outcome. As with the operations analysis mentioned earlier in this chapter, the elements to be measured should relate to desired operational performance and achievement of organizational strategic objectives.

There is a wide array of data available for benchmarking operational performance in hospitals or hospital departments, as long as the limitations of comparisons among hospitals mentioned earlier are kept in mind. However, comparing between inherently similar hospitals or hospital departments can be difficult using the individual operational metrics described in this text. For example, is a hospital pharmacy with lower doses per FTE performing better than another hospital pharmacy that generates the same number of doses in a smaller amount of square footage (with less opportunity to hold inventory), or worse off than a hospital pharmacy generating higher margins with fewer doses? Comparing with peer organizations on relevant operational metrics can help identify areas to improve performance on a given metric. Knowing how one hospital pharmacy generates more doses per FTE (perhaps through use of technology or specific department physical layout and traffic flows) can help improve performance on that metric. A tougher challenge can be to assess the combination of multiple operating metrics in order to determine which peer organization represents the one "best" standard.

Other than simple comparison of the types of metrics or ratios described in the *Operational Metrics and Health Care Organization* chapter, techniques such as ordinary least squares (OLS), **linear regression**, total factor productivity (TFP), stochastic frontier analysis (SFA), or **data envelopment analysis (DEA)** can be used to consolidate the results of multiple ratios of input per unit of output into a single "best" performance benchmark (Ozcan, 2008). OLS is a technique familiar to managers who have taken a business statistics course and can be fairly easy to calculate. However, for benchmarking applications, OLS is limited in that it assumes a linear relationship between all input and output variables, accepts some degree of central tendency and normality of all variables, and cannot differentiate poor-performing entities from high-performing ones. TFP can be useful if all inputs are translated to a dollar value and related to a unit of output. This may be helpful as long as the dollar values used in comparisons between hospitals are not biased by market or hospital conditions (such as use of group purchasing organizations). This may not be a valid assumption if hospitals in a comparison vary significantly in their staffing or supply chain practices. SFA addresses some of the weaknesses of OLS and TFP but also places a high degree of reliance on cost data to calculate its benchmarks. Only DEA allows use of benchmarking using unit of input data and can be used even with a mix of unit and cost measurements for inputs and outputs. DEA is also able to normalize wider variations in data points used to create a benchmark, such as departments with high volumes of output in large physical spaces with varying labor inputs (Galterio, Helton, Langabeer, & DelliFraine, 2009; Langabeer & Helton, 2012; Ozcan,

2008). DEA is a recommended technique for hospital managers attempting to create a benchmark with data from organizations of varying scale.

DEA uses a linear programming technique to create multiple ratios of input to outputs and then calculate a unique "best" solution that identifies the optimally efficient mix of inputs and output levels and determines high- and low-performing entities in the benchmark data. The calculation of a DEA benchmark is beyond the normal capabilities of a microcomputer spreadsheet such as Microsoft Excel. There are software add-ins that, when combined with an Excel spreadsheet, can perform the calculation of a DEA benchmark. A commonly used spreadsheet add-in for DEA is DEA Frontier (www.deafrontier.net). In addition, many common statistical software packages such as SAS (www.sas.com) or Stata (www.stata.com) have the ability to complete DEA benchmark calculations. The following is an example of the use of DEA as a technique to develop a performance benchmark for a hospital department.

Assume that the management of Baptist Hospital is concerned about the operational performance of its pharmacy department and wants to benchmark its performance with the other three hospitals with which it competes against: Memorial Hospital, County General Hospital, and Doctors Hospital. Data to create a benchmark for the pharmacy at Memorial can be obtained from publicly available data in the Centers for Medicare and Medicaid Services Medicare Cost Report Database (www.cms.gov/Research-Statistics-Data-and-Systems/Files-for-Order/CostReports/index.html). In this example, Memorial will benchmark its pharmacy department operations using inputs of department FTE, department square footage, salary expense, and nonsalary expenses. Department outputs are the number of orders filled and departmental operating margin. Operating margin can be considered as an output, especially in view of the need for an organization to generate profits to sustain ongoing operations. The benchmarking data for this example are listed in **Table 16–4**.

Table 16–4 Data Envelopment Analysis Benchmarking Example

Hospital	Full-Time Equivalent	Square Feet	Salary Expense	Nonsalary Expense	Orders Filled	Department Operating Margin
Memorial	35.1	4,415	$2,296,540	$6,200,658	87,714	$12,467,190
Baptist	52.9	6,012	$3,929,803	$12,182,390	93,329	$10,590,703
County	57.2	7,954	$4,185,166	$13,392,532	117,160	$9,925,790
Doctors	14.7	3,625	$945,938	$2,743,220	64,733	$11,237,105

Table 16–5 Relative Efficiency Comparison from Data Envelopment Analysis

Hospital	Efficiency
Memorial	1.00000
Baptist	0.78137
County	0.75631
Doctors	1.00000

The DEA model shown here is based on an input-oriented model, where managers are able to control inputs used and have no control over the number of outputs demanded (as is usually the case in a hospital where pharmacy order volumes depend on patient severity and physician treatment decisions). The model also assumes a constant return to scale, where the department does not get more efficient as it gets larger. Because a hospital pharmacy generally handles all orders in the same fashion with the same resources (a pharmacist, technician, medication inventory, compounding and dispensing equipment), economies of scale in the short term are assumed flat. A DEA calculation yields multiple useful outputs beginning with an expression of relative efficiency among the facilities in the analysis. The relative efficiency comparison among the four hospitals in this example is shown in **Table 16–5**.

Based on this analysis, it appears that management at Baptist Hospital had some reason for concern as the pharmacy at that hospital is operating at 78.1% of the efficiency of its competitors at Memorial and Doctors Hospitals. In this example, the operations at Memorial and Doctors Hospitals are the benchmarks in this analysis as they are the most efficient, while County Hospital is the least efficient in the market, operating at 75.6% of the efficiency of benchmark facilities. This can lead the management at the poorer-performing hospitals to look to the efficient operations at Memorial and Doctors for ideas on how to improve efficiency. But in the absence of visiting those hospitals and observing operations, measuring traffic patterns, and reviewing accounting records (which may be very unlikely to occur in a competitive hospital market), how can the management at Baptist know what can be done to raise the relative efficiency of its pharmacy to be on par with the leading facilities in the market? DEA can also provide guidance in this respect by offering targeted input levels for managers to aim for at their current levels of output. An example of the calculated targets for Baptist and County Hospitals is shown in **Table 16–6**.

Table 16–6   Input Targets Calculated Using Data Envelopment Analysis

Hospital	Full-Time Equivalent	Square Feet	Salary Expense	Nonsalary Expense
Memorial	35.1	4,415	$2,296,540	$6,200,658
Baptist	37.3	4,697	$2,443,552	$6,597,592
County	43.3	6,015	$2,825,374	$7,689,675
Doctors	14.7	3,625	$945,938	$2,743,220

The DEA calculation points out to Baptist Hospital's management that the following changes are needed to bring the efficiency of its pharmacy up to that of its local benchmark:

- FTE must be reduced from 52.9 to 37.3.
- Department square footage must be reduced from 6,012 to 4,697.
- Salary expenses must be reduced from $3,929,803 to $2,443,552.
- Nonsalary expenses must be reduced from $12,182,390 to $6,597,592.
- All of these changes would occur at the same level of outputs (93,329 orders filled and $10,590,703 operating margin) for the Baptist Hospital pharmacy.

Meeting these targets would likely represent some significant changes for Baptist Hospital, but they can give managers there some areas to examine in greater detail in order to improve operational efficiency. For example, the staffing pattern at Baptist may not flex downward during seasonal reductions in volume and so the FTE inputs and salary expenses appear higher than necessary. A corrective action to implement a variable staffing plan to reduce labor hours during periods of low medication orders (such as holidays, nights, and weekends) could improve efficiency at Baptist. Of course, a reduction in FTE inputs would also result in lower salary expenses, which would improve operating margins.

The change in square footage for the pharmacy department could easily prompt management at Baptist to critically evaluate the physical layout of that part of the hospital. It may be that the department occupies a large footprint on the hospital campus and due to this size it necessitates long walks by staff that take up time that could be otherwise used to produce valuable outputs for the pharmacy. Perhaps the large department size also encourages larger inventory holdings than necessary, which could result in supply waste due to expiration of stock. The extra space in the department could also provide room for staff functions that do not add value to department outputs and that could be eliminated. It is certainly possible that the department staff could increase to fill vacant space in the department, and a critical look at the department size and layout could yield further improvements to efficiency in the Baptist Hospital pharmacy.

Finally, reductions in nonsalary expenses would likely arise from changes in the costs of medications dispensed in the pharmacy. Upon investigation, management could discover increased costs from expired medications (as noted earlier) or that it has not conducted an evaluation of its group purchasing organization agreements in several years and may be losing valuable discounts on medications. Either intervention could yield immediate cost savings to the hospital. Other potential areas of cost reduction could be found in evaluation of repair and maintenance costs for old or outdated medication preparation technologies (such as IV admixture hoods, pneumatic tubes to send medication orders to patient care areas, or refrigerators). A critical evaluation of the costs of maintaining old equipment could reduce nonsalary expenses at Baptist and potentially reduce supply costs and improve patient care at the same time. Given the extent of reduction needed in this example to meet the efficiency benchmark (45.8%), there may be a variety of different cost-saving opportunities in this hospital pharmacy—with supplies and repairs likely being among the greatest opportunities for improvement.

DEA does have its limitations, primarily in not being able to account for nuanced variations among organizations being evaluated, such as differences in technologies in use, skill levels of staff, or pay practices. It also cannot account for quality in outputs. However, this tool provides a reliable benchmark target that can guide managers to look for opportunities to improve or identify the magnitude of opportunities available. Rather than aiming for performance on a variety of different ratios, a DEA benchmark can provide a useful synthesis of multiple ratios that can support operations mangers in setting clear and objective performance targets that lead to achievement of an organization's strategic objectives.

CHAPTER SUMMARY

Operations analysis is a useful exercise for health care managers to direct the organization's activities toward the meeting of strategic objectives. The analysis requires some degree of decision-making acumen to understand which elements of the operation should be measured, which metrics should be used to measure operational performance, and which time frames should be used. The time frame for analysis must balance the need to account for seasonal variations in volumes against the value of timely feedback to managers on operational results. Comparison of observed results in an operations analysis helps to provide some context to the analysis in terms of defining performance as "better" or "worse." Those comparisons can be for the current period against the same period in the prior year, the current fiscal year to date against the same time frame in the prior year, or a trended analysis of several smaller time periods (usually months). Financial budgets may also provide some context to the operations analysis but must be used with caution to avoid treating low efficiencies memorialized in budgets as "normal." As a result, benchmarking performance against external sources is a recommended way of using operations analysis to identify areas of favorable performance and potential improvement. A variety of benchmarking sources and tools exists to assist managers in operations analysis.

KEY TERMS

Benchmarking

Data envelopment analysis (DEA)

External benchmark

Internal benchmark

Linear regression

Operations analysis

DISCUSSION QUESTIONS

1. Why should an operations analysis consider the organization's strategic objectives?
2. What are the important things to consider in selecting operational metrics to use in an operations analysis?
3. What are seasonal variations in hospital volume? Give an example, and explain how seasonal variations can affect an operations analysis.
4. Differentiate between internal and external benchmarks, and give an example of each.
5. Name some sources of external benchmarks, which data are available, and what their potential uses can be.
6. Describe the various quantitative tools used to develop benchmarks, including their relative merits and drawbacks.

REFERENCES

Copp, N. A. (2002). Benchmarking in ambulatory surgery. *AORN Journal, 76*(4), 643–647.

Galterio, L., Helton, J., Langabeer, J., & DelliFraine, J. (2009). Data envelopment analysis: Performance normalization and benchmarking in healthcare. *Journal of Healthcare Information Management, 23*(3), 38–43.

Gapenski, L. C. (2013). *Fundamentals of healthcare finance* (2nd ed.). Chicago, IL: Health Administration Press.

Gott, K. J. (2010). *A productivity practicum.* Brentwood, TN: Applied Health Sciences Consulting.

Langabeer, J., & Helton, J. (2012). Longitudinal changes in the operating efficiency of public safety net hospitals. *Journal of Healthcare Management, 57*(3), 214–225.

Ozcan, Y. (2008). *Health care benchmarking and performance evaluation: An assessment using data envelopment analysis (DEA).* New York, NY: Springer Science+Business Media.

Tweet, A., & Gavin-Marciano, K. (1997). *The guide to benchmarking in healthcare: Practical lessons from the field.* New York, NY: Productivity Press.

CHAPTER 17

Best Practices for Health Care Operations Management

GOALS OF THIS CHAPTER

1. Describe the best practices for health care organizations.
2. Explore recent trends and opportunities in health care operations management.
3. Align your own career and organization with the future strategic position of health care.

Hospitals and health care systems have been showing signs of improved profitability. This reverses a trend of declining and predominantly negative margins that have saddled the industry for much of the past decade. This will not continue for long, however. Economics dictate that the long-term profitability of all industries will continue to diminish until normal profits approximate zero and that pricing, competition, and industry structure will evolve to make this happen. Many signs of this are occurring already.

Government policy and payers are continuously searching for reimbursement mechanisms and models that shift the burden of health care off the government and toward consumers and businesses. The Affordable Care Act of 2010 introduced health insurance exchanges, medical care homes, individual mandates for insurance coverage, and greater focus on quality and prevention. Other policy issues, such as incentives, pay for performance (i.e., aligning reimbursement levels with outcomes), changing access mechanisms, and other macro political issues, continue to evolve, focused on long-term cost reductions but felt by health care organizations in terms of reduced profit margins. Spiraling costs will eventually force a wide-scale effort that will reduce revenues and create greater pressure on cost-effectiveness and efficiency. Operations management plays a key role in this transformation. Management must continue to evolve, innovate, and differentiate if it expects profits or returns that are greater than the normal, long-run expectations for the industry. This chapter discusses the future of operations management in health care and summarizes the trends discussed in this text.

BEST PRACTICES FOR SUCCESSFUL OPERATIONS MANAGERS

This text provided a foundation for readers to learn about the administrative, clinical, and supply infrastructure of hospitals and health care organizations. Operations managers will continue to become more integral to the future of the health care industry. It is necessary and vital for managers in health care organizations to fully understand how clinical processes are paid for, supplies and products are moved between units, billing and cost management are connected, and facility layouts can improve patient flow.

The types of operations and productivity analyses described in this book are perfectly aligned with the evolving direction of health care in the United States, which is being shaped by several trends. Many of these have been discussed elsewhere in this text, such as procurement or pharmacy. This chapter focuses on the macro-level changes that are affecting operations management as a whole. There are eight broad trends in operations management, as shown in **Figure 17–1**.

Remain Strategically Focused on Agility, Speed, and Transparency

One of the biggest challenges in large hospitals and systems is the inability to know where patients and expensive resources are at all times, which effectively reduces capacity and causes excessive amounts of resources to be deployed. Imagine, however, the following scenario. A new patient is finalizing registration in admissions; subsequently, an order is given to housekeeping to make the room ready; a request also is made to materials management to order the typical procedural supplies required for the patient's stay and to simultaneously update the census, electronic medical records, and other key systems. If this same hospital tracks the flow and movements of all wheelchairs, infusion pumps, medications, crash carts,

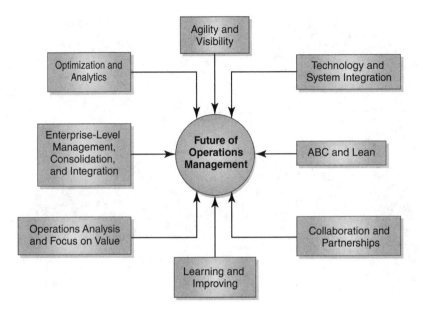

FIGURE 17–1 The Future of Health Care Operations Management

and other key resources as well, there would be higher utilization and throughput with reduced level of investments. All of the manual bed boards, tracking sheets, and paper processes could be discontinued, and in their place would be real-time visibility shared by all clinical and support services.

Health care business strategy is moving toward greater agility and speed in business processes in an effort to improve throughputs and service simultaneously. These strategic capabilities will drive decision-making processes and ultimately result in greater operational excellence.

In the long run, hospitals will evolve over time much the same way that other low-margin, operationally focused industries have, such as telecommunications, retail, and energy. The technology and processes in these industries have evolved to where a continuous, real-time monitoring environment is used to manage the key aspects of the business. In health care, the use of scorecards (or dashboards) is primarily retrospective, in that it looks back over the previous day or month for metrics and results. As health care improves its operational focus, a control center concept using tracking technologies supports:

- Radio frequency identification tags for use on key resources.
- Visibility of patients from admit to discharge—and all departments that are visited in between.
- Movement of expensive drugs and supplies to reduce the risk of theft or loss.

FIGURE 17–2 Visibility and Tracking in Health Care Control Centers
© Viappy/ShutterStock, Inc.

Health care is in the early phases of this evolution. Organizations are selectively putting tracking technologies such as patient bar coding and radio frequency identification on equipment and simultaneously implementing real-time clinical systems to improve processes such as discharge planning. These systems will prove useful, have a limited return on investment, but eventually dictate the need for further system integration (discussed later) to achieve greater benefits throughout the entire organization. This will eventually lead to the need for a new, integrated department that can monitor and control the flow and throughput of resources throughout the entire system. A control center concept—staffed by professionals focused on operational efficiencies and driven by new metrics of speed, agility, and acuity—will be implemented that can significantly decrease the organizational barriers and process inefficiencies. **Figure 17–2** shows a conceptual control center concept, where multiple systems and technologies are utilized to manage key resources.

Embrace and Integrate Technology into Operations

When harnessed, data is converted into useful information. But, what do we do with all of this data? Technology plays a vital role in integrating disparate processes and automating manual ones. As operations management begins to understand and influence the infrastructure to produce better costs and outcomes, technology will become even more pervasive. Much of this technology will be focused less on clinical needs than on business needs.

Technology deployment will continue to rise. Consumer-based technology that allows patients access to better information will prevail, but management technology—which supports evidence-based medicine, reporting, and better operations—is starting to reach a tipping point. These technologies are being pushed from clinic managers, physicians, and information technology executives. This will involve much more than just electronic medical records to include mobile apps, tele-medicine, analytics, and population health.

Most large hospitals have hundreds of enterprise and stand-alone systems, many of which are interdependent. Health care in the future will have much broader integration of these key systems and technology to allow for sharing and linking of data so that applications can operate as one large system. This is called **interoperability**, and extensive work is currently under way to define integration standards, middleware, and platforms on which this can occur. Interoperability ensures that all key systems—such as electronic medical records, a picture archiving and communication system, medication administration, enterprise resource planning, Charge Description Master, and many more—work together seamlessly. This interoperability will allow the first trend (strategy) to be fully realized. Interoperability is also encouraging connections between different hospital systems via health information exchange. A **health information exchange** is the electronic movement of patient records between hospital systems.

Integrate Service Delivery with Activity-Based Costing and Lean

Health care organizations are moving away from vertical, stand-alone, silo-based business units, where patients are treated differently at each department or clinic. More streamlined business processes will result in an integrated, or horizontal, service delivery. The current redundancy that exists—where each unit captures similar patient data, creates its own schedules, and manages separate systems—will be replaced by a more holistic and integrated service line approach.

This new approach will help drive improved throughput and patient flow through Lean and Six Sigma, but it will do little to reduce costs if it is not paired with an activity-based costing approach. **Activity-based costing** defines total costs at a detailed level, where activity drivers and resource consumers are used. Understanding the costs at an activity level is necessary because, in most health care organizations, there has been very little work done to understand what drives costs and where the true costs lie. Many of the hidden or fixed costs that are dormant in vertical processes are more easily exposed in a horizontal cross-functional approach, which is why activity-based costing should be used in conjunction with integrated service delivery.

Work Toward Greater Collaboration

New forms of partnerships and collaborations will focus on interorganizational processes. Once you have your own internal operations mastered, be prepared to understand and improve on these boundary-spanning processes. This also includes enhancing the continuum of care, and vertically or horizontally integrating with other practices, payers, and acute services. There are opportunities in the health care value chain for significantly higher levels of collaboration, both internally with physicians and providers and externally with vendors and payers. Interactions with all of these stakeholders today are still highly manual and do not involve electronic commerce and collaborative processes. Collaboration can take the form of automated reconciliations of charges and patients, shared business plans, and collocation of employees.

In many large facilities, limited outsourcing is already in use for support services such as gift shops and cafeterias. As health care continues to focus on operational efficiencies, many organizations will discover that their **core competency** (or expertise that underlies their reason for existing and the source of the competitive advantage) does not involve operating all aspects of a business process directly. A shift toward more selective outsourcing, in both clinical and business areas, will be significantly greater in the future than what currently exists.

Vendors will also control much more of the supply chain in many areas. Vendors possess more specialized knowledge and technology, which will penetrate deeper into many organizations, and complicated mechanisms will be used to better align incentives between vendors and providers—much different than the cost–plus arrangement that is common today. The large health care distributors will have an expanded role. Incentive payments for improved bottom-line performance in key metrics will be used, and vendors will offer more attractive solutions that include labor, technology, and process.

Different managerial skills are required to manage vendor arrangements such as these, and operational managers must also include business acumen such as contract administration, performance management, and vendor collaboration.

Continue Learning and Improving

A continuous improvement mentality is necessary in today's postmodern health care enterprise. A change will occur in how health care is operationalized. There will be plenty of hospital beds and clinical treatment rooms, but there will also be ways to explore use of improved technologies that allow patients to treat themselves or provide health care at home. The rise of chronic conditions will encourage a change in how care is delivered—and from where. Tele-medicine, for example, might allow patients to communicate directly with their providers without leaving the confines of their homes. Emergency medical services will also begin employing field-based medicine and using emergency medical technicians to provide care proactively (in advance of a 911 call) instead of waiting for the emergency to happen. Changes in how care is delivered are coming, and operations managers must be in a position to support these changes. Many administrators can benefit from improved management and business education. There are nearly 75 accredited graduate-level programs in health care administration, yet far too many programs focus predominantly on public and social policy and not enough on management, financial, and business issues. While most health care degree programs are centered on the health care enterprise as a governmental organization, this will change as programs evolve to teach a broader curriculum focusing on operations, finance, and technology. In those facilities governed by physicians, the pursuit of MBA degrees has risen steadily: An estimated 22% of physician executives in large medical centers have dual MD–MBA degrees (Westfall, 2005). Yet far too many physicians are relatively inexperienced in business practices that will help improve financial and operational performance.

As the health care industry continues to change into a more dynamic one, where financial pressures force administrators to act as true business managers, there will be a much higher need for well-rounded graduates with advanced business skills. Being able to use accounting and financial data to help drive improved decision making and processes currently relies on skills that are better developed outside of health care. Having and using these skills, however, is necessary if hospitals are to manage increasing scale, horizontal integration, and effective operations.

Conduct Operations Analysis and Demonstrate Financial Value

Operations analysis is fundamental to understanding an organization's or department's performance and to continue to focus on improving productivity and combating downward margin pressures. Clinical and support services need to continuously measure and improve the financial value offered. As health care becomes more sophisticated, organizations will be managed much more like a financial portfolio, where departments and units that offer the greatest value at the lowest risk are cultivated, while those that destroy value (i.e., where total costs of operations are greater than the returns provided) are mitigated or eliminated. As health care organizations continue to measure performance more holistically, the emphasis on tracking return on investment and value creation will force differential management of service lines. This emphasis on financial value will ultimately help each unit deliver better and more competitive services.

Manage the Enterprise Through Consolidation and Horizontal Management Processes

New payment and practice models will continue to be created. These are highly experimental, so operations managers should be prepared to have multiple types of contracts in place. Insurance exchanges will mean a different set of payer plans and models, but there will also be other forms of experimentation from payers. These should be viewed as positive because they foster an understanding of how to use simulation, forecasting, and demand utilization to comprehend the financial effect on operations.

The health care industry will most likely continue to consolidate, as it has over the past few decades. Horizontal integration—through mergers, acquisitions, and joint ventures—will probably be used (much more than vertical integration) to create integrated delivery networks, as organizations attempt to use their current skills to manage similar operations in other geographic areas. This will require management of the health care organization as an **enterprise**, or a complex, multidimensional, interconnected whole (not just specific departments or activities).

This consolidation will create the need for a systems approach that can manage the interrelated facilities to achieve better results. Standardization, aggregation, and alignment are all necessary if hospitals are to achieve any synergistic effects from integration. Operational management, therefore, has to evolve from a narrow perspective to a much larger network view that can take disparate operations and connect them to achieve better results. This will require better leadership skills and the ability to manage and align processes that are expansive and currently decentralized.

Deploy Big Data and Analytical Techniques

Data are collected everywhere. From patients (in electronic medical records and registration systems), to payers (in payer databases), to activities and events (from radio frequency identification tags on equipment and devices), to procedures (activities performed on patients). Harnessing this large amount of data—or **big data**—is challenging because it derives from multiple sources and is extremely large and complex to manage with traditional tools. Health care has significantly greater potential for utilization of optimization and analytical techniques. As discussed in this text, all of the key operational processes in most health care organizations have developed over time using trial and error and do not deliver optimal results. The use of game theory, process engineering, Six Sigma, and other techniques will help augment the deployment of analytical techniques. Use of linear programming, simulation modeling, and other mathematical tools will become much more widespread in hospitals of the future than they are today. The use of analytics and optimization in the future will support a broad range of processes, including labor scheduling, patient routing, wait line and service delivery, and department or resource location analysis, to name just a few.

ACHIEVING SUCCESS IN OPERATIONS MANAGEMENT

With the concepts and tools learned from this text, there should be several opportunities for improvement that can quickly be addressed. Here are some final thoughts on how operations managers can get started in the process of improvement and change by applying their knowledge to achieve better results quickly.

1. *Learn as much as possible about the organization*, and develop a list of the high-priority problems that it faces. Create a list or a plan of the processes that need the most improvement. Chart those initiatives that have the highest value and that can be achieved with minimal risks and faster time lines. This will allow for some "quick hits" or initial success to build an improvement program, one process at a time.

2. *Innovate and challenge the status quo.* To a large extent, health care organizations are governed by the people who are the most averse to change or who do not understand the financial or business reasons that make change necessary. Many clinicians and administrators will not see the need for continuously improving processes, managing performance on a routine basis, and identifying opportunities for breaking down barriers to increase throughput and operational efficiencies. Challenging this behavior and thought process is required if health care is to improve cost and quality simultaneously. Operations managers must be change agents.

3. *Comprehensively analyze and improve everything.* In quality and continuous improvement projects, it is important to encourage team-based decision processes that are **mutually exclusive and collectively exhaustive (MECE)**. MECE is a systems-oriented approach to decision making whereby each idea is distinct and can stand on its own; it also completely covers the range of possibilities for that issue (Rasiel, 1999). The MECE approach ensures that managers fully explore all issues yet are clear and separate in their thought processes, ensuring comprehensive coverage. MECE should be used in all process engineering and project management methodologies to develop the broadest and clearest depiction of the relative topics.

4. *Always look for analytical or quantitative approaches to problems.* Operations managers should not settle for outdated **heuristics** (i.e., rules of thumb) or other biased methods for making decisions. Quantitative techniques, wherever possible, should be used to model processes, productivity, and performance and to substantially improve decision-making processes. Quantitative data form the bases for many operations techniques, such as forecasting demand and capacity and then aligning health care operations strategies accordingly.

5. *Measure everything important, graphically, in scorecards.* Relying on text reports and tables makes trends and changes over time very difficult to identify and measure. Whether looking at statistical control charts of clinical procedures or financial outcomes, viewing data graphically in a scorecard puts things in perspective. All key processes and business units should have scorecards developed, so that pre- and postproject performance can be measured and planned results can be achieved. Comparison of trends to published benchmarks or targets helps instantly focus management on opportunity areas.

Of course, these are just some of the things that must be done if operations management is to be successful in transforming health care organizations. Remember, there are always new tools and techniques that can be adopted to improve outcomes. Good luck on the journey!

CHAPTER SUMMARY

Operations management in health care will continue to evolve over time. Eight key trends were identified that will further drive operational excellence: increased visibility of patients and resources; expansive system integration; integrated service delivery; greater collaboration with payers and vendors; additional business education for administrators; strategic focus on achieving financial value in all parts of the organization; consolidation of competition and the need for improved horizontal management processes; and broader use of optimization and analytics. It is important that operations managers, at all points in their careers, develop a comprehensive plan for identifying and improving operations. Lastly, several suggestions for how to comprehensively begin incorporating operations management into daily practice were provided.

KEY TERMS

Activity-based costing	**Heuristics**
Big data	**Interoperability**
Core competency	**Mutually exclusive and collectively**
Enterprise	**exhaustive (MECE)**
Health information exchange	

DISCUSSION QUESTIONS

1. What are some of the key trends that are evolving in health care operations management?
2. Which best practices should operations managers follow?
3. Discuss the rationale behind systems interoperability.
4. How might an operational control center work in health care?
5. Why should administrators and medical executives continue developing business skills?
6. What are five initial steps that can be taken to begin the operations management process?

REFERENCES

Rasiel, E. M. (1999). *The McKinsey way.* New York, NY: McGraw-Hill.

Westfall, C. (2005, November–December). 2005 compensation survey. *The Physician Executive,* 32–37.

Major Teaching Hospitals

ALABAMA

1. Birmingham Veterans Affairs Medical Center
2. UAB Health System, University of Alabama at Birmingham
3. University of Alabama Hospital
4. University of South Alabama Medical Center

ARIZONA

1. Banner Good Samaritan Medical Center
2. Banner Health
3. Department of Veterans Affairs, Veterans Integrated Service Network, VISN 18
4. Maricopa Medical Center
5. Mayo Clinic Hospital
6. Scottsdale Healthcare Osborn Medical Center
7. Southern Arizona Veterans Affairs Health Care System
8. St. Joseph's Hospital and Medical Center
9. The University Medical Center

ARKANSAS

1. Arkansas Children's Hospital
2. Central Arkansas Veterans Healthcare System
3. University of Arkansas for Medical Sciences

CALIFORNIA

1. California Pacific Medical Center
2. Cedars–Sinai Medical Center
3. City of Hope National Medical Center
4. Community Health Network
5. Community Regional Medical Center
6. Department of Veterans Affairs, Veterans Integrated Service Network, VISN 22
7. Dignity Health
8. Harbor–UCLA Medical Center
9. Jerry L. Pettis Memorial Veterans Affairs Medical Center
10. Kaiser Foundation Hospital, Los Angeles
11. Kaiser Foundation Hospitals, Northern California
12. Kaiser Permanente Foundation Hospitals, Southern California
13. LAC + USC Medical Center
14. Loma Linda University Medical Center
15. Long Beach Memorial Medical Center
16. Ronald Reagan UCLA Medical Center
17. San Francisco General Hospital and Trauma Center
18. Scripps Green Hospital
19. Scripps Health
20. Stanford Hospital and Clinics
21. Tenet Healthcare Corporation
22. UC Davis Health System
23. UC Irvine Medical Center
24. UCLA Health System
25. UC San Diego Medical Center
26. UCSD Health System
27. UCSF Medical Center
28. VA Sierra Pacific Network (10N21), Department of Veterans Affairs, VISN 21

29. Veterans Affairs, Greater Los Angeles Healthcare System
30. Veterans Affairs, Long Beach Healthcare System
31. Veterans Affairs, San Diego Healthcare System

COLORADO

1. Denver Health and Hospital Authority
2. National Jewish Health
3. University of Colorado Health
4. University of Colorado Hospital

CONNECTICUT

1. Bridgeport Hospital
2. Danbury Hospital
3. Greenwich Hospital
4. Norwalk Hospital
5. Saint Francis Care
6. Saint Francis Hospital and Medical Center
7. Stamford Health System
8. Stamford Hospital
9. University of Connecticut Health Center/John Dempsey Hospital
10. VA Connecticut Healthcare System
11. Yale–New Haven Health System
12. Yale–New Haven Hospital

DELAWARE

1. Christiana Care Health System
2. Veterans Affairs, Medical and Regional Office Center

DISTRICT OF COLUMBIA

1. Children's National Medical Center
2. Georgetown University Hospital

3. George Washington University
4. Hospital Howard University Hospital
5. Universal Health Services Inc., George Washington University Hospital
6. Washington Hospital Center

FLORIDA

1. All Children's Hospital
2. Department of Veterans Affairs, Veterans Integrated Service Network, VISN 8
3. Florida Hospital Orlando
4. Jackson Memorial Hospital
5. Miami Children's Hospital
6. Mount Sinai Medical Center
7. Orlando VA Medical Center
8. Tampa General Hospital
9. UF Health Jacksonville
10. UF Health Shands Hospital
11. Veterans Affairs Medical Center, James A. Haley Veterans' Hospital
12. West Kendall Baptist Hospital

GEORGIA

1. Athens Regional Medical Center
2. Atlanta Medical Center
3. Atlanta VA Medical Center
4. Augusta Veterans Affairs Medical Center
5. Central Georgia Health Systems
6. Children's Healthcare of Atlanta
7. Children's Healthcare of Atlanta (Includes Egleston and Scottish Rite)
8. Department of Veterans Affairs, Veterans Integrated Service Network, VISN 7
9. Emory Healthcare
10. Emory University Hospital
11. Emory University Hospital Midtown

12. Georgia Regents Medical Center
13. Grady Memorial Hospital–Atlanta
14. MCG Health, Inc.
15. Medical Center of Central Georgia
16. Memorial Health, Inc.
17. Memorial Health University Medical Center

ILLINOIS

1. Advocate Christ Hospital and Medical Center
2. Advocate Health Care
3. Advocate Illinois Masonic Medical Center
4. Advocate Lutheran General Hospital
5. Captain James A. Lovell Federal Health Care Center
6. Children's Memorial Hospital
7. Department of Veterans Affairs, Veterans Integrated Service Network, VISN 12
8. John H. Stroger, Jr. Hospital of Cook County
9. Loyola University Health System
10. Loyola University Medical Center
11. MacNeal Hospital
12. Memorial Health System
13. Memorial Medical Center
14. Mount Sinai Hospital
15. NorthShore University HealthSystem
16. Northwestern Memorial Hospital
17. OSF HealthCare
18. OSF Saint Francis Medical Center
19. Rehabilitation Institute of Chicago
20. Rush System for Health
21. Rush University Medical Center
22. Sinai Health System
23. University of Chicago Hospitals and Health System
24. University of Chicago Medical Center
25. University of Illinois at Chicago Medical Center
26. Veterans Affairs Chicago Health Care System

INDIANA

1. Eskenazi Health
2. Richard L. Roudebush Veterans Affairs Medical Center
3. St. Vincent Hospitals and Health Services, Inc.

IOWA

1. Iowa City Veterans Affairs Medical Center
2. UnityPoint Health–Des Moines
3. University of Iowa Hospitals and Clinics

KANSAS

1. University of Kansas Hospital

KENTUCKY

1. University of Kentucky Hospital
2. U of L Health Care University Hospital

LOUISIANA

1. Baton Rouge General Medical Center
2. General Health System
3. Interim LSU Hospital
4. Ochsner Clinic Foundation
5. Our Lady of the Lake Regional Medical Center
6. Southeast Louisiana Veterans Health Care System
7. Tulane Medical Center

MAINE

1. Maine Medical Center

MARYLAND

1. Department of Veterans Affairs, Veterans Integrated Service Network, VISN 5
2. Franklin Square Hospital
3. Holy Cross Hospital
4. Johns Hopkins Bayview Medical Center
5. Johns Hopkins Health System
6. Johns Hopkins Hospital
7. MedStar Health
8. Mercy Medical Center
9. The National Institutes of Health Clinical Center
10. University of Maryland Medical Center
11. University of Maryland Medical System
12. Veterans Affairs Maryland Health Care System

MASSACHUSETTS

1. Baystate Health System
2. Baystate Medical Center
3. Berkshire Medical Center
4. Beth Israel Deaconess Medical Center
5. Boston Children's Hospital
6. Boston Medical Center
7. Brigham and Women's Faulkner Hospital
8. Brigham and Women's Hospital
9. Cambridge Health Alliance
10. Cambridge Health Alliance–Cambridge Hospital Campus
11. CareGroup, Inc.
12. Dana-Farber Cancer Institute
13. Department of Veterans Affairs, Veterans Integrated Service Network, VISN 1
14. Lahey Hospital and Medical Center
15. Massachusetts General Hospital
16. Mount Auburn Hospital
17. Partners HealthCare System, Inc.
18. St. Elizabeth's Medical Center

19. Steward Health Care System
20. Tufts Medical Center
21. UMass Memorial Health Care
22. Veterans Affairs Boston Healthcare System
23. Veterans Affairs Medical Center (West Roxbury/Brockton)

MICHIGAN

1. Department of Veterans Affairs, Veterans Integrated Service Network, VISN 11
2. Detroit Medical Center
3. Henry Ford Health System
4. Henry Ford Hospital
5. Hurley Medical Center
6. McLaren Healthcare Corporation
7. McLaren Regional Medical Center
8. Oakwood Healthcare System
9. Oakwood Hospital and Medical Center
10. St. John Hospital and Medical Center
11. St. John Providence Health System
12. St. Joseph Mercy Health System
13. Trinity Health
14. University of Michigan Health System
15. University of Michigan Medical Center
16. Veterans Affairs Ann Arbor Healthcare System
17. William Beaumont Health System
18. William Beaumont Hospital

MINNESOTA

1. Abbott Northwestern Hospital
2. Allina Hospitals and Clinics
3. Fairview Health Services
4. HealthPartners, Inc.
5. Hennepin County Medical Center
6. Mayo Clinic Health System

7. Minneapolis Veterans Affairs Medical Center
8. Regions Hospital
9. Saint Mary's Hospital
10. University of Minnesota Medical Center, Fairview

MISSISSIPPI

1. University Hospitals and Clinics/University of Mississippi Medical Center

MISSOURI

1. Barnes-Jewish Hospital
2. BJC HealthCare
3. Children's Mercy Hospital
4. Mercy Hospital St. Louis
5. Saint Louis University Hospital
6. Saint Luke's Health System
7. Saint Luke's Hospital of Kansas City
8. St. Louis Children's Hospital
9. Truman Medical Center–Hospital Hill
10. University of Missouri Health Care

NEBRASKA

1. Department of Veterans Affairs, Veterans Integrated Service Network, VISN 23
2. The Nebraska Medical Center
3. VA Nebraska–Western Iowa Health Care System: Omaha Division

NEW HAMPSHIRE

1. Dartmouth–Hitchcock Alliance
2. Dartmouth–Hitchcock Medical Center

NEW JERSEY

1. Atlantic Health System
2. Barnabas Health
3. Cooper University Hospital
4. Hackensack University Medical Center
5. Jersey Shore University Medical Center
6. Meridian Health System
7. Monmouth Medical Center
8. Morristown Memorial Hospital
9. Newark Beth Israel Medical Center
10. Overlook Medical Center
11. Robert Wood Johnson Health System
12. Robert Wood Johnson University Hospital
13. Saint Barnabas Medical Center
14. Saint Peter's University Hospital
15. University of Medicine and Dentistry of New Jersey–University Hospital

NEW MEXICO

1. New Mexico Veterans Affairs Medical Center
2. University of New Mexico Hospital

NEW YORK

1. Albany Medical Center Hospital
2. Albany Veterans Affairs Medical Center
3. Bassett Healthcare Network
4. Beth Israel Medical Center
5. Brooklyn Hospital Center
6. Continuum Health Partners, Inc.
7. Department of Veterans Affairs, Veterans Integrated Service Network, VISN 2
8. Hospital for Special Surgery
9. James J. Peters VA Medical Center
10. Lenox Hill Healthcare Network

11. Lenox Hill Hospital
12. Long Island Jewish Medical Center
13. Maimonides Medical Center
14. Mary Imogene Bassett Hospital
15. Memorial Sloan Kettering Cancer Center
16. Montefiore Medical Center
17. Mount Sinai Hospital
18. New York Methodist Hospital
19. NewYork–Presbyterian Healthcare System
20. NewYork–Presbyterian Hospital: The University Hospital of Columbia and Cornell
21. North Shore–Long Island Jewish Health System
22. North Shore University Hospital
23. NYU Hospitals Center
24. NYU Langone Medical Center
25. Roswell Park Cancer Institute
26. Staten Island University Hospital
27. St. Luke's–Roosevelt Hospital Center
28. Stony Brook University Hospital
29. Strong Health System
30. Strong Memorial Hospital
31. SUNY Downstate Medical Center/University Hospital of Brooklyn
32. Syracuse Veterans Affairs Medical Center
33. United Health Services Hospitals
34. University Hospital, SUNY Upstate Medical University
35. Veterans Affairs New York Harbor Healthcare System–New York Campus
36. Veterans Affairs Western New York Healthcare System
37. Westchester Medical Center
38. Winthrop South Nassau University Health System, Inc.
39. Winthrop–University Hospital

NORTH CAROLINA

1. Carolinas HealthCare System
2. Carolinas Medical Center
3. Department of Veterans Affairs, Veterans Integrated Service Network, VISN 6
4. Duke University Health System

5. Duke University Hospital
6. Durham Veterans Affairs Medical Center
7. UNC Health Care System
8. University of North Carolina Hospitals
9. Vidant Health
10. Vidant Medical Center
11. Wake Forest Baptist Medical Center

NORTH DAKOTA

1. Sanford Medical Center

OHIO

1. Akron Children's Hospital
2. Akron General Medical Center
3. Arthur G. James Cancer Hospital and Richard J. Solove Research Institute
4. Cincinnati Children's Hospital Medical Center
5. Cincinnati Veterans Affairs Medical Center
6. Cleveland Clinic Foundation
7. Cleveland Clinic Health System
8. Dayton Veterans Affairs Medical Center
9. Department of Veterans Affairs, Veterans Integrated Service Network, VISN 10
10. Good Samaritan Hospital (TriHealth)
11. Grant–Riverside Methodist Hospitals, Grant Medical Center Campus
12. Grant–Riverside Methodist Hospitals, Riverside Campus
13. Kettering Medical Center
14. Louis Stokes Cleveland Veterans Affairs Medical Center
15. MetroHealth Medical Center
16. MetroHealth System
17. Miami Valley Hospital
18. OhioHealth
19. Ohio State University Health SystemSumma Health System
20. UC Health
21. University Hospitals Case Medical Center

22. University Hospitals HealthSystem
23. University of Cincinnati Medical Center
24. University of Toledo Medical Center
25. Wexner Medical Center at The Ohio State University

OKLAHOMA

1. Oklahoma City Veterans Affairs Medical Center
2. OU Medical Center

OREGON

1. Oregon Health & Science University
2. Portland Veterans Affairs Medical Center

PENNSYLVANIA

1. Albert Einstein Medical Center (Albert Einstein Healthcare Network)
2. Allegheny General Hospital
3. Children's Hospital of Philadelphia
4. Crozer–Chester Medical Center
5. Crozer–Keystone Health System
6. Department of Veterans Affairs, Veterans Integrated Service Network, VISN 4
7. Fox Chase Cancer Center
8. Geisinger Medical Center
9. Hospital of the University of Pennsylvania
10. Jefferson Health System
11. Lankenau Hospital
12. Lehigh Valley Health Network
13. Lehigh Valley Hospital–Cedar Crest
14. Main Line Health
15. Penn State Milton S. Hershey Medical Center
16. Philadelphia Veterans Affairs Medical Center
17. St. Christopher's Hospital for Children

18. St. Luke's Hospital
19. Temple University Health System
20. Temple University Hospital
21. Tenet Health System, Hahnemann University Hospital
22. Thomas Jefferson University Hospital
23. University of Pennsylvania Health System
24. University of Pittsburgh Medical Center
25. University of Pittsburgh Medical Center Hamot
26. University of Pittsburgh Medical Center Shadyside
27. Veterans Affairs Pittsburgh Healthcare System
28. WellSpan Health
29. WellSpan York Hospital
30. Western Pennsylvania Hospital
31. West Penn Allegheny Health System

PUERTO RICO

1. San Juan Veterans Affairs Medical Center

RHODE ISLAND

1. Care New England Health System
2. Lifespan, Inc.
3. Memorial Hospital of Rhode Island
4. Miriam Hospital
5. Rhode Island Hospital
6. Roger Williams Hospital
7. Women and Infants Hospital of Rhode Island

SOUTH CAROLINA

1. Greenville Health System
2. Medical University of South Carolina Medical Center
3. Palmetto Health
4. Palmetto Health Alliance
5. Ralph H. Johnson Veterans Affairs Medical Center

SOUTH DAKOTA

1. Sanford USD Medical Center
2. Sioux Falls VA Health Care System
3. Sioux Valley Hospitals and Health System

TENNESSEE

1. Department of Veterans Affairs, Veterans Integrated Service Network, VISN 9
2. Erlanger Health System
3. Erlanger Medical Center
4. Johnson City Medical Center
5. Le Bonheur Children's Hospital
6. Memphis Veterans Affairs Medical Center
7. Methodist Healthcare–University Hospital
8. Mountain States Health Alliance
9. Regional Medical Center at Memphis
10. University of Tennessee Medical Center
11. Vanderbilt University Medical Center
12. Vanguard Health Systems
13. Veterans Affairs Tennessee Valley Healthcare System

TEXAS

1. Baylor St. Luke's Medical Center
2. Baylor University Medical Center
3. Central Texas Veterans Health Care System
4. Children's Medical Center of Dallas
5. Department of Veterans Affairs, Veterans Integrated Service Network, VISN 17
6. Harris Health System
7. The Methodist Hospital System (Houston, Texas)
8. John Peter Smith Hospital (Tarrant County Hospital District)
9. Medical Center Hospital
10. Memorial Hermann–Texas Medical Center

11. Methodist Dallas Medical Center
12. Parkland Health & Hospital System
13. Scott & White Hospital–Temple
14. South Texas Veterans Health Care System
15. St. Luke's Episcopal Health System
16. Texas Children's Hospital
17. University Health System
18. University Medical Center Health System
19. University Medical Center of El Paso
20. University of Texas Health Science Center at Tyler
21. University of Texas MD Anderson Cancer Center
22. University of Texas Southwestern Medical Center

UTAH

1. University of Utah Health System
2. University of Utah Hospital

VERMONT

1. Fletcher Allen Health Care
2. White River Junction VA Medical Center

VIRGINIA

1. Carilion New River Valley Medical Center
2. Hunter Holmes McGuire Veterans Affairs Medical Center
3. INOVA Fairfax Hospital
4. INOVA Health System
5. Salem Veterans Affairs Medical Center
6. Sentara Norfolk General Hospital
7. University of Virginia Medical Center
8. VCU Medical Center

WASHINGTON

1. Harborview Medical Center
2. University of Washington Medical Center
3. UW Medicine
4. Veterans Affairs Puget Sound Health Care System
5. Virginia Mason Medical Center

WEST VIRGINIA

1. Cabell Huntington Hospital
2. CAMC Health System
3. Charleston Area Medical Center
4. West Virginia United Health System
5. West Virginia University Hospitals, Inc.

WISCONSIN

1. Aurora Health Care
2. Froedtert Hospital
3. Gundersen Health System
4. Gundersen Lutheran Medical Center
5. Sinai Samaritan Medical Center
6. St. Luke's Medical Center
7. University of Wisconsin Hospital and Clinics

Source: Association of American Medical Colleges. Reprinted with Permission.

Answers to Selected Chapter Exercise Problems

CHAPTER 1

1. Some questions to consider include the following:

   - What is the current level of productivity in terms of packages per hour?
   - What is the cost of the new software? How long is its useful life? What is the amortized cost?
   - What is the expected level of productivity postimplementation?
   - Does the delta in productivity metrics justify the cost?

CHAPTER 3

1. Average deduction rate is 52%.
2. Thirty days of working capital.
3. The return on capital is 3.6%.

CHAPTER 5

1.a Five-day moving average forecast is 28.2.

1.b Three-day moving average forecast is 29.3.

2. Using the calculation of $W = \dfrac{L}{\lambda}$, average wait time is 15 minutes: $(10 \div 40) \times 60 = 15$ minutes. Note that this is not the same as the total wait in the system (W_q).

3. The standard time is 21.25, or $\dfrac{17}{1 - 0.2}$

CHAPTER 6

1. The single-factor productivity rate is 12.2 (190,000 square feet ÷ 15,570 hours worked).
2. Productivity has decreased by 6.9% from the previous month.
3. Yes, this would be a good use of capital. The total annual cost would be $20,000 ($60,000 ÷ 3) and total annual savings would be $285,450 ($23,787.50 per month × 12 months). Therefore, the total monthly benefit is $22,120.83.

CHAPTER 8

1. The program evaluation and review technique calculation is 26.3 days.
2. The program evaluation and review technique calculation is higher by 1.3 days.

CHAPTER 9

1. The program would break even at 1,000 procedures.
2. The new breakeven point is 857 procedures.
3. The second option should be chosen.

CHAPTER 10

1. The net present value is $1,243. Yes, the project should be accepted because it is greater than $0.
2. The payback period is 2.85 years.

CHAPTER 13

1. The total annual cost of supplies is $1,800,000 (15% × $1 million × 12 months).
2. The net realizable value is $87.50 ($100 sales price − $12.50 cost to sell).
3. Current replacement cost falls between the ceiling and the floor, so $40 is the lower of cost or market.

4. Debit cost of goods sold, credit inventory.
5. Days of inventory on hand is 72 days.
6. The economic order quantity is 223, calculated as follows:

$$\sqrt{(2 \times 1{,}000 \times 50) \div (20 \times 0.1)}$$

CHAPTER 14

1. Yes, this is an increasing trend.
2. This is calculated using $y = a + bx$, with a slope equal to 10 and an intercept of 50. The forecast for Period 2 is 70.

Glossary of Terms

ABC classification	A classification scheme where inventories or supplies are grouped according to usage or sales volumes, typically in terms of quantities or dollar volumes. "A" items tend to be the highest-usage or highest-dollar items and typically represent about 80% of the usage but only 20% of the items.
Academic medicine	Clinical patient care that occurs in a teaching hospital or one of its facilities. Care delivered by the faculty, residents, fellows, or students of an affiliated medical school as part of a formal training program.
Accountable care organization (ACO)	A group of various healthcare providers (sometimes referred to as a network) that shares financial responsibility for the care of a designated group of patients on behalf of an insurer.
Acquisition	A type of growth strategy in which one organization acquires another organization. Examples include a hospital purchasing a physician practice, or a large, investor-owned hospital purchasing a small, rural, independent hospital.
Act	Enacted healthcare law.
Actionable	The ability of an organization to execute the proposed changes and quickly address priorities.
Activity-based costing (ABC)	Defines total costs at a detailed level where activity drivers and resource consumers are used.

Acute care Focused on a specific episode or event requiring care.

Adjusted average daily census (AADC) A calculation of adjusted patient days.

Adjusted discharge A calculation that measures hospital volumes of inpatient discharges in terms of the hospital's overall inpatient and outpatient outputs. Calculated as total gross revenue divided by total inpatient revenue, multiplied by the number of inpatient discharges.

Adjusted occupied bed (AOB) A calculation of actual occupied beds in a given hospital adjusted for patients who are admitted for less than 24 hours or who were not inpatients when the census was taken.

Adjusted patient day A calculation that measures hospital volumes where both inpatient and outpatient volumes are incorporated. Calculated as total gross revenue divided by total inpatient revenue, multiplied by the number of inpatient days.

Admission When a patient enters the hospital for an inpatient stay.

Admixture The pharmaceutical process of combining multiple fluids.

Allowances Deductions or discounts from gross patient revenues that reduce the amount of charges to be collected. Typically, these are contractually negotiated (for managed care) or regulated (for government payers).

Ambulatory Payment Classification (APC) A billing mechanism in which outpatient per-procedure fees may be adjusted to reflect the relative severity or resource intensity of services.

As-is process A process map that depicts the actual, current process in place prior to any process engineering.

Asset Anything the hospital owns that has immediate or long-term monetary value.

Attributes Characteristics that describe an item.

Audit	An examination or verification of finances, compliance, and/or operations. The most common audits are financial in nature, assuring adherence to generally accepted accounting principles, thus ensuring that the organization is materially correct and that internal controls are adequate.
Audit trail	The ability to maintain details on all transactions processed in information systems used to process purchasing.
Auto-correlated demand	Where the value of demand in one period is related to the demand for itself in previous periods.
Average daily census (ADC)	An average number of patient days in a time period to gauge the level of inpatient activity for that period.
Average length of stay (ALOS)	The average number of days a patient stays, from admission to discharge. An inpatient metric, which is calculated as the number of patient days during a period divided by the number of discharges.
Balance sheet	One of the three most common financial statements that shows the financial position of a hospital at a specific point in time. Key elements focus on the accounting equation of Assets = Liabilities + Net assets.
Bar code	A single- or two-dimension machine-readable code that contains several key pieces of information. Also called a *license plate*, it is visually represented by either an array of bars linearly or a matrix diagram of dots.
Bar code reader	A scanning device that can be used to scan, decode, and interpret the contents of a bar code.
Base staffing	When some areas of the hospital can flex their labor hours while maintaining a minimal level of staff regardless of patient visits produced.
Benchmarking	Comparison of a key performance measurement relative to the competition or other leading organizations. The process of seeking best practices among better-performing organizations, with intentions of applying those internally.

Benefit	A gain or positive change in an outcome, often called the *cash inflow* or *return*.
Big data	A term used to describe the large amount of data derived from multiple sources.
Bill of material	A listing or recipe that defines the specific raw materials in or components of a finished good.
Biometric methods	Newer security systems that use physiological characteristics, such as fingerprints or retinal scans, to uniquely identify an individual.
Bonds	Debt instruments issued by a healthcare organization to the public; the organization is obligated to repay the original principal plus interest for the period the debt was outstanding.
Bottleneck	A choke point, or a point in a process where capacity is limited and effectively reduces the number of outputs due to physical or logical constraints.
Brand equity	The combination of assets and liabilities unique to each teaching hospital that determines its overall image or perception in the marketplace.
Breakeven analysis	Analyzes cost structures and volumes to identify at which point total returns equal total costs.
Breakeven point	A point of activity where total revenues equal costs, thus yielding a net income of zero.
Budget	A quantitative plan that represents management's plans and typically converts patient activities into associated revenues, costs, and margins.
Bulk replenishment	Occurs when items are simply augmented to the existing cart.
Bullwhip effect	A term used to describe a phenomenon whereby demand varies or fluctuates significantly as the demand is viewed or interpreted further upstream. Although the actual consumer demand might be fairly constant, the effect of promotions, nonsystematic ordering, and other factors tend to cause the upstream supply chain to interpret downstream

demand as highly variable. Caused by lack of visibility into actual consumer demand, among other factors.

Business plan
The written, detailed plan for an existing or proposed program, facility, service line, or other operation. Typically used to assess financial practicality as well as detail key strategies.

Business strategy
The managerial process responsible for formulating dynamic decisions about critical elements of the business that establishes hospital direction, creates a significantly differentiated competitive game plan, and results in a competitive advantage. Also called *competitive strategy* or simply *strategy*.

Buy-in
When sponsors and managers craft a story or vision for their change and then obtain support from others to ensure that no organizational obstacles prevent the project's advancement.

Cannibalize
To draw demand away from another product. For example, when a cellular phone manufacturer introduces a new model, this new model cannibalizes or diminishes sales for existing models.

Capacity
The amount of resources or assets that exist to serve the demand.

Capacity planning
The process of aligning capacity with demand.

Capital
Investments in assets to offset labor, or assets used to produce even more assets.

Capitalized
Recognized as an asset on the balance sheet.

Capital substitution
Spending capital on a service or product that would replace a service or employee.

Capitation
A method of physician or provider reimbursement that transfers financial risk of care to physicians and away from health plans or insurers. Standard primary care capitation in health plans reimburses the provider on a per-member, per-month basis, such that a flat payment is made per capita to a defined population over a certain period of time.

Carousel
Automated pickers that help select single- and small-dose packages, label them, and store them in the right location using technology and large mechanized systems.

Case mix index (CMI)
A measurement that shows the complexity of a procedure. It is used to normalize data so that comparisons can be made relative to other procedures and perform benchmarking against competitive hospitals. Adjusting supply expenses by case mix index is one common use.

Case rate
A prospectively determined amount that is paid for all services associated with a hospital admission, regardless of the costs for that occasion of care. Often used for specific types of services such as childbirth or organ transplants.

Cash inflow
A gain or positive change in an outcome; also called *benefit*.

Cash outflow
Costs for an organization that include things such as labor, hardware, software, implementation support (consulting, training), communications and infrastructure, and miscellaneous.

Category
A classification determined by a variety of attributes.

Causal factor
A data series that is used to help improve product forecasts because it has a suspected strong relationship with the item. For example, "new building starts" is often used to help improve the prediction of demand for "lumber," because the quantity of lumber consumed has a strong tie to the number of houses or buildings being built.

Chain of custody
The handling audit trail, which details who has handled specific items, when, and where the transfers of physical products occurred.

Channel
A type of outlet for selling hospital services, or a specific set of processes and parties that gets products from source of supply to end consumer. Hospital channels include clinics, hospitals, mobile clinics, and even in-store retail locations. A type of facility where patient care is provided.

Chargeable	If the purpose of the material is to charge it back, directly or indirectly to patients, and if it is not consumed by the end of the period, it is held as inventory.
Charge Description Master (CDM)	A hospital's master list of prices for all procedures, services, and supplies provided to patients.
Collaboration	Working jointly with others in an endeavor to accomplish similar goals. Fundamental to effective operations and supply chain management.
Collaborative	Open, participative process and environment where internal and extended supply chain partners work together to share common information formats (such as point-of-sale data), languages, and processes to achieve a common goal (increase profitability and improve demand).
Collaborative planning, forecasting, and replenishment (CPFR)	A process deployed in consumer industries where the entire extended supply chain network uses a specific collaborative planning and forecasting framework to improve inventory and sales plans. A partnership for sharing information about consumer point-of-sale data between suppliers and retailers.
Commercial insurers	Nongovernment payers that collectively fund between 30% and 40% of the nation's hospital services.
Commodity economics	An industry condition affecting product profitability where specific characteristics (e.g., excess supply, multiple strong competitors, fragmented markets) force the average price of a product to be driven continually lower, until eventually price is equal to the marginal cost of a product.
Community hospital	A term used to describe facilities that are available for use by the entire community. It represents the majority of hospitals in the United States and includes all nonfederal, short-term hospitals of either for-profit or nonprofit status.
Competition	A term used to describe the existence of substitute providers of a product or service. In most industries, the greater the intensity of the competition, the greater the need for business strategy, because heightened competition leads to reduced margins over time.

Competitive advantage	Differential outcome or differential performance achieved by an organization relative to the competition. A competitive advantage is a result of the activities and processes that are performed significantly better than the competition.
Competitive bidding	A formalized process that engages multiple vendors simultaneously to ensure a competitive marketplace, improve economies of scale, and possibly lower total cost of ownership for products.
Competitiveness	Management's ability to respond to environmental changes (such as changes in reimbursement practices) as well as competitor's actions (such as adding new facilities or expanding existing service lines).
Compounding	A pharmaceutical process of breaking down tablets or solid substances.
Comprehensive	Taking into account all of the factors involved and including all of the data in the ratios so as not to oversimplify the calculation at the expense of meaningful and reliable data.
Concentration	A term used to describe the existence of competition, in terms of size and distribution, in a market. Typically expressed in a ratio format from 0 to 1, where a number closer to 0 would indicate an extremely fragmented and competitive market, while a number closer to 1 would indicate a near monopoly environment.
Consignment in	Measures someone else's inventory that is being held or stored on the hospital's facility at no charge until sold.
Consignment out	Reflects the hospital's inventory that is placed elsewhere for sale.
Consistent	To do the same things the same way repeatedly over time.
Continuous demand	Evenly dispersed usage throughout all time periods.
Continuous improvement	A constant focus on achieving better outcomes.

Contract labor	Staffing obtained from outside sources.
Control chart	A chart that shows process data values over time, relative to both mean and standard deviations.
Controlled drugs	Drugs that are tightly controlled around usage and distribution by the U.S. Drug Enforcement Agency because of potential for misuse and abuse.
Controlling	All tasks to monitor and track progress toward goals, ensure performance improvement, and make corrective changes in strategy where necessary.
Core competency	Expertise that underlies an organization's reason for existing, and the source of its competitive advantage.
Cost of capital	The actual cost of money. If capital is borrowed the interest charge is included in this.
Cost of goods sold (COGS)	The total cost of the inventory sold in a specific period.
Cost–quality continuum	A theoretical trade-off in which a focus on one side of the equation leads to diminishing returns on the other. A focus on costs might lead a hospital to reduce services provided, which might affect overall quality.
Cost report	An institutional report that details the financial and operational transaction summary for a hospital, such as revenues and expenses by key services, as well as balance sheet and activity information.
Council of Teaching Hospitals (COTH)	A group of major hospitals that plays a significant role in educating future medical providers and providing basic and advanced research as well as patient care. An organization of the Association of American Medical Colleges with restricted membership to only those hospitals with primary missions in academic health care.
Counterbalancing error	When an inventory error corrects itself (generally at the end of the second period).
Critical path method	A technique that helps identify the longest path in a project, which therefore makes it the most critical.

Current asset
An asset (something producing a future benefit) that is expected to be converted to cash through sales or consumption in the next 12 months, or operating cycle, whichever is longer. Cash, accounts receivable, and inventory are current assets.

Current liability
A liability (obligations owed to another party) that is expected to become due or be paid in the next 12 months. Accounts payable is a current liability.

Current Procedural Terminology (CPT)
The code that describes the types of services provided by hospitals. Often used interchangeably with Health-care Common Procedure Coding System codes.

Current ratio
The relationship between current assets divided by current liabilities.

Customer
Within health care, a customer is a potential, current, or previous user, consumer, or other interested party involved in the exchange of healthcare services. The primary customer is the patient (i.e., the individual receiving care), but many secondary customers of hospitals exist, such as payers, communities, patients' families, government, or other key stakeholders in the healthcare transaction.

Customer service
The means by which a provider attempts to keep customers happy and loyal while differentiating itself from others.

Customer service level
A measure of the probability that product will be available when the customer demands it.

Cycle count
Periodic and physical counts of inventory on hand.

Cycle inventory
The inventory that accrues over time due to supply chain production or a procurement process that is tied to inflexible lot sizes. For example, if demand in Period A was 10,000 units, but the retailer can only purchase from its supplier in a 20,000-unit lot size, the difference between the two over time becomes the average cycle inventory.

Cyclical demand
When naturally occurring cycles tend to result in a predictable ebb and flow in the demand.

Data envelopment analysis (DEA) Allows use of benchmarking using unit of input data, can be used with a mix of unit and cost measurements for inputs and outputs, and is able to normalize wider variations in data points used to create a benchmark.

De-bottleneck To eliminate constraints or obstacles that limit capacity or throughput.

Decision A choice between two or more alternatives.

Decision making A process in an organization in which decisions are made and reflect the major processes involved in managing the work of organizations.

Decreasing demand When consumers demand a smaller quantity of items than before.

Deductions Similar to allowances. Adjustments, whether for contractual, regulatory, or charitable care provided, that reduce gross patient revenues.

Defect An instance in a process where the customer requirement has not been met.

Defects per million opportunities (DPMO) A ratio of defects that actually occurs per million opportunities where they could have occurred.

Deliverable The tangible outcome that results from the project.

Demand The need for a specific product at a specific time. In a perfect world, demand would equal sales, but in reality they can be significantly different. As an example, if sales were 500 in Period X but two manufacturing plants were down and thus the firm had no inventory to sell, the lost demand plus actual sales would equal demand.

Demand association A process that allows planners to estimate the demand for new products, or to estimate demand for current products at new selling locations, by associating the historical demand of one product to another. This process brings a degree of analytical validation to and otherwise judgmental means for estimating demand, especially for new product introductions. Also called *product chaining* or *demand chaining*.

Demand chain	As opposed to a supply chain, *demand chain* is a relatively new term that focuses on the more complex set of business processes and activities that help firms understand, manage, and ultimately create consumer demand. Tends to focus more on generating demand than fulfilling supply.
Demand forecast	A collaborative process that estimates the quantity of items that will be used or required over a specific time period. Projection of demand by item, location, and time dimensions.
Depreciation	A decline in value over time, or an allocation of the original cost of an asset during the total productive or useful life of that asset.
Design capacity	Maximum stated or theoretical output for a resource.
Diagnosis	The physician's or medical provider's explanation for the cause or source of the problem or symptoms.
Diagnosis-related group (DRG)	A classification system for illnesses that comprises 495 groups of medical conditions, each of which has a different reimbursement schedule for Medicare payments. Used by the Centers for Medicare and Medicaid Services to standardize payments and promote more efficient patient care.
Differentiation	The ability of an organization to fundamentally offer different products, serve different markets, or otherwise perform differently than others in the marketplace.
Discharge	When the patient who was admitted leaves the hospital.
Distinctive competency	Something that the organization does really well relative to other organizations.
Distributors	Brokers, intermediaries, or other middlemen that aggregate supply, store inventory, and serve to connect the manufacturer with retailers and consumers.
Division of labor	Continued specialization that helps to produce well-defined roles and tasks, concentrated work efforts, and higher efficiencies.
Downstream	On a supply chain, the zone closer to final consumption or use.

Drilldown	Allows users to continuously explore data more deeply by making finer adjustments and moving lower in the hierarchy, helping to further understand and analyze data at more descriptive levels using narrowly defined attributes.
Drug	A substance that is intended for use in the diagnosis, cure, mitigation, treatment, and prevention of disease.
Durable medical equipment (DME)	Equipment used in the delivery of patient care that meets several criteria: it is used repeatedly for multiple patients, is used for a medical necessity, is appropriate for use outside of the hospital, and is no longer beneficial to patients once they resume normal health.
Economic order quantity	A calculation that represents the "best" solution to the offsetting priorities of minimizing the amount of inventory on hand, the costs of ordering goods, and the carrying costs of inventory.
Economic performance	The financial viability and outcomes measured over the long term. Often measured by multiple metrics, such as return on capital. Typically, economics refers to true cash operating position after the costs of the capital employed have been extracted.
Economies of scale	Synergies or reductions in total costs due to purchase and usage of larger bulk quantities.
Effective capacity	Adjusts the design capacity with average expected utilization rates.
Effectiveness	Measures "doing the right things," which relates to strategy and planning.
Efficiency	One of the primary goals of operations management. Measures the degree of resources and costs consumed per unit of output.
Electronic data interchange (EDI)	The standardization of specific, common data through common message formats, such as invoices, point-of-sale data, and shipping notices, that helps simplify exchanges and electronic transfer between different components of the supply chain. EDI is used to enable tracking of point-of-sale demand to

synchronize the supply chain, thus reducing overall inventories, decreasing planning response cycle times, and improving overall collaboration.

Enterprise

A complex, multidimensional healthcare organization that is interconnected as a whole.

Enterprise resource planning (ERP) system

The primary "system of record" to track products or services provided, costs, customers, and cash associated with the entire operation.

Evidenced-based medicine

Medicine that follows the scientific method to medical practice and seeks to quantify the true outcomes associated with certain medical practices by applying statistical and research methods.

Exchange cart

A large, moveable, steel structure carrying replenishments for pars.

Exclusions

Services for which an insurer or payer will not provide reimbursement.

Extended supply chain management

A term used to describe the internal hospital supply chain as well as channel partners external to the firm. Also referred to as the supply chain network, this can include manufacturers, wholesalers, distributors, brokers, retailers, dealers, third-party logistics providers, transportation carriers, and public warehouses.

External benchmark

A benchmark that is established based on objective data obtained from comparison with peer organizations.

External environment

Includes all forces external to the industry that potentially influence business strategy; can be broken down into customer, competitor, industry, and environment.

Facilitator

A person who guides the discussion around core themes, maintains independence and integrity of the process, and helps to remove barriers.

Fee for service (FFS)

An approach where a hospital charges additionally for each service provided. It is becoming less common as managed care and indemnity providers contractually negotiate bundled services for fixed fees in efforts to reduce overall costs.

Finished good	An item that is in its final stage for consumption or utilization.
First in, first out (FIFO)	An accounting method for inventory where the first item purchased and received is the first item used, and therefore ending inventory consists of the most recently purchased items.
Fiscal year	An accounting period of 1 year, used for financial reporting and budgeting purposes. May be the same as a calendar year but could be any 12-month period.
Fixed costs	All the expenses necessary to deliver services. They do not vary with total services provided.
Fixed staffing	When labor hours are not able to vary with outputs.
Forecasting	A projection or estimate of future demand. Forecasting can be created using a variety of qualitative and quantitative methods.
Forward positioning	The placement of medications (or other inventory) near the point of use, prior to their actual usage based on forecasted needs.
Full-time equivalent (FTE)	A unit of workload of an employed person based on a full-time employee.
Full-time equivalent employees per adjusted occupied bed (FTE/AOB)	A calculation of the ratio of labor inputs per until of total output for the hospital.
Full-time equivalent employees per occupied bed (FTE/OB)	A calculation of the average number of FTE hours for every inpatient served in the hospital each day.
Future value	The future value of a payment received today.
Game theory	An economic technique whereby the organization attempts to estimate how the competition will respond to its strategies and what the effect on performance will be.
Gantt chart	Shows activities as blocks or bars over time. An intuitive chart used to show resources for time allocations for key tasks and that supports monitoring of activities during the management phase.

Generally accepted accounting principles (GAAP)

Represents the accounting principles required for use by public companies.

Group physician practice

An organized group of physicians that comes together to leverage economies of scale in administrative and facility infrastructures. Typically involves management of all back-office and financial functions so that physicians can focus on providing care and not on the daily aspects of business management.

Group purchasing organization (GPO)

A collaborative arrangement where multiple parties (buyers) unite for purposes of increasing their collective bargaining power with vendors (sellers).

Hawthorne effect

A phenomenon where individuals perform differently than in normal situations when they are given attention or are being observed.

Healthcare Common Procedure Coding System (HCPCS)

A system that uses a code, often used interchangeably with Current Procedural Terminology codes, that describes the types of services provided by a hospital.

Health care operations management

A discipline that integrates scientific principles of management to determine the most efficient and optimal methods to support patient care delivery. The quantitative management of the supporting business systems and processes that transforms resources (or inputs) into health care services (outputs).

Health information exchange

The electronic movement of patient records between hospital systems.

Health Information Technology for Economic and Clinical Health (HITECH) Act

Intended to stimulate and encourage greater efficiencies in health care for the United States by developing a national health information technology infrastructure.

Health Insurance Portability and Accountability Act (HIPAA) of 1996

This act established national standards to protect personal health information and outlined safeguards for transmitting and storing protected health information.

Health maintenance organization (HMO)	A health plan that represents a managed care alternative delivery system. Offers enrollees unlimited access to care from a qualified, select list of providers.
Herfindahl-Hirschman index (HHI)	An index that measures market concentration. It is used primarily by the Department of Justice and the Federal Trade Commission to assess the effect of a merger on that market's competitive dynamics. Calculated by a sum of the squares of the individual market shares for each of the hospitals in the market. The higher the number, the closer the healthcare market is to being a monopoly. Alternatively, the lower the concentration, the more competitive the market.
Heuristic	A rule of thumb or general guideline.
Hierarchy	A classification system that organizes data around common attributes.
Horizontal integration	Consolidations, mergers, acquisitions, or alliances among several competitive or cooperative hospitals.
Hospital	An organization devoted to delivering patient care, which provides services centered on observation, diagnosis, and treatment.
Hurdle rate	The cost of capital. Also the minimum rate of return required on projects.
Improve	To make something better.
Income statement	Measures a hospital's profitability by tracking revenues, expenses, and margins and works off of the basic accounting principle of revenues minus expenses equals profit margin.
Increasing demand	When consumers demand a larger number of items than before.
Innovation	The continuous search for doing new things, or just doing current things better. Often a driver of industry economics.
Input	All resources to be used or consumed in a process, such as labor hours, staff, supplies, space or facilities, information systems, and other resources.

Integrated delivery network
Any combination or integration between a hospital and other providers or partners in the healthcare industry that work together collaboratively across a spectrum of care to provide more competitive and comprehensive services.

Interest
The payment received by those who hold money to forgo current consumption.

Intermediate good
An item that needs further processing or transformation.

Intermittent demand
Demand that is not dispersed evenly over time but tends to occur only at specific periods in batches or lumps.

Internal benchmark
A benchmark that is established based on objective data obtained from historical performance data in the organization's internal records.

Internal rate of return (IRR)
A computation in which the net present value of a project is equal to zero in order to gauge the return on a project.

Interoperability
The integration of technology to allow for the sharing and linking of data so that applications behave as one large system.

Inventory
Materials that are available for sale and therefore represent future benefits for an organization. Requires special financial accounting treatment to determine proper valuation. Buffer against demand variability.

Item
Any physical good that is procured for ultimate use or consumption.

Item master
Stores item-level data necessary for both transactional processing and analytical reporting.

Joint venture
A type of growth strategy in which two or more organizations unite financial and operating resources to create a new jointly owned entity for a specific project or purpose.

Just in time (JIT)
The process of moving goods (either finished, semi, or materials) to the next stage of the supply chain just at the point in time when they are required for

use in the process or consumption by the customer. The goals of just-in-time programs typically are to reduce or eliminate inventory levels, minimize process cycle times, and increase the level of responsiveness and flexibility in the manufacturing and logistics processes. The contrary philosophy of supply to stock.

Key performance indicator (KPI) A limited number of performance metrics that quantify operating results in critical areas, typically focused around strategic outcomes or productivity.

Labor The productive work being performed by employees.

Last in, first out (LIFO) An inventory accounting method that states that the oldest items purchased and received are the last to be sold, or that newer items purchased are the first ones sold.

Laundry management The process of collecting, processing, transporting, and replenishing linens during the linen life cycle, from acquisition to final disposition.

Leading Motivating employees, building support for ideas, and generally getting things done through people.

Lean process A process focused on quality improvements that increase speed, improve flexibility, reduce lot sizes, expand customization, and reduce waste.

Liabilities The claims of all vendors and creditors against the assets of the business, representing all debts owed by the hospital.

Linear programming A mathematical technique designed to make decisions that optimize trade-offs necessary for resource allocation.

Linear regression A technique that assumes a linear relationship between all input and output variables, accepts some degree of central tendency and normality of all variables, and cannot differentiate poor-performing entities from high-performing ones.

Linens Fabrics used for healthcare purposes, including scrubs, pillows and cases, sheets, blankets, towels, lab coats, rags, protective gear, and gowns.

Logistics	The efficient coordination and control of the flow of all operations, including patients, personnel, and resources.
Longitudinal basis	To observe processes over an extended time period.
Loss leader	An item that is sold by a vendor at a loss in order to attract customers to buy other premium items. Loss leaders are usually either very early or late stage, have poor growth prospects under normal conditions, or might not otherwise sell well.
Lower of cost or market (LCM)	A concept used in inventory accounting that states that inventory must be capitalized at whichever price is lower—cost or market.
Lowest unit of measure (LUM)	A practice where items are purchased and stored in the unit in which they will ultimately be consumed.
Managed care	Organized efforts to achieve cost containment in health care. Typically, managed care has two key characteristics: structurally integrated alternative delivery systems (such as health maintenance or preferred provider organizations) and different reimbursement mechanisms and financial incentives that change provider and patient behaviors toward less utilization and less expensive treatments.
Managed care organization (MCO)	An organization that is designed to capture the benefits of managed care. A generic term that includes health maintenance and preferred provider organizations.
Managed competition	The application of managed care principles within a competitive environment.
Management	Makes the basic decisions about staffing levels and mix, compensation and motivation of employees, locations to serve, technology to put in place, and where to focus efforts.
Manufacturers	Companies that produce goods or transform raw materials and components into usable finished products.
Markup	The difference between the invoice cost and the price charged to patients, typically expressed as a percentage. Used to generate reasonable returns or margins.

Mass production	The concept of the creation of rapid production processes through the use of assembly-line techniques.
Materials management	The department in a hospital typically responsible for supply chain management, including the business processes associated with acquiring, storing, distributing, and replenishing supplies and other resources.
Mean absolute deviation (MAD)	A calculation of the amount of error in a forecast. Calculated as the sum of the absolute difference between the average of the actual values and the forecasted values, divided by the number of observations.
Measurable	Refers to how inputs and outputs are readily observed and calculated.
Medicaid	A health insurance program for low-income persons who are aged, blind, disabled, or are members of families with dependent children. Medicaid is funded and controlled primarily by individual states, although the U.S. government does share in providing resources.
Medical record	The formal auditable account and history of a patient's encounters in the hospital, including description of illnesses, procedures performed, supplies provided, medications administered, provider notes, and discharge procedures.
Medicare	A federally funded national health insurance program for persons aged 65 and older and for disabled persons regardless of income or age.
Midnight census	An official count of patients in beds in the inpatient care units at midnight on a given day.
Milestone	A key date by which a major project deliverable should be achieved.
Monte Carlo simulation	An analysis that combines probability theory with random number generation and defined distribution patterns to iteratively simulate outcomes.
Multivariate	A forecasting approach that relies on multiple data series to predict future demand.

Mutually exclusive and collectively exhaustive (MECE)	A systems-oriented approach to decision making where each idea is distinct and stands on its own and also completely covers the range of possibilities for that issue.
National drug code	A ten-digit pharmaceutical industry identifier that uniquely identifies each drug.
Net patient revenue	The difference between gross patient revenues less discounts and deductions. Also called *operating revenue*.
Net present value (NPV)	The present value of all cash inflows less expected cash outflows. A measure of the relative profitability of a project over the long term, after full consideration of the time value of money.
Net realizable value	A ceiling or upper limit, defined as selling price minus all cost to sell the items.
Net revenue per full-time equivalent	A calculation to determine the amount of net revenue created on average by each employee in the organization.
Network	A group of providers—including doctors, clinics, academic medical centers, and hospitals—that is contractually organized, either loosely or formally, to provide a full range of integrated healthcare services to enrolled members and patients.
Nonproductive hours	Includes vacation, sick time, holiday pay, and other hours paid to employees while they were not engaged in their normal work.
Observation	Analyzing or studying patients and running tests and checks—all of which ultimately lead to a diagnosis.
Obsolete	When the useful life of a product has expired.
Occupancy percentage	A calculation of the average number of patients in inpatient care in a hospital for a given day divided by the number of beds in operation in that hospital used to determine the percentage of a hospital's inpatient capacity in use.
Operating expense per adjusted discharge	A calculation of the ratio between total operating expense and adjusted discharge.

Operating expense per adjusted occupied bed	A calculation of the ratio between total operating expense and adjusted patient days.
Operating expense per discharge	A calculation of the ratio between total operating expense and discharge.
Operating expense per occupied bed	A calculation of the ratio between total operating expense and patient days.
Operating margin	The difference between net patient revenue and total operating expense. Reflects the profits cleared in the course of normal business operations. As a percentage, it is calculated by dividing profit margin by net revenues.
Operational excellence	A term used to describe an organization that continuously seeks to improve its productivity, business processes, and overall effectiveness.
Operations analysis	A valuable management tool that measures progress toward strategic objectives and identifies ways to improve performance that meets those objectives.
Operations effectiveness	A measure of how well an organization is managed.
Operations management	Quantitative management of the supporting business systems and processes that transform resources (or inputs) into healthcare services (outputs). A discipline of management that integrates scientific principles to determine the most efficient and optimal methods to support patient care delivery.
Operations research	The discipline of applying advanced analytical methods to help make better decisions.
Optimization	A mathematical approach to solving a problem in which an optimal solution can be reached given the constraints and parameters defined.
Organizing	Making decisions about which tasks will be done, where, when, and by whom.
Outcome	The result, end point, or change in performance from a project.

Output	The result of the transformation or conservation process such as patient day, surgical procedure, diagnostic test, meals for patients or visitors, and a claim for reimbursement.
Outsourcing	Contracting an outside firm to perform services that were once handled internally.
Pareto chart	A graphical representation of the vital few issues that exist. Based on the 80-20 concept, that 80% of the cumulative percentage of problems are caused by 20% of the issues.
Par level	An inventory location that holds a specific product mix with minimum quantities that will cover the location for a predetermined number of hours or days. Used for supplies, pharmaceuticals, and linens.
Partnering	Establishing mutually beneficial and cooperative relationships with others where trust and teamwork help create synergies.
Patient day	The most common measure of output for a hospital over time. Represents one patient staying in the hospital's inpatient care units at midnight on a given day. Based on the hospital's midnight census.
Payback	The number of periods required to complete the return of the original investment.
Payer	A party to a hospital transaction that provides financial reimbursement through specific mechanisms and protocols, typically based on negotiated or settled pricing.
Payoff	Payback on return.
Penetration	A term used in procurement to represent the percentage of usage or purchases against a specific contract.
Per diem	A method of reimbursement where payers will compensate hospitals a flat reimbursement amount each day, regardless of actual services performed or resources consumed.
Performance scorecard	A tool to visualize measurements of key performance indicators for an organization relative to time, targets, or other baselines.

Periodic inventory	Does not keep a running record of items that are sold or purchased, and relies heavily on physical counting and observation of goods because no system is used to track balances.
Perpetual	The ability to know, at all points in time, actual balances due to continuous tracking of inventory receipts and issues.
Perpetual inventory	A running record of the inventory balance on hand at all times.
Pharmacy	A facility that exists to fill and dispense drugs and medications that are prescribed by physicians or other caregivers.
Physician preferences	A situation in which a provider chooses established vendors and known products based on existing comfort level and a possible reluctance to change.
Pilot	An initial test of the proposed new process, under limited conditions, to help gauge issues and success in achieving the desired goals.
Planning	Involves the establishment of goals and a strategy to achieve them. In health care, planning can be strategic (such as deciding which geographic region to invest in a new facility), or operational (such as how many employees to have on staff for each shift).
Point-of-use (POU) system	Similar to a vending machine in that it allows automation to drive replenishment, charging supplies to a patient account, and inventory calculations.
Policy	Provides broad guidelines that are used to create specific procedures within a system.
Portfolio	A collection of investments grouped by different categories that are selected to help ensure a balanced and systematic approach to improving overall outcomes.
Postponement	A supply chain concept where one procures goods at the latest point in the process, which helps to reduce inventory levels and encourage rapid response on the part of vendors.

Preferred provider organization (PPO)	A health plan that contracts with a limited panel of independent providers. Patient care services are offered with little or no out-of-pocket expenses for enrollees when all patient care has been performed by members of this network of preferred providers.
Prescription	A doctor's written order for medication, or other course of treatment.
Present value	The value today of a future payment.
Price elasticity	The responsiveness of the market to changes in prices. The relationship between pricing variability and demand variability.
Price per unit	The fee that will be charged to payers or customers in order to receive the service. Typically, it does not vary.
Procedures per employee	A calculation of how many procedures or units of output are produced per employee based on the ratio between the number of procedures in a department and the productive labor hours divided by the number of hours a full-time employee works in one year.
Process	A set of activities and tasks that are performed in sequence to achieve a specific outcome.
Process capability index	A measure for gauging the extent to which a process meets the customer's expectations.
Process engineering	The careful scrutiny of a current state process to identify value creation opportunities, such as eliminating hand-offs or steps in the process.
Process flowchart	A diagram depicting the flows or activities in a process.
Production function	A mathematical equation ($P = O \div I$) used to determine how efficiently an organization is producing services for patients.
Productive hours	Those that can be controlled by management and are used to directly provide patient care. Includes regular paid hours, overtime and callback hours, and hours paid for training and orientation.

Productive hours per unit
A calculation of productive hours in a time period divided by the number of procedures produced in that time period to determine the number of labor hours it takes to produce a unit of output in a specific department or hospital.

Productivity
The ratio of outputs to inputs for a specific process. One of the primary goals in operations management is to increase this ratio on a continuous basis.

Product life cycle
A process and an indicator that defines the major phases involved in the development and deployment of a product. The major phases of the life cycle include pre-launch, introduction, growth, maturity, decline, and retirement (or death).

Profit center
Organizational units that generate revenues and are expected to earn reasonable returns on those revenues after considering all costs of operations.

Profit margin
The excess of revenues less expenses, which represents the residual value of a hospital that is available for funding future operations.

Program evaluation and review technique (PERT)
A diagram that requires estimates for three cases: best case, worst case, and most likely case.

Project
An organized effort involving a sequence of activities that are temporarily being performed to achieve a desired outcome.

Project management
The application of knowledge, skills, tools, and techniques to a project in order to achieve project success.

Project manager
The individual who leads the planning and daily activities to achieve the project deliverables.

Prospective payment
A generic term for a payment methodology where fee schedules are calculated based on treatment type or illness classifications and are paid prospectively (i.e., in advance of the treatment) without regard to actual costs incurred.

Protected health information (PHI)	Includes any information that can be used to discover the identity of an individual patient.
Quality	High standards, excellence, and the ability to meet and exceed customers' expectations.
Quality management	The application of quantitative and qualitative methods to ensure that healthcare services and products possess the characteristics necessary to completely satisfy the needs that they are designed to serve.
Quantitative	When data and numbers are used for measurement purposes.
Quick response	A process where lead times are minimized, rapid processing of orders occurs, and changes in demand and business requirements are instantly communicated over the supply chain via collaborative information systems.
Radar diagrams	Graphical analyses that show target versus actual performance in key internal areas and identify potential problem areas.
Radio frequency identification (RFID)	Technology that uses small radio transponders to read and transmit data over existing wireless standards and frequencies.
Rapid prototyping	A concept whereby ideas and solutions can be targeted toward a very small sample to see if the solution improves results prior to wide-scale implementation.
Realization	Mitigating the risks of a project and adapting to changes that arise during the project.
Receipt	Physical documentation of actual quantities of goods that were delivered. Often receiving documents are called *proof of delivery*. Receipts must be matched against orders prior to payment.
Regulation	Authorized instructions for how something should be carried out.
Reimbursement	Payments to the provider that pays for the cost of rendering care.
Reliable	When the productivity figures yield stable and uniform results over time.

Request for information (RFI)   Used by a potential buyer to obtain vendor information that can be used to compile a list of qualified vendors for a purchase or procurement.

Request for proposal (RFP)   A formal process used to solicit binding bids from vendors for a specific purchase or contract.

Request for quotation (RFQ)   A sourcing approach where purchasing sends a simple request to suppliers known to offer a certain product, spelling out any particular specifications and minimum terms and conditions required in the purchasing transaction.

Requisition   A request for an item from a user or consumer of goods and services. The first step in the purchasing process.

Retrospective   To look backward at all costs incurred. In this type of reimbursement, insurers would fully compensate actual costs plus a component to represent a small profit margin.

Return on investment (ROI)   A ratio calculated as total amount of profits earned from a project or investment, divided by the total cost of that investment. ROI typically looks at profits and expenses over a specific time period, such as 3 or 5 years, to capture the time value of money.

Revenue code   Classifications on a hospital bill by which hospital supplies are billed to payers.

Revenue cycle management   The process of managing claims processing, setting payment practices, and revenue generation.

Reverse logistics   The process and methods by which hospitals reverse the physical flow of goods, returning them back internally to the originating department or all the way back up the chain to distributors and suppliers.

Risks   The factors that jeopardize project success or that cause potential impairment or delay.

Robot   An automated picker that selects single- and small-dose packages, labels them, and stores them in the right location using technology and large mechanized systems.

Rollup	An aggregation in a hierarchy.
Root cause analysis	A process for identifying and correcting the major issues causing problems.
Safety stock	Inventory carried in excess of forecasted demand to help manage unexpected variability or uncertainty in demand behavior. Also referred to as inventory buffer or reserve stock.
Sales and operations planning (S&OP)	The process used in many industrial, process, and manufacturing industries to help plan production around demand estimates derived collaboratively by multiple internal departments, such as sales, marketing, and logistics.
Satisficing	A process of making a less than optimal decision, but one that can be supported and is acceptable because it meets the minimal criteria (e.g., decision is reached quickly, is adequate, and/or is the result of consensus between parties).
Scheduled drug	A drug that is tightly monitored around usage and distribution because of potential for misuse and abuse.
Scorecard	A quantitative evaluation tool that lists the key attributes or decision criteria and forces weighted scoring across several areas. Typically used for either evaluating vendors or projects.
Seasonal demand	Spikes in the Christmas months for toys, the sale of chocolate at Easter time, or even seasonal patterns when events are repetitive and periodic in nature (holidays, timing of specific promotions, and climate or weather).
Sensitivity analysis	A simulation tool that allows a user to change key variables and assumptions using known mathematical relationships to estimate the effect on a dependent variable.
Service-level agreement (SLA)	A formal agreement that clearly communicates the types of services to be offered, performance expectations, hours services are to be provided, inputs or resources to be committed, and payments, if any.

Service line	A discrete group of closely related product items. In health care, a service line is equivalent to the number of medical offerings available in the portfolio. Also referred to as health care services or product lines.
Shrinkage	A loss due to failure to charge out properly to patients as drugs or supplies were dispensed or utilized, misplacement or overuse of drugs or supplies, items that have passed the expiration date or are obsolete and have no value, loss due to theft, pricing or value decreases, or any other general loss.
Simulation model	A computer model that predicts the behavior or performance of a process or how something might perform in the real world.
Six Sigma	A methodology focused on improving processes and quality by eliminating defects and reducing outcome variability or volatility.
Slice and dice	A term used in information technology to describe the process of breaking data down into component parts using different perspectives and dimensions to view data.
Slope	The tilt or angle of the rise (or fall) over the run.
Software maintenance	Upgrades to and enhancements of software systems.
Soiled linen	Dirty or used laundry and linens.
Specialization	Suggests that if individuals repeatedly perform just one task, they will be able to perform that task faster and with higher quality than others, because they have repeated exposure to the process and have learned from their experiences.
Spectrum analysis	An analysis of the electromagnetic spectrum to assess waves, ensure that there will be no interference from other equipment or devices, and confirm that channels and frequencies are clear. Used prior to implementation of radio frequency identification technology.

Spend analysis	An in-depth comprehensive analysis of a hospital's expenditures, primarily of routine operating expenses, focused on what, how, and with whom an organization spends dollars.
Square root law of inventory	Suggests that the total costs will increase dramatically as the number of stocking points increases.
Standard deviation	A statistical measure of the degree of fluctuation or dispersion around the mean.
Standardization	A common goal in logistics and supply chain processes to use standard procedures, resources, items, and services to achieve consistent results across multiple departments.
Statement of cash flows	Represents all of the cash inflows a hospital receives from its ongoing business activities and investments, as well as its cash outflows for expenditures, labor, and other activities. Shows both sources and uses of funds and reconciles the income statement and the balance sheet back to changes in cash flow.
Statement of financial position	A balance sheet designed to show how a hospital's assets, liabilities, and equity are distributed at a specific point in time, usually prepared at regular intervals and especially at the end of an accounting year.
Stock-keeping unit (SKU)	The combination of the specific end item sold in a particular location. Typically the lowest level in the product hierarchy of a planning system.
Stock-out	A shortage of a specific product in inventory resulting from lack of adequate understanding of demand. Results if an order arrives and no product is available. Also called a *sellout* in certain industries.
Strategic alliance	An often ambiguous term used to imply any number of working relationships between two or more organizations. Often results in a joint venture or merger.
Strategic management	The process for orchestrating organizational resources toward the development of an alignment between business strategies and the environment in order to improve financial performance. Involves the

behavior of complex organizations in responding to turbulent environments and aligning teaching hospitals' services with market needs.

Strategic planning	The process of formulating competitive strategies that determine a hospital's overall direction and approach.
Strategic pricing analysis	The application of differential pricing markups to each drug based on its potential for reimbursement, usage, the item's history and life cycle, payer mix, and other factors.
Strengths, weaknesses, opportunities, and threats (SWOT) analysis	A thorough review of an organization's combination of strengths, weaknesses, opportunities, and threats. Generates questions to address to match strategy to situation.
Supply chain	The activities, people, facilities, and process involved in moving products through a network in order to procure, assemble, manufacture, distribute, and sell products to consumers.
Supply chain management (SCM)	The integration of supply and demand management within and across companies.
Supply to stock (STS)	A philosophy where larger quantities of materials are purchased and placed into an inventory location for storage and distribution. The contrary philosophy of just in time.
System	A set of connected parts that fit together to achieve a purpose.
System integration	The integration of all pharmacy systems from the point of order through administration.
Teaching hospital	A major healthcare organization offering observation, diagnosis, and treatment through the practice of academic medicine via a variety of distribution channels. A limited number of large, complex hospitals that have a major commitment to the missions of academic medicine, including graduate medical education, medical research, and patient care. These organizations are the primary training grounds for future medical doctors, as well as nurses and other allied health professionals.

Temporary price reductions	Decreasing prices temporarily in order to generate additional demand.
Three-way match	A basic way of limiting risk of bribery or unethical buyers by ensuring that the three key documents in the procure-to-pay process are performed by different individuals, therefore segregating duties and responsibilities.
Throughput	The rate or velocity at which services are performed, or goods are delivered. Refers to the amount of outputs that a process can deliver over a specific time period and is used in both productivity analysis and process engineering.
Time and motion study	An analysis of the details of a process to identify the total amount of time and effort required to perform a procedure.
Time series	A set of values or observations at successive points in time.
Time value of money	A financial concept stating that money received in the present is worth more than the same amount received in the future.
Timing	Represents the difference between when a supply is purchased and when it is consumed.
To-be process	A version of a process map that depicts the future state, or after design and process engineering.
Total costs	The sum of both fixed and variable costs.
Tracking system	Tools that monitor the position, flow, and movement of resources. Both radio frequency identification and bar-coding systems fall within this category.
Treatment	The course of action that the hospital will take to make the patient better, lessen the symptoms, or otherwise care for the patient.
United Nations Standard Products and Services Code (UNSPSC)	A classification system to describe item-level data that is used worldwide. Supports standardization among vendors and providers about items.

Univariate	Refers to dependence on a single variable, where demand forecasts are based on only one historical data series.
Upstream	On a supply chain, the zone closer to the manufacturer of a good.
Utilization	Refers to the usage patterns of linens.
Valuation	An assessment of the financial value of an asset.
Value chain	The collection of activities that define how work is accomplished in an organization, from inputs to final outputs. In the healthcare industry, the value chain comprises the parties and activities involved in delivering patient care. This includes the procurement of materials from suppliers, the delivery of care by physicians and nurses, the financing of care by third-party payers, and the receipt of care by patients.
Variability	Inconsistency or dispersion of results. Variability in process outcomes is the major source of operational inefficiency and should be minimized as much as possible. Measured by standard deviation.
Variable costs	The costs that vary directly with production.
Vendor	Any party that sells goods to others irrespective of ownership of assets.
Vendor-managed inventory (VMI)	A process whereby a supplier manages the inventory stock levels for its customers based on forecasted demand. The process is designed to be proactive by the supplier, which controls the distribution plans and sends out orders with minimal involvement from the customer.
Vendor master	A continuous review process of vendors and items purchased, as well as careful examination of vendor listings in both purchasing and the accounts payable areas for incomplete and suspicious information.
Vertical acquisition	A type of growth strategy in which one organization acquires another organization—usually a key supplier or a buyer. An example is if a teaching hospital purchased a health insurance plan.

Vertical integration	The acquisition or alliance of other parties involved in other phases of the healthcare value chain, such as payers, clinics, or physicians.
Voluntary Interindustry Commerce Standards (VICS)	An association focused on creating voluntary standards within the industry that all parties would use to share data in a consistent manner in order to collectively improve the supply chain coordination among retailers, manufacturers, and suppliers.
Wait time	A time interval during which there is a temporary cessation of service.
Weighted average	Assumes that the cost should reflect the averages of all items purchased over time.
Work breakdown structure (WBS)	A key aspect of project planning that decomposes project activities into more detailed components to allow for better planning.
Working capital	A valuation metric that defines the excess of current assets (including cash, accounts receivable, and inventories) less current liabilities (primarily trade and other payables). It measures liquidity and the ability to cover short-term debt.

INDEX